Beginning Greek with Homer

An Elementary Course based on Odyssey V

by

Frank Beetham

Bristol Classical Press

First published in 1996
by Bristol Classical Press
an imprint of
Gerald Duckworth & Co. Ltd
61 Frith Street
London W1D 3JL
e-mail: inquiries@duckworth-publishers.co.uk
Website: www.ducknet.co.uk

Reprinted with corrections, 1998
This impression 2002

© 1996 by Frank Beetham

All rights reserved. No part of this publication
may be reproduced, stored in a retrieval system, or
transmitted, in any form or by any means, electronic,
mechanical, photocopying, recording or otherwise,
without the prior permission of the publisher.

A catalogue record for this book is available
from the British Library

ISBN 1-85399-480-4

Printed in Great Britain by
Antony Rowe Ltd, Eastbourne

Contents

Preface	page	i	Section 13	page	86
Section 1	page	1	Section 14	page	94
Section 2	page	6	Section 15	page	103
Section 3	page	11	Section 16	page	113
Section 4	page	18	Section 17	page	119
Section 5	page	26	Section 18	page	127
Section 6	page	32	Section 19	page	131
Section 7	page	42	Section 20	page	137
Section 8	page	48	Section 21	page	145
Section 9	page	60	Section 22	page	150
Section 10	page	66	Section 23	page	160
Section 11	page	71	Section 24	page	171
Section 12	page	80	Section 25	page	178

Appendix A - Moods & Tenses	page 186
Appendix B - Rules of Contraction	page 193
Conspectus of grammar	page 202
Elisions	page 240
Answers	page 241
Word list	page 251
Indices	page 262

PREFACE

Beginning Greek with Homer.

This is a quick course for those who wish to read Homer in the original tongue but know no Greek, or are only just beginning to work through a course in Classical Greek and wish to read Homer from a very early stage. It assumes no previous knowledge of Greek. The first six sections deal with the fundamental elements of grammar that are necessary as a preliminary, and from section 7 the course proceeds through Odyssey, book five, with grammatical explanations and exercises.

The beginning of Odyssey V is a good place to start reading Homer. The Odyssey opens, after an invocation of the Muse, with a council at which all the Olympian gods except Poseidon are present. Zeus, who is in the chair, complains that mortals are apt to bring misfortunes on themselves and then blame the gods. Athene raises the case of Odysseus, of all the Achaean chiefs who survived the Trojan War and are still alive the only one who has not yet returned home, and who is detained against his will by Calypso on a sea-girt island. (We note that the Trojan War ended ten years previously,[1] and that Odysseus has been Calypso's prisoner for seven years.[2]) Athene points out that Zeus is under an obligation to Odysseus for being scrupulous in performing sacrifices at Troy. Zeus replies that Odysseus has brought his troubles on himself in so far as he has offended Poseidon by blinding Polyphemus, the Cyclops, who is Poseidon's son;[3] nevertheless Poseidon, who is not destined to kill Odysseus but only to keep him from home, will eventually relent, and so the other gods may plan how to get Odysseus home. Athene asks Zeus to send Hermes, the messenger god, to tell Calypso to let Odysseus go. Then she leaves for Ithaca, where Telemachus, the only son of Odysseus and Penelope, is in serious difficulty with the suitors who wish to marry Penelope. The first four books are concerned with how Athene helps him, and how he makes a journey in search of news of his father.

There is another meeting of the gods at the beginning of Odyssey V. Poseidon is still absent. Athene complains that Odysseus is still the

---
[1] Odyssey II, 175.
[2] Odyssey VII, 259.
[3] It really was Odysseus' fault; his companions tried to persuade him not to wait in the cave until the Cyclops came, and afterwards not to boast and give his name to the Cyclops; but Odysseus would not listen to them, and caused his own troubles with Poseidon as well as the death of some of his companions. See Odyssey X, 437, cited by M. Finkelberg, *Patterns of Human Error in Homer*, Journal of Hellenic Studies CXV, 1995, pp.17-18.

prisoner of Calypso, and at last Zeus sends Hermes with a message to release him. The first half of the book tells how Calypso finally lets Odysseus go and helps him on his way. The second half tells how Poseidon discovers Odysseus at sea and of the terrible storm which ensues, how Odysseus is helped by Leucothea, a sea goddess, and how after much suffering he reaches Phaeacia from where he is destined to be taken home. The following books (VI-VIII) are about Odysseus' welcome in Phaeacia where he is rescued by Nausicaa, the king's daughter; in books IX-XII Odysseus himself, at a banquet in the palace of king Alcinous, describes his own voyage home beginning with his departure from Troy and including his adventures with Polyphemus, Aeolus, the Laestrygonians and Circe, his visit to the underworld, Scylla and Charybdis, and the catastrophic wrecking of his last ship, from which he is the only survivor, after his companions had killed the cattle of the sun. In Odyssey XIII Odysseus reaches Ithaca, is disguised, and begins his struggle to regain his kingdom.

The function of Odyssey V is to introduce the hero. He has, as is usual in epic, key epithets. These are: *dios* ("noble"), *theios* ("divine", "more than human"), *talasiphron* ("patient of mind", "stout hearted"), *megaletor* ("great hearted"), *polymechanos* ("resourceful"), *polymetis* ("of many counsels", "shrewd"). His characteristic is his single-minded determination to return home, and he will not be put off by temptation (for instance, to settle for an easy life and marry Nausicaa) any more than by danger and suffering. He is a king, and will at all costs return to claim his wife, his home and his kingdom. Odyssey V sets out the magnitude of the task.

Calypso

As Hainsworth explains,[4] Calypso has no myth and no cult. In this, she is unlike the sea goddess Leucothea who was worshipped in several places including Pyrgi on the coast of Etruria[5] and whose son, Melicertes, was associated with the Isthmian Games at Corinth.[6] Most of what is known about Calypso comes from Odyssey I (45-62 and 80-95), where Athene says that she lives in a palace on a remote, wooded, sea-girt island called Ogygia located at the navel of the sea, and that she is the daughter of baleful Atlas "who knows all the depths of the sea and himself holds the tall pillars which separate earth and heaven". She

---

[4] *A Commentary on Homer's Odyssey*, ed. Heubeck, (Oxford, Clarendon Press, 1988) vol. i, p.250.
[5] *Le Città Etrusche*, F. Boitani, M. Cataldi & M. Pasquinucci, Mondadori (1973) p.175.
[6] Elisabeth R. Gebhard in *Greek Sanctuaries*, ed. Marinatos & Hägg, Routledge (1993), p.171.

charmed Odysseus with sweet and wheedling words to try to make him forget Ithaca. From Odyssey V 71 we learn that Calypso's palace is a cave with four springs nearby flowing in different directions. Line 277 implies that Odysseus sailed eastwards on his way from Ogygia to Phaeacia.

Ogygia has never been identified, and even its name has not been explained.[7] Some have found a connection between the myth of Calypso, the daughter of Atlas, and early Greek voyages into the western Mediterranean,[8] and a suitable cave with four springs nearby has been found on the Moroccan coast opposite Gibraltar; this is not in the middle of the sea, or even on an island. On the other hand, in the Odyssey it looks as if Atlas himself may not be connected with the Atlas mountains, but thought of as in the middle of the ocean. Others have seen a connection between Calypso and Siduri the alewife, a divine figure living near the sea in the ancient Akkadian epic of Gilgamesh,[9] in which the hero also makes a long journey and visits the underworld and, soon after meeting Siduri, has to fell trees and build a boat.

The name Calypso is cognate with the Greek verb *kalupto*, "I conceal", and West and Hainsworth[10] think she may have been invented to fill the gap of seven years in Odysseus' story. In the Odyssey she is made to resemble Circe in some ways; for instance, both live on islands and both are singing at their loom when visitors call.[11] Invented or not, she is a lively personality, kindly but with a touch of menace. She certainly does not shrink from expressing her indignation and her tirade against Zeus and the other gods (Odyssey V, 118-144) shows her as the predecessor of those heroines in Greek literature, such as Medea or the daughters of Danaus, who were outraged by male unreasonableness and cruelty towards females, and some of whom went on to do terrible things themselves. That she does not tell the whole truth is probably not a fault in the context of the Odyssey, where the hero himself often tells lies and gets

---

[7]See Hainsworth's note, *op. cit.*, p.304. It might mean "primeval" which would perhaps add a touch of mystery to Calypso.
[8]See "Kalypso" in Pauly-Wissowa, *Real-Encyclopädie d. klassischen Altertumswissenschaft*.
[9]S. Dalley, *Myths from Mesopotamia* (Oxford, 1988) pp.48 and 99-105.
[10]*A Commentary on Homer's Odyssey*, vol. i, pp.81 and 249.
[11]Hesiod made them even more alike; at *Theogony* 1017 he says that Calypso, like Circe, had two sons by Odysseus. (He also mentions another Calypso, "lovely Calypso", among the nymphs and river goddesses, daughters of Oceanus and Tethys, at 359.) See also Michael N. Nagler, *Dread Goddess Revisited* in *Reading the Odyssey*, Seth L. Schein (Princeton, 1996).

credit for it.[12]   Odysseus twice calls her "terrible" (Odyssey VII 246 and 255) and once "wily" (245) when explaining himself to Nausicaa's father, Alcinous. The character of Calypso may have been created out of scanty and diverse materials, but its importance for later literature is considerable. The scene in Odyssey V when Odysseus and Calypso part has been described as delicate and subtle, such as would not seem out of place in Sophocles.[13]

The question of authorship[14]
"Longinus" *on the Sublime*[15] 9, 12-13: "The Odyssey is an epilogue of the Iliad ... he (sc. Homer) made the whole structure of the Iliad, which he was writing at the height of his powers, dramatic and full of action; but the greater part of the Odyssey full of talk,[16] which is characteristic of old age." Most, but not all, readers of Homer in antiquity agreed that the Iliad and Odyssey were the work of the same poet, and that the Iliad was the older. Since the late eighteenth century, the Homeric question has been revived, and some have even doubted whether either the Iliad or the Odyssey is the work of a single poet. Heubeck reviews the controversy in the general introduction to *A Commentary on Homer's Odyssey* and concludes that the epics are by different poets; while the author of the Iliad is still referred to as "Homer", he calls the other "the Poet of the Odyssey", concluding firmly that there was a single author of the Odyssey, though he would have worked with earlier materials, and that the Poet of the Odyssey knew the Iliad; the Odyssey is therefore later. Furthermore, Heubeck sees the hand of a young poet in the skill and vigour with which the Odyssey was composed.

Heubeck's general introduction does not discuss when the Odyssey might have been composed, but Rutherford[17] gives c. 750 B.C. as the traditional date for the Iliad, and perhaps 700 for the Odyssey. It seems not long

[12]Occasionally the bard himself may be inconsistent. For instance, Odysseus tells Alcinous (Odyssey VII, 263) that Calypso had set him free only after a message from Zeus, but Calypso does not say so in Odyssey V. How did Odysseus know?
[13]R.B. Rutherford, *Homer: Odyssey books XIX and XX* (Cambridge, 1992), p.55.
[14]There is a fuller discussion in A.F. Garvie, *Homer Odyssey Books VI-VIII* (Cambridge, 1994) pp.1-18.
[15]An anonymous Greek work of literary criticism, probably of the 1st century AD.
[16]Odyssey IX-XII are, of course, a continuous tale told by Odysseus himself.
[17]*Odyssey XIX & XX*, p.39. Rutherford notes that many of the arguments for these dates are indecisive.

before this that alphabetic writing was introduced in Greece.[18] Heubeck (p.12) is certain that neither epic could have been created at all without the aid of writing. Nevertheless, the formulaic style of the poetry itself indicates that both the Iliad and the Odyssey come after a succession of orally composed poems, perhaps very long ones, whose bards had passed on their skill from one generation to another. In these circumstances, it is to be expected that though the poems might be about particular heroic deeds of hundreds of years before (such as the Trojan War), they would contain some inconsistencies in details, for instance the shape of shields or whether things were made of iron or bronze,[19] because of the incorporation of formulae or traditional descriptions from different periods; the bards may also have known and used stories or poems from other cultures.

The Epic Dialect

The Iliad and Odyssey are composed in a literary dialect, Epic, which was regarded as the only one appropriate for epic poetry.[20] It is an ancient dialect and contains many archaisms. While some of its features may[21] have originated in the Greek dialect used in the Mycenaean palaces in the bronze age and preserved in Linear B tablets, Epic is a composite of Aeolic (spoken in the region of Lesbos and in parts of mainland Greece) and of Ionic (spoken mainly in some of the islands and the southern seaboard of Asia Minor), to which the Athenian dialect (Attic) is related, with some elements of Arcado-Cypriot.

Because of the composite nature of the dialect, there are often alternative endings in the cases of nouns and the persons of verbs. This would have been a considerable help to a bard in making the verse scan. The

---

[18]"The earliest surviving Greek inscriptions range round (roughly) the middle of the eighth century." L.H. Jeffery, *Archaic Greece* (Methuen, 1976), p.26. There were at first various versions of the alphabet, and that in which all Greek is now written was only adopted at Athens at the end of the fifth century BC, in 403, in the archonship of Eucleides. Even if it were known that the Odyssey had been written or dictated by the author, the original spelling would have shown differences from the present text.
[19]D.H.F. Gray, *Metal Working in Homer*, Journal of Hellenic Studies LXXIV, 1954, p.1.
[20]This tradition was maintained in later centuries, e.g. by Apollonius Rhodius' *Argonautica*, dating from the 3rd century BC. The *Argonautica* is in the Epic dialect, although its style is different (see e.g. R.L. Hunter, *Apollonius of Rhodes, Argonautica book III* (Cambridge, 1989) pp. 39-41).
[21]P. Chantraine, *Grammaire Homérique* (Librarie C. Klincksieck, Paris, 1958), vol.i, p.509, notes, however, that many Mycenaean words are entirely absent from the vocabulary of Homer, and some of the archaic expressions in the tablets are not found in Epic.

endings-system therefore tends to be more complex than in Attic. However, the structure of sentences in Epic is often simpler than in other Classical Greek dialects (especially Attic, which particularly influenced later Greek) because it is paratactic; i.e. clauses are presented side-by-side as often in English, rather than one inside another like a nest of boxes. The structure of sentences in Epic is influenced by the availability of formulae; these are conventional expressions which fit into a line and are familiar to an audience. The simplest consist of a name and epithet; for instance, "rosy-fingered dawn". A longer formula, filling a whole line, is: "but when rosy-fingered dawn, child of morn, appeared."[22]

The grammar in this course covers everything needed to read books V and VI. The order in which the grammar is presented is naturally influenced by the need to begin reading Odyssey V as soon as possible. The word list contains words which occur at least twice in Odyssey V and VI. All other words are explained in the footnotes, which also explain all grammatical points not already covered.[23] The exercises, where appropriate, cover points from the lines of Odyssey V which follow. If, having completed books V and VI, the reader should go on from book VII to book XII this would complete the reading of what amounts to a mini-epic, books V-XII, the wanderings of Odysseus.

The contents of the course are as follows:
Section 1: The alphabet.
Section 2: Nouns: the three declensions: the nominative case (singular, dual and plural). The verb "to be" (present and imperfect). Adjectives (first and second declension).
Section 3: Homeric endings for active verbs: the present tense active. Nouns and adjectives, the accusative case.
Section 4: Verbs, the middle and passive voices; the present tense, middle and passive; present infinitives.
Section 5: Nouns and adjectives, the genitive case. First and second person pronouns. The dactylic hexameter.
Section 6: Verbs: the imperfect tense. Nouns, personal pronouns and adjectives: the dative and vocative cases.

---
[22]This is found 18 times in the Odyssey and twice in the Iliad.
[23]Except for parts of λύω, other pattern verbs and nouns and adjectives used as patterns, word forms not actually found in Homer are generally enclosed in square brackets.

Section 7: The Greek verb - the functions of the moods and tenses briefly described. The present optative. Purpose clauses (1). *Odyssey V, 1-20; Athene addresses the renewed Council of the Gods.*

Section 8: The demonstrative and relative pronouns; αὐτός and other third person pronouns. *Odyssey V, 21-42; Zeus decrees that Odysseus must return home.*

Section 9: The weak aorist tense, active and middle. *Odyssey V, 43-58; Hermes flies to Calypso's island.*

Section 10: The strong aorist tense, active and middle. *Odyssey V, 59-74; Hermes marvels at the beauty of Calypso's cave.*

Section 11: Present and aorist participles, active and middle. *Odyssey V, 75-96; Calypso greets Hermes and offers him hospitality.*

Section 12: The future tense, active and middle. *Odyssey V, 97-117; Hermes tells Calypso of Zeus' decision.*

Section 13: The imperative mood. *Odyssey V, 118-144: Calypso protests at Zeus' double standard for gods and goddesses.*

Section 14: The subjunctive mood. Purpose clauses (2). *Odyssey V, 145-170; Hermes departs, and Calypso seeks Odysseus out and tells him he is to go home.*

Section 15: Future and aorist infinitives. The verb τίθημι. *Odyssey V, 171-200; Calypso assures Odysseus that she is not leading him into a trap.*

Section 16: The verb εἶμι (I (shall) go). Personal possessive adjectives. *Odyssey V, 201-227; Calypso tries to convince Odysseus that he should stay with her.*

Section 17: Clauses of time. *Odyssey V, 228-261; Odysseus builds his raft.*

Section 18: Verbs: the aorist passive tense. *Odyssey V, 262-281; Odysseus sets sail.*

Section 19: The aorist passive tense (continued). *Odyssey V, 282-296; the god Poseidon sees Odysseus and determines to make trouble for him; he raises a great storm.*

Section 20: Verbs: the perfect tense, active, middle and passive. *Odyssey V, 297-332; the raft is severely damaged in the storm, and Odysseus washed overboard.*

Section 21: Perfect tense verbs with present tense equivalents in English. *Odyssey V, 333-353; a sea goddess comes to help Odysseus.*

Section 22: Verbs: (a) The perfect participle active, and middle and passive (b) the pluperfect tense. *Odyssey V, 354-387; the raft is finally wrecked, and Odysseus has to swim for it.*
Section 23: Adjectives of mixed and third declension. *Odyssey V, 388-423; Odysseus nears land but the coast is unexpectedly dangerous.*
Section 24: Clauses expressing conditions. *Odyssey V, 424-457; how Odysseus comes ashore at last.*
Section 25: Comparison of adjectives. *Odyssey V, 458-493 (the end of the book); Odysseus, exhausted, falls asleep under a twin olive tree.*

There are two editions of Odyssey VI in print; one, with Odyssey VII, by G.M. Edwards (1915) (Bristol Classical Press) has elementary notes and a vocabulary. The other, with Odyssey VII and VIII, by A.F. Garvie (Cambridge University Press, 1994), is intended both for those beginning their study of Homer and for more advanced students, and contains an introduction dealing with Homer, with the Phaeacian books of the Odyssey, with metre and with the text, the text itself, and a commentary in which questions of interpretation, grammar and style are discussed fully. It has no vocabulary. Odyssey IX, edited by J.V. Muir (Bristol Classical Press, 1981) has a facing vocabulary and an introduction but no commentary. The whole Odyssey is available in the two-volume edition with introduction (especially helpful on Homeric grammar) and notes by W.B. Stanford (1965) (formerly Nelson, now Bristol Classical Press (Duckworth), 2nd edition (revised)). Odyssey I and II (edited, with a translation, by P.V. Jones, 1991) is published by Aris & Phillips, and Odyssey XIX & XX (edited by R.B. Rutherford, 1992, in the same series as Garvie's *Odyssey VI-VIII*) by Cambridge University Press.

There is a two-volume edition of the Iliad (Willcock, 1978 and 1983) published by Nelson, and separate editions of Iliad I (Harrison & Jordan, Bristol Classical Press, 1983), Iliad III (with vocabulary, ed. Hooker, Bristol Classical press, 1979), Iliad VI (with vocabulary, ed. Harrison & Jordan, Bristol Classical press, 1985), and Iliad XXIV (ed. MacLeod, Cambridge University Press, 1982).

Autenrieth's *Homeric Dictionary for use in Schools & Colleges*, tr. R.P. Keep, and N. Marinone, *All the Greek Verbs* are both published by Bristol Classical Press and are invaluable for continuing to read Homer. Clyde Pharr, *Homeric Greek - A Book for Beginners* (revised by J. Wright, University of Oklahoma Press, 1985) has a full elementary account of Homeric grammar. It is based on Iliad I, and has exercises for translation into and out of Greek. References to Liddell & Scott are to *A Greek-English Lexicon* by H.G. Liddell and R. Scott, ninth edition, revised by Sir H. Stuart Jones, with supplement (1968) (Oxford University Press).

I have most frequently consulted *A Commentary on Homer's Odyssey* ed. A. Heubeck (Oxford, Clarendon Paperbacks, 1990), especially the section by J.B.Hainsworth on Odyssey V-VIII, and P.Chantraine, *Grammaire Homérique* (Librarie C. Klincksieck, Paris, 1958). I have also consulted Stanford's edition of the Odyssey, Pfarr's *Homeric Greek* and A. Gehring, *Index Homericus* (Georg Olms, 1970). The text has been reprinted from the Oxford Classical Texts edition of Homer edited by Thomas W. Allen (2nd. ed. 1917) by permission of Oxford University Press and downloaded (with permission) from *Thesaurus Linguae Graecae*.[24] I should like to express my gratitude to both, and to Dr. Hainsworth for his assistance with my enquiries. I am also grateful to Mrs. Jean Dodgeon for proof reading and many helpful suggestions. I must thank my wife, Gwynneth, for her constant help and support.

---

[24]There are the following alterations: at line 458, I have printed ἄμπνυτο (following TLG (*Thesaurus Linguae Graecae*) and most mss.) instead of ἔμπνυτο. At 471 I have printed μεθείη (following Chantraine) instead of Allen's μεθήῃ, and at 490 I have printed αὖοι instead of Allen's αὖῃ. I have printed ἕως for ἧος at 123 and εἷος for ἧος elsewhere, following TLG. See p.119, footnote 2.

The Greek Alphabet

Capital	Small	Name	English sound
A	α	alpha	a
B	β	beta	b
Γ	γ	gamma	g[1]
Δ	δ	delta	d
E	ε	epsilon	e (short)
Z	ζ	zeta	z
H	η	eta	e (long)[2]
Θ	θ	theta	th
I	ι	iota	i
K	κ	kappa	k
Λ	λ	lambda	l
M	μ	mu	m
N	ν	nu	n
Ξ	ξ	xi	x
O	o	omicron	o (short)
Π	π	pi	p
P	ρ	rho	r
Σ	σ	sigma	s
	ς	" "	s (at end of word)

[1] γγ is pronounced "ng".
[2] English also has short and long vowels: so a in "bat" is short, while a in "balm" is long. η is pronounced like ai in "hair" and ω like aw in "saw" (but some pronounce it like o in "go").

Τ	τ	tau	t
Υ	υ	upsilon	u
Φ	φ	phi	ph
Χ	χ	khi	kh
Ψ	ψ	psi	ps
Ω	ω	omega	o (long)

Section 1
The alphabet and punctuation.
The Greek alphabet has 24 letters.[1] Of these, seven are vowels:
α ε η ι ο υ ω.
The names of all Greek letters begin with the sound that they make. Some of the vowel-names are also descriptive; thus, as ψιλόν ("psilon") means, in Greek, "a plain thing", epsilon means "plain e" and upsilon means "plain u". In the same way, μικρόν ("mikron") means "a small thing" and μέγα ("mega") means "a great thing"; so omicron means "small o" and omega means "great o".

Three of the remaining letters (the consonants) are **aspirated**:
θ = th   φ = ph   χ = kh.
The aspiration was light: θ stands for th as in Thomas, φ for ph as in clap hands (rather than ph as in photograph) and χ for kh as in khaki (or as ch in chaos and chasm).

Three letters include a **sibilant:**
ζ (although we tend to pronounce it like dz in "adze") more probably stood for sd as in "asdic" or "Esdras".

ξ stands for ks or x, as in "sticks" or "Styx".

ψ stands for ps as in "pseudo". ζ, ξ and ψ count as double letters when scanning Greek verse.

---

[1] The Greek alphabet was developed from the north Semitic one, probably in the eighth century B.C. Different Greek states had their own variations of it (the Latin alphabet, which is our own, is a cousin, probably coming via the Etruscans) and the East Ionic alphabet which was officially accepted at Athens (403/2 B.C.) gradually became the standard for all Greeks. Since the letters of the alphabet were used also for numerals (e.g., α = 1, β = 2, ι = 10, ια = 11), as 27 numerals were needed, 3 obsolete letters were retained as numerals: ϛ (waw) or ϝ (digamma) as 6, ϟ (koppa) as 90 and ϡ (sampi) as 900. (See Lilian H. Jeffery, *Archaic Greece*, pp.25-6, and the articles on the two alphabets in *The Oxford Classical Dictionary*.) Digamma is occasionally found in texts of Homer (e.g. *The Cambridge Homer*, ed. A. Platt, 1892 & 1894) to separate vowels not pronounced together e.g. ϝιϕιϝάνασσα for 'Ιϕιάνασσα, one of the daughters of Agamemnon mentioned at Iliad IX, 145.

When the Iliad and the Odyssey were divided into 24 books in the time of Zenodotus of Ephesus, the first librarian at the Great Library at Alexandria, each book was named after a letter of the Greek alphabet. These letters are not numerals; consequently Iliad I and Odyssey ι refer to the *ninth* books of the Iliad and Odyssey respectively.

Of the eleven other letters,   β closely resembles b,
                               δ closely resembles d,
                               κ closely resembles k
                               τ closely resembles t.
The remaining seven are: γ = g
                               λ = l
                               μ = m
                               ν = n
                               π = p
                               ρ = r
                               σ (ς at the end of a word) = s.

There are some Greek words which have been taken over unchanged, except for the alphabet, into English. These include:

ψεύδω   χαρακτήρ   στίγμα

κρατήρ   καταστροφή   ψυχή[2]

μανία   διάγνωσις   φλόξ

παρθενών   μητρόπολις   θερμός
and the following names from Greek mythology
Ζεύς   Στύξ   Νέστωρ

Καλυψώ   Ζέφυρος[3]   Ποσειδάων

Βορέης[4]   Τηλέμαχος   Κύκλωψ

Ναυσικάα   Κίρκη   Πηνελόπεια.

Several letters in our alphabet have no counterparts in Greek: c is redundant, as it can always be replaced by k or s. W is not a frequent sound in Greek, and when it occurs is expressed by ου.[5] There are one or two others[6] the most important of which is h. The East Ionic dialect of Greek lacked a sound corresponding to h, and the aspirate letter H

---

[2]In transliteration (i.e., changing alphabets) υ often becomes y in English.
[3]The west wind.
[4]The north wind, whose name usually ends -as in English.
[5]e.g. for the Latin v - Octavia, in Plutarch's Life of Antony, is Ὀκταουία.
[6]e.g. f and v. These sounds are more important in modern Greek, and are accommodated in various ways; for instance, ευ has changed from expressing "eu" to "ef", so that the modern Greek for "thank you!" (εὐχαριστῶ) is pronounced "efkharisto". Also, β is more equivalent to the English v. βῆμα (the Greek for "step" or "tribune") is now pronounced "vema", and "banana" is written μπανάνα.

was taken over for eta (long e). When the East Ionic alphabet was officially adopted at Athens, an arrangement was needed to indicate vowels which are aspirated at the beginning of words; hence the system of **breathings**.

A rough breathing ʽ is placed over a vowel which is aspirated at the beginning of a word.

A smooth breathing ʼ is placed over a vowel which is not aspirated at the beginning of a word.

Thus Ἑλένη (rough breathing) = Helen

and Ἀγαμέμνων (smooth breathing) = Agamemnon.

Put the following into English letters:

ἅλμα   ἰδέα   ἦθος

ἕλιξ   Ὠρίων   ὕδρα

ἐπιδερμίς   ὑποθέσις   ἱπποπόταμος

ἰσοσκελής   ἀήρ   ὁρίζων.

Two vowels pronounced together are known as diphthongs (from the Greek δίς (= twice) and φθόγγος (= voice, sound). The commonest diphthongs are:-

αι = ai, as in aisle
αυ = ow, as in cow
ει = ey, as in grey
ευ (pronounce ε and υ separately)
οι as in "ahoy!"
ου = ou, as in soup.

ι does not usually form a diphthong with long α, η and ω, but remains silent, and is written underneath (iota subscript), as

ᾳ   ῃ   ῳ

Breathings are placed over the second vowel in a diphthong that begins a word, e.g.:-

Εὐφράτης   αὐτόματον   αἱμορραγία⁷

It will be seen that the second ρ in αἱμορραγία has a rough breathing. ρ normally has a rough breathing at the beginning of a word, and, as here, when it follows another ρ later in a word. What are:

ῥυθμ[ός]   ῥοδόδενδρον   ῥευματισμ[ός]

The English equivalents of the following Greek words (most of which have Greek endings lost in English) should now be clear:

ἀριστοκρατία   ὑποκριτής   ἀμφιθέατρον

ἀπάθεια   ῥαψῳδία   ᾠδή

αὐστηρός   συμπάθεια   ἀποπληξία

as should the following names from Greek mythology:

Ὀδυσσεύς   Παλλὰς Ἀθήνη   Ἑρμείας or Ἑρμῆς

Ἄρτεμις   Δημήτηρ   Ἥφαιστος

Ἰθάκη   Οὔλυμπος   Ἡρακλῆς

When two successive letters are vowels, but are to be pronounced separately, the second has a diaeresis mark ¨ above it, e.g. in Ὀϊλεύς, Oileus, the father of the lesser Ajax in the Iliad. If there is a breathing, it is attached to the first vowel.

Punctuation

Ancient Greek was written on papyrus, and punctuation consisted chiefly of occasional full stops. Words were not separated, and the letters were all capitals. The use of minuscule (small) letters came in with parchment, as did more punctuation. The following four signs are used:-

. is a full stop   , is a comma

· is a colon or semicolon   ; is a question mark.

Accents   There are three accents:
an acute (´), at which the voice was raised
a grave (`) at which the voice was lowered
a circumflex (ˆ) at which the voice was first raised and then lowered.[8]

---

[7] -ια is a Greek first declension termination (as in γαῖα, see Section 2, page 6).
[8] An acute accent is called in Greek "oxytone", a grave accent "barytone", and a circumflex "perispomenon".

Section 1

An acute or a grave accent is found on either a short or a long vowel. A circumflex is only found on a long vowel (a diphthong counts as a single long vowel). Most Greek words have only one accent; this is on one of the last three syllables.

(a) If the accent is on the third syllable from the end of a word, it is acute, and the last syllable normally has a short vowel, e.g. Πηνελόπεια.[9]

(b) If the accent is on the second syllable from the end, it may be acute or circumflex. If this syllable has a short vowel, the accent must be acute. If this syllable has a long vowel,
    (i) if the accent is acute e.g. Ποσειδάων, the last syllable must have a long vowel or a diphthong;
    (ii) if the accent is circumflex e.g. Γαῖα (Gaia, Earth); the last syllable must have a short vowel.

(c) If the accent is on the last syllable of a word, it may be acute e.g. Καλυψώ or circumflex e.g. Ἡρακλῆς. However, if a word is not followed by a break (a full stop, question mark, colon or comma) an acute accent on the last syllable becomes grave, e.g. Παλλάς in Παλλὰς Ἀθήνη. This is the only situation in which a grave accent is found.

Certain words ("enclitics") throw their accent forward onto the last syllable of the word in front. Two accents may then appear on the word in front of the enclitic[10] provided that two acute accents do not appear on successive syllables e.g. if an enclitic follows Ποσειδάων, the accent from the enclitic just disappears. If an enclitic follows a word ending with a grave accent, the grave accent becomes acute.

There are relatively few situations when accents affect the meaning.[11]

---

[9]There are exceptions, e.g. ῥινόκερως ("rhinoceros").
[10]The ending -δέ, meaning "towards", although not a separate word, is treated as an enclitic. So from θῶκος ("meeting") we have θῶκόνδε ("to a meeting") at line 3 and from οἶκος ("home"), at line 204 and at Odyssey VI, 159, οἶκόνδε ("homewards", "to home").
[11]Greek accents were probably first written in the 2nd century B.C. to record the tonic accent of ancient Athenian speech. They affect the pitch, not the pronunciation. For the peculiarities of accentuation in the traditional text of Homer (which are few) see Chantraine, *Grammaire Homérique* vol.i, pp.189-192.

Section 2
Part A - Nouns.

Nouns are words that name things and people, e.g. god in English (θεός in Greek) or island in English (νῆσος in Greek). Names of individuals or places are proper nouns and begin with a capital letter, e.g., Zeus (Ζεύς in Greek), or Ithaca in English (Ἰθάκη in Greek).

There are three declensions (groups of nouns according to the pattern of their endings) in Greek. First declension nouns have endings containing an a or e sound (α or η).

Greek has singular, plural and dual in both nouns and verbs. However, although duals are found in later writers (e.g. Plato and the tragedians) they are rare in Homer and can be noted rather than learned. All duals in the tabulations are printed in smaller type. There are no duals in the feminine nouns of the first declension.[1]

Singular nouns (first declension):

γαῖα (feminine)	θάλασσα (fem)	νύμφη (fem)	ἱκέτης (masculine)
land, earth	sea	nymph	suppliant

Their plurals:

γαῖαι	θάλασσαι	νύμφαι	ἱκέται
lands	seas	nymphs	suppliants

Second declension nouns have endings containing an o sound (o or ω).

Singular nouns, second declension:

ἑταῖρος (masculine)	νῆσος (feminine)	τέκνον (neuter)
companion	island	child

Their duals

ἑταίρω	νήσω	τέκνω
two companions	two islands	two children

Their plurals:

ἑταῖροι	νῆσοι	τέκνα
companions	islands	children

---

[1]For the masculines, see p. 231.

Section 2

All other nouns are in the third declension.

Singular nouns, third declension:

| πατήρ (masculine) father | πατρίς (feminine) fatherland | πῆμα (neuter) woe | λέχος (neuter) bed |

Their duals:

| πατέρε two fathers | πατρίδε two fatherlands | πήματε two woes | λέχεε two beds |

Their plurals:

| πατέρες fathers | πατρίδες fatherlands | πήματα woes | λέχεα beds |

All first declension nouns are feminine except those ending -ης, which mostly stand for classes of men (e.g. the ending -δης in Ἀτρείδης, meaning "son of Atreus"), and are masculine.

Although many second declension nouns ending -ος are masculine, some are feminine.

Second declension nouns ending –ον are all neuter.

The third declension includes masculine, feminine and neuter nouns. Note that there is a large class of 3rd declension nouns ending -ος which are neuter.

Neuter plurals end -α.

New words:
ἀκουή (1 fem) = report
μοῖρα (1 fem) = fate
θεά (1 fem) = goddess
θεός (2 masc) = god, (2 fem) = goddess
ἄγγελος (2 masc) = messenger
οἶκος (2 masc) = home or room or house
δῶμα (3 neuter) = hall (when plural, a king's palace)

NB, "the" is seldom expressed in Homer; e.g. ἀκουή can mean "a report" or "the report". *What is the English for*: 1.μοῖραι. 2.οἶκοι. 3.ἀκουαί. 4.ἄγγελος. 5.δώματα. 6.θεαί. 7.ἄγγελοι. 8.θεοί. 9.θεά. 10.θεός. 11.θεώ(NB, dual). 12. δῶμα. (Two meanings for each.)

Part B - Adjectives.

Adjectives qualify nouns, e.g. "good" in "a good thing".

Many Greek adjectives are of the first and second declension; adjectives are of the same gender as the nouns they qualify. Adjectives with the second declension ending -ος are *masculine*; those with the first declension ending -α or -η are *feminine*, and those with the second declension neuter ending -ον are *neuter*, as follows:

φίλος, φίλη, φίλον friendly, dear (*also* own, belonging to oneself)

masculine	feminine	neuter
φίλος	φίλη	φίλον
(a) friendly (man)	(a) friendly (woman)	(a) friendly (thing)

δῖος, δῖα,[2] δῖον heavenly, noble

masculine	feminine	neuter
δῖος	δῖα	δῖον
(a) noble (man)	(a) noble (woman)	(a) noble (thing)
	(a) heavenly (goddess)	

Compound adjectives, e.g. σκηπτοῦχος, "sceptre-bearing", which are made up of two or more words combined, have feminine endings like masculines,[3] e.g. καλλίσφυρος in Κάδμου θυγάτηρ, καλλίσφυρος Ἰνώ ("Cadmus' daughter, fair-ankled Ino") (Odyssey V, 333).[4] Similarly, εὔσκοπος ("keen-eyed", from εὖ = well and σκοπέω = I look) is masculine and feminine:

εὔσκοπος	εὔσκοπος
(a) keen eyed (man)	(a) keen-eyed (woman)

but in Homer, ἀθάνατος ("immortal"), from α- (= "un")[5] and θάνατος ("death"), can also have distinct masculine, feminine and neuter endings:

ἀθάνατος	ἀθάνατος	ἀθάνατον
	or ἀθανάτη	
(an) immortal (man)	(an) immortal (woman)	(an) immortal (thing)

New words: κακός, κακή, κακόν = bad, evil
καλός, καλή, καλόν = beautiful, fine

---

[2] Only a few adjectives have feminine singular ending -α. Most have -η.
[3] Such two-termination adjectives are given in lexica as ending -ος, -ον, to show that the feminine ending is -ος like the masculine. (A lexicon is a Greek dictionary.)
[4] Made up from κάλλος (beauty) and σφυρόν (ankle). (Κάδμου = of Cadmus, θυγάτηρ = daughter, καλλίσφυρος -ον = fair-ankled, Ἰνώ: Ino)
[5] The prefix α- meaning "un-" is called α-privative because it cancels the meaning of what immediately follows.

Section 2

What is the English for: 1.γαῖα καλή. 2.φίλος ἑταῖρος. 3.θεοὶ σκηπτοῦχοι. 4.μοῖρα κακή. 5.δῖον τέκνον. 6.ἀθάνατοι θεαί. 7.πήματα κακά. 8.δῖος ἱκέτης. 9.φίλη πατρίς. 10.ἀκουαὶ καλαί.

Part C - the verb "I am".

Present tense		Imperfect tense	
singular			
1 εἰμί	I am	ἦα[6]	I was
2 ἐσσί[7]	you are	ἦσθα[8]	you were
3 ἐστί(ν)[9]	he/she/it is	ἦεν[10]	he/she/it was
dual			
2 ἐστόν	you two are	ἦστον	you two were
3 ἐστόν	the two of them are	ἤστην	the two of them were
plural			
1 εἰμέν[11]	we are	ἦμεν	we were
2 ἐστέ	you are	ἦτε	you were
3 εἰσί(ν)[12]	they are	ἦσαν[13]	they were

The imperfect also means "I used to be" and "I was beginning to be". It is the only past tense of "to be" in Greek.

Neuter plurals. A neuter plural noun can have a singular verb in Greek; this sounds rather like "things is" in English.

New word: οὐ = not. (οὐκ before a smooth breathing,
                    οὐχ before a rough breathing)
What is the English for: 1.οἶκος ἐστὶ καλός. 2.ἀκουή οὐκ ἐστὶ κακή. 3.φίλοι δῖοι ἦσαν. 4.θεοί ἀθάνατοί εἰσι. 5.ἀθάνατος ἐσσί; 6.ἀθανάτω ἐστόν; (NB, dual) 7.ἀθανάτω ἤστην;(NB, dual) 8.κακά ἐστι τέκνα. 9.ἄγγελοι ἀθάνατοι οὐκ εἰσιν. 10.πατρὶς φίλη ἦεν. 11.νύμφαι δῖαί εἰσι. 12.δώματα κακὰ οὐκ ἦεν. 13.δώματα κακὰ οὐκ ἦσαν. 14.πῆμα κακόν ἐστι.

[6]Sometimes ἔα or ἔον.
[7]Sometimes εἰς. Attic & the Common Greek (koiné) of the New Testament have εἶ.
[8]Sometimes ἔησθα.
[9]ν can be added if the next word begins with a vowel and a hiatus is not wanted.
[10]Sometimes ἔην, ἤην or ἦν.
[11]Attic & koiné have ἐσμέν.
[12]Sometimes ἔασι(ν).
[13]Sometimes ἔσαν.

15. λέχος κακὸν ἦεν; 16. λέχος κακόν οὐκ ἐστί.

17. πατὴρ ὡς ἤπιος ἦεν. (Odyssey V, 12) (ὡς = as, like ἤπιος = kind)

18. Ζεὺς ὑψιβρεμέτης, οὗ κράτος ἐστὶ μέγιστον (Odyssey V, 4, altered)
(οὗ = whose κράτος = power μέγιστος = very great
ὑψιβρεμέτης = (1 masc.) the high thunderer)
(What declension does κράτος belong to?)

19. ἵκετο δ' εἰς Αἰγάς, ὅθι οἱ κλυτὰ δώματ'[14] ἔασιν. Odyssey V, 381 (about Poseidon, going home to his temple at Aegae) (ἵκετο = he arrived δὲ (δ') = and εἰς Αἰγάς = at Aegae ὅθι = where οἱ = to him κλυτός = famous) Note that "there is/ there are to him" = "he has".

20. δώματα πατρὸς ἐμοῦ μεγαλήτορος Ἀλκινόοιο ῥεῖα ἀρίγνωτ' ἐστί Odyssey VI, 299-300, adapted) (said by Nausicaa) (πατρός = of father ἐμοῦ = of my μεγαλήτορος = of great-hearted ' Ἀλκινόοιο = of Alcinous ῥεῖα = easily ἀρίγνωτος = recognisable

21. γαῖα Φαιήκων, ὅθι τοι μοῖρ' ἐστὶν ἀλύξαι (Odyssey V, 345; the goddess Leucothea to Odysseus) (Φαιήκων = of the Phaeacians τοι = for you ἀλύξαι = to escape)

---

[14]δώματ' ἔασιν stands for δώματα ἔασιν. When a word ending with a vowel stands immediately before a word beginning with a vowel, in order to avoid a hiatus or gap between the vowels, the final vowel of the first word can be omitted, and the omission is marked by an apostrophe (rather as in English, "don't" contains an apostrophe to show that it stands for "do not", and that the second o has been omitted). Such omissions in Greek are called *elisions* from the Latin verb *elido*, which means "I knock out". In δ', which stands for δὲ, ε has been elided.

If the word after the elision begins with a rough breathing, e.g. ἱκέτης, this may affect the word before. ἔπειτα ἱκέτης, "then a suppliant" becomes ἔπειθ' ἱκέτης because when α is elided from ἔπειτα, τ (t) is left adjacent to the rough breathing at the beginning of ἱκέτης and becomes θ (th). Similarly, if an elision leaves κ immediately before a rough breathing, it becomes χ, and π becomes φ.

Elision is common in Homer. ἀρίγνωτ' ἐστί which stands for ἀρίγνωτα ἐστί and μοῖρ' ἐστὶν which stands for μοῖρα ἐστὶν (both below) are other examples.

Section 3
Part A - Verbs

All sentences have subjects and predicates. The subject tells you what the sentence is about; e.g.
the gods were sitting down for a council
is about the gods; they are the subject. "were sitting down for a council" is the predicate; it says something about the gods, namely what they were doing, that they were sitting down for a council.

The Greek for this sentence is:
θεοί (*the gods*) θῶκόνδε (*for a council*) καθίζανον (*they were sitting down*).

The subject (*the gods*) is a plural noun; here, the predicate consists of *for a council*, which is an adverbial phrase, and *they were sitting down*, which is a verb.

Verbs show what a subject is doing, did, or will do, or what is being done to a subject, or was done to a subject, or will be done to a subject.

When the subject is *I*, a verb is said to be in the first person singular; when the subject is *we*, it is said to be in the first person plural.

When the subject is *you*, a verb is said to be in the second person, and can be either singular, or dual ("*both of you*"), or plural.

When the subject is *he, she* or *it*, a verb is said to be in the third person singular; if the subject is *both of them*, or *they both*, a verb is said to be in the third person dual, and if the subject is *they*, it is said to be in the third person plural.

When a verb in English shows what a subject is doing, will do, did or was doing it is said to be *active*.

When a verb shows what a subject is doing or does customarily, it is said to be in the present tense, and when it shows what a subject was doing, in the imperfect tense. When it shows what a subject will do, it is said to be future.

When a verb in Greek denotes a single, isolated action, usually in the past, it is said to be in the aorist tense.

Homeric Greek ending pattern for active verbs

person	present endings		past endings		
			weak aorist	imperfect and strong aorist	
	-ω verbs	-μι verbs	-ω and -μι verbs	-ω verbs	-μι verbs
1st singular (*I*)	-ω	-μι	-(σ)α	-ον	-ν
2nd singular (*you*)	-εις	-ς (or -σθα)	-(σ)ας	-ες	-ς (or -σθα)
3rd singular (*he/she/it*)	-ει	-σι	-(σ)ε	-ε	-
2nd dual (*you both*)	-ετον	-τον	-(σ)ατον	-ετον	-τον
3rd dual (*they both*)	-ετον	-τον	-(σ)ατην	-ετην	-την
1st plural (*we*)	-ομεν	-μεν	-(σ)αμεν	-ομεν	-μεν
2nd plural (*you*)	-ετε	-τε	-(σ)ατε	-ετε	-τε
3rd plural (*they*)	-ουσι	-(α)σι	-(σ)αν	-ον	-σαν

Present tense active verbs

λύω	I am loosing, I loose	φέρω	I am carrying, I carry
λύεις	you are loosing	φέρεις	you are carrying
λύει	he/she/it is loosing	φέρει	he/she/it is carrying
λύετον	you both are loosing	φέρετον	you both are carrying
λύετον	they both are loosing	φέρετον	they both are carrying
λύομεν	we are loosing	φέρομεν	we are carrying
λύετε	you are loosing	φέρετε	you are carrying
λύουσι	they are loosing	φέρουσι	they are carrying
ὄρνυμι	I am arousing,	φημί	I am saying (yes), affirming
ὄρνυς	you are arousing	φῄς[1]	you are saying (yes)
ὄρνυσι	he/she/it is arousing	φησί	he/she/it is saying (yes)
ὄρνυτον	you both are arousing	φατόν	you both are saying (yes)
ὄρνυτον	they both are arousing	φατόν	they both are saying (yes)
ὄρνυμεν	we are arousing	φαμέν	we are saying (yes)
ὄρνυτε	you are arousing	φατέ	you are saying (yes)
ὀρνύασι	they are arousing	φασί	they are saying (yes)

The first person singular ending in the present tense in most verbs is -ω, but in some is -μι. -μι verbs are called "athematic" because they lack the "thema", the <u>vowel which begins the ending</u>, in the present and

---
[1] or φῆσθα.

Section 3

imperfect tenses. Thus in -ω verbs, the ending for "we" is -ομεν, but in -μι verbs is -μεν. Notice that this is true of the second person singular, the first and second person endings in the plural, and the dual of athematic verbs in the present and imperfect tenses; the 3rd person singular ending of athematic verbs in the present tense is -σι(ν) and the 3rd person plural ending is -ασι(ν)

New words:
αἰεί = always
ἔχω = I have
ὄλλυμι = I destroy
χαίρω = I rejoice

ἐθέλω = I want, I wish
ἴσχω = I hold (back)
ὄμνυμι = I swear (a solemn oath)

Examples of the present tense:
(a) continuous action:
ἄγγελος ἀκουὴν φέρει - the messenger is bringing the report
(b) customary action:
πατέρες τέκνα αἰεὶ ἔχουσι - fathers always have children.

What is the English for:
1.λύομεν. 2.λύομεν; 3.ἐθέλουσι. 4.ἔχει. 5.χαίρομεν. 6.ἴσχεις. 7.ὄλλυσι. 8.ὀλλύασι. 9.ὄρνυς; 10.θεὸς ὄμνυσι. 11. οὐκ ἐθέλομεν. 12.οὐ χαίρω; 13.ἑταῖροι οὐ χαίρουσι. 14.ἄγγελοι φασί. 15.ἀγγέλω φατόν. (NB, dual)

16.χαίρουσί δὲ πατὴρ καὶ πότνια μήτηρ. (Odyssey VI, 30) (δέ = and, but καί = and ποτνία = lady μήτηρ = mother) (understand "your" with πατήρ and μήτηρ).

17.οἱ δὲ αἰεὶ ἐθέλουσι νεόπλυτα εἵματα (Odyssey VI, 64)
(οἱ = they νεόπλυτα εἵματα = freshly washed clothes).

18.ἔνθα Καλυψὼ ναίει, ἐϋπλόκαμος, δεινὴ θεός. (Odyssey VII, 244-5)
(ἔνθα = there. ναίω = I dwell. ἐϋπλόκαμος (two termination adjective): with beautiful tresses. δεινός, δεινή, δεινόν: terrible)

Part B - the Accusative Case
The Object
A subject and verb may make complete sense by themselves, e.g., *The sun is rising.* Such a verb is called intransitive. On the other hand, many verbs are transitive; that is, to complete the meaning of the sentence they need some expression to indicate what their action affects directly, e.g. *know* in *I know a bank where the wild thyme blows.* In

this sentence, *a bank* is directly affected by the verb *know*, which is transitive. A *bank* is the object of *know*.

When a noun is used as an object in Greek, the ending shows this. (Neuter nouns are an exception.) In the first and second declension, masculine and feminine nouns used to denote singular objects end -ν, and those used to denote plural objects end -ς. In the third declension, masculine and feminine nouns used to denote singular objects regularly end -α, and plural objects regularly end -ας.

The subjects are said to be in the nominative case,[2] and the objects in the accusative case. With duals and neuter nouns, the endings of the nominative and accusative cases are the same.

Singular, first declension nouns:
Nominative case (subject):

γαῖα	θάλασσα	νύμφη	ἱκέτης
land, earth	sea	nymph	suppliant

Accusative case (object)

γαῖαν	θάλασσαν	νύμφην	ἱκέτην
land, earth	sea	nymph	suppliant

Plural, first declension nouns:
Nominative case (subjects):

γαῖαι	θάλασσαι	νύμφαι	ἵκεται
lands	seas	nymphs	suppliants

Accusative case (objects)

γαίας	θαλάσσας	νύμφας	ἱκέτας
lands	seas	nymphs	suppliants

Singular, second declension nouns
Nominative case (subjects):

ἑταῖρος	νῆσος	τέκνον
companion	island	child

Accusative case (objects)

ἑταῖρον	νῆσον	τέκνον
companion	island	child

---

[2]The nominative case has other uses as well as to denote subjects. It is, for instance, the "naming" case, and is used as such after the verb "to be", e.g. εἰμὶ Ὀδυσεὺς Λαερτιάδης ("I am Odysseus, son of Laertes") at Odyssey IX, 19.

Section 3

Dual, second declension nouns
Nominative case (subjects):
ἑταίρω	νήσω	τέκνω
two companions	two islands	two children

Accusative case (objects):
ἑταίρω	νήσω	τέκνω
two companions	two islands	two children

Plural, second declension nouns
Nominative case (subjects):
ἑταῖροι	νῆσοι	τέκνα
companions	islands	children

Accusative case (objects):
ἑταίρους	νήσους	τέκνα
companions	islands	children

Singular, third declension nouns
Nominative case (subjects):
πατήρ	πατρίς	πῆμα	λέχος
father	fatherland	woe	bed

Accusative case (objects)
πατέρα	πατρίδα	πῆμα	λέχος
father	fatherland	woe	bed

Dual, third declension nouns
Nominative case (subjects):
πατέρε	πατρίδε	πήματε	λέχεε
two fathers	two fatherlands	two woes	two beds

Accusative case (objects)
πατέρε	πατρίδε	πήματε	λέχεε
two fathers	two fatherlands	two woes	two beds

Plural, third declension nouns
Nominative case (subjects):
πατέρες	πατρίδες	πήματα	λέχεα
fathers	fatherlands	woes	beds

Accusative case (objects)
πατέρας	πατρίδας	πήματα	λέχεα
fathers	fatherlands	woes	beds

Word order. In English, the word order decides the function of a word in a sentence: *the cat catches a mouse* is not the same as *a mouse catches the cat*. In Greek, because there are different cases for subjects and objects, it is the ending, not the word order, which indicates the function of a noun in a sentence. The word order can affect the emphasis, but will not tell you which nouns are subjects and which are objects.

What does this mean? Ὀδυσσεὺς πατέρα ἔχει.

What does this mean? πατέρα ἔχει Ὀδυσσεύς.

Do they mean the same? What about these two?

νύμφη ἄνθρωπον φιλέει (φιλέω = I like, I love, am a friend of)
νύμφην ἄνθρωπος φιλέει (ἄνθρωπος = man)

New words:
αἰέν (like αἰεί) = always   ἄλλος, ἄλλη, ἄλλο = other
ἀνάγκη 1f = necessity   ἄνθρωπος 2m = man
λαός (m) = the people
χαλεπός, χαλεπή, χαλεπόν = difficult, dangerous, rugged, bitter, hostile, cruel
γάρ = for (for the reason that) (2nd word in clause)
δέ = and, but, however (2nd word in clause)
ἠδέ = and   καί = and, also, indeed

What is the English for:
1.οἶκον καλὸν ἔχω. 2.πατέρα χαλεπὸν ἔχεις. 3.πατὴρ Ζεὺς ἄλλα τέκνα ἔχει. 4.κακοὺς ἑταίρους ἔχετε. 5.χαίρει λαός· θαλάσσαν γὰρ ἴσχει ἡ γαῖα. 6.θάλασσα γαῖαν οὐκ ὄλλυσι. 7.Ἀθήνη Ναυσικάαν πρῶï (early in the morning) ὄρνυσιν, ἄλλοι δὲ θεοί μιν (her) οὐκ ὀρνύασιν. 8.Ναυσικάα χαίρει· καλὸν γὰρ πατέρα ἔχει, καὶ καλὴν μητέρα. 9.τέκνα νεόπλυτα εἵματα ἐθέλουσι; πατὴρ καὶ πότνια μήτηρ φασίν. 10.ὄμνυσι Ζεύς, μοῖραν δὲ οὐκ ἴσχει. 11.θεοὶ ἠδὲ θεαὶ θῶκόνδε καθιζάνουσιν. (See p.11. καθιζάνω: I sit down.) 12.ἀνθρώπους καὶ ἀθανάτους μοῖρα ἴσχει.

Movement towards
Prepositions are used to indicate the relationship of nouns, e.g., *in* in the phrase *a ship in a bottle*. After most prepositions indicating movement towards, e.g. *towards the sea*, the accusative follows in Greek.
New words:
εἰς or ἐς (with accusative) = into, to   ἐπί (with accusative) = over, against, to
πρός (with accusative) = to, towards   πέμπω = I send.

What is the English for:
1.Ὀδυσσεὺς ἑταίρους ἐπὶ θαλάσσαν πέμπει. 2.νύμφη ἑταίρους εἰς δῶμα οὐ πέμπει. 3. ἀθάνατοι ἀγγέλους πρὸς ἀνθρώπους αἰὲν πέμπουσιν. 4.πρὸς φίλην πατρίδα ἀγγέλους οὐ πέμπομεν.

Section 3

First and second person pronouns
Nominative:
ἐγώ = I   σύ *or* συ = you   ἡμεῖς *or* ἄμμες   ὑμεῖς *or* ὔμμες
                                   = we   = you (plural)
Accusative:
ἐμέ *or* με   σέ *or* σε   ἥμας *or* ἥμεας   ὑμέας *or* ὔμμε
= me   = you   *or* ἄμμε   = you (plural)
                               =us

What is the English for: 1.σὺ πρὸς θεοὺς ἄγγελον πέμπεις; 2.εἰς δώματα ἐμὲ νύμφη οὐ πέμπει. 3.οἴμοι·[3] Ὀδυσσεύς καὶ Ἀγαμέμνων ἡμας ἐπὶ θαλάσσαν πέμπουσι. 4.ὑμέας δὲ πρὸς Σκύλλην ἡδὲ Χάρυβδιν πέμπουσι. 5.ἐγὼ καὶ σὺ χαίρομεν· ἀκούη γὰρ ἀληθινή[4] οὐκ ἐστί.

6.σχέτλιοί ἐστε, θεοί (Odyssey V, 118)[5] (Calypso is speaking to Hermes)
7.Διογενὲς Λαερτιάδη, πολυμήχαν' Ὀδυσσεῦ,
οὕτω δὴ οἰκόνδε φίλην ἐς πατρίδα γαῖαν
αὐτίκα νῦν ἐθέλεις ἰέναι;[6] (Odyssey V, 203-5; Calypso to Odysseus)
8.χαλεπὸν δέ με πένθος ἰκάνει.[7] (Odyssey VI, 169) (Odysseus to Nausicaa)
9.ξεῖνος... πομπὴν ὀτρύνει (Odyssey VIII, 28-30)[8]
(King Alcinous to his court.)
10.ἐμὲ ... Διὸς θυγάτηρ Ἀφροδίτη αἰὲν ἀτιμάζει
φιλέει δ' ἀΐδηλον Ἄρηα.[9] (Odyssey VIII, 308-9)
(Hephaestus' complaint in the lay of Demodocus.)
11. Οὖτιν δὲ μὲ κικλήσκουσι
μήτηρ ἠδὲ πατὴρ ἠδ' ἄλλοι πάντες ἑταῖροι[10] (Odyssey IX 366-7)
(Odysseus to Polyphemus, the Cyclops.)
12.παῖδά τε σὸν φιλέει καὶ ἐχέφρονα Πηνελόπειαν. (Odyssey XIII, 406)[11]
(Athene speaking to Odysseus about Eumaeus, the faithful swineherd.)

[3]Alas!
[4]ἀληθινός, ἀληθινή, ἀληθινόν = true.
[5]σχέτλιος = hardhearted, cruel.
[6]Διογενης = descended from Zeus. Λαερτιάδης = son of Laertes. πολυμήχαν' Ὀδυσσεῦ stands for πολυμήχανε Ὀδυσσεῦ, O resourceful (*literally*, of many devices) Odysseus! Διογενὲς and Λαερτιάδη, and πολυμήχαν' and Ὀδυσσεῦ are vocative; see p.41. οὕτω = so, in this way. δή = indeed, really. οἰκόνδε = homewards (cf θῶκόνδε, towards a meeting). αὐτίκα = all at once. νῦν = now. ἰέναι = to come, to go.
[7]πένθος 3 neuter (like λέχος) = sorrow, misfortune. ἰκάνω = I arrive at, I reach.
[8]ξεῖνος = stranger πομπή = escort ὀτρύνω = I request urgently.
[9]Διός = of Zeus. θυγάτηρ (3rd declension) = daughter. ἀτιμάζω = I dishonour. φιλέω = I love. ἀΐδηλος = destructive. Ἄρης (accusative, Ἄρηα) 3rd declension = Ares.
[10]Οὖτις (accusative, Οὖτιν) = Noman. κικλήσκω = I call. ἠδ' stands for ἠδὲ. πάντες = all.
[11]παῖς (accusative, παῖδα) 3rd declension: son. σός, σή, σόν = your. τε ... καὶ ... = both ... and ... ἐχέφρων (accusative singular ἐχέφρονα) 3rd declension: prudent. φιλέω = I love.

Section 4
Part A - Verbs (Middle & Passive)

In the sentence *I know a bank where the wild thyme blows,* "know" says what I do and "blows" says what the wild thyme does. Both are active verbs; they express something that a subject does.

In the sentence *O my Luve's like a melody that's sweetly played in tune* "is played" does not express what the melody does, but what is done to the melody. "is played" is a *passive* verb.

In Greek, there are *middle* verbs, which express what one does or gets done to or for oneself. The English "I get my hair cut" would in Greek be expressed by a middle verb; it is something I get done to myself.

In early Greek the middle was probably not distinguished from the passive, and in Homer the middle and passive endings, except for the aorist, are the same.

active		middle & passive	
λύω	I am loosing	λύομαι	I am loosing for myself *or* I am being loosed
λύεις	you are loosing	λύεαι *or* λύῃ	you are loosing for yourself *or* being loosed
λύει	he/she/it is loosing	λύεται	he/she/it is loosing for himself, herself, itself *or* being loosed
λύετον	you two are loosing	λύεσθον	you two are loosing for yourselves *or* being loosed
λύετον	those two are loosing	λύεσθον	those two are loosing for themselves *or* being loosed
λύομεν	we are loosing	λυόμε(σ)θα	we are loosing for ourselves *or* being loosed
λύετε	you are loosing	λύεσθε	you are loosing for yourselves *or* being loosed
λύουσι(ν)	they are loosing	λύονται	they are loosing for themselves *or* being loosed

Section 4

The endings are as follows:- -ω verbs

	active	middle & passive
singular	-ω = I	-ομαι = I
	-εις = you	-εαι or -ῃ = you
	-ει = he, she, it	-εται = he, she, it
dual	-ετον = you two	-εσθον = you two
	-ετον = those two	-εσθον = those two
plural	-ομεν = we	-ομε(σ)θα = we
	-ετε = you	-εσθε = you
	-ουσι(ν) = they	-ονται = they

-μι verbs

	active	middle & passive
singular	-μι = I	-μαι = I
	-ς = you	-σαι = you
	-σι = he, she, it	-ται = he, she, it
dual	-τον = you two	-σθον = you two
	-τον = those two	-σθον = those two
plural	-μεν = we	-με(σ)θα = we
	-τε = you	-σθε = you
	-ασι(ν) = they	-νται = they

Compare:

	active		middle & passive	
singular	ὄρνυμι	I arouse	ὄρνυμαι	I arise, arouse myself, am aroused
	ὄρνυς	you arouse	ὄρνυσαι	you arise
	ὄρνυσι(ν)	he, she, it arouses	ὄρνυται	he, she, it arises
dual	ὄρνυτον	you two arouse	ὄρνυσθον	you two arise
	ὄρνυτον	those two arouse	ὄρνυσθον	those two arise
plural	ὄρνυμεν	we arouse	ὀρνύμε(σ)θα	we arise
	ὄρνυτε	you arouse	ὄρνυσθε	you arise
	ὀρνύασι(ν)	they arouse	ὄρνυνται	they arise

NB (1) Some English active verbs (e.g. "arise") are equivalent to Greek middle verbs. (2) In Odyssey V, φέρομαι (from φέρω) is found in its passive sense, "I am carried, borne".

What is the English for:
1.λύεαι. 2.λυόμεθα. 3.λύεται. 4.φέρεται. 5.ὄρνυται. 6.φερόμεθα. 7.ὄρνυσθε. 8.ὄρνυσαι. 9.φέρεαι. 10.φέρονται. 11.ὄρνυσθε; 12.ὀρνύμεθα. 13.φέρεσθε. 14.φέρουσιν. 15.ὀρνύασιν. 16.ὄρνυσιν. 17.φέρεσθε; 18.οὐ φερόμεθα. 19.οὐκ ὄρνυσθε; 20.οὐκ ὀρνύμεθα.

Passive verbs
Passive verbs are found in this striking description of the home of the happy gods on top of Mount Olympus:

ἡ μὲν ἄρ᾽ ὣς εἰποῦσ᾽ ἀπέβη γλαυκῶπις Ἀθήνη
Οὔλυμπόνδ᾽, ὅθι φασὶ θεῶν ἕδος ἀσφαλὲς αἰεὶ
ἔμμεναι· οὔτ᾽ ἀνέμοισι τινάσσεται οὔτε ποτ᾽ ὄμβρῳ
δεύεται οὔτε χιὼν ἐπιπίλναται, ἀλλὰ μάλ᾽ αἴθρη
πέπταται ἀννέφελος, λευκὴ δ᾽ ἐπιδέδρομεν αἴγλη·
τῷ ἔνι τέρπονται μάκαρες θεοὶ ἤματα πάντα. (Odyssey VI, 41-47)

ἡ = she μέν = in truth ἄρ᾽ stands for ἄρα = then ὣς = so εἰποῦσ᾽ stands for εἰποῦσα = saying (feminine) ἀπέβη = went away γλαυκῶπις = with gleaming eyes Οὔλυμπόνδ᾽ stands for Οὔλυμπόνδε = towards Olympus ὅθι = where θεῶν = of the gods ἀσφαλὲς ἕδος (neuter) = safe seat ἔμμεναι = to be οὔτ᾽ stands for οὔτε οὔτε ... οὔτε ... = neither ... nor ... ἀνέμοισι = by winds τινάσσω = I shake ποτ᾽ (stands for ποτε) = ever ὄμβρῳ = by rain δεύω = I wet χιών (3rd declension, feminine, nominative) = snow ἐπιπίλναμαι (middle) = I come near ἀλλά = but μάλ᾽ stands for μάλα = utterly αἴθρη = clear sky πέπταται = has been spread ἀννέφελος = cloudless (fem., qualifies αἴθρη) λευκή = white δ᾽ stands for δὲ ἐπιδέδρομεν = has spread over αἴγλη = radiance τῷ ἔνι = in it τέρπω = I delight (τέρπομαι is middle, I enjoy myself) μάκαρ (3) = happy ἤματα πάντα = all (their) days

New words:
καίω = I light, burn up   πῦρ (3, neuter) = fire
καίομαι (passive) = I burn (intransitive, i.e. with no object)
καίομαι (middle) = I light for myself
μάκαρ (3, adjective) = happy, blessed (plural, μάκαρες)

Section 4

What is the English for:
1. νύμφη πῦρ καίει.
2. πῦρ καίεται.
3. νύμφη πῦρ καίεται.

N.B. καίομαι (passive) is translated by an English active verb.

Some verbs are found in the passive, but can have active meanings, as καίομαι can mean "I am burning". Others can be middle or passive, e.g. τέρπομαι = I enjoy myself (middle) or I am delighted (passive).

What is the English for:
4. θεὸς τέρπεται ἰδὼν (seeing) οἶκον Καλυψοῦς (of Calypso).

Middle verbs

Middle verbs are more found more often than passive in Homer, and many are used simply as conveying their own meanings like active verbs. Among the most common are:-

ἀμείβομαι = I answer, reply
γίγνομαι = I become, happen
δύναμαι = I can
ἔρχομαι = I come, go
ἱκνέομαι = I come, arrive at, approach as suppliant
κεῖμαι = I lie (down)

δύναμαι	κεῖμαι	μέμνημαι
= I can	= I lie (down)	= I remember
δύνασαι	κεῖσαι	μέμνησαι
= you can	= you lie	= you remember
δύναται	κεῖται	μέμνηται
= he, she, it can	= he, she, it lies	= he, she, it remembers
δύνασθον	κεῖσθον	μέμνησθον
= you two can	= you two lie	= you two remember
δύνασθον	κεῖσθον	μέμνησθον
=those two can	= those two lie	= those two remember
δυνάμε(σ)θα	κείμε(σ)θα	μεμνήμε(σ)θα
= we can	= we lie	= we remember
δύνασθε	κεῖσθε	μέμνησθε
= you can	= you lie	= you remember
δύνανται	κείαται *or* κέαται *or*	μέμνηνται
= they can	κέονται = they lie	= they remember

μέμνημαι is perfect middle from μιμνήσκω ("I remind") and means "I have reminded myself" (Chantraine, *Grammaire Homérique* vol.i, p.436).

δύναμαι and κεῖμαι are middle verbs of the -μι type.[1] κεῖμαι also means "I have been put".[2]

New word: λέγω = I say, speak.

What is the English for (a): 1.τέρπεαι. 2.δύνασαι. 3.μέμνησαι. 4.ἀμείβεαι. 5.ἔρχεαι. 6.ὄρνυσαι. 7.οὐκ ἀμείβεαι. 8.ἔρχεαι; 9.οὐ μέμνησαι. 10.οὐ τέρπεαι; (b): 1.κείμεθα. 2.κέαται. 3.δύνασθε. 4.ἀμείβεται. 5.ἔρχονται. 6.καίεαι. 7.οὐ μεμνήμεθα. 8.ὄρνυσαι; 9.πῦρ καίεαι; 10.πῦρ ἤδη (already) καίεται. (c): 1.χαίρομεν 2.τερπόμεθα. 3.τέκνα ὄρνυμεν. 4.τέκνα ὄρνυται. 5.'Ηὼς (the Dawn) ὄρνυται. 6.θεοὶ θῶκόνδε[3] ἔρχονται. 7. 'Αθηναίη (Athene) λέγει. 8.Ζεὺς ὑψιβρεμέτης ἀμείβεται; 9.οὐκ αἰεὶ χαλεπός ἐστιν. 10. ἀνάγκη καὶ θέμις (right, as opp. to wrong) θεοὺς ἴσχουσιν· ἀνάγκῃ (by necessity) ἴσχεται Ζεύς.

Part B - The Infinitive

The infinitive is expressed in English most often by *to ...*, as in *to be or not to be, that is the question*. It is a verbal noun, and can be the subject of a sentence, or the object: *I do not like to see this kind of thing*. In Greek, it often goes with δύναμαι, as we say "I am able to..." in English.

Infinitives (present)

The infinitive of -ω verbs ends -ειν, or -εμεν or -εμεναι; so
to loose can be λύειν, λύεμεν or λυέμεναι.
The present active infinitive ending of -μι verbs is -ναι or -μεναι or -μεν:[4] so

"to be" = εἶναι or ἔμμεναι

"to arouse" = ὀρνύμεναι

(φάναι = to affirm is not found in Homer).

---

[1] The aorist of δύναμαι is found at line 315 with an aorist passive ending, but this is an exception. (The aorist is the only distinctively passive tense form found in Homer; see Sections 18 and 19.)
[2] It is used as the perfect passive of τίθημι (= I put) (Section 15).
[3] See p.5.
[4] See Chantraine, *op. cit.* vol.1, pp.485-493. The various forms of the infinitive are drawn from different dialects; -ειν is Ionic-Attic, -ναι is Ionic, while -εμεν and -εμεναι are Aeolic.

Section 4

Middle and passive present infinitives end -σθαι; so we have:
λύεσθαι = to loose for oneself, to be loosed
φέρεσθαι = to carry for oneself, be carried, borne
ὄρνυσθαι = to arise, to be aroused
γίγνεσθαι = to become, to happen.

What is the English for: 1.οἶκον καλὸν ἔχειν ἐθέλω. 2.πατὴρ κακὸν τέκνον ἴσχειν ἐθέλει. 3.πατὴρ κακὸν τέκνον ἴσχεμεν οὐ δύναται. 4.Ὀδυσσεύς εἰς πατρίδα φίλην ἱκνεῖσθαι (contracted from ἱκνέεσθαι) ἐθέλει. 5.μοῖραν οὐ δύναται ἴσχειν Ζεύς ὑψιβρεμέτης. 6.πῦρ καίειν οὐ δύναμεθα· ψύχει (by cold) ὀλλύμεθα. 7.ἄγγελοι ἵππους (horses) οὐκ ἔχουσιν· ἔρχεσθαι οὐ δύνανται. 8.ἄγγελοι οὐκ ἀμείβονται· "μέμνησθαι γὰρ οὐ δυνάμεθα," λέγουσιν. 9. Ὀδυσσεύς ἑταίρους ὀρνύμεναι οὐ δύναται. 10.ἱκέτην εἰς πατρίδα φίλην ἱκνεῖσθαι οὐκ ἐθέλουσιν ἀθάνατοι. 11.θεοὶ μάκαρες εἶναι λέγονται. 12.Ζεὺς ὑψιβρεμέτης θεῶν (of the gods) πατὴρ εἶναι λέγεται.

Part C - The Homeric hexameter[5]

The Iliad and the Odyssey are composed in dactylic hexameters. Each line is scanned according to the length of the syllables. A long syllable contains *either* a long vowel (η, ω, or long α, ι, or υ), *or* a diphthong (two vowels sounded together) *or* a short vowel followed by more than one consonant. Other syllables are short.

Each line contains six feet, and each of the first five feet is either a <u>dactyl</u> (δάκτυλος: finger), a long syllable followed by two short syllables (-◡◡), or a <u>spondee</u>, two long syllables (- -). However, because of the inevitable slight lengthening of the final syllable of each line before the next one begins, the spondee in the sixth foot can be long + short (- ◡).

The pattern of feet can be shown as follows:

  -◡◡ -◡◡ -◡◡ -◡◡ -◡◡ -◡
  - -   - -   - -   - - (- -) - -.

Points to note:
- the fifth foot is almost always a dactyl.
- <u>many, but not all lines</u> end either with a two or a three syllable word.

[5]For a fuller discussion, see Rutherford, *Odyssey XIX & XX* pp.78-85, Garvie, *Odyssey VI-VIII* pp.31-33 and Jones, *Odyssey 1&2* pp.24-25.

- sometimes a syllable with a short vowel followed by two successive consonants is counted as short if the consonants are a mute (κ, π, τ or χ, φ, θ) followed by a liquid (λ, μ, ν or ρ), e.g. the first syllable of τέκνον may be counted either long or short in scanning. (In Homeric verse occasionally in other circumstances a long vowel will be shortened[6] or a short vowel lengthened or merged into a following long vowel in order to scan.)

- a hiatus (where a word ending in a vowel is followed by a word beginning with a vowel) is sometimes allowed, but often avoided by eliding[7] the vowel at the end of the first of the two words:

ἡ μὲν ἄρ' ὣς εἰποῦσ' ἀπέβη γλαυκῶπις 'Αθήνη

where α has been elided from εἰποῦσα.

- in every line there must be a break between words within either the third or fourth foot. These breaks are called *caesurae*.

The "masculine" caesura[8] occurs after the first syllable of the third foot, e.g.

_ ᴗ ᴗ _ _ _ ᴗ ᴗ _ _ _ ᴗ ᴗ _ _

ἡ μὲν ἄρ' ὣς εἰποῦσ' | ἀπέβη γλαυκῶπις 'Αθήνη

The "feminine" caesura occurs after the first *short* syllable of the third foot, which is a dactyl, e.g.

_ _ _ ᴗ ᴗ _ ᴗ | ᴗ _ ᴗ ᴗ _ ᴗ ᴗ _ _

Οὔλυμπόνδ', ὅθι φασὶ θεῶν ἕδος ἀσφαλὲς αἰει

Occasionally, the caesura is after the first syllable of the fourth foot, e.g.

_ ᴗ ᴗ _ _ _ ᴗ _ | ᴗ ᴗ _ ᴗ ᴗ _ _

Διογενὲς Λαερτιάδη, πολυμήχαν' 'Οδυσσεῦ (Odyssey V, 203)

If the following two lines are translated, in the same word order, into Greek, each will form a Homeric hexameter:

[6]When a long vowel or diphthong is scanned as short before a hiatus, this is called "correption".
[7]See p.10.
[8]Rutherford, *op. cit.* p.81.

1. The most handsome (κάλλιστοι) fathers handsome children not always they have.[9] (The most handsome fathers do not always have handsome children.)
2. Zeus (the) High-thunderer (ὑψιβρεμέτης) (NB ι is long), of whom (οὗ) assuredly (τε) (the) power (κράτος) is very great (μέγιστον).

The influence of the Homeric poems and of Hesiod is found in many later poets. Dactylic hexameters were used by the 6th and 5th century philosophers Parmenides and Empedocles, and were revived for epic by Apollonius of Rhodes in the 3rd century. Ennius (born 239 B.C.), who claimed that Homer had acknowledged him in a dream as his own reincarnation, adopted dactylic hexameters for Latin epic. The greatest Latin poets followed, including Lucretius (in philosophy) and Vergil. Compare Odyssey VI, 41-47, quoted on p. 20, with this:

> apparet divum numen sedesque quietae
> quas neque concutiunt venti nec nubila nimbis
> aspergunt neque nix acri concreta pruina
> cana cadens violat semperque innubilus aether
> integit, et largo diffuso lumine ridet.
> <div align="right">Lucretius, <i>de Rerum Natura</i>
("concerning the nature of the universe") III, 18-22</div>

(There) appears the godhead of the divine beings and their tranquil seats
which neither do winds shake nor clouds with cloudbursts
spatter nor does snow fixed hard with sharp frost
falling white disturb, and always cloudless sky
covers, and laughs with generous outpoured light.

Homeric images appear in other languages in poetry of later times. The safe seat of the gods, for instance, is reflected in the nineteenth century English poem *Morte d' Arthur* by Tennyson:
> the island-valley of Avilion;
> where falls not hail, nor rain, nor any snow,
> nor ever wind blows loudly; but it lies
> deep-meadow'd, happy, fair, with orchard-lawns
> and bowery hollows crown'd with summer sea...

---
[9]Translate "handsome" as καλά (to qualify τέκνα). Use αἰέν for "always", and elide α from τέκνα in front of οὐκ. The caesura is masculine, after πατέρες.

Section 5
Possessives - The Genitive Case.

There are three more cases to learn: the genitive, the dative and the vocative.

The genitive case is used to indicate possession (in English, 'of'), or source (e.g. with prepositions showing separation, *from, out of*).

Singular, first declension nouns:
Nominative case (subject):
γαῖα	θάλασσα	νύμφη	ἱκέτης
land, earth	sea	nymph	suppliant

Accusative case (object)
γαῖαν	θάλασσαν	νύμφην	ἱκέτην
land, earth	sea	nymph	suppliant

Genitive case
γαίης[1]	θαλάσσης	νύμφης	ἱκέταο or ἱκέτεω[2]
of land	of sea	of nymph	of suppliant

Plural, first declension nouns:
Nominative case (subjects):
γαῖαι	θάλασσαι	νύμφαι	ἵκεται
lands	seas	nymphs	suppliants

Accusative case (objects)
γαίας	θαλάσσας	νύμφας	ἱκέτας
lands	seas	nymphs	suppliants

Genitive case
γαιάων	θαλασσάων	νυμφάων	ἱκετάων
of lands	of seas	of nymphs	of suppliants

Singular, second declension nouns
Nominative case (subject):
ἑταῖρος	νῆσος	τέκνον
companion	island	child

Accusative case (objects)
ἑταῖρον	νῆσον	τέκνον
companion	island	child

Genitive case
ἑταίροιο or	νήσοιο or	τέκνοιο or
ἑταίρου	νήσου	τέκνου
of companion	of island	of child

[1] The genitive singular of feminine first declension nouns ends -ης in Homer except for θεᾶς ("of (the) goddess").
[2] The Attic form is ἱκέτου.

Dual, second declension nouns
Nominative case (subjects):
ἑταίρω   νήσω   τέκνω
two companions   two islands   two children
Accusative case (objects):
ἑταίρω   νήσω   τέκνω
two companions   two islands   two children
Genitive case
ἑταίροιιν   νήσοιιν   τέκνοιιν
of two companions of two islands   of two children

Plural, second declension nouns
Nominative case (subjects):
ἑταῖροι   νῆσοι   τέκνα
companions   islands   children
Accusative case (objects):
ἑταίρους   νήσους   τέκνα
companions   islands   children
Genitive case
ἑταίρων   νήσων   τέκνων
of companions   of islands   of children

Singular, third declension nouns
Nominative case (subjects):
πατήρ   πατρίς   πῆμα   λέχος   'Οδυσσεύς[3]
father   fatherland   woe   bed   Odysseus
Accusative case (objects)
πατέρα   πατρίδα   πῆμα   λέχος   'Οδυσσῆα[4]
father   fatherland   woe   bed   Odysseus (object)
Genitive case
πατρός   πατρίδος   πήματος   λέχεος   'Οδυσσῆος[5]
(rarely πατέρος) of fatherland of woe   of bed   of Odysseus
of father

Dual, third declension nouns and accusative case (objects)
Nominative case (subjects):
πατέρε   πατρίδε   πήματε   λέχεε
two fathers   two fatherlands   two woes   two beds
The 3rd declension genitive and dative dual ending (rare) is –οῖιν.[6]

---

[3] Also sometimes spelled 'Οδυσεύς.

[4] Also 'Οδυσσέα.

[5] Also often 'Οδυσῆος. Once 'Οδυσσέος (Iliad iv, 491) and once 'Οδυσεῦς (note circumflex accent), at Odyssey XXIV, 398.

[6] It is found most often in the dative e.g. at Iliad xviii, 537 ἕλκε ποδοῖιν, "she (fate) was dragging (a dead man) by his two feet" (ἕλκω = I drag, πούς, ποδός (masculine) = foot).

Plural, third declension nouns

Nominative case (subjects):
πατέρες	πατρίδες	πήματα	λέχεα
fathers	fatherlands	woes	beds

Accusative case (objects)
πατέρας	πατρίδας	πήματα	λέχεα
fathers	fatherlands	woes	beds

Genitive case
πατέρων *or*	πατρίδων	πημάτων	λεχέων
πατρῶν	of fatherlands	of woes	of beds
of fathers			

Summary of genitive endings (singular):
    first declension   -ης (feminine)   -αο (masculine)
    second declension -οιο or -ου
    third declension   -ος
The genitive plural ending is -ων (-αων in the first declension).[7]

Third declension nouns are given in lexica in two cases, nominative singular followed by genitive singular e.g.
    πατρίς, πατρίδος (feminine), fatherland.
    Ζεύς, Διός (more rarely, Ζηνός) (masculine), Zeus.
The stem of a noun is the part left when any prefixes or endings have been taken off. πατριδ- is the stem of πατρίδος, the genitive ending -ος having been removed. The genitive case is given in lexica because the other cases (except the nominative singular) are generally found by removing -ος and substituting the ending of the case wanted; e.g. πατρίδος (genitive singular) - ος = πατρίδ-. πατρίδ- +α gives πατρίδα, the accusative singular. A few third declension nouns have stems in the genitive singular unlike the nominative singular. In those examples, the usual rule is still that the other cases are found by using the genitive singular stem; e.g. the usual accusative of Ζεύς is Δία (Διός - ος leaves Δί. Δί + α = Δία). Alternatively, the accusative is Ζῆνα (from Ζηνός).

Give the case of the following 3rd declension nouns and adjectives, and say which are singular and which plural. Give also the nominative singular.
1.λέχεος. 2.πήματα (two possibilities, because neuter). 3.δωμάτων. 4.πατέρα. 5.λεχέων. 6.πατέρας. 7.πατέρες. 8.πατρίδα. 9.δώματος. 10.δώματα (NB., neuter). 11.μακάρων. 12.'Οδυσσῆος.

---

[7]The ending -θεν is sometimes used to indicate a genitive, e.g. ἐμέθεν ("of me") and σέθεν ("of you") on p.29. -θεν also means "from"; see p.136, footnote 30.

Section 5

New words:
Ἠώς (3 fem) = Dawn[8]
ὀφθαλμός (2 masc) = eye
πόντος (2 masc) = the open sea
τις, τινος = anybody
τίς, τίνος; = who?

θεῖος -α -ον = godlike, marvellous, superhuman
σχεδίη (1 fem) = raft
τι, τινος = anything
τί, τίνος; = what?

The pronoun τις is third declension. When it is indefinite ("somebody", "anybody", neuter "something", "anything") it appears unaccented because the accent is placed on the preceding word.[9] τις, as an adjective, means "any". ἄγγελός τις means "some messenger" or "any messenger". τίς accented normally is the interrogative pronoun.

Say which the case of each of the following is, and whether it is singular or plural:
1.τινος. 2.τινες. 3.τίνας; 4.τι (two possibilities). 5.τινα (three possibilities).

What is the English for:
1.ἔρχεταί τις. 2.τίς ἔρχεται; 3.τίς λέγει; 4.τί λέγει; 5.τίνος οἰκός ἐστιν; 6.οἰκός ἐστί τινος. 7.θεός τις.

When τις is used to qualify an adjective, it makes the meaning less precise: κακός τις - a kind of bad (man).

First and second person pronouns

Nominative:
ἐγώ = I	σύ = you	ἡμεῖς *or* ἄμμες = we	ὑμεῖς *or* ὕμμες = you

Accusative:
ἐμέ *or* με =me	σέ *or* σε = you	ἥμας *or* ἤμεας *or* ἄμμε = us	ὑμέας *or* ὕμμε = you

Genitive:
ἐμεῖο *or* ἐμέο *or* ἐμεῦ *or* μευ *or* ἐμέθεν	σεῖο *or* σέο *or* σέθεν *or* σευ	ἡμείων *or* ἡμέων	ὑμείων *or* ὑμέων
= my, of me	= your, of you	= our, of us	= your, of you

---
[8]Only found in the nominative singular in Homer. The genitive of Ἠώς would be Ἠόος but is contracted to Ἠοῦς. The accusative is Ἠῶ, contracted from Ἠόα, and the dative is Ἠοῖ. There is no plural.
[9]i.e. it is enclitic (see Section 1, p.5).

Genitives indicating possession. *What is the English for*:
1.τίνος οίκός έστιν; δῶμα νύμφης. 2.οίκος ίκέταο. 3.δῶμα θεοίο. 4.δῶμα θεοῦ τινος. 5.οίκος ἡμέων. 6.λέχος τέκνοιο. 7.λέχος τέκνου. 8.λέχος Ἠοῦς. 9.δώματα θεάων. 10.δώματα θεῶν. 11.νῆσος νύμφης. 12.ὀφθαλμός μου. 13.ἕταιροι' Ὀδυσσῆος. 14.' Ὀδυσσῆος σχεδίη. 15.εἰς πατρίδα ὑμείων. 16.θέαι ἠδὲ θεοὶ γαίης μάκαρές εἰσι. 17.δώματα νύμφης καλά ἐστι. 18. ὑμεῖς, τίνες ἐστέ; ἡμεῖς ἑταῖροι θείου' Ὀδυσσῆός εἰμεν. σὺ δέ, τίς ἐσσί; 19.τίνος ἄγγελος ἐσσί σύ; 20.ἄγγελός εἰμι Διός ὑψιβρεμέταο ἠδ' ἄλλων μακάρων θεῶν. 21.τίς πόντου κρείων[10] ἐστιν; Ποσειδάων ἐνοσίχθων (the earth-shaker)· ' Ὀδυσσῆος φίλος οὐκ ἔστιν.

Other uses of the genitive case.
1. The genitive case is used to imply **separation**,

e.g. χῶρος λεῖος πετράων (Odyssey V, 442-3)
a place free from rocks
(χῶρος = place λεῖος –α –ον = free[11] πέτρα = rock)

The genitive is therefore used with prepositions which imply separation
e.g. ἀπὸ = from, ἐκ or ἐξ = out of, and παρά = from beside.

λαχὼν ἀπὸ ληίδος αἶσαν (Odyssey V, 40)
having obtained a share from the booty
(λάχων = having obtained ληίς, ληίδος 3fem. = booty αἶσα 1fem. = share[12])

ἐκ πόντου βὰς ἰοειδέος ἠπειρόνδε (Odyssey V, 56)
having gone out of the violet coloured sea towards the dry land
(βὰς = having gone ἰοειδής (3) = violet coloured ἤπειρος (2fem.) = dry land, mainland
–δε = towards)

ἐγὼ δ' ἄορ ὀξὺ ἐρυσσάμενος παρὰ μηροῦ (Odyssey XI, 24)
and I, a sharp sword having drawn from beside my thigh
(ἄορ (3neut.) = sword ὀξύς, ὀξεῖα, ὀξύ = sharp ἐρυσσάμενος = having drawn μηρός (2 masc.) = thigh)

The genitive is also used with many prepositions when the idea of separation is not apparent, or perhaps has been replaced by the idea of "cause", e.g. ἐπί + genitive = "on" or "upon", perhaps with the connotation of "supported from".

ἐπὶ θρόνου (Odyssey V, 195)
on a chair
(θρόνος (2 masc) = chair)

---

[10]κρείων, κρείοντος (3 masc.) = lord.
[11]literally, smooth.
[12]Sometimes personified as Αἶσα, fate (rather like Μοῖρα), the goddess of lottery.

Section 5

2.The genitive can be used to show what comparisons arise from, like the English "than":[13]

'σχέτλιοί έστε, θεοί, ζηλήμονες έξοχον άλλων," (Odyssey V, 118) (Calypso speaks.)
"you are merciless, gods, jealous more than others"
(σχέτλιος -α -ον = merciless ζηλήμων (3) = jealous έξοχον (adverb) = standing out from, more than)

3.The genitive can be used with some verbs that refer only to parts or aspects of things or people, e.g.

αύτάρ έπεί τάρπησαν έδητύος ήδέ ποτήτος (Odyssey V, 201)
but when they were delighted[14] with (literally, of) the eating and drinking
(αύτάρ = but έπεί = when έτάρπησαν = they were delighted έδητύς, έδητύος (3 fem) = food, eating ποτής, ποτήτος (3 fem) = drink, drinking)

4. μέμνημαι is found with the genitive meaning "I remember", because it is the thought or memory of someone or something that you have in your mind.

What is the English for:

1.θεοί ύμέων ού μέμνηνται. 2.τίς όφθαλμόν σευ όλλυσι, Κύκλωψ; Ούτις;[15]
3.πατρίς ήμέων τηλόθι[16] θαλάσσης κείται.
4.έξ Αίθιόπων. (Odyssey V, 282) (Αίθίοπες = Ethiopians)
5.Ήώς δ' έκ λεχέων παρ' άγαυού Τιθωνοίο[17]
όρνυται. (Odyssey V 1-2, altered)
άγαυός -ή -όν = illustrious, noble
6.('Οδυσσήα) πέμπει άπό νήσου δία Καλυψω. (Odyssey V, 263, altered)
7.ού τις μέμνηται 'Οδυσσήος θείοιο. (Odyssey V, 11)
8.τήλε δ' άπό σχεδίης αύτός πέσε, πηδάλιον δέ
έκ χειρών προέηκε. (Odyssey V, 315-6)
(τήλε = far αύτός = he himself πέσε = fell πηδάλιον (2 neut) = steering oar, rudder χείρ, χειρός 3(fem) = hand προέηκε = he let go)

---

[13]See also Section 25.
[14]It means: "When they had been delighted ...", i.e. had had enough.
[15]Ούτις, literally "notsomebody", i.e. "Noman", the false name by which Odysseus made himself known to the Cyclops.
[16]τηλόθι + genitive = far from.
[17]δ' stands for δέ. λεχέων is a poetical plural: translate as if singular (λέχεος). παρ' stands for παρά. Tithonus was the brother of Priam, king of Troy. His wife, Eos, obtained the gift of immortality for him, but not that of eternal youth. See Section 13, end.

Section 6
Part A - The Imperfect Tense[1]

<u>The Greek verb - tenses</u> Verbs are found in the following tenses:-

the **present**, which represents the English "I do", I am doing", and "I do do." In Greek, the present is essentially a continuous tense; "I am loosing" is nearer to the Greek λύω than "I loose".

the **imperfect**, which is essentially the past continuous "I was doing", though it is often equivalent to the English past continual "I used to do", and to the inceptive "I began to do".

the **future**

the **aorist**, or "undelimited" tense, named from ἀ- ("un") + ὁρίζω ("I delimit").[2] This tense is used for isolated events that are complete in themselves, especially to denote simple actions occurring in the past; but some parts of the aorist (e.g. the infinitive) do not have past significance.

The **perfect** is used, like the English perfect with "have" for the present state resulting from past actions; e.g., "I have gone". ("I went" is aorist in Greek.)

The **pluperfect** which, like the English "I had gone" represents an action previous to another.

<u>Aspect.</u> Verbs may express *continuous* action ("I am laughing") or *momentary* action ("the bubble burst"). In general, the present and imperfect tenses express continuous action, and the aorist expresses momentary action.

<u>Primary and secondary tenses.</u>
The present, future and perfect are regarded as *primary* tenses.
The imperfect, aorist and pluperfect are regarded as *historic* or *secondary* tenses.

---

[1] See also Appendix A.
[2] The English "horizon" is derived from ὁρίζω.

Section 6

The Greek imperfect tense covers the English past continuous ("I was baking bread"), past continual ("I used to bake bread") and inceptive ("I was just beginning to bake bread"). It is a past (or secondary) tense but has the same aspect as the present tense and is formed from the stem[3] of the present tense, which in the case of λύω is λυ-.

The imperfect tense of λύω, I loose:

active		middle/passive	
(ἔ)λυον	I was loosing	(ἐ)λυόμην	I was loosing(for myself), I was being loosed
(ἔ)λυες	you were loosing	(ἐ)λύεο[4]	you were loosing (for yourself), you were being loosed
(ἔ)λυε	he/she/it was loosing	(ἐ)λύετο	he/she/it was loosing for himself/ herself/ itself, he/she/it was being loosed
(ἐ)λύετον	you two were loosing	(ἐ)λύεσθον	you two were loosing for yourselves, you two were being loosed
(ἐ)λυέτην	those two were loosing	(ἐ)λυέσθην	those two were loosing for themselves, those two were being loosed
(ἐ)λύομεν	we were loosing	(ἐ)λυόμε(σ)θα	we were loosing for ourselves, we were being loosed
(ἐ)λύετε	you were loosing	(ἐ)λύεσθε	you were loosing for yourselves, you were being loosed
(ἔ)λυον	they were loosing	(ἐ)λύοντο	they were loosing for themselves, they were being loosed.

---
[3] A verb stem is what remains after the removal of any prefixes and suffixes.
[4] Or ἐλύευ.

Imperfect tenses of -μι verbs:

active		middle (& passive)	
[ὤρνυν]	I was arousing	[ὠρνύμην]	I was arising
[ὤρνυς or ὤρνυσθα]	you were arousing	[ὤρνυσο]	you were arising
[ὤρνυ] or ὤρνυε	he/she/it was arousing	ὤρνυτο	he/she/it was arising
[ὤρνυτον]	you two were arousing	[ὤρνυσθον]	you two were arising
[ὠρνύτην]	those two were arousing	[ὠρνύσθην]	those two were arising
[ὤρνυμεν]	we were arousing	[ὠρνύμε(σ)θα]	we were arising
[ὤρνυτε]	you were arousing	[ὤρνυσθε]	you were arising
[ὤρνυσαν] they were arousing or ὤρνυον[5]		ὤρνυντο	they were arising

Imperfect of φημί:[6]

singular		plural	
(ἔ)φην	I affirmed	(ἔ)φαμεν	we affirmed
(ἔ)φης or (ἔφησθα)	you affirmed	[(ἔ)φατε]	you affirmed
(ἔ)φη	he, she, it affirmed	(ἔ)φασαν or ἔφαν or φάν[7]	they affirmed

A past tense in Greek which states an action as a fact[8] is normally signalled by prefixing the augment ε if a verb stem begins with a consonant or otherwise by lengthening the opening vowel. Thus λύομεν = "we are loosing", while ἐλύομεν = "we were loosing"; ἀκούομεν = "we are hearing", while ἠκούομεν = "we were hearing". The augment ε was originally an auxiliary word used to mark the sense of "past" more exactly.[9] It is almost always used in Attic Greek and in Common Greek (koiné), but the augment is optional in Epic and often omitted in Homer.

If a verb has a preposition prefixed, e.g. εἰσφέρω, I carry in, from εἰς = into and φέρω = I carry, the augment follows the prefix: εἰσφέρομεν = we are carrying in, εἰσεφέρομεν = we were carrying in.

---

[5]or ὄρνυν, ὄρνυς, ὄρνυ (ὄρνυε), ὄρνυμεν, ὄρνυτε, ὄρνυσαν (ὄρνυον) if the augment is not used. -μι verbs are sometimes found with the same endings in the imperfect active as -ω verbs.
[6]ἔφασκον, ἔφασκες ... (like the imperfect of an -ω verb) can be used for this tense.
[7]The middle (ἐ)φάμην is sometimes used for "I affirmed (spoke)", (ἐ)φάτο for "he/she affirmed" and ἔφαντο for "they affirmed". The dual of φημί is not found in Homer.
[8]i.e. an indicative. See p.42.
[9]Chantraine, *Grammaire Homérique* vol i, p.479.

Section 6

Give the tense and person of the following verbs, and say whether they are active or middle/passive: 1.ἔλυες. 2.ἐλύετε. 3.λύει. 4.λύες. 5.ἔλυε. 6.λύομαι. 7.ἐλυόμην. 8.λυόμην. 9.φέρουσιν. 10.φέρον (two possibilities). 11.ἔφερον (two possibilities). 12.ὀρνύασι. 13.ὄρνυντο. 14.ὤρνυντο. 15.χαίρεις. 16.χαῖρες. 17.χαίρομεν (two possibilities). 18.γίγνεται. 19.γίγνετο. 20.ὤρνυε. 21.ἔρχοντο. 22.ἤρχοντο. 23.φασί. 24.φάσαν. 25.ἔφη.

New words:
ἀλλά = but[10]   αὖ, αὖτε = again, furthermore
ἔπειτα (ἔπειτ') = then, next
οὐδέ = and not, but not, nor, not even
οὔτε ... οὔτε ... = neither ... nor ...
τε... καὶ ... = both ... and ...   τε = and (τε is enclitic and follows the
τε ... τε ... = both ... and ...   word after "and" in English, e.g.
   θάλασσά τε = "and the sea".)

What is the English for:
1.ἔλυες. 2.ἔλυες; 3.λύεις. 4.λύες. 5.πῦρ ἔκαιον. 6.πῦρ ἐκαίετο. 7.πῦρ καίεται. 8. πῦρ ἔκαιον ἐγώ. 9.πῦρ ἐκαιόμην. 10.αὖτε πῦρ ἐκαίοντο. 11.οὔτε μοῖραν οὔτε ἀνάγκην ἴσχει Ζεύς. 12.οὔτε μοῖραν οὔτε ἀνάγκην ἴσχε Ζεύς. 13.ἄγγελοι ἤρχοντο ἀλλ' ἀκούην οὐκ ἔφερον, οὐδ' ἀμείβοντο. 14.'Αθηναίη λέγεν, ἀλλ' ἀθάνατοι ἀκούειν οὐκ ἐδύναντο. 15.πρῶτον (at first) ἔχαιρόν τε καὶ ἐτέρποντο μάκαρες ἀθάνατοι. 16.ἔπειτα χαλεποὶ ἐγίγνοντο. 17.θεοί τε καὶ θεαὶ ἠμείβοντο· ἡμεῖς 'Οδυσσῆος οὐ μεμνήμεθα, οὐδὲ τὸν(him) οἴκαδε (homewards) πέμπειν (to send) ἐθέλομεν.

Part B - The Dative Case

The dative case has two main functions:-
(a) it is used for the **indirect object**, the equivalent of "to" or "for" in English, as when we say "the mother gives the child a sweet", or "the mother gives a sweet to the child", or "I am doing this for you",
  e.g. τοῖσι δ' 'Αθηναίη λέγε
   "and to them Athene was telling..." (Odyssey V, 5)
(b) it is used for the **instrument**, the equivalent of the English "by",
  e.g. ἡ δ' ἔνδον ἀοιδιάουσ' ὀπὶ καλῇ
   ἱστὸν ἐποιχομένη χρυσείῃ κερκίδ' ὕφαινεν[11]
   and she, indoors singing with a beautiful voice,
   plying the loom with a golden shuttle was weaving (Odyssey V, 61-62)

[10]Usually first word in a clause.
[11]ἔνδον = within, indoors   ἀοιδάουσα (fem. present participle active) = singing   ὄψ, ὀπός (3 fem) = voice   ἱστός (2 masc) = loom (also mast of ship, both of which stood upright)   ἐποιχομένη = plying (fem present participle middle) from ἐποίχομαι meaning "I go to and fro", as it was necessary to step sideways to follow the shuttle.   χρύσειος = golden.   κερκίς, κερκίδος (3 fem) = shuttle.   κερκίδ' stands for κερκίδι.   ὑφαίνω = I weave.

The dative singular ends -ι (ι subscript in the first and second declension). The dative plural ending is –σι (-ῃσι in the first, and –οισι in the second declensions, often shortened to –ῃς (or –αις)[12] and –οις respectively).

Singular, first declension nouns

Nominative case (subject):

γαῖα	θάλασσα	νύμφη	ἱκέτης
land, earth	sea	nymph	suppliant

Accusative case (object)

γαῖαν	θάλασσαν	νύμφην	ἱκέτην
land, earth	sea	nymph	suppliant

Genitive case

γαίης[13]	θαλάσσης	νύμφης	ἱκέταο
of land	of sea	of nymph	of suppliant

Dative case

γαίῃ	θαλάσσῃ	νύμφῃ	ἱκέτῃ
(to, for) by land	(to, for) by sea	to, for nymph	to, for suppliant

Plural, first declension nouns

Nominative case (subjects):

γαῖαι	θάλασσαι	νύμφαι	ἵκεται
lands	seas	nymphs	suppliants

Accusative case (objects)

γαίας	θαλάσσας	νύμφας	ἱκέτας
lands	seas	nymphs	suppliants

Genitive case

γαιάων	θαλασσάων	νυμφάων	ἱκετάων
of lands	of seas	of nymphs	of suppliants

Dative case

γαίῃσι	θαλάσσῃσι	νύμφῃσι	ἱκέτῃσι
or γαίῃς	or θαλάσσης	or νύμφης	or ἱκέτης
(to)/for, by lands	(to)/for, by seas	to/for nymphs	to/for suppliants

---

[12]e.g. θεαῖς at Odyssey V, 119 (θεαῖς ἀγάασθε "you have a grudge to goddesses").
[13]See footnote 1 on page 26. The dative ending is like the genitive in being formed from η.

Section 6

Singular, second declension nouns
Nominative case (subjects):
ἑταῖρος	νῆσος	τέκνον
companion	island	child

Accusative case (objects)
ἑταῖρον	νῆσον	τέκνον
companion	island	child

Genitive case
ἑταίροιο *or* ἑταίρου	νήσοιο *or* νήσου	τέκνοιο *or* τέκνου
of companion	of island	of child

Dative case
ἑταίρῳ	νήσῳ	τέκνῳ
to/for companion	to/for/by island	to/for child

Dual, second declension nouns
Nominative case (subjects) and accusative case (objects):
ἑταίρω	νήσω	τέκνω
two companions	two islands	two children

Genitive case and dative case
ἑταίροιιν	νήσοιιν	τέκνοιιν
of two companions, to/for two companions	of two islands, (to)/for/by two islands	of two children, to/for two children

Plural, second declension nouns
Nominative case (subjects):
ἑταῖροι	νῆσοι	τέκνα
companions	islands	children

Accusative case (objects):
ἑταίρους	νήσους	τέκνα
companions	islands	children

Genitive case
ἑταίρων	νήσων	τέκνων
of companions	of islands	of children

Dative case
ἑταίροισι *or* ἑταίροις	νήσοισι *or* νήσοις	τέκνοισι *or* τέκνοις
to/for companions	(to)/for, by islands	to/for children

Singular, third declension nouns
Nominative case (subjects):

πατήρ	πατρίς	πῆμα	λέχος	Ὀδυσσεύς
father	fatherland	woe	bed	Odysseus

Accusative case (objects)

πατέρα	πατρίδα	πῆμα	λέχος	Ὀδυσσέα
father	fatherland	woe	bed	Odysseus (object)

Genitive case

πατρός	πατρίδος	πήματος	λέχεος	Ὀδυσσῆος
of father	of fatherland	of woe	of bed	of Odysseus

Dative case

πατρί[14]	πατρίδι	πήματι	λέχει	Ὀδυσσῆι or Ὀδυσῆι
to/for father	to/for/by fatherland	to/for/by woe	to/for/by bed	to/for Odysseus

Plural, third declension nouns
Nominative case (subjects):

πατέρες	πατρίδες	πήματα	λέχεα
fathers	fatherlands	woes	beds

Accusative case (objects)

πατέρας	πατρίδας	πήματα	λέχεα
fathers	fatherlands	woes	beds

Genitive case

πατέρων or πατρῶν	πατρίδων	πημάτων	λεχέων
of fathers	of fatherlands	of woes	of beds

Dative case

πατράσι	πατρίσι	πήμασι	λεχέεσσι
to/for fathers	to/for/by fatherlands	to/for/by woes	to/for/by beds

It has been noted that the dual is seldom found in the third declension, most often with the names of parts of the body:[15] in the nominative and accusative,

ὄσσε = two eyes, χεῖρε = two hands

and in the (genitive and) dative

ποδοῖιν = (of), by two feet

---

[14] Rarely πατέρι.
[15] The dual of ἀνήρ (man) (Section 9) is ἀνέρε (or ἄνδρε) (Chantraine, *op. cit.*, vol. i, p. 215).

Section 6

The irregular noun νηῦς (= "ship").

Singular	nominative	νηῦς	ship (subject)
	accusative	νῆα (*rarely* νέα)	ship (object)
	genitive	νηός *or* νεός	of ship
	dative	νηΐ	(to, for) by ship
Plural	nominative	νῆες *or* νέες	ships (subject)
	accusative	νῆας *or* νέας	ships (object)
	genitive	νηῶν *or* νεῶν	of ships
	dative	νήεσσι *or* νηυσί (*or* νέεσσι)[16]	(to, for) by ships

First and second person pronouns

Nominative:
ἐγώ = I   σύ *or* συ = you   ἡμεῖς *or* ἄμμες = we   ὑμεῖς *or* ὕμμες = you

Accusative:
ἐμέ *or* με = me   σέ *or* σε = you   ἡμας *or* ἤμεας *or* ἄμμε = us   ὑμέας *or* ὕμμε = you

Genitive:
ἐμεῖο *or* ἐμέο *or* ἐμεῦ *or* μευ *or* ἐμέθεν = my, of me   σεῖο *or* σέο *or* σέθεν *or* σευ = your, of you   ἡμείων *or* ἡμέων = our, of us   ὑμείων *or* ὑμέων = your, of you

Dative:
ἐμοί *or* μοι = to/for me   σοί *or* σοι = to/for you   ἡμῖν *or* ἄμμι = to/for us   ὑμῖν *or* ὕμμι = to/for you

There are also dual first person pronouns, viz:
(nom. and acc.)   νώ *or* νῶϊ   the two of us
(gen. and dat.)   νῶϊν   of, or to/for the two of us

and dual second person pronouns:
(nom. and acc.)   σφώ *or* σφῶϊ   the two of you
(gen. and dat.)   σφῶϊ(ν)   of, or to/for the two of you

<u>With prepositions</u>, the dative case often indicates a state of rest; thus it is used after ἐν *or* ἐνί, which means "in" or "on". ἐπί meaning "on" can be

---

[16]ναῦφι is also found but only as an instrumental ("with ships"), Chantraine, *op. cit.* vol.i, p.225.

used with the genitive or dative. The meaning of many other prepositions changes according to the case of the nouns or pronouns they qualify; so μετά with the accusative means "after", but with the genitive means "with". μετά with the dative means "accompanied by".

What is the English for:
ἐν νήσῳ κεῖται (Odyssey V, 13)
ἐν νηί (Odyssey V, 27)

New words:
ἐς (alternative to εἰς) = into, to ἐν, ἐνί (+ dative) = in
ἐϋπλόκαμος, -ον (fem. as masc.) = with beautiful tresses
Ζεύς[17] = Zeus
ἤπιος -α -ον = kind, gentle κῦμα, κύματος (3 n) = wave
μετά (+ dative) = accompanied by νηῦς (irreg. fem.) = ship
χείρ, χειρός (3 fem) = hand[18] ὡς = as, how

What is the English for:
1.Δία θεοὶ ἠδὲ θεαὶ ἀμείβονται.[19] 2.ἑταῖροι Ὀδυσσῆος ἐν νηί εἰσιν. 3.ἀκούην ἀπὸ Διὸς νύμφῃ ἐϋπλοκάμῳ θεὸς φέρει. 4.ἐν ἄλλῃ νήσῳ Κύκλωψ ἐστι. 5.καλὰ δώματά ἐστιν Ὀδυσσῆι (='Οδυσσεὺς καλὰ δώματα ἔχει). 6.ἐνὶ πόντῳ κύματα χαλεπὰ ἐγίγνοντο. 7.ἐν χειρὶ μοῖραν ἀνθρώπων Ζεὺς ἔχει. 8.σχεδίη Ὀδυσσῆος κύμασιν ὤλλυτο. 9.δῖος Ὀδυσσεὺς αὖτε ἐκ τῆς θαλάσσης μοίρῃ σῴζεται. (σῴζω = I save.) 10.ὡς πατὴρ ἤπιος Ζεὺς ἱκέτῃσιν ἦεν. 11 Ὀδυσσεὺς ἐς πατρίδα γαῖαν μετὰ πολλὰ (many) πήματα ἔρχεται. 12. Ὀδυσσεὺς ἐς πατρίδα γαῖαν μετὰ πολλοῖς (many) πήμασιν ἔρχεται.

---

[17]Vocative Ζεῦ, accusative Δία or Ζῆνα, genitive Διός or Ζηνός, dative Διί or Ζηνί.
[18]Dative plural, χείρεσσι, χείρεσι or χερσί(ν). Dual, χειρέ (nom & acc), (genitive & dative not found in Homer).
[19]ἀμείβομαι is followed by an accusative, like the English "I answer".

Part C - The Vocative Case

The vocative case is used for calling. The vocative singular is like the nominative, with the following exceptions:
first declension: masculine vocative ends -α[20]
    e.g. ἱκέτα = O suppliant!
except that the vocative of names meaning "son of" (patronymics) ending -ιδης end -δη e.g. 'Ατρείδη : O son of Atreus!

second declension: masculine vocative ends -ε
    e.g. ἄνθρωπε = O man!

some third declension nouns and adjectives are shortened slightly to form the vocative:
    e.g. πατέρ = O father! Ζεῦ = O Zeus!
    χρυσόρραπι in 'Ερμεία χρυσόρραπι = O Hermes of the golden wand!
    (Odyssey V, 87) (χρυσόρραπις : with a golden wand)
    ('Ερμείας is 1st declension)
Plural vocatives are like nominatives.

What is the English for:
1.ὦ ἵκετα. 2.ὦ θεά. 3.ἄγγελε. 4.ὦ ἄγγελοι. 5.ἑταῖρε. 6.ὦ ἀθάνατοι. 7.Δαρδανίδη Πρίαμε (Iliad XXIV, 171). 8.διογενὲς Λαερτιάδη, πολυμήχαν' 'Οδυσσεῦ (Odyssey V, 203).[21]

---

[20]Short α if the nominative ending is -της, otherwise long α e.g. 'Ερμεία, O Hermes!
[21]διογενής : descended from Zeus (a conventional way to address kings). Laertes was Odysseus' father who was now very old and had remained on Ithaca when Odysseus had gone to Troy. πολυμήχανος -ov : of many devices, ingenious. The final ε of the second declension vocative singular is often elided before a vowel.

42 Beginning Greek with Homer
Section 7
The Present Optative

The Greek verb - moods[1]
The verbs met so far have been in the indicative mood. The indicative mood is used to make simple statements of fact, e.g. *It is raining*.

Verbs in the optative mood express wishes or remote contingencies.

The present optative - -ω verbs

	active endings		middle/passive endings	
singular	–οιμι	λύοιμι O that I might loose	–οιμην	λυοίμην O that I might loose for myself, be loosed
	–οις (–οισθα)	λύοις (λύοισθα) O that you might loose	–οιο	λύοιο O that you might loose for yourself, be loosed
	–οι	λύοι O that he/she/it might loose	–οιτο	λύοιτο O that he/she/it might loose for him/her/itself, be loosed
dual	–οιτον	λύοιτον O that you two might loose	–οισθον	λύοισθον O that you two might loose for yourselves, be loosed
	–οιτην	λυοίτην O that those two might loose	–οισθην	λυοίσθην O that those two might loose for themselves, be loosed
plural	–οιμεν	λύοιμεν O that we might loose	–οιμε(σ)θα	λυοίμε(σ)θα O that we might loose for ourselves, be loosed
	–οιτε	λύοιτε O that you might loose	–οισθε	λύοισθε O that you might loose for yourselves, be loosed
	–οιεν	λύοιεν O that they might loose	–οιατο	λυοίατο O that they might loose for themselves, be loosed

[1] See also Appendix A.

The present optative (active) -μι verbs (εἰμί - I am)

Singular
-ιην	εἴην	O that I might be
-ιης	εἴης	O that you might be
-ιη	εἴη²	O that he/she/it might be

Dual
-ιτον	εἴτον	O that you two might be
-ιτην	εἴτην	O that those two might be

Plural
-ιμεν	[εἶμεν]	O that we might be
-ιτε	[εἶτε]	O that you might be
-ιεν	εἶεν	O that they might be

The present optative (middle) -μι verbs (δύναμαι - I can)

Singular
-ιμην	δυναίμην	O that I might be able
-ιο	δύναιο	O that you might be able
-ιτο	δύναιτο	O that he/she/it might be able

Dual
-ισθον	[δύναισθον]	O that you two might be able
-ισθην	[δυναίσθην]	O that those two might be able

Plural
-ιμε(σ)θα	[δυναίμε(σ)θα]	O that we might be able
-ισθε	[δύναισθε]	O that you might be able
-ιατο	[δυναίατο]	O that they might be able

A negative wish is expressed by μή + optative. μὴ λύοις : O that you might not loose! μὴ εἴης : O that you might not be! μὴ δύναιο : O that you might not be able!
The optative mood is used in main clauses
   for wishes (hence its name), e.g. *O that this too too solid flesh*
                                        would melt,
   and for more remote suppositions, e.g. *I might do it if I could.*

A Greek verb in the optative can often be translated in English by a verb with "might".
In sentences where in English the main verb would be past, the optative mood is often³ used for purposes in past time,
e.g. they were telling you *so that you might know.*

---

²Occasionally ἔοις is found for εἴης and ἔοι for εἴη.
³Alternatively, a verb in the subjunctive mood may be used (Section 14).

Clauses expressing purpose in the past
In "the gods were sending a messenger to bring the report", "to bring the report" expresses the purpose the gods had in sending the messenger. In Homeric Greek the purpose could be expressed in the form "the gods were sending a messenger in order that he might bring the report."

"he might bring" may[4] in Greek be expressed by a verb in the optative mood; here, φέροι, the 3rd person singular of the present optative active of φέρω can be used.

"in order that" is expressed in several ways:-
ἕως (with indicative, "until"), ὡς (with indicative, "as"), ὅπως (with indicative, "how"), and, most often, ἵνα (with indicative, "where") and ὄφρα (with indicative, "while", "until").
The gods were sending a messenger to bring the report can be translated:
  θεοὶ ἄγγελον ἔπεμπον ἕως ἀκουὴν φέροι or
  θεοὶ ἄγγελον ἔπεμπον ὡς ἀκουὴν φέροι or
  θεοὶ ἄγγελον ἔπεμπον ὅπως ἀκουὴν φέροι or
  θεοὶ ἄγγελον ἔπεμπον ἵνα ἀκουὴν φέροι or
  θεοὶ ἄγγελον ἔπεμπον ὄφρα ἀκουὴν φέροι.

A negative purpose is expressed by μή, either alone or in combination with ὄφρα μή, ὡς μή or ἵνα μή, e.g., "the gods were keeping the messenger back so that he might not bring the report" would be
  θεοὶ ἄγγελον ἴσχον μὴ ἀκουὴν φέροι,
or θεοὶ ἄγγελον ἴσχον ὄφρα (or ὡς) (or ἵνα) μὴ ἀκουὴν φέροι.

Remote eventualities
An optative verb sometimes expresses a remote eventuality, usually with a condition "if ... " either expressed or understood, e.g.
("if you only knew what trouble awaits you")
  ἐνθάδε κ' αὖθι μένων σὺν ἐμοὶ τόδε δῶμα φυλάσσοις (Odyssey V, 208)
"in that case remaining here in this place with me you would guard this hall."
ἐνθάδε: here κ' stands for κε: in that case αὖθι: in this place μένων:remaining σύν (with dative): with τόδε (neuter): this φυλάσσω: I guard

---
[4]See footnote 3.

Section 7   45

New words:
Ἀθηναίη (sometimes spelled Ἀθήνη) (1 fem) = Athene
ἄλγος (3 neuter) = pain, woe   βροτός (2 m. or f.) = mortal, human
εὐρύς, εὐρεῖα, εὐρύ = wide
ἕως, εἷος or εἵως (with indicative) = while, until, so that[5]
κῆδος (3 neuter) = anxiety, grief   κράτος (3 neuter) = power
μέν = indeed   μετά + accusative = after
νῦν, νύ = now   νῶτον (2 neuter) = back[6]
ὁ = he
παῖς, παιδός (3 masc. or fem.) (dative plu. παίδεσσι) = child, son, daughter
πάσχω = I suffer   πολλοί, πολλαί, πολλά = many
ῥέζω = I perform   φρήν, φρενός (3 fem) = heart, mind[7]

Give the mood and person of the following verbs:
1.ἐθέλοιτε 2.γιγνοίμην 3.ἐρχοίατο 4.ἔχοιεν 5.λέγεις 6.εἴης 7.ἐσσί
8.δυναίμην 9.δύνασθε 10.πέμποισθε.
What is the English for:
1.λέγοιμι. 2.ἀμειβοίατο. 3.χαίροις. 4.τερποίμην. 5.μὴ ἔρχοιτο.
6.μάκαρ εἴης, ὦ Ὀδυσσεῦ. 7.ἤπιος εἴη ἡμῖν ὑψιβρεμέτης Ζεύς.
8.νύμφη ἀμφίπολον (maidservant) πέμπειν ἤθελεν εἰς δώματα ἵνα πῦρ καίοι.
9.νύμφη ἀμφίπολον πέμπειν ἤθελεν εἰς δώματα ὅπως πῦρ καίοιτο.
10.ἀμφίπολος ἐκ λέχεος οὐκ ὤρνυτο μὴ πῦρ καίοι.

Homer, Odyssey V, 1-20
Ἠὼς δ'[8] ἐκ λεχέων παρ' ἀγαυοῦ Τιθωνοῖο
ὤρνυθ',[9] ἵν' ἀθανάτοισι φόως[9] φέροι ἠδὲ βροτοῖσιν·
οἱ δὲ θεοὶ θῶκόνδε[10] καθίζανον, ἐν δ' ἄρα[11] τοῖσι[12]

---
[5]See also pp.97-8 and p.119, footnote 2.
[6]Often νῶτα (plural) even when singular in English.
[7]Original meaning "midriff". Often found in plural (φρένες, φρένας, φρενῶν, φρεσί(ν)) even when the English meaning is singular. A person's φρένες are the seat of the emotions, and also where one makes plans.
[8]For lines 1-2, see also p. 31. δ' stands for δὲ (a very frequent elision, e.g. at lines 12, 15 & 19).
[9]ὤρνυθ' stands for ὤρνυτο, 3rd person singular, imperfect middle of ὄρνυμι. ἀγαυός is also used of the Phaeacians at VI, 55. φόως (also φάος) 3 neuter : "light". The dative singular is φάει. ἵν' stands for ἵνα.
[10]οἱ δὲ θεοὶ ... = "but they, the gods..." (οἱ = they). θῶκόνδε : for a council meeting (θῶκος is a seat of office). This was the second council of the gods about Odysseus; the first is at Odyssey I, 1-95. καθιζάνω : I sit down.
[11]ἄρα : there and then, straightaway.
[12]ἐν τοῖσι : among them. Understand ἦεν ("was") (Ζεὺς ὑψιβρεμέτης is the subject).

Beginning Greek with Homer

Ζεὺς ὑψιβρεμέτης, οὖ[13] τε κράτος ἐστὶ μέγιστον.[14]
τοῖσι[15] δ' Ἀθηναίη λέγε κήδεα πόλλ' Ὀδυσῆος   5
μνησαμένη·[16] μέλε[17] γάρ οἱ ἐὼν ἐν δώμασι νύμφης·
"Ζεῦ πάτερ ἠδ' ἄλλοι μάκαρες θεοὶ αἰὲν ἐόντες,[18]
μή[19] τις ἔτι πρόφρων[20] ἀγανὸς[21] καὶ ἤπιος ἔστω
σκηπτοῦχος βασιλεύς,[22] μηδὲ[23] φρεσὶν αἴσιμα εἰδώς,
ἀλλ'[24] αἰεὶ χαλεπός τ' εἴη καὶ αἴσυλα ῥέζοι,   10
ὡς[25] οὔ τις μέμνηται Ὀδυσσῆος θείοιο
λαῶν, οἷσιν ἄνασσε,[26] πατὴρ δ' ὣς[27] ἤπιος ἦεν.

[13]οὗ: whose. τε: in fact; cf. τε ... καὶ ... o r τε ... τε ... : both ... and ... (p.35).
[14]μέγιστον: very great *or* greatest (neuter).
[15]τοῖσι : to them. NB λέγε (3rd person singular) is imperfect (without augment). λέγει would be present. λέγω with an object means "I mention, I relate".
[16]μνησαμένη : having remembered (aorist middle participle, nominative feminine singular, μιμνήσκω). πολλ' : πολλά (neuter plural accusative), qualifying κήδεα. (The accent has moved to πόλλ' because α has been elided.)
[17]μέλε (imperfect of μέλει) : he mattered, was a care to (οἱ: to her). ἐών: being (nominative singular masculine of the participle of "be"). "being" is equivalent here to "because he was". νύμφης refers to Calypso, whose prisoner Odysseus had been for seven years.
[18]ἠδ' stands for ἠδὲ. ἐόντες is the participle of "be" (nominative plural masculine). "being always" means "living for ever", equivalent to "who live for ever".
[19]Translate in the order: μή τις σκηπτοῦχος βασιλεύς ἔστω ἔτι πρόφρων ἀγανὸς καὶ ἤπιος: "let not any sceptre-bearing king be ..." ἔστω is 3rd person singular imperative of εἰμί; μή is the negative for an imperative. One papyrus has εἴη for ἔστω (Hainsworth), which gives: "O that no sceptre-bearing king might be ...".
[20]ἔτι: still, yet (with μή, "no longer"). πρόφρων: kindly, gracious (literally, "with forward mind").
[21]ἀγανός : mild, gentle.
[22]σκηπτοῦχος βασιλεύς : sceptre-bearing king.
[23] μηδε αἴσιμα εἰδώς: nor right-minded. αἴσιμος, αἴσιμον (fem as masc) : agreeable to the will of the gods, destined, agreeable to the decrees of fate, meet, fitting. (αἴσιμα is neuter plural, "fitting things".) εἰδώς : knowing (masculine singular nominative participle of οἶδα, I know). φρεσὶν αἴσιμα εἰδώς: "knowing fitting things in his heart". (φρεσίν (dative plural) indicates place where.)
[24]ἀλλ' stands for ἀλλά. αἴσυλος, αἴσυλον (fem as masc): godless, unseemly (αἴσυλα is neuter plural: "unseemly things"). NB, εἴη and ῥέζοι are optative (3rd person singular).
[25]ὡς means "as" (μέμνηται is indicative). Translate in the order: ὡς οὔ τις λαῶν οἷσιν ἄνασσε μέμνηται Ὀδυσσῆος θείοιο ... λαῶν is a poetic plural for λαοῦ.
[26]οἷσιν: over whom (dative plural referring to λαῶν). ἄνασσε is 3rd person singular, imperfect active of ἀνάσσω: I am chieftain (cf. λέγε in line 5).
[27]πατὴρ δ' ὣς = ὡς δὲ πατήρ. ὡς (meaning "as") is accented when it follows the noun to which it refers.

Section 7

ἀλλ' ὁ μὲν[28] ἐν νήσῳ[29] κεῖται κρατέρ'[30] ἄλγεα πάσχων,
νύμφης ἐν μεγάροισι[31] Καλυψοῦς, ἥ[32] μιν ἀνάγκῃ
ἴσχει· ὁ δ' οὐ δύναται ἥν πατρίδα γαῖαν ἱκέσθαι·[33]   15
οὐ γάρ οἱ πάρα[34] νῆες ἐπήρετμοι[35] καὶ ἑταῖροι,
οἵ[36] κέν μιν πέμποιεν ἐπ' εὐρέα[37] νῶτα θαλάσσης.
νῦν αὖ παῖδ' ἀγαπητὸν[38] ἀποκτεῖναι μεμάασιν[39]
οἴκαδε[40] νισόμενον· ὁ δ' ἔβη[41] μετὰ πατρὸς ἀκουὴν
ἐς Πύλον ἠγαθέην[42] ἠδ' ἐς Λακεδαίμονα δῖαν."   20

---

[28]ἀλλ' stands for ἀλλά. ὁ: he.
[29]P.Grimal, *The Dictionary of Classical Mythology*, tr. Maxwell-Hyslop, Blackwell, 1986, p.86-7, identifies Calypso's isle, called Ogygia e.g. at Odyssey I, 85, with Ceuta, a peninsula opposite Gibraltar, but this identification (originally by Bérard) has been challenged by Stanford, *Journal of Hellenic Studies* vol. LXXXI (1961) p.160 both because Ceuta is not an island and because the four springs there are not "turned to face this way and that" as described at Odyssey V, 71.
[30]κρατέρ' stands for κρατέρα, qualifying ἄλγεα. κρατερός, κρατερά, κρατερόν: strong, mighty, harsh, rough, fierce. πάσχων ("suffering") is masculine singular nominative of the present participle of πάσχω, I suffer. κρατέρ'ἄλγεα πάσχων is a Homeric formula found again in this book at line 395.
[31]Dative plural of μέγαρον (2n): hall. ἐν μεγάροισι: in the palace. Καλυψοῦς (contracted from Καλυψόος, 3rd declension genitive): of Calypso.
[32]ἥ: who (feminine). μιν: him.
[33]ὁ δ' = but he ... ἱκέσθαι: to reach (the aorist middle infinitive of ἱκνέομαι). ἥν: his (qualifies πατρίδα γαῖαν).
[34]Note that this is πάρα, not παρά. πάρα stands for πάρεισι "there are at hand". (οἱ is dative singular, meaning "for him"). "There are ships at hand for him" = "he has ships."
[35]ἐπήρετμος, ἐπήρετμον (fem as masc): equipped with oars.
[36]οἵ : who. κέν: in that case. μιν: him. πέμποιεν: might send. "who" followed by an optative verb expresses the purpose that companions might serve if he had them.
[37]εὐρέα is accusative plural of εὐρύς, "broad", qualifying νῶτα. Lines 16 and 17 are formulaic, being identical with Odyssey IV 559-560 and XVII 145-146, and almost identical with lines 141-142 in this book; lines 17 and 142 are the same, and 141 only differs from 16 in having γάρ in the place of κεν and μοι instead of οἱ. ἐπ' εὐρέα νῶτα θαλάσσης is an example of a Homeric formula. It is found also at Odyssey IV, 313 and 362, and Iliad ii, 159, viii, 511 and xx, 228. ἐπ' stands for ἐπί.
[38]παῖδ' stands for παῖδα. ἀγαπητός -ή, -όν: beloved. Understand "his", i.e. "belonging to Odysseus", qualifying παῖδα, the object of ἀποκτεῖναι: to kill (aorist infinitive).
[39]μεμάασιν : they are eager, intend, strive (irregular, from *μάω, a defective verb not found in the present tense). μεμάασιν is perfect with present sense; see Section 21, p.145. "they" refers to a new subject, the suitors of Penelope. Translate in the order νῦν αὖ μεμάασιν ἀποκτεῖναι ἀγαπητὸν παῖδα νισόμενον οἴκαδε.
[40]νισόμενον (masculine accusative singular, qualifying παῖδα): coming. οἴκαδε : homewards. Odyssey III-IV describe how Telemachus visited Nestor at Pylos (on the west coast of the Peloponnese) and Menelaus at Lacedaemon (Sparta), both of whom had returned from the Trojan War, enquiring about Odysseus. IV ends with an ambush laid for Telemachus by the suitors of Penelope.
[41]ὁ δ' ἔβη: and he went (equivalent to the English "and he had gone"). Translate in the order: μετὰ ἀκουὴν πατρός.
[42]ἠγάθεος, ἠγαθέη, ἠγάθεον : most holy. Πύλος is feminine. ἠδ': ἠδὲ.

Section 8
The demonstrative and relative pronouns
ὀ, ἡ, τό = "that", 'this'; "he", "she", "it", "they"; "the"; "who", "which"

	masculine	feminine	neuter
singular			
nom	ὁ = that, he	ἡ = that, she	τό = that, it
acc	τόν = that, him	τήν = that, her	τό = that, it
gen	τοῦ = that's, his *or* τοῖο	τῆς = that's, her	τοῦ = that's[1] *or* τοῖο
dat	τῷ = to/for that, him	τῇ = to/for that, her	τῷ = by that, it
dual			
nom/acc	τώ = those two, they (all genders)		
gen/dat	τοῖιν = of/to those two, them (all genders)		
plural			
nom	οἱ *or* τοί = those, they	αἱ *or* ταί = those, they	τά = those, they
acc	τούς = those, them	τάς = those, them	τά = those, them
gen	τῶν = of those, their	τῶν *or* τάων = of those, their	τῶν = of those, their
dat	τοῖσι(ν) *or* τοῖς = to/for them	τῇσι(ν) *or* τῇς = to/for them	τοῖσι(ν) *or* τοῖς = by them

In the dialect of Classical Athens (Attic), and in the later Common Greek, ὁ, ἡ, τό are masculine, feminine and neuter of the definite article "the". In those dialects, ὁ θεός = the god, ἡ ἀκουή = the report, and τὸ νῶτον = the back.

However, this is only occasionally so (see (a) below) in Homeric Greek. It seems that originally ὁ, ἡ, τό were the masculine, feminine and neuter genders of a pronoun meaning "this", "that".[2] Later, they were

---
[1] *or* its.
[2] Chantraine, *Grammaire Homérique*, vol.ii, pp.158-168.

Section 8 49

used also as pronouns³ meaning "he", "she" "it" respectively, and in Homer as pronouns meaning "who", "which" in relative clauses.⁴

Examples: (a) ὁ, ἡ, τό means "the" (rare in Homer)
τῷ δ' ἄρα πέμπτῳ πέμπ' ἀπὸ νήσου δῖα Καλυψώ (Odyssey V, 263)
and on the fifth (day) then noble Calypso was sending (him) away from the island
(πέμπτος -η -ον = fifth πέμπ' stands for (ἔ)πεμπε)

(b) ὁ, ἡ, τό sometimes is associated with a noun and has a meaning close to "the", but is a demonstrative:
οἱ δὲ θεοὶ θῶκόνδε καθίζανον (Odyssey V, 3)
but they, the gods, were sitting down for a council

(c) ὁ, ἡ, τό = "he", "she", "it", (in plural, "they")
(i)τοῖσι δ' Ἀθηναίη λέγε κήδεα πόλλ' Ὀδυσῆος
and to them Athene was telling many woes of Odysseus (Odyssey V, 5)
(ii)ἀλλ' ὁ μὲν ἐν νήσῳ κεῖται = but he indeed is lying in an island (Odyssey
V, 13)
(d) ὁ, ἡ, τό = "that", "those"
ἀλλ' ὅτε δὴ τὴν νῆσον ἀφίκετο
but when, finally, he reached that island (Odyssey V, 55) (i.e. the island where Calypso lived) (ὅτε = when, δή = finally, ἀφίκετο = he reached)

(e) ὁ, ἡ, τό = "who", "which"
καλὰ πέδιλα, ἀμβρόσια χρύσεια, τά μιν φέρον
fine sandals, immortal golden ones, which used to carry him (Odyssey V, 44-45)
(πέδιλον = sandal (2 neuter), ἀμβρόσιος –ον = immortal, χρύσειος –η –ον = golden
μιν = him)

What is the English for:
1.οἱ θεοὶ μέμνηνται Ὀδυσσῆος θείοιο.
2.ὁ μὲν ἐθέλει εἰς πατρίδα γαῖαν ἱκέσθαι, νῆας δὲ καὶ ἑταίρους οὐκ ἔχει.
3.τὴν νῆσον ἔχει νύμφη ἐϋπλόκαμος.
4.θεοὶ καθιζάνουσι τοῖς λέγει Ἀθηναίη.
5.θεοὶ καθιζάνουσι τῶν Ζεὺς ὑψιβρεμέτης ἐστι πατήρ.
6.τίνος ἐστιν ἡ νῆσος; νύμφης ἐϋπλοκάμου ἐστιν.

---
³i.e. to stand for a noun or proper noun, as "he" can stand for "the god" or "Zeus".
⁴i.e., clauses that relate to a noun or pronoun in another part of a sentence: distinguish "the long-remembered beggar was his guest
    whose beard descending swept his aged breast" (relative, whose : τοῦ)
from   "Whose is this hat?" (interrogative, whose : τίνος;).

The relative pronoun, "who", "which"
The following relative pronoun specifically means "who", "which":

	masculine	feminine	neuter
		singular	
nominative	ὅς (who)	ἥ (who)	ὅ (which)
accusative	ὅν (whom)	ἥν (whom)	ὅ (which)
genitive	οὗ (whose)	ἧς (whose)[5]	οὗ (of which)
dative	ᾧ (to whom)	ᾗ (to whom)	ᾧ (by which)
		dual	
nom & acc	ὥ	[ᾥ]	[ᾥ]
gen & dat	[οἷιν]	[οἷιν]	[οἷιν]
		plural	
nominative	οἵ (who)	αἵ (who)	ἅ (which)
accusative	οὕς (whom)	ἅς (whom)	ἅ (which)
genitive	ὧν (whose)	ὧν (whose)	ὧν (of which)
dative	οἷς or οἷσι (to whom)	ᾗσι (to whom)	οἷσι (by which)

(The feminine singular genitive is ἕης at Iliad xvi 208.)

NB(i) ὅς ἥ ὅ has an acute accent in the nominative masculine and feminine, whereas ὁ ἡ τό does not.

NB(ii) ὅς ἥ ὅ has a rough breathing in all cases, singular and plural, whereas ὁ ἡ τό begins with τ in all cases except the nominative masculine and feminine.

In English, "who" or "which" is used to introduce an adjectival clause, i.e. one which qualifies a noun; in the sentence *A king sate on the rocky brow which looks o'er sea-born Salamis*, the clause *which looks o'er sea-born Salamis* qualifies *the brow*.

In the following Greek sentence:
οὔ τινα οἶδα
ἀνθρώπων, <u>οἵ</u> τήνδε[6] πόλιν καὶ γαῖαν ἔχουσιν. (Odyssey VI, 176-7)
I do not know any of the men <u>who</u> own this city and land
οἵ τήνδε πόλιν καὶ γαῖαν ἔχουσιν "who own this city and land" qualifies ἀνθρώπων "of the men". (οἶδα = I know πόλις = (the) city)
In the sentence κεῖται... νύμφης ἐν μεγάροισι Καλυψοῦς, <u>ἥ</u> μιν ἀνάγκῃ ἴσχει *(Odyssey V, 13-15)*
(he lies ... in the halls of the nymph Calypso <u>who</u> him by necessity controls)
which noun does ἥ μιν ἀνάγκῃ ἴσχει *qualify?*

---
[5]ἕης at Iliad xvi, 208.
[6] See ὅδε ἥδε τόδε, p. 52.

Section 8

The relative pronoun (*who, which*) has the same gender and number as the noun qualified by the clause it introduces, but its case may be different, as required by the meaning of its own clause; so both ἀνθρώπων and οἵ are masculine plural, but ἀνθρώπων is genitive while οἵ is nominative, and νύμφης Καλυψοῦς and ἥ are feminine singular, but νύμφης Καλυψοῦς is genitive while ἥ is nominative. What are the cases of the words (both of which are masculine plural) underlined in the following sentence? οὔ τις μέμνηται Ὀδυσσῆος θείοιο <u>λαῶν</u>, <u>οἷσιν</u> ἄνασσε (Odyssey V, 11-12). (ἀνάσσω, I am chieftain over, is equivalent to "I am chieftain for".)

<u>ὅς τε</u> ὅς, ἥ, ὅ is frequently found before τε to show that there is a connection which holds in fact, or as it happens, e.g.
Ζεὺς ὑψιβρεμέτης, οὗ τε κράτος ἐστι μέγιστος
Zeus the high thunderer whose power is (in fact) very great (Odyssey V, 4)

What is the English for: 1.νύμφη ἣ ἐϋπλόκαμός ἐστι νῆσον ἔχει.
2.Ὀδυσσεὺς ἐν νήσῳ κεῖται ἣν νύμφη ἐϋπλόκαμος ἔχει.
3.Ὀδυσσεὺς ἑταίρους οὐκ ἔχει οἵ αὐτὸν ἐπ᾽ εὐρέα νῶτα θαλάσσης πέμποιεν.
4.Ζεὺς ὑψιβρεμέτης οὗ κράτος ἐστι μέγιστον ἄλλοις θεοῖς ἀνάσσει.
5.Ἀθηναίη κήδεα Ὀδυσσῆος λέγε ὧν οὔ τις μέμνηται.
6.Ἑρμείας ἔρχεται ὅς τε ἀθανάτων ἄγγελός ἐστι. (Ἑρμαίας: Hermes)

<u>ὅς τις</u> (ὅς, "who" and τις, "someone") together mean "whoever" e.g.
αἰδοῖος μέν τ᾽ ἐστὶ καὶ ἀθανάτοισι θεοῖσιν,
ἀνδρῶν ὅς τις ἵκηται ἀλώμενος (Odyssey V, 447-8)
Indeed, in fact he is to be respected even to the immortal gods,
whoever of men may arrive wandering
(αἰδοῖος : to be respected, ἀνδρῶν : of men, ἵκηται : may arrive, ἀλώμενος : wandering)

(ἵκηται is aorist subjunctive: see footnote 38 below and Section 14.)

Both ὅς and τις have their own endings, and so the accusative is ὅν τινα, the nominative plural οἵ τινες and the accusative plural οὕς τινας.[7] The feminine is ἥ τις, ἥν τινα and (plural) αἵ τινες, ἅς τινας.

---

[7]There is, however, a shortened form in which ὅς and τις are written as one word as follows: ὅτις (nominative singular, masculine & feminine), ὅτι or ὅττι (neuter singular, nom. & acc.), ὅτινα (accusative singular, masculine), ὅττεο or ὅττευ or ὅτευ (genitive singular), ὅτῳ (dative singular), ὅτινας (accusative plural, masculine), ὅτεων (genitive plural) and ὁτέοισι (dative plural). The neuter plural (accusative) is sometimes ἅσσα. (Chantraine, *op. cit.* vol.i, p.280)

ὅς τις is sometimes used for "who" or "which" if the essential nature of a connection is stressed, e.g. a cause, a condition or a purpose, or if it introduces a clause which defines the answer to a question:-
σὺ δὲ τρίτον ἄνδρ' ὀνόμαζε,
ὅς τις ἔτι ζωὸς κατερύκεται εὐρέϊ πόντῳ (Odyssey IV, 551-2)
but as for you, name the third man
who still alive is held prisoner (in) the wide open sea.
(τρίτον (acc.) : third, ἄνδρ' (ἄνδρα) : man (acc.), ὀνόμαζε : name! (imperative, see Section 13), ἔτι : still, ζωός : alive, κατερύκεται : is held prisoner.)

What is the English for:
1. πέμψει δέ τοι οὖρον ὄπισθεν
ἀθανάτων ὅς τις σὲ φυλάσσει (Odyssey XV, 34-5)
(πέμψει : will send (3rd singular), τοι : look you, οὖρος : a following wind, ὄπισθεν : behind, φυλάσσω : I protect)
2. ἄγγελοι οὐκ ἐθέλουσι λέγειν οἵ τινες εἰσίν.

The possessive adjective ὅς, ἥ, ὅν or ἑός, ἑή, ἑόν (= his, her, its (own))
ὅς ἥ ὅν is an adjective meaning "his", "her", "its". As an adjective, it has the same gender, number and case as the noun it qualifies; so
ἥ γαῖα = his own land *or* her own land *or* its own land
ὅς ἑταῖρος = his companion *or* her companion *or* its companion
ὅν νῶτον = his own back *or* her own back *or* its own back
ὅν λέχος = his own bed *or* her own bed *or* its own bed. (λέχος is *neuter*.)

ὅς ἥ ὅν has exactly the same endings as ὅς ἥ ὅ except that the neuter singular (nominative, vocative and accusative) ends ν.

What is the English for:
1. νύμφη ὃν ἑταῖρον ἀνάγκη ἴσχει.
2. νύμφη τὸν ἐν οἷσι μεγάροις ἴσχει.
3. Ὀδυσσεὺς δ' οὐ δύναται ἣν πατρίδα γαῖαν ἱκέσθαι. (cf. Odyssey V, 15)
4. Ἡὼς ἐξ οὗ λέχεος ὄρνυται.
5. Τιθωνὸς ἐξ οὗ λέχεος οὐκ ὄρνυται.
6. ἕταιροι Ὀδυσσῆος ἐν ἑῇ νηὶ ἐπὶ νῶτα εὐρέα θαλάσσης φέρονται.

ὅδε, ἥδε, τόδε = this
With the suffix -δε, ὁ, ἡ, τό always means "this". So ὅδε = "this man", ἥδε = "this woman" and τόδε = "this thing", e.g. τίς δ' ὅδε Ναυσικάᾳ ἕπεται; = "but who is this man following Nausicaa?" (Odyssey VI, 276) (ἕπομαι + dative = I follow)

ὅδε, ἥδε, τόδε can qualify a noun, e.g. ἥδε πόλις = this city.[8]

<u>οὗτος, αὕτη, τοῦτο = this, that</u>[9]
is the normal Greek pronoun for "this" when mentioning something perhaps not quite as near as is meant by ὅδε, and can be used for more distant things where we might use "that". οὗτος ("this") tends to refer to something already mentioned, ὅδε to something that follows.

	masculine	feminine	neuter
singular			
nominative	οὗτος = this (man)	αὕτη = this (woman)	τοῦτο = this(thing)
accusative	τοῦτον = this (man)	ταύτην = this (woman)	τοῦτο = this (thing)
genitive	τούτου = of this (man)	ταύτης = of this (woman)	τούτου = of this (thing)
dative	τούτῳ = to/for this (man)	[ταύτῃ] = to/for this (woman)	[τούτῳ] = by this (thing)
dual			
nom/acc	τούτω = these two (men)	–	τούτω = these two (things)
gen/dat	[τούτοιιν] = of/to/for these two (men)	–	[τούτοιιν] = of/by these two (things)
plural			
nominative	οὗτοι = these (men)	[αὗται] = these (women)	ταῦτα = these (things)
accusative	τούτους = these (men)	[ταύτας] = these (women)	ταῦτα = these (things)
genitive	τούτων = of these (men)	[ταυτάων] = of these (women)	τούτων = of these (things)
dative	τούτοισι(ν) = to/for these (men)	[ταύτῃσι(ν)] = to/for these (women)	[τούτοισι(ν)] = by these (things)

[8]cf. τήνδε πόλιν (accusative), p.50.
[9]Chantraine, op. cit., vol.ii, pp.168-9.

The origin of οὗτος αὕτη τοῦτο may have been the repetition of ὁ, ἡ, τό for emphasis, as can be seen e.g. from the genitive singular τούτου. In Homer, οὗτος, αὕτη, τοῦτο most often qualifies a noun, e.g.

οὐκ ἔσθ' οὗτος ἀνήρ (Odyssey VI, 201)

there is not this man (this man does not exist)

(ἀνήρ (3 masculine) = man)

and is more rarely used as a pronoun, e.g. οὗτος = this man, αὕτη = this woman, τοῦτο = this thing. The phrase ἐκ τούτων (Odyssey VI, 29), where τούτων is the neuter genitive, means "from these things".

What is the Greek for:
1. τίς ἐστιν οὗτος ἀνήρ; 2. τίς ἐστιν οὗτος;
3. νύμφη αὕτη Καλυψώ ἐστιν. 4. ταῦτα μέγαρα Καλυψοῦς ἐστιν.
5. τίς ἐστιν οὗτος νόος ὃν 'Αθηναίη ἔχει; (νόος (2 masculine) = intention)
6. τοῦτον νόον ὃν 'Αθηναίη ἔχει οὐκ οἶδα. (οἶδα = I know)

(ἐ)κεῖνος, (ἐ)κείνη, (ἐ)κεῖνο (in Attic prose, ἐκεῖνος, ἐκείνη, ἐκεῖνο) = that. (ἐ)κεῖνος is used to refer to distant things, either in space or time. The endings are like φίλος, except that the nominative and accusative singular neuter lack final ν.

(ἐ)κεῖνος, (ἐ)κείνη, (ἐ)κεῖνο are often used as pronouns, e.g. (ἐ)κεῖνος = that man, (ἐ)κείνη = that woman, (ἐ)κεῖνο = that thing.

ἐρρέτω, εἴ μιν κεῖνος ἐποτρύνει (Odyssey V, 139)

let him (Odysseus) begone, if that one (i.e. Zeus) urges him

(ἐρρέτω : let him begone (to his ruin), εἰ : if, ἐποτρύνω : I urge, μιν : him)

What is the Greek for:
1. κεῖνος πατὴρ ὡς ἤπιος ἦεν. 2. (ἐ)κείνην ἀμείβεται Ζεὺς ὑψιβρεμέτης.
3. ἐκεῖνοι οὐ μέμνηνται 'Οδυσσῆος. 4. κείνοις ἀνάσσει 'Οδυσσεύς.
5. κείνους οὐ πέμπει Ζεὺς εἰς ἣν πατρίδα γαῖαν.
6. ἐκ τοῦ δ' οὔτ' 'Οδυσῆα ἐγὼν ἴδον οὔτ' ἐμὲ κεῖνος. (Odyssey I, 212)

(ἐκ τοῦ = since then οὔτ': οὔτε ἐγών: ἐγώ ἴδον = I saw (Section 10, p.67))

Section 8   55

αὐτός, αὐτή, αὐτό
αὐτός, αὐτή, αὐτό = (he) himself, (she) herself, (it) itself, as in "he himself has said it". "Autograph" in English comes from αὐτὸς (or αὐτὴ) γράφει, "he himself or she herself writes". If the verb is 1st person, the nominative means "I myself" or "we ourselves", and if 2nd person, "you yourself" or "you yourselves". The endings are like ἐκεῖνος.
Examples:
μή[10] τί σοι αὐτῷ πῆμα κακὸν βουλευσέμεν ἄλλο. (Odyssey V, 187)
(I promise) not to devise any other evil trouble for you yourself
(βουλευσέμεν : to be about to plan)

αὐτὴ δ' ἀντίον ἷζεν 'Οδυσσῆος θείοιο (Odyssey V, 198)
and she herself was sitting opposite godlike Odysseus
(ἵζω = I sit. ἀντίον + genitive = opposite)

What is the English for:
1.οἶδα[11] καὶ αὐτός. (Odyssey V, 215)   2.'Αθηναίη αὐτὴ λέγε.
3."Διὸς αὐτοῦ τέκνον εἰμι," λέγει.   4.μνηστῆρες[12] αὐτοὶ ἐν νηΐ εἰσιν.
5.'Ερμεία,[13] σὺ αὐτος ἀγγελὸς ἀθανάτων ἐσσι.

<u>Third person pronoun</u>   In the Epic dialect, a third person pronoun "him", "her", corresponds to ἐμέ, με (= "me") and σέ, σε (= "you" (singular)). This pronoun, not found in the nominative. has two forms:
accusative   ἕ   μιν[14]   both = him, her
genitive   εἷο[15]   ἕο   both = of him, of her
dative   ἑοῖ or οἷ   οἱ   both = to/for him, to/for her
Its plural is:
accusative   σφέας   σφε[16]   = them
genitive   σφῶν   σφεων or σφείων = their, of them
dative   σφίσι(ν)   σφι(ν) or σφισι(ν) = to, for by them

---
[10]μή is the negative with an infinitive. βουλεύσεμεν (future infinitive of βουλεύω : I plan, devise) : to be about to devise. NB the accent on τί is caused by σοι, which is enclitic. τί is not interrogative.
[11]οἶδα : I know. καί can mean "even" or "also" as well as "and".
[12]μνηστῆρες (3, masculine) = (the) suitors, referred to as "they" in line 18. See p.47, footnote 39.
[13]Vocative of 'Ερμείας (1, masculine) : Hermes
[14]μιν, ἑο and οἱ are enclitic.   εὑ or ἕθεν sometimes stand for ἑο.
[15]also ἕο, εὗ
[16]σφε, σφεων and σφι(ν) or σφισι(ν) are enclitic.   σφεων is always a monosyllable.

There is a dual: accusative σφ' (standing for σφε) or σφωε "those two"
genitive & dative σφωιν "of, or to, for, by those two"
which is enclitic and can be distinguished from σφῶι(ν) "of, or to, for, by you two" (see p. 39, above) by the accent.

Examples:

ἐν μεγάροισι Καλυψοῦς, ἥ μιν ἀνάγκῃ ἴσχει· (Odyssey V, 14-5)
in the palace of Calypso, who is holding him by necessity

οἵ κέν μιν πέμποιεν ἐπ' εὐρέα νῶτα θαλάσσης.(Odyssey V, 17)
who might send him over the wide back of the sea

(Καλυψώ) δῶκέ οἱ πέλεκυν μέγαν (Odyssey V, 234)
(Calypso) gave to him a large axe
δῶκε = she gave   πέλεκυν (acc. sing.) = axe   μέγαν (masc. acc. sing.) = large

ἀτὰρ ἐν νόστῳ 'Αθηναίην ἀλίτοντο,
ἥ σφιν ἐπῶρσ' ἄνεμόν τε κακὸν καὶ κύματα μακρά. (Odyssey V, 108-9)
But on their way home they offended Athene, who for them raised up both an evil wind and long waves.
(ἀλίτοντο, 3rd plu. aorist indicative of ἀλιταίνομαι, I offend against ἐπῶρσ' stands for ἐπῶρσε, raised up (3rd person singular, aorist indicative, ἐπόρνυμι (for aorist of ὄρνυμι, see p.62)) ἄνεμος 2 masc. = wind, μακρός, μακρή, μακρόν = long)

New words:
ἀντίον = opposite (with genitive)   αὐδάω = I utter, speak (to), address
αὖτε = furthermore, also   βουλή = will, plan, design
γε (enclitic) = indeed   δή = at that point, in fact, finally
ἐμός, ἐμή, ἐμόν = my, mine
ἔπος, ἔπους (neuter) = word, statement (*also* saying, poem)
ἦμαρ, ἤματος (neuter) = day   ἦ τοι, ἦ γάρ = of a certainty
θνητός, θνητή, θνητόν = mortal (subject to θάνατος, death)
κε or κεν = in that case[17]   κῆρ (neuter) = heart[18]
νημερτής (accusative singular νημερτέα) = sure and true
νόστος (masc) = voyage home
περί (+ acc, gen or dat) = around   περὶ κῆρι = very dear[19]

[17]κε is enclitic. It is used in suppositions and sometimes in expressing purpose; it has the effect of the English "would". See line 36 and footnotes 55 and 57 below.
[18]Found only in nominative, accusative and dative singular (or locative, κῆρι : in the heart). To be distinguished from κήρ (feminine) : doom.
[19]περί in this phrase is an adverb, and κῆρι is locative (p.134). Chantraine, *op. cit.*, vol. ii, p.126.

Section 8 57

περ = (1) very much, by all means (2) though[20]
πομπή (1 fem) = a sending home, an escort
προσφημί = I speak to
ὑψόροφος, -ov = high-roofed[21]   χρυσός (2 masc) = gold

What is the English for:
1. οὗτος ἀνήρ ἐστιν Ὀδυσσεύς· πρός ἑο ὑψόροφα δώματα ἱκνέεσθαι ἐθέλει. (ἀνήρ : man)
2. Ἀθηναίη, σὺ πέμπεις μιν οἴκαδε; δύνασαι γάρ.
3. πέμπω· μοῖρα γάρ οἱ ἐστι πρὸς ἣν πατρίδα γαῖαν ἔρχεσθαι.
4. Ζεὺς ὑψιβρεμέτης Ἑρμείαν, τέκνον ἐόν, ἀντίον ηὔδα.[22]
5. "νύμφῃ ἐϋπλοκάμῳ ἐθέλω σε νημερτέα βουλὴν λέγειν," ἔφη.
6. Ἑρμείας ἐδήσατο[23] καλὰ πέδιλα[24] ἀμβρόσια χρύσεια, τά μιν φέρον.
(Odyssey V, 44-45)

Homer, Odyssey V, lines 21-42
τὴν δ' ἀπαμειβόμενος προσέφη[25] νεφεληγερέτα Ζεύς·[26]
"τέκνον ἐμόν, ποῖόν[27] σε ἔπος φύγεν[28] ἔρκος[29] ὀδόντων.
οὐ γὰρ δὴ τοῦτον μὲν ἐβούλευσας[30] νόον[31] αὐτή,

[20]With a participle (see Section 11, p.76). περ is enclitic.
[21]Not found in the feminine.
[22]3rd person singular imperfect active of αὐδάω (contracted from ηὔδαε). ηὔδα- is αὐδα- augmented.
[23]ἐδήσατο (3rd singular, aorist middle of δέω) : "he tied on for himself".
[24]πέδιλα : sandals ἀμβρόσιος : divinely fair χρύσειος -η -ov : golden.
[25]ἀπαμειβόμενος προσέφη is a very common formula: "answering spoke to".
[26]νεφεληγερέτα Ζεύς, "Zeus the cloud-gatherer" is a Homeric formula, and the vocative is used instead of the nominative probably because this was the familiar form of the phrase. This formula is used also at Iliad I, 517, where Zeus responds to Thetis' request on behalf of Achilles:
τὴν δὲ μέγ' ὀχθήσας προσέφη νεφεληγερέτα Ζεύς (μέγα : greatly, ὀχθήσας : annoyed) her, however, greatly annoyed, did address cloud-gatherer Zeus.
(Iliad I, 511, where Zeus refuses to speak, ends οὐ τι προσέφη νεφεληγερέτα Ζεύς.)
[27]ποῖος, ποίη, ποῖον : what kind of? Translate with ἔπος.
[28]φύγεν : escaped (3rd singular aorist active of φεύγω, I flee).
[29]ἔρκος (3n, like λέχος) : fence ὀδόντων is genitive plural of ὀδούς, ὀδόντος (masculine): tooth. Hainsworth, *A Commentary on Homer's Odyssey* vol.i, p.256 notes σε φύγεν ἔρκος ὀδόντων "escaped you with respect to the fence of (your) teeth" as a kenning, or colourful paraphrase, more common in Germanic poetry, where it helps with alliteration, than in Greek. Zeus has already used this phrase to Athene at Odyssey I, 64, (see West, *op. cit.*, p.83). It is a reproof: her teeth should have kept back what she said.
[30]"you devised" (2nd person singular aorist indicative active from βουλεύω, I devise).
[31]τοῦτον qualifies νόον. νόος (2m) : plan (purpose, thought, intention).

ὡς³² ἦ τοι κείνους 'Οδυσεὺς ἀποτείσεται³³ ἐλθών·³⁴
Τηλέμαχον δὲ σὺ πέμψον³⁵ ἐπισταμένως,³⁶ δύνασαι γάρ, 25
ὥς κε μάλ' ἀσκηθὴς³⁷ ἣν πατρίδα γαῖαν ἵκηται,³⁸
μνηστῆρες³⁹ δ' ἐν νηὶ παλιμπετὲς⁴⁰ ἀπονέωνται."⁴¹
  ἦ ῥα,⁴² καὶ 'Ερμείαν,⁴³ υἱὸν⁴⁴ φίλον, ἀντίον ηὔδα·
"Ἑρμεία· σὺ γὰρ αὖτε τά τ' ἄλλα⁴⁵ περ ἄγγελός ἐσσι·
νύμφῃ ἐϋπλοκάμῳ εἰπεῖν⁴⁶ νημερτέα βουλήν, 30
νόστον 'Οδυσσῆος ταλασίφρονος,⁴⁷ ὥς κε νέηται,⁴⁸
οὔτε θεῶν πομπῇ οὔτε θνητῶν ἀνθρώπων·
ἀλλ' ὅ γ' ἐπὶ σχεδίης πολυδέσμου⁴⁹ πήματα πάσχων⁵⁰
ἤματι εἰκοστῷ⁵¹ Σχερίην ἐρίβωλον⁵² ἵκοιτο,

³²Here, with a subjunctive, ὡς means "so that".
³³κείνους is the object of ἀποτείσεται, 3rd person singular aorist subjunctive middle of ἀποτίνω, I pay back. ὡς ἀποτείσεται: "so that he may avenge himself on". (For subjunctives, see Section 14.)
³⁴Nominative masculine singular of the participle of ἦλθον, "I came", which is the aorist of ἔρχομαι. ἐλθών means "having come", i.e "when he comes".
³⁵2nd person singular aorist imperative active of πέμπω, "send!" "You" is often put in with Greek imperatives, almost always left out with English ones.
³⁶ἐπισταμένως : skilfully.
³⁷μάλ' stands for μάλα ("very much"). μάλ' ἀσκηθής : quite unharmed.
³⁸ὥς κε ... ἵκηται: so that he may reach (ἵκηται is 3rd person singular, aorist subjunctive of ἱκνέομαι. κε ("in that case") reinforces the subjunctive. ὥς κε : so that.
³⁹See footnote 12.
⁴⁰παλιμπετές : back again
⁴¹ἀπονέωνται: (they) may depart (3rd person plural present subjunctive of ἀπονέομαι, I depart).
⁴²ἦ ῥα is a formula used at the end of a speech "thus he spake". ἦ is 3rd singular imperfect from ἠμί, a cognate form of φημί. ῥα is an abbreviation of ἄρα: then.
⁴³ 'Ερμείας (vocative,'Ερμεία): Hermes.
⁴⁴υἱός (2 masculine): son. φίλος (here, and in line 37) = his own.
⁴⁵αὖτε here: "for your part". τά τ' ἄλλα is accusative: "of course in respect of other matters". Such a use of the accusative case is sometimes called the accusative of respect (cf. ἕρκος ὀδόντων, line 22). Among Hermes' other functions was conducting the souls of the dead to Hades. τ' stands for τε (τε : of course). περ: indeed.
⁴⁶εἰπεῖν: "say!" (the infinitive active of εἶπον, the aorist of λέγω, I say, which is an irregular verb, used for an imperative). Understand "my" with νημερτέα βουλήν. νόστον, in the following line, is in apposition to βουλήν. The νόστος is Zeus' βουλή.
⁴⁷Masculine genitive singular of ταλασίφρων: patient of mind, stout hearted.
⁴⁸3rd person singular present subjunctive of νέομαι, I go, (here) return (home). For ὥς κε, see footnote 38. The subject is "he" (Odysseus) - "so that he may return".
⁴⁹γ' stands for γε. πολύδεσμος (feminine as masc.) : fastened with many bonds.
⁵⁰πάσχων : "suffering" (masculine nominative singular of the present participle of πάσχω).
⁵¹εἰκοστός εἰκοστή εἰκοστόν : twentieth. The dative (ἤματι εἰκοστῷ) expresses time when, "on" in English.
⁵²ἐρίβωλος: very fertile. ἵκοιτο "(so that) he might reach" is 3rd person singular, aorist optative of ἱκνέομαι.

Section 8

Φαιήκων ἐς γαῖαν, οἳ ἀγχίθεοι⁵³ γεγάασιν·⁵⁴   35
οἵ⁵⁵ κέν μιν περὶ κῆρι θεὸν ὣς⁵⁶ τιμήσουσι,⁵⁷
πέμψουσιν⁵⁸ δ' ἐν νηΐ φίλην ἐς πατρίδα γαῖαν,
χαλκόν⁵⁹ τε χρυσόν τε ἅλις⁶⁰ ἐσθῆτά⁶¹ τε δόντες,⁶²
πόλλ', ὅσ' ἄν⁶³ οὐδέ ποτε⁶⁴ Τροίης⁶⁵ ἐξήρατ⁶⁶ Ὀδυσσεύς,
εἴ περ ἀπήμων⁶⁷ ἦλθε,⁶⁸ λαχὼν⁶⁹ ἀπὸ ληΐδος⁷⁰ αἶσαν.   40
ὣς⁷¹ γάρ οἱ μοῖρ' ἐστὶ φίλους τ' ἰδέειν⁷² καὶ ἱκέσθαι⁷³
οἶκον ἐς ὑψόροφον καὶ ἑὴν ἐς πατρίδα γαῖαν."

⁵³ἀγχίθεος: near the gods, i.e. akin to them or like them.
⁵⁴γεγάασιν: (they) have become (3rd person plural perfect of γίγνομαι).
⁵⁵The accent on οἵ ("who") (line 35) is grave, as ἀγχίθεοι follows without a punctuation break. The accent on οἵ ("they") in line 36 is acute because it is affected by κέν which is enclitic. The acute accent on κέν is from μιν, also enclitic.
⁵⁶Translate in the order ὡς θεὸν.
⁵⁷κεν = "would". τιμήσουσι: (they) would honour (3rd person plural future indicative active, τιμάω : I honour). For the effect of κεν with future indicative, see p.186.
⁵⁸πέμψουσιν, they would send (3rd person plural future indicative active of πέμπω, also affected by κεν).
⁵⁹χαλκός: bronze. χαλκόν τε χρυσόν τε ἅλις ἐσθῆτά τε are the object of δόντες, which qualifies οἵ, the subject of τιμήσουσι πέμψουσι δέ.
⁶⁰ἅλις : enough
⁶¹ἐσθής, ἐσθῆτος (fem): clothing. Hainsworth (*op. cit.*, p.258) refers to Odyssey VIII, 387ff and XIII 10ff. At Odyssey VIII 387, Alcinous, the ruler of the Phaeacians, himself gives Odysseus a tunic and a cloak and a talent of gold, and tells 12 other "kings" of the Phaeacians to do the same; so Odysseus arrives on Ithaca with 13 changes of clothes and 13 talents of gold. To have arrived home empty handed would have been dishonourable in a returning warrior, and Zeus' arrangements for Odysseus take advantage of the custom of giving expensive presents to departing guests (this increased the prestige of the giver). In Odyssey IV, at 125-132 Helen and Menelaus display lavish presents they received when they left Egypt, and at 589-592 Telemachus, when leaving Sparta, is offered expensive gifts by Menelaus.
⁶²having given (nominative masculine plural of the aorist participle active of δίδωμι, I give).
⁶³πόλλ' stands for πολλά, "many things", summing up χαλκόν τε χρυσόν τε ἅλις ἐσθῆτά τε. ὅσ'stands for ὅσα (neuter plural accusative) : how many, as many as.
⁶⁴οὐδέ ποτε stands for οὐδέποτε: never.
⁶⁵This genitive means "from Troy".
⁶⁶ἐξήρατ' stands for ἐξήρατο (3rd person singular aorist middle of ἐξαίρω, I lift up. ἐξαίρομαι: I carry off). ἄν ... ἐξήρατο: "he would have carried off". (ἄν: "would.")
⁶⁷ἀπήμων: without trouble.
⁶⁸εἴ περ: if indeed. ἦλθε (3rd person singular of ἦλθον, the aorist of ἔρχομαι): he had come.
⁶⁹λαχών: having received as his portion (nominative masculine singular of the aorist participle active of λαγχάνω, I receive as my portion or lot).
⁷⁰ληΐς, ληΐδος (fem): booty. αἶσα (1 fem.): a share.
⁷¹ὥς = so, thus. Note the accent; compare ὡς ("as", "like").
⁷²μοῖρ' stands for μοῖρα. ("Fate is for him" = "it is his destiny".) ἰδέειν: to see (aorist infinitive active of ὁράω (irregular): I see.
⁷³ἱκέσθαι to arrive (aorist infinitive of ἱκνέομαι). ἱκέσθαι ἐς + acc. : to arrive at.

Section 9
The Weak Aorist Tense.

The aorist tense, which in the indicative mood most often corresponds with the English past definite, has two patterns in Greek, as the past definite does in English. In English, if we wish to change the present tense verb "I cook" into the past definite tense, we add the suffix -ed, and say, "I cooked". The modification which gives the weak aorist indicative ending in Greek may be thought of as similar to the English suffix -ed. There are, however, English verbs where this is not done, and instead there is a different form of the verb stem to express a past action (e.g., "I sing" is present, and "I sang" is past). The Greek strong aorist involves a comparable change in the verb stem and the use of an ending like the imperfect. All strong and many weak aorists have aorist stems which differ from the present, though in the weak aorist the difference is sometimes slight; e.g. corresponding to the present, λύω (I am loosing) is the aorist ἔλῡσα, in which υ is long, not short.

The weak aorist ending system is based on -α or -σα. The following are the weak aorist indicative active and middle patterns:

        active   middle

singular
    (ἔ)λυσα = I loosed   (ἐ)λυσάμην = I loosed for myself
    (ἔ)λυσας = you loosed   (ἐ)λύσαο (or (ἐ)λύσω) = you loosed for yourself
    (ἔ)λυσε(ν) = he/she/it loosed   (ἐ)λύσατο = he/she/it loosed for him/her/itself

dual
    (ἐ)λύσατον = you two loosed   (ἐ)λύσασθον = you two loosed for yourselves
    (ἐ)λυσάτην = those two loosed   (ἐ)λυσάσθην = those two loosed for themselves

plural
    (ἐ)λύσαμεν = we loosed   (ἐ)λυσάμε(σ)θα = we loosed for ourselves
    (ἐ)λύσατε = you loosed   (ἐ)λύσασθε = you loosed for yourselves
    (ἔ)λυσαν = they loosed   (ἐ)λύσαντο = they loosed for themselves

Section 9

In the aorist, the temporal augment is only found in the indicative. The same rules for the augment apply as in the imperfect tense (p.34). However, in Homer the augment is often omitted, and then the tense must be recognised from the ending.

In some verbs the aorist endings are formed by variations of –σα e.g. -ψα for –πσα or –ξα for –γσα or –κσα (-σα is sometimes called the sigmatised aorist), but σ is not found with verbs whose stems end in λ, ν or ρ because of the desire to avoid the combinations λσ, νσ and ρσ. α is the characteristic vowel of weak aorist endings, as follows:

	active	middle
singular	-(σ)α	-(σ)αμεν
	-(σ)ας	-(σ)αο *or* -(σ)ω
	-(σ)ε	-(σ)ατο
dual	-(σ)ατον	-(σ)ασθον
	-(σ)ατην	-(σ)ασθην
plural	-(σ)αμεν	-(σ)αμε(σ)θα
	-(σ)ατε	-(σ)ασθε
	-(σ)αν	-(σ)αντο

The aorist passive has its own system of endings (see Sections 18 & 19).[1]

Verbs ending -αω or -εω in the present indicative active have aorists ending -ησα, and verbs ending -οω have aorists ending -ωσα, e.g.

τιμάω = I honour   (ἐ)τίμησα = I honoured
ποιέω = I do, make   (ἐ)ποίησα = I did, made
χολόω = I anger   (ἐ)χόλωσα = I angered.

Some other weak aorist indicatives:

active verbs		middle verbs	
present	aorist	present	aorist
ἀπιθέω *I disobey*	ἀπίθησα	ἀμείβομαι *I answer*	ἠμειψάμην
βουλεύω *I plan*	(ἐ)βούλευσα		*or* ἀμειψάμην
δεύω *I dip, wet*	ἔδευσα	δέομαι *I tie on myself*	ἐδησάμην
δέω *I tie, bind*	(ἔ)δησα	ὀχέομαι *I ride*	ὀχησάμην
ἐγείρω *I awaken*	ἤγειρα (ἔγειρα)	σεύομαι *I dart*	(ἐ)σευάμην[2]
ἐθέλω *I want, wish*	ἐθέλησα[3]		
θέλγω *I charm*	ἔθελξα		
καίω *I set on fire*	(ἔ)κηα		
ὄλλυμι *I destroy*	ὤλεσα (ὄλεσ(σ)α)		

[1]See also Appendix A (Voices). An aorist middle may still seem passive in English.
[2]It also has a poetical strong aorist (Section 10) as follows: [ἐσσύμην], ἔσσυο, ἔσσυτο, ἐσσύμεθα (2nd and 3rd persons plural and dual not found in Homer).
[3]In later Greek, ἠθέλησα, but not found augmented in Homer.

present	aorist
ὄμνυμι *I swear*	ὤμοσ(σ)α (ὄμοσα *or* ὄμοσσα)
ὄρνυμι *I arouse*	ὧρσα
πέμπω *I send*	(ἔ)πεμψα
ῥέζω *I perform*	(ἔ)ρεξα *or* ἔρρεξα

Which of these verbs are aorist, and which imperfect?
1.ἔλυσα. 2.ἔλυον. 3.ἔλυσας. 4.ἔλυσε. 5.ἔλυε. 6.ἐλύσατο. 7.ἐλύετο. 8.ἔθελον. 9.ἐθέλησαν. 10.ὦρσεν. 11.ὤρνυτο. 12.ὄμοσαν.

The aorist optative

The aorist optative expresses a wish, purpose or contingency regarded as a simple action.

aorist optative active   aorist optative middle

λύσαιμι = might I loose   λυσαίμην = might I get loosed
λύσαις = might you loose   λύσαιο = might you get loosed
 or λύσαισθα *or* λύσειας
λύσαι = might he/she/it loose   λύσαιτο = might he/she/it get loosed
 or λύσειε
λύσαιμεν = might we loose   λυσαίμε(σ)θα = might we get loosed
λύσαιτε = might you loose   λύσαισθε = might you get loosed
λύσαιεν = might they loose   λυσαίατο = might they get loosed
 or λύσειαν

The aorist optative dual is active: [λύσαιτον, λυσαίτην], middle: [λύσαισθον, λυσαίσθην].

What is the English for:
1.λύσαμεν. 2.ἐλύσαν; 3.ἐλύσαο. 4.λύσω; 5.λύσαιτο. 6.ἀμειψαίατο. 7.ἔπεμψαν. 8.ἔκαιον. 9.ἔκηαν. 10.ἀπίθησε (ἀπιθέω = I disobey) 11.ἐδήσατο. (δέομαι = I tie on (myself) 12.σεύατο. (σεύομαι : I dart) 13.ὀχήσατο. (ὀχέομαι : I ride) 14.ἄνθρωπος πῦρ ἔκηε.
15.ἄνεμοι[4] κύματα ὦρσαν.
16.ἑταίρους ἐς τοῦτο σπέος⁵ ἐπέμψατε;
17.ἑταίρους ἐς τοῦτο σπέος ἐπέμπετε;
18.ἑταίρους ἐς τοῦτο σπέος πέμψατε;
19.ὑπὸ ποσσὶν[6] ἐδήσω καλὰ πέδιλα, Ἑρμεία;
20.ἐν πόντῳ ὄρνις σεύατο ἐπὶ κύματα.
21.ἐν πόντῳ ὄρνις σεύεται ἐπὶ κύματα.
22.ἐν πόντῳ ὄρνις σεύετο ἐπὶ κύματα.

---
[4]See "new words" below.
[5]For σπέος and ὄρνις, see the list of new words below.
[6]See "new words" and footnote 13 below.

Section 9

New words:

ἅλς, ἁλός (3 m) = salt, sea
ἄνεμος (2 m) = wind
ἀπιθέω = I disobey

αὐτίκα = immediately
δέομαι = I tie on myself
ἐγείρω = I awaken
ἔνθα = there, thither, where
θέλγω = I charm, bewitch
κατά (+ accusative) = down, along, throughout, at, in (the heart)
ναίω = I dwell, inhabit
ὅτε = when, at the time when
πυκινός, -ή, -όν = close set
σπέος, σπείους (3 n) = cave[10]
τότε = then

ὥς = thus, so (NB accent)

ἅμα = at the same time
(+ dative) = together with
ἀνήρ, ἀνδρός or ἀνέρος (3 m) = man[7]
ἀτρύγετος, ἀτρύγετον = harvestless, barren[8]
δεινός, δεινή, δεινόν = terrible
δέω = I tie, bind
ἐνδόθι = within, at home
ἐπιβαίνω[9] = I set foot on

ὄρνις, ὄρνιθος (3m or f) = bird
ὀχέομαι = I ride
σεύομαι = I dart
τηλόθι = afar, at a distance
ὑπό (+ genitive or dative) = under, (+ genitive) by the agency of

---

[7]The vocative is ἄνερ. The accusative singular is ἀνέρα or ἄνδρα. The genitive singular is ἀνδρός or (less frequently) ἀνέρος. The dative singular is ἀνδρί or less frequently, ἀνέρι. The nominative plural is ἀνέρες or ἄνδρες, and the accusative plural is ἀνέρας or ἄνδρας. The genitive plural is always ἀνδρῶν, and the dative plural is ἀνδράσι or ἀνέρεσσι. (Chantraine, *Grammaire Homérique*, vol. i, p.214.)
[8]Homeric epithet of the sea.
[9]Aorist, ἐπέβην "I stepped on", [ἐπέβης], [ἐπέβη], ἐπέβημεν "we stepped on", [ἐπέβητε], ἐπέβησαν "they stepped on". (For the endings, see p.83, footnote 12.) ἐπιβάς (masculine), ἐπιβᾶσα (feminine), ἐπιβάν (neuter) = "having stepped on". "on" is normally expressed by the genitive. Here and at Iliad xiv 226, the accusative is used; in the Iliad, of Hera: Πιερίην δ' ἐπιβᾶσα καὶ Ἠμαθίην ἐρατεινὴν σεύατο ... "having set foot on Pieria and lovely Emathia, she darted ..."
[10]Sometimes σπεῖος, as at line 194 (p.112). The dative singular is σπῆι and the dative plural σπέσσι *or* σπήεσσι.

Odyssey V, 43-58

ὣς ἔφατ',[11] οὐδ' ἀπίθησε διάκτορος Ἀργεϊφόντης.[12]
αὐτίκ' ἔπειθ' ὑπὸ ποσσὶν[13] ἐδήσατο καλὰ πέδιλα,[14]
ἀμβρόσια χρύσεια, τά μιν φέρον ἠμὲν[15] ἐφ' ὑγρὴν[16]   45
ἠδ' ἐπ' ἀπείρονα[17] γαῖαν ἅμα πνοιῆσ'[18] ἀνέμοιο.
εἵλετο[19] δὲ ῥάβδον,[20] τῇ[21] τ' ἀνδρῶν ὄμματα[22] θέλγει,[23]
ὧν ἐθέλει, τοὺς δ' αὖτε καὶ ὑπνώοντας[24] ἐγείρει·[25]
τὴν μετὰ χερσὶν ἔχων πέτετο[26] κρατὺς[27] Ἀργεϊφόντης.

[11]ἔφατ' stands for ἔφατο = "he said" (see p.34). οὐδ' stands for οὐδὲ.
[12]For ἀπίθησε (3rd person singular), see p.61. διάκτορος Ἀργεϊφόντης is a formulaic title, repeated at lines 75 and 94. (κρατὺς Ἀργεϊφόντης is found at line 49.) διάκτορος was later explained as meaning "messenger" or "servant" (cf. διάκονος, from which the English word "deacon" is derived). Ἀργεϊφόντης is often translated "slayer of Argus", and the meaning "slayer" is implied by φόντης (from φονεύω = I murder) but the meaning of Ἀργεϊ- is obscure; in a non-Homeric myth Hermes slew a hundred-eyed monster named Argus that had been set by Hera to watch over the hapless princess Io after Zeus had seduced her, but the legend may have been invented to explain Ἀργεϊφόντης after the original meaning had been forgotten. (Stanford suggests also an alternative derivation, from ἀργός ("shining") and φαίνω ("I am appearing"), giving the meaning "brightly appearing", and notes that Chantraine, *Mélanges Navarre* (1935) p.69 ff. considered Ἀργεϊφόντης an inexplicable pre-Greek name.)
[13]αὐτίκ' stands for αὐτίκα. ἔπειθ' stands for ἔπειτα. ποσσὶν is dative plural from ποῦς, ποδός (m) = foot. For ἐδήσατο (3rd person singular, middle), see p. 61.
[14]For πέδιλον and χρύσειος, see page 49. ἀμβρόσιος, ἀμβροσίη, ἀμβρόσιον (= immortal), is derived from α- = un- (see p.8, footnote 5) and βροτός (= mortal).
[15]ἠμὲν ... ἠδὲ ... = both ... and ...
[16]ἐφ' stands for ἐπί. ὑγρή = the sea (fem. of ὑγρός, ὑγρή, ὑγρόν) = "moist").
[17]ἐπ' stands for ἐπὶ. ἀπείρων (masc & fem), ἀπεῖρον (neuter) (3rd declension) = boundless.
[18]πνοιῆσ' stands for πνοιῆσι (dative plural). πνοιή (1 feminine) = breath.
[19]εἵλετο (he took up) is 3rd person singular aorist indicative middle of αἱρέω, I take. (This is a strong aorist; see section 10.)
[20]Hermes' ῥάβδος (2 feminine) or herald's staff was a permanent part of his equipment like the *caduceus* of his Latin counterpart, Mercurius (Hainsworth, *A Companion to Homer's Odyssey* vol.i, p.259).
[21]τῇ here is relative (see p. 49, (e)) and refers to ῥάβδον. τ' stands for τε.
[22]ὄμμα, ὄμματος (neuter) = eye.
[23]θέλγω = I enchant.
[24]ὑπνώοντας (3rd declension, masculine accusative plural) = "drowsing", from the present participle of ὑπνώω = I am drowsy. (For participles, see Section 11.) τοὺς ὑπνώοντας: those drowsing.
[25]ἐγείρω = I arouse. Line 48 is repeated at Odyssey XXIV, 4 where Hermes is conducting the souls of the dead suitors to Hades.
[26]πέτομαι = I fly. πέτετο (NB, unaugmented) is imperfect, 3rd person singular. τὴν = it (the rod); see p.48. ἔχων = holding (present participle of ἔχω).
[27]κρατύς = strong, mighty (a masculine adjective, used as an epithet of Hermes).

Section 9   65

Πιερίην²⁸ δ' ἐπιβὰς²⁹ ἐξ αἰθέρος³⁰ ἔμπεσε³¹ πόντῳ·   50
σεύατ'³² ἔπειτ' ἐπὶ κῦμα λάρῳ³³ ὄρνιθι ἐοικώς,³⁴
ὅς τε³⁵ κατὰ δεινοὺς κόλπους³⁶ ἁλὸς ἀτρυγέτοιο
ἰχθῦς³⁷ ἀγρώσσων³⁸ πυκινὰ πτερὰ³⁹ δεύεται⁴⁰ ἄλμῃ·⁴¹
τῷ ἴκελος⁴² πολέεσσιν⁴³ ὀχήσατο⁴⁴ κύμασιν Ἑρμῆς.
ἀλλ' ὅτε δὴ τὴν νῆσον ἀφίκετο⁴⁵ τηλόθ'⁴⁶ ἐοῦσαν,⁴⁷   55
ἔνθ'⁴⁸ ἐκ πόντου βὰς⁴⁹ ἰοειδέος⁵⁰ ἠπειρόνδε
ἤϊεν,⁵¹ ὄφρα⁵² μέγα⁵³ σπέος ἵκετο, τῷ ἔνι νύμφη
ναῖεν ἐϋπλόκαμος· τὴν δ' ἔνδοθι τέτμεν⁵⁴ ἐοῦσαν.

---

²⁸Pieria is a mountainous district in Macedonia, north of Mount Olympus.
²⁹See p.63, footnote 9.
³⁰αἰθήρ, αἰθέρος (fem. in Homer, in later prose masc.) = the ether, the sky.
³¹"fell upon", 3rd person singular aorist indicative of ἐμπίπτω (followed by dative) (πέσε is a strong aorist; see Section 10). The dative (πόντῳ) expresses end of motion - literally, "he fell upon (i.e., swooped down on) the sea".
³²σεύατ' stands for σεύατο (3rd person singular, aorist indicative of σεύομαι, p.61).
³³λάρος: "a ravenous sea bird, perhaps a sea mew or gull" (Liddell & Scott).
³⁴ἐοικώς: "like" (with dative, as old English "like unto"). ἐοικώς is masculine nominative singular of ἐοικώς, ἐοικυῖα, ἐοικός, "like", and qualifies "he" (Ἀργειφόντης).
³⁵ὅς τε ... "one which, in fact..." See p.51, above.
³⁶κόλπος, 2 masculine = gulf (literally "lap", "bosom").
³⁷Accusative plural of ἰχθύς (3 masc.) = "fish" (ἰχθῦς is the object of ἀγρώσσων).
³⁸ἀγρώσσων = catching (nominative masculine singular, present participle active of ἀγρώσσω). It qualifies ὅς (line 52), "which", standing for the sea bird.
³⁹πτερόν (2 neuter) = feather.
⁴⁰δεύω = I wet. δεύεται is 3rd person singular, present indicative middle - "gets its close-set feathers wet".
⁴¹ἄλμη = sea water, brine, spray.
⁴²ἴκελος, ἰκέλη, ἴκελον (+ dative) = like, resembling. τῷ ("to that") refers to λάρῳ.
⁴³Dative plural of πολύς (= "many"). πολέεσσιν qualifies κύμασιν, and πολέεσσιν κύμασιν (dative indicating place) indicates what Hermes rode on.
⁴⁴ὀχέομαι = I ride, am carried (see p. 61). Ἑρμῆς is an alternative for Ἑρμείας.
⁴⁵ἀφίκετο is 3rd person singular of ἀφικόμην, the strong aorist indicative (see Section 10) of ἀφικνέομαι, I arrive at, reach, and means "he reached".
⁴⁶τηλόθ' stands for τηλόθι, meaning "afar".
⁴⁷Feminine accusative singular of ἐών, "being" (= "which is"), qualifying νῆσον.
⁴⁸ἔνθ' stands for ἔνθα, meaning "there".
⁴⁹βάς (masculine), βᾶσα (feminine), βάν (neuter) = "having stepped", nominative singular, aorist participle of βαίνω, I step, go (for which, see p.83, footnote 12).
⁵⁰See page 30.
⁵¹ἠπειρόνδε: inland. ἤϊεν: "he went", 3rd person singular imperfect of εἶμι = "I go" (Section 16)
⁵²ὄφρα with indicative, "until". ἵκετο is 3rd person singular of ἱκόμην, the strong aorist indicative of ἱκνέομαι, I reach, and means "he reached".
⁵³Accusative neuter singular of μέγας = "great", qualifying σπέος. τῷ ἔνι = ἐν τῷ. τῷ is relative ("which") (p. 49). In line 58, τήν is demonstrative: "her", (p.48). ναῖεν is 3rd person singular imperfect of ναίω: its subject is νύμφη ἐϋπλόκαμος.
⁵⁴"he found" (3rd person singular of τέτμον, I found). For ἐοῦσαν (here qualifying τήν) see footnote 47. "her being inside" = "that she was inside".

Section 10
The strong aorist.

The strong aorist (sometimes called "the second aorist") indicative is formed by adding endings like the imperfect to a changed form of the stem. Sometimes the change is comparatively minor: compare
(ἔ)βαλλον = I was throwing (imperfect)
with (ἔ)βαλον = I threw (aorist).
However, sometimes an altogether different stem is used for the aorist, e.g., from ἔρχομαι, ἠρχόμην = I was coming (imperfect)
but the aorist is ἦλθον = I came.[1]

Some verbs with strong aorists:

αἱρέω = I take	εἷλον = I took
αἱρέομαι = I choose[2]	εἱλόμην = I chose
ἀφικνέομαι = I arrive at,[3] reach	ἀφικόμην = I arrived at, reached
βάλλω = I throw, hit, put	(ἔ)βαλον = I threw, hit, put
γίγνομαι = I become, happen	(ἐ)γενόμην = I became, happened
ἔρχομαι = I come, go	ἦλθον or ἤλυθον = I came, went[4]
εὑρίσκω = I find	εὗρον = I found
ἔχω = I have	ἔσχον = I had, held, kept[5]
ἱκνέομαι = I arrive at, reach	ἱκόμην = I arrived at, reached
-	κατέπεφνον = I slew[6]
-	(ἔ)λαβον = I took, accepted[7]
-	ἐλαβόμην = I took hold of (+ genitive)
λέγω = I say, speak, tell	ἔειπον = I said, spoke, told[8]

[1] There are similar stem changes in English. The past of "I go" is "I went", from a different verb stem "wend" ("the ploughman homeward wends his weary way").
[2] An excellent example of the middle voice: "I choose" = "I take for myself".
[3] Almost always with accusative in Homer, not requiring a separate word for "at".
[4] Often prefixed, e.g. by ἐξ (ἐξῆλθον, I went out), ἐπί (ἐπῆλθον, I went against, attacked) and παρά (παρῆλθον, I passed by, slipped past).
[5] The imperfect is εἶχον. Care is needed to distinguish this from the aorist.
[6] Often found simply as (ἔ)πεφνον, I slew. This is an example of an archaic reduplicated type of aorist (the reduplication is επεφνον), and is connected with the present tense verb θείνω, I strike. (Chantraine, Grammaire Homérique vol.i, pp.342 &396-7).
[7] The normal Attic present (λαμβάνω, I take) is not found in Homer where a related form λάζομαι is found, e.g. Odyssey III, 483: ἐς δίφρον ἀνέβαινε καὶ ἡνία λάζετο χερσί ("he began to get up on the chariot and began to take the reins with his hands"). (δίφρος 2 masc.: chariot, ἡνία, 2 neuter plural: reins)
[8] εἴπομεν is found instead of ἐείπομεν for "we said", and εἶπον instead of ἔειπον (3rd person plural, "they spoke" at Odyssey VI, 223). εἴπας is sometimes found for ἔειπες (e.g. at Iliad i, 106) meaning "you said".

Section 10

ὁράω = I see   εἶδον or ἴδον = I saw
πάσχω = I suffer   (ἔ)παθον = I suffered
πίπτω = I fall   (ἔ)πεσον = I fell[9]
    -                       (ἔ)τετμον = I found, came across[10]
τρέπομαι = I turn   (ἐ)τραπόμην = I turned[11]
φεύγω = I flee   (ἔ)φυγον = I fled

Which of these verbs are aorist, and which imperfect?
1.ἔλεγον 2.ἔλαβον 3.ἔπαθον 4.ἔπασχον 5.ἔφευγον 6.ἔφυγον 7.ἔσχον 8.εἶχον 9.ἱκόμην 10.τρεπόμην 11.βάλλον 12.βάλον.

The strong aorist indicative:

	active	middle
singular	(ἔ)λαβον = I took	(ἐ)λαβόμην = I got hold of
	(ἔ)λαβες = you took	(ἐ)λαβέο = you got hold of
	(ἔ)λαβε = he/she/it took	(ἐ)λάβετο = he/she/it got hold of[12]
dual	(ἐ)λάβετον = you two took	(ἐ)λάβεσθον = you two got hold of
	(ἐ)λαβέτην = those two took	(ἐ)λαβέσθην = those two got hold of
plural	(ἐ)λάβομεν = we took	(ἐ)λαβόμε(σ)θα = we got hold of
	(ἐ)λάβετε = you took	(ἐ)λάβεσθε = you got hold of
	(ἔ)λαβον = they took	(ἐ)λάβοντο = they got hold of

What is the English for:
1. ἔβαλε. 2.ἐγὼ ἔβαλλον. 3. ἑταῖροι χρυσὸν ἔλαβον. 4.χρυσὸν εἰς τὴν θάλασσαν ἔβαλον. 5.χρυσὸν ’Οδυσσῆος ἐλάβομεν. 6.χρυσὸν αὐτοῦ λάβομεν. 7.ἔπος ’Αθηναίης ἕρκος ὀδόντων φύγεν. 8.‘Ερμείας σπέος νύμφης εἶδεν. 9.ἔπειτ’ ἔπος νύμφῃ ἔειπεν. 10.ἀπὸ σχεδίης πέσεν ’Οδυσεύς αὐτός. 11.σχεδίης αὖ λάβεο, ’Οδυσεῦ; 12.σχεδίης ἐλάβετο ’Οδυσεύς;

The strong aorist optative

aorist optative active	aorist optative middle
λάβοιμι = might I take	λαβοίμην = might I get hold of
λάβοις = might you take	λάβοιο = might you get hold of
λάβοι = might he/she/it take	λάβοιτο = might he/she/it get hold of
λάβοιτον = might you two take	λάβοισθον = might you two get hold of
λαβοίτην = might those two take	λαβοίσθην = might those two get hold of
λάβοιμεν = might we take	λαβοίμε(σ)θα = might we get hold of
λάβοιτε = might you take	λάβοισθε = might you get hold of
λάβοιεν = might they take	λαβοίατο = might they get hold of

[9]Sometimes prefixed by ἐν (ἔμπεσον, I fell in) or κατά (κάππεσον, I fell down).
[10]Aorist without any present.
[11]Intransitive, as in "he turned and fled".
[12]ἐλλάβετ’ (standing for ἐλλάβετο) is found instead of ἐλάβετο at Odyssey V, 325.

Occasionally an alternative form where the ending is based on –οιη is found in Homer, e.g. at Iliad xiv, 241 ἐπισχοίης πόδας ("you might rest your feet") where ἐπισχοίης is 2nd person singular, aorist optative active of ἐπέχω, I hold upon, I rest. (Chantraine, *Grammaire Homérique* vol.I, p.464).
The strong aorist optative expresses a wish, purpose or contingency regarded as a simple action rather than as continuous. The endings are the same as the present optative, but the stem is the aorist stem, e.g.

        present optative active   aorist optative active
        βάλλοιμι   βάλοιμι

New words:
αἴγειρος (2f) = black poplar   αἱρέω (aorist εἷλον) = I take, grasp
αἱρέομαι (aorist εἱλόμην) = I choose, take (for myself)
ἀλλήλους –ας –α = each other
ἀμφί + accusative or dative = around, concerning
ἀνά + accusative = up, along
ἀφικνέομαι (aorist ἀφικόμην) = I reach, arrive at
βάλλω (aorist (ἔ)βαλον = I throw, hit, put
γλαφυρός –ά –όν = hollow[13]
ἔνδον = inside   θηέομαι = I gaze at, admire
εὑρίσκω (aorist εὗρον) = I find
ἱστός (2m) = loom, mast   κλήθρη (1f) = alder
ὁράω (aorist, εἶδον) = I see[14]
πίπτω (aorist (ἔ)πεσον) = I fall   (ἔ)τετμον = I found
τρέπομαι (aorist (ἐ)τραπόμην) = I turn (intransitive)
ὕδωρ, ὕδατος (3n) = water   ὕλη (1f) = wood
φεύγω (aorist (ἔ)φυγον) =I flee, escape

What is the English for:
1.θεὸς ἐκ πόντου ἰοειδέος ἠπειρόνδε ἦλθεν. (see p.30) 2.ἐν δέ νήσῳ ὄρνιθας τανυσιπτέρους[15] εὗρεν. 3.Ἑρμῆς μέγα σπέος ἵκετο. 4.νύμφην ἔνδοθι τέτμεν. 5.ὄρνιθες τανυσίπτεροι οὐκ ἔφυγον. 6.τί εἶδες περὶ σπείους νύμφης; 7. τί ἔειπες νύμφῃ ἐϋπλοκάμῳ; 8. νημερτέα βουλὴν Διὸς Ἑρμείας νύμφῃ ἐϋπλοκάμῳ ἔειπεν ἐν σπέει γλαφυρῷ ἐν τῷ αὐτὴ ἔναιεν. 9. Ἑρμῆς ῥάβδον ἑὴν εἵλετο. 10.Ποσειδάων χερσὶ τρίαιναν εἷλεν. (τρίαινα: trident)

[13]γλαφυρός applies to Calypso"s cave in Odyssey V, though elsewhere it applies to other things, especially ships.   σπέος γλαφυρόν "hollow cave" is a doublet (all caves are hollow). Such doublets are not uncommon in Homeric poetry; see K. O'Nolan, *Doublets in the Odyssey* (Classical Quarterly (1978) p.23).
[14]See also p.201.
[15]τανυσίπτερος, τανυσίπτερον (fem. as masc.) = with extended wings, long winged.

Section 10 69

Odyssey V, 59-74

πῦρ μὲν ἐπ' ἐσχαρόφιν¹⁶ μέγα¹⁷ καίετο, τηλόσε¹⁸ δ' ὀδμὴ¹⁹
κέδρου τ' εὐκεάτοιο θύου²⁰ τ' ἀνὰ νῆσον ὀδώδει²¹   60
δαιομένων·²² ἡ δ' ἔνδον ἀοιδιάουσ' ὀπὶ καλῇ
ἱστὸν ἐποιχομένη χρυσείῃ κερκίδ' ὕφαινεν.²³
ὕλη δὲ σπέος ἀμφὶ πεφύκει²⁴ τηλεθόωσα,²⁵
κλήθρη τ' αἴγειρός τε καὶ εὐώδης²⁶ κυπάρισσος.²⁷
ἔνθα δέ τ' ὄρνιθες τανυσίπτεροι εὐνάζοντο,²⁸   65
σκῶπές²⁹ τ' ἴρηκές³⁰ τε τανύγλωσσοί τε κορῶναι
εἰνάλιαι,³¹ τῇσίν τε θαλάσσια ἔργα μέμηλεν.³²

¹⁶ἐπ' ἐσχαρόφιν: on the hearth. ἐσχαρόφιν is an Epic form of the (genitive and) dative singular of ἐσχάρη, hearth. The ending -φι(ν) is an archaism in Homer, used for singular and plural, and also for the ablative, instrumental and locative cases (obsolete in Greek: see p.134, footnote 14). (Chantraine, op. cit. vol i, pp.234-241)
¹⁷μέγα, great (neuter singular nominative of μέγας) qualifies πῦρ.
¹⁸τηλόσε = to a great distance (literally, "to afar").
¹⁹ὀδμή (1f) = smell, scent. κέδρος (2f) = cedar. εὐκέατος, εὐκέατον (fem. as masc.) = easily split. τ' ... τ' ... stands for τε ... τε ... ("both ... and ...") linking κέδρου εὐκεάτοιο and θύου.
²⁰θύον (2n) = thyme (which grows as a woody shrub). ἀνά here means "up along", i.e. "throughout".
²¹ὀδώδει is 3rd person singular pluperfect of ὄζω (I reek, smell of) used as the imperfect.
²²δαιόμενος, δαιομένη, δαιόμενον = kindled (genitive plural here because applied to genitive singular nouns, κέδρου and θύου).
²³For lines 61-62, see p.35.
²⁴Translate in the order ἀμφὶ σπέος. πέφυκα is perfect of φύω with present meaning, "I am growing". πεφύκει (3rd singular pluperfect) means "was growing".
²⁵τηλεθόωσα, "luxuriant", is the feminine of τηλεθάων, the present participle of τηλεθάω, "I am flourishing", and qualifies ὕλη. τηλεθάω is a lengthened form of θάλλω, I bloom. τηλεθάων is almost always used to describe vegetation, but at Iliad xxii, 423, lamenting the death of Hector, Priam uses it to describe all his sons grown up straight and tall (παῖδας τηλεθάοντας) whom Achilles has killed.
²⁶εὐώδης (masculine & feminine), εὐῶδες (neuter) (3rd declension) = sweet scented.
²⁷κυπάρισσος : cypress. Though κλήθρη and αἴγειρος grow in wet ground, κυπάρισσος prefers dry (Hainsworth, A Commentary on Homer's Odyssey vol.i, p.262, notes that the poet is above such niceties).
²⁸τανυσίπτερος, τανυσίπτερον (feminine as masculine) = with long wings. εὐνάζομαι = I have my bed, i.e. roost. εὐνάζοντο is 3rd person plural, imperfect.
²⁹σκώψ, σκωπός = little horned owl ("owl" in Greek is γλαύξ, γλαυκός, not in Homer).
³⁰ἴρηξ, ἴρηκος = hawk (in later Greek, ἱέραξ). κορώνη = cormorant (Hainsworth, and Autenreith) (cormorants often perch on rocks stretching their wings out to dry and sometimes nest in trees). τανύγλωσσος, –ον = long-tongued.
³¹εἰνάλιος, εἰναλίη, εἰνάλιον = found in the sea, maritime (compared with πόντος, ἅλς often refers to coastal waters). τῇσιν = "to which" (refers to κορῶναι).
³²μέμηλεν: "are a care" (3rd person singular of μέμηλα, perfect indicative of μέλω, I am a care to, with present meaning). The subject is θαλάσσια ἔργα ("tasks in the sea"). ἔργον (2 neuter) = task.

ἡ δ' αὐτοῦ³³ τετάνυστο³⁴ περὶ σπείους γλαφυροῖο
ἡμερὶς³⁵ ἡβώωσα, τεθήλει δὲ σταφυλῇσι.³⁶
κρῆναι³⁷ δ' ἑξείης πίσυρες ῥέον ὕδατι λευκῷ,　　　70
πλησίαι³⁸ ἀλλήλων τετραμμέναι³⁹ ἄλλυδις ἄλλη.⁴⁰
ἀμφὶ⁴¹ δὲ λειμῶνες⁴² μαλακοὶ ἴου ἠδὲ σελίνου⁴³
θήλεον. ἔνθα κ'ἔπειτα καὶ ἀθάνατός περ ἐπελθὼν⁴⁴
θηήσαιτο ἰδὼν⁴⁵ καὶ τερφθείη⁴⁶ φρεσὶν ᾗσιν.

---

³³αὐτοῦ = just there. ἡ is the demonstrative pronoun (feminine because referring to ἡμερίς (line 69)), used here to reinforce αὐτοῦ - "there (it was), just there!"
³⁴τετάνυστο is 3rd person singular pluperfect passive of τανύω, I stretch out, and means "had been stretched out", i.e. "was spreading".
³⁵ἡμερίς, genitive ἡμερίδος, (3f) = cultivated vine. ἡβώωσα, flourishing, is the present participle (feminine nominative singular, qualifying ἡμερίς) of ἡβάω, I am in my prime. cf. ἥβη (in English, Hebe), youthfulness.
³⁶τεθήλει is 3rd person singular pluperfect of θάλλω (see footnote 25 above) used as an imperfect and means "it was blooming". σταφυλή (1f) = bunch of grapes.
³⁷κρήνη (1 fem) = spring, fountain. ἑξείης = in a row. πίσυρες = four (the normal Greek for four is τέσσαρες). ῥέω = I flow (ῥέον is 3rd person plural, imperfect active; its subject is κρῆναι). λευκός -ή -όν = white, clear. λευκῷ qualifies ὕδατι.
³⁸πλησίος, πλησίη, πλησίον (+ genitive) = near.
³⁹τετραμμέναι is feminine nominative plural of the perfect participle passive of τρέπω, I turn, and means "(having been) turned", i.e. "facing". πλησίαι and τετραμμέναι qualify κρῆναι.
⁴⁰ἄλλυδις ἄλλη = one hither, another thither, this way and that. ἄλλη is singular because it qualifies κρῆναι distributively; it applies to each single fountain. ἄλλυδις means "in another direction", and ἄλλυδις ἄλλη means "another in another direction" applied to each of them, i.e. "this way and that".
⁴¹ἀμφί is used here as an adverb - "around" means "on either side of the mouth of the cave".
⁴²λειμών, λειμῶνος (3m) = meadow. μαλακός -ή -όν = soft.
⁴³ἴον (2n) = violet. σελίνον (2n) = celery. θηλέω + genitive : I abound in. θήλεον, 3rd person plural imperfect of θηλέω, meaning, with the genitive, "I abound in". The genitives with θήλεον are ἴου and σελίνου.
⁴⁴ἐπελθών is the masculine nominative singular of the (strong) aorist participle of ἐπέρχομαι, and means "having come upon"; it is the subject: "a visitor" (one who has come upon Calypso's home). κ' stands for κε. κε changes the sense of an optative to "would". κε here goes with θηήσαιτο, 3rd person singular, aorist optative of θηέομαι. κε θηήσαιτο: would wonder. καὶ here means "even" and should be taken with περ: "even though ἀθάνατός". For περ meaning "although" see p.76.
⁴⁵ἰδών is the (strong) aorist participle (masculine nominative singular) of ὁράω, and means "having seen". It has the force of a condition, "if he saw (it)", or can be expressed in English by "seeing it".
⁴⁶τερφθείη is 3rd person singular aorist optative passive of τέρπω and is also taken with κε. It means "would be delighted". φρεσὶν, which is qualified by ᾗσιν (possessive: see p.52) is the dative plural of φρήν. It is a dative expressing location: in his heart.

Section 11
Participles - Present and Aorist, Active and Middle

A participle is an adjective connected with a verb. Active participles in English are formed by adding -**ing** to the verb stem, e.g., "burning", formed from the verb "burn", in *Tiger, tiger, burning bright*.

The participles of Greek verbs ending -μαι in the 1st person singular are easily formed by substituting –μενος, –μενη, –μενον for -μαι. Thus from ἀμείβομαι (I answer) we have ἀμειβόμενος = answering, from μέμνημαι (I remember) we have μεμνημένος = remembering, and from τέρπομαι (I enjoy myself) we have τερπόμενος = enjoying oneself. Each of these has masculine, feminine and neuter genders like φίλος (page 8). So ἀνὴρ ἀμειβόμενος means "an answering man", νύμφη ἀμειβομένη means "an answering nymph" and δῶμα καιόμενον means "a house being set alight".

What is the English for: 1.'Οδυσσεύς ἐπ' ἀκτῆς κλαῖε καθήμενος.
(κλαίω = I weep κάθημαι = I sit ἀκτη = headland)
2.θεὸς θεὰν ἔπεσσιν ἀμειβόμενος προσέφη.
3.πῆμα ἐρχόμενον ὁρόω. 4. 'Ερμείας νύμφην ἱστὸν ἐποιχομένην εἶδεν.

Present active participles of verbs ending -ω are formed by substituting –ων, –ουσα, –ον for ω. Thus, from λύω = I loose we have λύων, λύουσα, λύον = loosing, and from βάλλω = I throw we have βάλλων, βάλλουσα, βάλλον = throwing. So ἀνὴρ βάλλων = man throwing, νύμφη βάλλουσα = nymph throwing, and κῦμα βάλλον = wave throwing. Note that the masculine and neuter participles are 3rd declension, while the feminine is 1st.[1]

The present participle active (singular):

	masculine	feminine	neuter
nominative	λύων	λύουσα	λύον
	(loosing)	(loosing)	(loosing)
accusative	λύοντα	λύουσαν	λύον
	(loosing)	(loosing)	(loosing)
genitive	λύοντος	λυούσης	λύοντος
	(of loosing)	(of loosing)	(of loosing)
dative	λύοντι	λυούση	λύοντι
	(to/for loosing)	(to/for loosing)	(by loosing)

---
[1]Present participles active of -μι verbs, e.g. ὀλλύς, ὀλλῦσα, [ὀλλύν], destroying, from ὄλλυμι, I destroy, are like τιθείς, τιθεῖσα, τιθέν (p.220).

(dual)
nominative & accusative
     λύοντε   λυούσα   λύοντε
     (two loosing) (two loosing) (two loosing)
genitive & dative
     λυόντοιιν   λυούσηιν   λυόντοιιν
     (of/to two   (of/to two   (by two
     loosing)   loosing)   loosing)

(plural)
nominative λύοντες   λύουσαι   λύοντα
     (loosing)   (loosing)   (loosing)
accusative λύοντας   λυούσας   λύοντα
     (loosing)   (loosing)   (loosing)
genitive λυόντων   λυουσάων   λυόντων
     (of loosing)   (of loosing)   (of loosing)
dative   λύουσι[2]   λυούσησι(ν)   λύουσι
     (to/for loosing) (to/for loosing) (by loosing)

The present participle ("being") of the verb εἰμι ("I am") is
ἐών (masculine) ἐοῦσα (feminine) ἐόν (neuter)

A present participle is used when the action mentioned is going on at the same time as another, e.g.

  ἡ δ' ἔνδον <u>ἀοιδιάουσ</u>'[3] ὀπὶ καλῇ
 ἱστὸν <u>ἐποιχομένη</u> χρυσείῃ κερκίδ' ὕφαινεν. (Odyssey V, 61-2)
  ("but she, indoors, <u>singing</u> in a beautiful voice,
   <u>plying</u> the loom was weaving with a golden shuttle").

What is the English for:
1.πάσχων. 2.νύμφη ἀοιδιάουσα (ἀοιδιάω = I sing). 3.τέκνον ἀοιδίαον. 4.πῦρ καιόμενον. 5.ὄρνις ἰχθῦς ἀγρώσσων. (ἰχθῦς (accusative plural) = fish, ἀγρώσσω = I catch) 6.νῆσος τηλόθ' ἐοῦσα. 7. Ὀδυσσεὺς ἄλγεα πάσχων.
8.Ὀδυσσεὺς ἐν νήσῳ κεῖται ἄλγεα πάσχων.
9. Ἑρμείας νύμφην ἔτετμεν ὀπὶ καλῇ ἀοιδιάουσαν. 10.θεοὶ τέρπονται ἀλλήλους ὁρῶντες.[4] 11.Ἑρμῆς νήσους ἀφικνέεται τηλόθ' ἐούσας.
12.νύμφης ἀπόπροθι (ἀπόπροθι = far away) ναιούσης εἰς εὐρὺ σπέος ἦλθεν διάκτορος ἀργειφόντης.
13.Ὀδυσσῆα ἄλγεσι θύμον (θύμος = spirit, heart) ἐρέχθοντα (ἐρέχθω = I rend, break) οὐκ ἔτετμεν Ἑρμῆς.
14.ἡ δὲ Καλυψὼ ἐπ' ἀκτῆς κλαίουσα οὐ κάθητο. (for κάθημαι, see p. 71)
15.ὀρνίθων ἰχθῦς ἀγρωσσόντων πυκινὰ πτερὰ δεύεται ἅλμῃ. (cf. line 53)

[2]or λυόντεσσι(ν) (also neuter).
[3]ἀοιδιάουσ' stands for ἀοιδιάουσα.
[4]Contracted from ὁράοντες.

Section 11   73

16. ὄρνιθας ἐν ὕλῃ εὐναζομένους θηεῖτο διάκτορος ἀργειφόντης. (θηεῖτο (3rd person singular, imperfect of θηεοομαι, contracted from θηέετο. εε has become ει.)

Aorist participles have no augments.
(i) The aorist participle expresses the pure action of the verb, without any necessary indication of time. For instance, we may say "planning to get past the sentries, Odysseus disguised himself as a beggar". "Planning", since it describes simply what was going on in Odysseus' head, is, in Greek, an aorist participle, βουλεύσας.
(ii) But the aorist participle is sometimes used for an anterior action, i.e. one which happens beforehand: ἐγείρας τὸν δράκοντα, ὁ παῖς ἔφυγεν "having awakened the dragon, the child ran away."[5]

The aorist active participle The endings of the weak aorist participle active are similar to the present participle endings, but formed with α instead of ο or ου.
The weak aorist active participle, *loosing*, or *having loosed*:

	masculine	feminine	neuter
(singular)			
nominative	λύσας	λύσασα	λῦσαν
accusative	λύσαντα	λύσασαν	λῦσαν
genitive	λύσαντος	λυσάσης	λύσαντος
dative	λύσαντι	λυσάσῃ	λύσαντι
(dual)			
nominative & accusative	λύσαντε	λυσάσα	λύσαντε
genitive & dative	λυσάντοιιν	λυσάσῃιν	λυσάντοιιν
(plural)			
nominative	λύσαντες	λύσασαι	λύσαντα
accusative	λύσαντας	λυσάσας	λύσαντα
genitive	λυσάντων	λυσάσων	λυσάντων
dative	λύσασι(ν)[6]	λυσάσῃς[7]	λύσασι(ν)

---
[5] Chantraine, *Grammaire Homérique* vol.ii, p.188.
[6] or λυσάντεσσι(ν) (also neuter plural dative).
[7] or λυσάσῃσι.

Examples:
(type i) καί μιν φωνήσας ἔπεα πτερόεντα προσηύδα[8] (Odyssey V, 172)
"and her, uttering winged (πτερόεντα) words, did he begin to address"
(type ii) Πιερίην δ' ἐπιβὰς[9] ἐξ αἰθέρος ἔμπεσε πόντῳ· (Odyssey V, 50)
"and he, having set foot on Pieria, plummeted from the sky down to the sea."

The weak aorist middle participle is formed on the same lines as the present middle participle: -αμενος, -αμενη, -αμενον is substituted for the first person singular ending -αμην.

What is the English for:
1.φώνησας. 2.φωνήσασα. 3.πέμψαν. 4.πεμψάσης. 5.πέμψαντος. 6.ἀμειψαμένη.
7.κῇας. 8.κήασα. 9.κήασαι. 10.πέμψαντες. 11.πεμψάσῃσι. 12.ταῦτα φωνήσασα, εἰς σπέος ἦλθε νύμφη.
13.ὣς ἄρα φωνήσασα νύμφη τράπεζαν οἱ παρέθηκε.[10]
14.Φαίηκες κακὰ ἔπαθον Ὀδυσσῆα πέμψαντες ἐν νηὶ φίλην ἐς πατρίδα γαῖαν.
15.θεοῖσι δ' Ἀθηναίη λέγε κήδεα πολλὰ Ὀδυσῆος μνησαμένη.
16.αὐτῇ ταῦτα φωνησάσῃ ἠμείβετο νεφεληγερέτα Ζεύς.

Strong aorist participles
The strong aorist active participle (e.g. ἰδών, *seeing*, or *having seen*,
from εἶδον, the aorist of ὁράω) has endings exactly like present participles[11] (i.e. the endings are formed with ο or ου) but the aorist stem, not the present, is used. With very irregular verbs like ὁράω, where the aorist (εἶδον) is quite different, it is easy to distinguish the aorist participle (ἰδών, *seeing* or *having seen*) from the present participle (ὁρόων, *seeing*). But with some verbs, the difference is subtle and care is needed to distinguish, for instance, βάλλων (throwing, the participle of βάλλω), I throw, and βαλών, (*throwing* or *having thrown*, the participle of ἔβαλον, I threw).

[8]προσηύδα (contracted from προσηύδαε) is an inceptive imperfect (p.33). προσαυδάω = I address. φωνέω (p.76) = I speak, call out, utter.
[9]For ἐπιβάς, see p.63, footnote 9. For πόντῳ, see p.65, footnote 31.
[10]παρέθηκε is 3rd person singular aorist active of παρατίθημι (for τίθημι, see Section 15). The meaning is "she put beside (him)". τράπεζα (1f) = table.
[11]Except that the accent is on the ending.

Section 11

Example:

πόσε φεύγετε φῶτα ἰδοῦσαι; (Odyssey VI, 199)[1][2]
"Where are you fleeing to, seeing a man?"

ἰδών, ἰδοῦσα, ἰδόν, *seeing* or *having seen*

	masculine	feminine	neuter
(singular)			
nominative	ἰδών	ἰδοῦσα	ἰδόν
accusative	ἰδόντα	ἰδοῦσαν	ἰδόν
genitive	ἰδόντος	ἰδούσης	ἰδόντος
dative	ἰδόντι	ἰδούσῃ	ἰδόντι
(dual)			
nominative & accusative	ἰδόντε	ἰδούσα	ἰδόντε
genitive & dative	ἰδόντοιιν	ἰδούσῃιν	ἰδόντοιιν
(plural)			
nominative	ἰδόντες	ἰδοῦσαι	ἰδόντα
accusative	ἰδόντας	ἰδούσας	ἰδόντα
genitive	ἰδόντων	ἰδουσάων	ἰδόντων
dative	ἰδοῦσι(ν)	ἰδούσης *or* ἰδούσῃσι(ν)	ἰδοῦσι(ν)

What is the English for:
1.ἰδόντα. 2.ἰδοῦσι(ν). 3.φυγών. 4.φεύγων. 5.ἐλθοῦσα. 6.ἐλθόν. 7.πάσχων.
8.παθοῦσα. 9.εἰπών.[13] 10.σχών. 11. εὑροῦσα. 12.ἱκομένη. 13.λαβόντες.
14.εἰς νῆσον ἐλθὼν οἶκον Καλυψοῦς[14] θηεῖτο διάκτορος ἀργειφόντης.
15.θεὸν ἰδοῦσα νύμφη μιν οὐκ ἡγνοίησεν. (ἀγνοιέω = I do not know, fail to recognise)

[12]Nausicaa to her handmaidens, on the appearance of Odysseus. (πόσε; = where to? φώς, φωτός = man (not to be confused with φάος (sometimes φόως), φῶτος = light)).
[13]εἰπών is not augmented. In Attic, the aorist of λέγω is εἶπον, but in Homer ἔειπον.
[14]For Καλυψοῦς, see p.47, footnote 31.

Greek phrases containing participles can often be translated better in English by using "who/which", "when", "because", "as" or "although" clauses. For example:

νῦν αὖ παῖδ' ἀγαπητὸν ἀποκτεῖναι μεμάασιν
οἴκαδε νισόμενον· (Odyssey V, 18-19)

(ἀγαπητός: beloved ἀποκτεῖναι (aorist infinitive): to kill μεμάασιν (perfect tense): they are eager οἴκάδε: homewards νίσομαι: I return)

is literally, in English,
"now again they are eager to kill the beloved son returning home".

This is ambiguous in English but not in Greek, where the ending of νισόμενον clearly goes with παῖδα ἀγαπητόν and not with "they", the subject of μεμάασιν. In order to avoid the ambiguity, it is necessary to use a temporal clause in English, such as: "now again they are planning to kill the beloved son as he returns home."

περ (= although) is regularly accompanied by a participle, e.g. θεός περ ἐών = though being a god = although he is (was) a god.

ἱμειρόμενός περ ἰδέσθαι σὴν ἄλοχον: though desiring to see your wife = though you desire to see your wife (Odyssey V, 209-10)
(ἱμείρομαι = I desire ἄλοχος (2 fem.) = wife)

New words:
αἰδοῖος -α -ον = to be respected[15]
ἄρα = then, there and then, so
δάκρυον (2 neuter)= the tear[16]
δέρκομαι = I see, look at
ἐπεί = when, since
ἔσθω or ἐσθίω = I eat[18]
θυμός (2m) = soul, mind, heart
μεγαλήτωρ[19] = great-hearted
πᾶς, πᾶσα, πᾶν = every (plu., all)[20]
τελέω = I fulfil, finish, complete
φρονέω = I think, I have in mind, *also* I am wise, I am sane.[21]

ἄντην (adverb) = face to face
ἀτάρ *or* αὐτάρ = but, besides, moreover
εἰ *or* αἰ = if
ἐρυθρός, ἐρυθρόν = red[17]
θρόνος (2m) = chair, seat
κάθημαι = I sit
πάρος (adverb) = formerly
πίνω (aorist ἔπιον) = I drink
φωνέω = I call out, speak, call by name

---
[15]Describes those who have a claim to regard or reverence: gods, kings, members of one's family, women generally, trusted old servants, strangers, guests, suppliants.
[16]The nominative and accusative singular are often δάκρυ and the dative plural δάκρυσι, as if 3rd declension, in poetry to fit the metre.
[17]The feminine is not found in Homer.
[18]The root is ἔδω (cf. ἐδωδή, food); the form ἐσθίω is usual in later Greek.
[19]Genitive μεγαλήτορος, a 3rd declension adjective found only in the masculine gender, and only with θυμός and proper nouns e.g. Πάτροκλος, Κύκλωψ, Ὀδυσσεύς.
[20]πάντα (neuter plural) = everything.
[21]Also μέγα φρονέω (literally, "I think big") = I am presumptuous.

Section 11   77

What is the English for:
1.Ζεὺς μοῖραν οὐκ ἴσχει θεός περ ἐών.
2.Καλυψὼ 'Ερμῆν οὐκ ἠγνοίησεν ἀπόπροθι[22] περ δώματα ναίουσα.
3.Καλυψὼ 'Ερμῆν ἰδοῦσα οὐκ ἐτέρπετο αἰδοῖόν τε φίλον τέ περ ὄντα.
4.στάς[23] περ θηεόμενος, αὐτίκ' ἄρ' εἰς εὐρὺ σπέος ἦλθεν διάκτορος ἀργειφόντης.
5.'Ερμῆς οὐκ ἄρ' 'Οδυσσῆα τέτμεν εἰς νῆσόν περ ἀφικόμενος.
6.'Ερμῆς οὐκ ἄρ' 'Οδυσσῆα ἔτετμεν ἐν νήσῳ περ ἐόντα.
7.ἐπ' ἀκτῆς καθήμενος δάκρυσι θύμον ἐρέχθει[24] 'Οδυσσεὺς μεγαλήτωρ.
8.πᾶσαν νῆσον δερκόμενος τέρπεται 'Ερμείας.
9.ἐπὶ θρόνου καθήμενος πῖνε καὶ ἦσθε διάκτορος ἀργειφόντης.
10.οὐδὲ ἀπόπροθι δώματα ναίοντες ἀλλήλους ἀγνοιέουσιν ἀθάνατοι.
11.νύμφην μιν ἐν θρόνῳ ἱδρύσασαν[25] 'Ερμείας προσέειπεν.[26]
12.ὣς ἄρα φωνήσασα θεὰ κέρασσε[27] νέκταρ[28] ἐρυθρόν.
13.δειπνήσας[29] δέ μιν ἔπεσσιν ἀμειβόμενος προσέειπεν διάκτορος ἀργεϊφόντης.

Odyssey V 75-96
ἔνθα στάς[30] θηεῖτο διάκτορος 'Αργεϊφόντης.   75
αὐτὰρ ἐπεὶ δὴ πάντα ἐῷ θηήσατο θυμῷ,
αὐτίκ' ἄρ' εἰς εὐρὺ σπέος ἤλυθεν.[31] οὐδέ μιν ἄντην
ἠγνοίησεν[32] ἰδοῦσα Καλυψώ, δῖα θεάων·
οὐ γάρ τ' ἀγνῶτες[33] θεοὶ ἀλλήλοισι πέλονται[34]
ἀθάνατοι, οὐδ'[35] εἴ τις ἀπόπροθι[36] δώματα ναίει.   80
οὐδ' ἄρ' 'Οδυσσῆα μεγαλήτορα ἔνδον ἔτετμεν,

[22]ἀπόπροθι = far away. Calypso's island (pp.iii and 47, footnote 29) is remote (Athene says at Odyssey I, 50, that Odysseus is a prisoner νήσῳ ἐν ἀμφιρύτῃ, ὅθι τ' ὀμφαλός ἐστι θαλάσσης "in a sea-girt island where in fact is the navel of the sea").
[23]στάς is masculine nominative singular of the participle of ἔστην, the strong aorist of ἵστημι, "I make to stand", used intransitively as "I came to a stand". στάς means "standing", "having stopped". ἄρ' stands for ἄρα = then, then and there.
[24]ἐρέχθω = I rend, I break.
[25]ἱδρύω = I make to sit down, I seat.
[26]προσέειπεν is the 3rd person singular of προσέειπον, the strong aorist indicative active of προσλέγω, I speak to.
[27]κέρασσε is 3rd person singular of (ἐ)κέρασσα the weak aorist indicative of κεράννυμι, "I mix", from the same root as κρατήρ (*crater*), a mixing bowl.
[28]νέκταρ, νέκταρος (3n) = nectar. Euripides (*Bacchae*, 143) some centuries later described honey as "the nectar of bees" (μελισσᾶν νέκταρ).
[29]δειπνέω = I feast.
[30]For στάς, see footnote 23 above. θηεῖτο, contracted from θηέετο, is 3rd person singular, imperfect of θηέομαι. θηήσατο (line 76) is 3rd person singular aorist indicative. An aorist is usual after ἐπεί where in English "had" follows "when".
[31]ἤλυθεν is 3rd person singular aorist indicative of ἔρχομαι (p.66).
[32]ἠγνοίησεν is 3rd person singular of ἠγνοίησα, the aorist indicative of ἀγνοέω, I fail to recognise (cf. English "agnostic").
[33]ἀγνώς, ἀγνῶτος (masculine and feminine adjective, 3rd declension) = unknown.
[34]3rd person plural present indicative of πέλομαι = I am (πέλω: I come into existence).
[35]οὐδέ here = not even.
[36]For ἀπόπροθι, see footnote 22 above.

ἀλλ' ὅ γ' ἐπ' ἀκτῆς³⁷ κλαῖε³⁸ καθήμενος, ἔνθα πάρος περ,³⁹
δάκρυσι καὶ στοναχῇσι⁴⁰ καὶ ἄλγεσι θυμὸν ἐρέχθων⁴¹
[πόντον ἐπ' ἀτρύγετον δερκέσκετο⁴² δάκρυα λείβων].⁴³
Ἑρμείαν δ' ἐρέεινε⁴⁴ Καλυψώ, δῖα θεάων, 85
ἐν θρόνῳ ἱδρύσασα⁴⁵ φαεινῷ⁴⁶ σιγαλόεντι·⁴⁷
"τίπτε⁴⁸ μοι, Ἑρμεία χρυσόρραπι,⁴⁹ εἰλήλουθας,⁵⁰
αἰδοῖός τε φίλος τε; πάρος γε μὲν οὔ τι θαμίζεις.⁵¹

³⁷ὅ ('he") refers to Odysseus. ἀκτή (1f) = headland.
³⁸κλαῖε is 3rd person singular imperfect of κλαίω = I weep.
³⁹E.V.Rieu (*Homer, The Odyssey*, Penguin Classics) translates ἔνθα πάρος περ as "in his accustomed place". ἔνθαπερ = just there where. πάρος ("formerly") has been inserted between ἔνθα and περ by the grammatical figure of speech called tmesis, or "cutting". The literal meaning is "just there where (he) formerly (was)".
⁴⁰στοναχή (1f) = groaning.
⁴¹For ἐρέχθω, see footnote 24 above.
⁴²The ending -σκω or –σκομαι is *iterative*; it means that an action happens repeatedly. So δερκέσκετο means "he kept on looking at". (See Stanford, *Odyssey 1-12*, foreword, p.lxviii and Chantraine, *Grammaire Homérique* vol.i, p.322.)
⁴³λείβω = I pour (forth). This line is bracketed because it is the same as 158 and could be omitted without leaving a noticeable gap. A scholium (an ancient note in mss., in Homer sometimes coming from the works of the great commentators in the Library at Alexandria) remarks that it is περιττός ("extra") "because the previous line is sufficient". (Buttmann, *Scholia Antiqua in Homeri Odysseam*, Berlin 1821, p. 182.) (See also Hainsworth, *A Commentary on Homer's Odyssey* vol.i, p.263.)
⁴⁴ἐρέεινε is 3rd person singular imperfect of ἐρεείνω = I ask.
⁴⁵For ἱδρύω, see footnote 25 above.
⁴⁶φαεινός, φαεινή, φαεινόν = shining, radiant (also used to describe Nausicaa's bedroom doors at Odyssey VI, 19).
⁴⁷φαεινῷ and σιγαλόεντι (dative singular of σιγαλόεις) both qualify θρόνῳ. σιγαλόεις, σιγαλόεσσα, σιγαλόεν = glossy, glittering. The stone judgement seat on which Nestor sat (Odyssey III, 406-8) was polished with anointing oil to mark its sanctity (West, *A Companion to Homer's Odyssey* vol.i, p.185), and so σιγαλόεντι here may mean "polished with oil". (In Homer, fabrics were sometimes treated with olive oil; see Hainsworth, note on Odyssey VII, 107 (*op. cit.*, p.328) and Janko's comment (*Journal of Hellenic Studies* vol.cx (1990) p.207). Perhaps this is why Nausicaa's neglected washing is referred to as εἵματα σιγαλόεντα at Odyssey VI, 26.)
⁴⁸Syncopated form of τί ποτε; = why ever? μοι (dative, with λέγε understood) = tell me.
⁴⁹χρυσόρραπις –ιδος = with wand of gold (epithet of Hermes). χρυσόρραπι is vocative (see p.41).
⁵⁰εἰλήλουθας = "have you come" (2nd person singular of εἰλήλουθα, the perfect of ἔρχομαι).
⁵¹τι has the force of "at all". θαμίζω = I come often (from θαμά = often). Calypso's greeting to Hermes is very similar to Charis' greeting to Thetis at Iliad xviii, 385-6:
τίπτε, Θέτι τανύπεπλε, ἱκάνεις ἡμέτερον δῶ
αἰδοίη τε φίλη τε; πάρος γε μὲν οὔ τι θαμίζεις.
"Why ever, Thetis of the long robe, are you coming to our home,
both respected and dear? Indeed, previously you haven't come at all often."
The present tense (θαμίζεις) emphasises the general nature of the remark, which relates to a state of affairs beginning in the past and continuing to the present. (See Chantraine, *op. cit.* vol.ii, p.191.)

αὔδα⁵² ὅ τι φρονέεις· τελέσαι⁵³ δέ με θυμὸς ἄνωγεν,⁵⁴
εἰ δύναμαι τελέσαι γε καὶ εἰ τετελεσμένον⁵⁵ ἐστίν. 90
ἀλλ' ἕπεο⁵⁶ προτέρω,⁵⁷ ἵνα τοι⁵⁸ πὰρ⁵⁹ ξείνια⁶⁰ θείω."
ὣς ἄρα φωνήσασα θεὰ παρέθηκε τράπεζαν⁶¹
ἀμβροσίης⁶² πλήσασα,⁶³ κέρασσε⁶⁴ δὲ νέκταρ⁶⁵ ἐρυθρόν·
αὐτὰρ ὁ⁶⁶ πῖνε καὶ ἦσθε διάκτορος Ἀργεϊφόντης.
αὐτὰρ ἐπεὶ δείπνησε⁶⁷ καὶ ἤραρε⁶⁸ θυμὸν ἐδωδῇ,⁶⁹ 95
καὶ τότε δή μιν ἔπεσσιν ἀμειβόμενος προσέειπεν·⁷⁰

---

⁵²2nd person singular imperative of αὐδάω (see Section 13): "say!", "tell (me)!"
⁵³τελέσαι: "to accomplish (it)" (weak aorist infinitive active (Section 15) of τελέω).
⁵⁴ἄνωγεν is 3rd person singular of ἄνωγα = "I bid" perfect tense, with present meaning, (Section 21). Understand "my" with θύμος. με is the object of ἄνωγεν.
⁵⁵Although τετελεσμένον is neuter nominative singular of the perfect participle passive of τελέω, and εἰ τετελεσμένον ἐστίν literally means "if it has been accomplished" Hainsworth (op. cit., p.264) notes that τετελεσμένον has to be translated "something that must come to pass". (Perhaps "something that has been brought to fulfilment by fate"?)
⁵⁶ ἕπεο : follow! is 2nd person singular imperative of ἕπομαι, I follow (Section 13). This line is bracketed by some editors and Allen notes, in the apparatus criticus of the Oxford Classical Text, several families of mss. which omit it. It is awkward because Hermes, having been made to sit down, is asked almost at once to get up again. As Hainsworth notes from Iliad xviii, when Thetis calls on Hephaestus to ask him to make armour for Achilles, she is greeted by Charis, Hephaestus' wife, who leads her indoors and *then* makes her sit down. After that, Charis calls Hephaestus. Here, Hermes is asked to sit down too soon. Line 86, not 91, causes the problem, but if the whole passage (85-96) is made up of conventional lines, Hainsworth (op. cit., pp. 263-4) suggests that it should not be scrutinised "with more care than the poet used in its composition". Even Homer sometimes nods.
⁵⁷προτέρω = "on ahead" (literally, "before").
⁵⁸τοι:"let me tell you", "indeed" (an old form of σοι with "let me say" understood).
⁵⁹πάρ is short for παρά, "beside (you)". ἵνα θείω : so that I may put. θείω is 1st person singular aorist subjunctive active of τίθημι. (See Sections 14 & 15, p.107.)
⁶⁰ξείνια (2 neuter plural) = guest-presents, provision made for a guest.
⁶¹See p.74, footnote 10.
⁶²ἀμβροσίη = ambrosia, the food of the gods. Liddell & Scott suggest "elixir of life". Hainsworth (op. cit., p.264) notes that ambrosia is sometimes mentioned as a liquid.
⁶³πλήσασα is the feminine nominative singular of the participle of ἔπλησα, the aorist active of πίμπλημι, I fill. With genitive, πίμπλημι = "I fill full of ..."
⁶⁴For κέρασσε, see footnote 27 above.
⁶⁵For νέκταρ, see footnote 28 above.
⁶⁶αὐτὰρ ὁ: moreover, he, the messenger, the slayer of Argus... πῖνε and ἦσθε are 3rd person singular imperfect: "began to ..."
⁶⁷For δειπνέω, see footnote 29 above.
⁶⁸"he (had) furnished" ἤραρε is 3rd person singular, strong aorist indicative active of ἀραρίσκω, "I fit, equip". For ἐπεί followed by an aorist, see footnote 30.
⁶⁹ἐδωδή (1f) = food.
⁷⁰For προσέειπεν, see footnote 26 above. μιν refers to Calypso.

Section 12
The Future Tense

The future tense is in principle very easily formed in Greek. The endings of the future active and middle of λύω are the same as the present, but after -σ-. In many verbs with weak aorists, the future and the aorist stems are formed similarly, e.g. λύσω (future active), (ἔ)λῦσα (aorist active) and λύσομαι (future middle), (ἐ)λυσάμην (aorist middle).

Future active
λύσω = I shall loose

λύσεις = you will loose

λύσει = he, she, it will loose

λύσετον = you two will loose
λύσετον = those two will loose

λύσομεν = we shall loose

λύσετε = you will loose

λύσουσι(ν) = they will loose

Future middle
λύσομαι = I shall loose for myself

λύσεαι = you will loose for
or λύσῃ yourself

λύσεται = he, she, it will loose for him, her, itself

λύσεσθον = you two will loose for yourselves
λύσεσθον = those two will loose for themselves

λυσόμε(σ)θα = we shall loose for ourselves

λύσεσθε = you will loose for yourselves

λύσονται = they will loose for themselves

The future *passive* in Attic Greek ends -ησομαι or -θησομαι, e.g. λυθήσομαι (I shall be loosed), but this tense is found only once in Homer, at Iliad x, 365.[1] Some futures of the middle type, however, are found with passive meanings, e.g. (from πέρθω, I destroy) πέρσεται ("(the city) will be destroyed") (Iliad xxiv, 729), (from φιλέω, I love) φιλήσεαι ("you will be loved") (Odyssey I, 123 and XV, 281).

---

[1] ἔμελλε μιγήσεσθαι φυλάκεσσι - he was intending to become mingled with the guards. μιγήσεσθαι is the infinitive of μιγήσομαι, I shall be mingled, from μίγνυμι, I mix. This line occurs in a passage which is suspected of being a later interpolation, and Chantraine, *Grammaire Homérique*, vol.i, p.447, considers that it was a new type. No future passive in -θησομαι occurs in Homer.

Section 12

Verbs in the following future tenses are found in Odyssey V and VI:[2]

ἀμφιέσω (from ἀμφιέννυμι) I shall clothe, put round (V, 167)
ἀναπλήσω (from ἀναπίμπληι) I shall fulfil (V, 302)
ἀποπέμψω (from ἀποπέμπω) I shall send away (V, 161)
βουλεύσω (from βουλεύω) I shall plot, devise (V, 179, 187)
δείξω (from δείκνυμι) I shall show (VI, 194)
δευήσομαι (from δεύομαι) I shall be in need of (with genitive) (VI, 192)
ἐνθήσω (from ἐντίθημι) = I shall put in (V, 166)
ἐνισπήσω (from ἐννέπω) = I shall tell (V, 98)
ἕξω (from ἔχω) = I shall have, keep (VI, 281) (NB future has rough breathing)
ἐπικεύσω (from ἐπικεύθω) = I shall hide (V, 143)
ἐρέω (used as future of λέγω) I shall say (VI, 285)
ἔρξω (from ἔρδω) I shall do (V, 360)
ἔσ(σ)ομαι (from εἰμί) I shall be (V, 416, VI, 33, 277) (3rd person singular is
                                                                   ἔσ(σ)εται or ἔσται)
ἕψομαι (from ἕπομαι) I shall follow (with dative) (VI, 32)
ἡγεμονεύσω (from ἡγεμονεύω) = I shall lead (VI, 261)
θήσω (from τίθημι) I shall put (here, "I shall make") (V, 136)
καταφθίσω (from καταφθίνω) I shall destroy utterly (V, 341)
μενέω (from μένω) I shall remain (V, 362)
μίξομαι (from μίσγω) I shall mingle (VI, 136)
νήξομαι (from νήχω) I shall swim (V, 364)
ὀνόσσομαι (from ὄνομαι) I shall blame, find fault with (V, 379)
παύσομαι (from παύομαι) I shall cease (VI, 174)
πείσομαι (from πείθομαι) I shall obey (V, 358)
πέμψω (from πέμπω) I shall send (V, 37, 140, 161, 167)
τιμήσω (from τιμάω) I shall honour (V, 36)
τλήσομαι (from τλάω[3]) I shall endure (V, 222, 362)
ὑποθήσομαι (from ὑποτίθεμαι) = I shall advise (V, 143)

NB1 There is essentially only one pattern of future endings used by Homer - -σω for active and -σομαι for middle verbs.[4] Verbs whose present active ends -μι have futures ending -σω (e.g. θήσω is the future of τίθημι and δείξω is the future of δείκνυμι). Of -μι verbs met so far,

---
[2]ἀποτίσεται (V, 24), ποιήσετε (V, 120), ἐφάψεαι (V, 348), παρανήξομαι (V, 417), πειρήσομαι (VI, 126), ἀπολούσομαι (VI, 219), χρίσομαι (VI, 220) and λοέσσομαι (VI, 221) are aorist subjunctives (for which, see Section 14, p.97). δήεις (VI, 291) is present with future significance: "you will find".
[3]Not found in the present tense except in late Greek; τολμάω is used instead.
[4]εἶμι, to be distinguished from εἰμί = I am, in Attic and Ionic prose is "I shall come", the future of ἔρχομαι; but εἶμι in Homer is normally present. (Section 16)

the future of ὄρνυμι is ὄρσω (Iliad xxi, 335) and the future of ὄλλυμι is ὀλέσω or ὀλέσσω. φήσω, the future of φημί, is not found in Homer.

NB2 Most verbs ending –αω or –εω in the present tense have futures ending –ησω (e.g. αἱρέω = I take, αἱρήσω = I shall take; τιμάω = I honour, τιμήσω = I shall honour). Verbs ending –οω in the present have futures ending -ωσω (e.g. χολόω = I anger, χολώσω = I shall anger).

NB3 Some verbs which are active in the present tense are middle in the future, e.g. νήχω, I swim, νήξομαι, I shall swim. Note especially that ἔσ(σ)ομαι (I shall be) is the future of εἰμί (I am).

NB4 If the stem of a verb ends γ, κ or χ in the present tense, in the future tense the stem ends ξ e.g. νήξομαι = I shall swim, and if β, π or φ in the present tense, in the future tense the stem ends ψ, e.g. πέμψω = I shall send.

NB5 Most verbs with stems ending λ, ν or ρ in the present tense have futures ending -εω instead of -σω, e.g

μένω (I wait) μενέω (I shall wait).
In the Ionian dialect,[5] to avoid λσ, νσ and ρσ, ε was inserted; afterwards, σ was dropped. We can imagine two stages: first, μενέσω, then μενέω.[6] However, some verbs with stems ending λ, ν or ρ in the present tense e.g. καταφθίνω (I destroy), by a change of stem, have futures with stems ending σ e.g. καταφθίσω (I shall destroy).

NB6 Verbs ending -σσω in the present tense mainly have futures ending -ξω, and so the future of ἀνάσσω, I am chief, is ἀνάξω, I shall be chief, e.g. Τρώεσσιν ἀνάξει, he will be chief of the Trojans (Iliad xx, 307). Verbs with stems ending ζ in the present tense mainly have futures with stems ending σ, e.g. from εὐνάζομαι, I roost, the future would be εὐνάσομαι, I shall roost.[7] But some verbs ending -ζω or -ζομαι in the present tense have futures ending -σσω or -σσομαι. The future of καθέζομαι, I

---

[5] The Aeolic dialect may have allowed futures ending –λσω and –ρσω. Consequently these are occasionally found in poetry; hence ὄρσω, I shall arouse, for the future of ὄρνυμι (Chantraine, op. cit. vol. i, p.449).
[6] In Attic, this gives rise to the contracted form μενῶ.
[7] E.g. σ' εὐνάσω "I shall find you somewhere to sleep" (Odyssey IV, 408) from εὐνάζω (I put to bed), the active of εὐνάζομαι.

Section 12	83

sit down,[8] would be καθέσσομαι, I shall sit down. Some verbs ending -ιζω in the present have futures ending -ῶ (contracted from -εω), e.g. from κομίζω = I bring, κομιῶ = I shall bring (contracted from κομιέω).[9]

What is the English for: 1.βουλεύσεις. (see p.81) 2.βουλεύσουσιν. 3.βουλεύσετε; 4.ἐσσόμεθα. 5.φίλοι ἔσεσθε; 6.δεινὸν ἔσσεται; 7.μένει. 8.μενέει. 9.πέμψουσι. 10.οὐ πέμψει. 11.'Οδυσσεῦ, ἡμῖν ἀνάξεις. 12.τλήσεαι. (see p. 81) 13.τλήσεται; 14.ἄλγος οὐ τλησόμεθα. 15.χρυσὸν ἕξετε. 16.χρυσὸν οὐκ ἔχομεν.

New words:

ἄγχι[10] = near
ἄστυ (3n) = town
ἔβην = I went[12]
ἐσθλός, ἐσθλή, ἐσθλόν = good, brave, noble.
κέλομαι (also κελεύω) = I order
μάλα = indeed, very
νόος (2m) = purpose, thought
πόλις (3f)[14] = city
ῥιγέω I shiver
τοι (enclitic) = let me tell you!

αἰγίοχος = aegis-bearing[11]
δεῦρο = hither, to here
ἔτι = still, yet

μακρός, μακρά, μακρόν = long, tall
μῦθος (2m) = word, speech, tale
οἴκαδε = homewards[13]
πῶς = how? (πως = in any way)
τῇδε = here (in this place)
look! (originally from a phrase like λέγω σοι)

What is the English for:
1.ῥιγήσω. 2.κελεύσεις. 3.νημερτέως[15] τοι τὸν μῦθον θεὸς ἐνισπήσει.[16]
4.'Αθηναίη σφιν ὄρσει ἀνεμόν τε κακὸν καὶ κύματα μακρά.
5. ἔνθ' ἀθάνατοι πάντας καταφθίσουσιν ἐσθλοὺς ἑταίρους. (see pp.81/2)

---

[8]Section 15. καθέσσομαι is not found, but ἐφέσσομαι "I shall seat someone upon (my knee)" is found at Iliad ix, 455.
[9]τόνδε τ' ἐγὼ κομιῶ "in fact, I shall bring this man" (Odyssey XV, 546). The other persons (singular and plural) of the future are not found in Homer, but would be: κομιεῖς, κομιεῖ, κομιοῦμεν, κομιεῖτε, κομιοῦσι(ν). For ε-contracted verbs, see p.197ff.

[10]Adverb, and preposition with genitive.
[11]The aegis was a goatskin shield.
[12]The strong aorist of βαίνω, I step, I go. (ἔβην, ἔβης, ἔβη, ἔβητον, ἐβήτην, ἔβημεν, ἔβητε, ἔβησαν.)
[13]The suffix –δέ means "towards" (see p.5).
[14]Accusative singular πόλιν, genitive singular πόλιος or πόληος, dative singular πόλει or πόληι. The plural is: πόλιες or πόληες (nominative), πόλιας or πόληας or πόλεις (accusative), πολίων (genitive), πολίεσ(σ)ι (dative).
[15]The suffix –ως marks an adverb, like the English "-ly".
[16]For ἐνισπήσω, see p.81.

Odyssey V, lines 97-117

εἰρωτᾷς[17] μ' ἐλθόντα θεὰ θεόν· αὐτὰρ ἐγώ τοι
νημερτέως τὸν μῦθον ἐνισπήσω· κέλεαι γάρ.
Ζεὺς ἐμέ γ' ἠνώγει[18] δεῦρ' ἐλθέμεν[19] οὐκ ἐθέλοντα·
τίς δ' ἂν[20] ἑκὼν[21] τοσσόνδε[22] διαδράμοι ἁλμυρὸν[23] ὕδωρ   100
ἄσπετον;[24] οὐδέ τις ἄγχι βροτῶν πόλις[25], οἵ τε[26] θεοῖσιν
ἱερά[27]τε ῥέζουσι καὶ ἐξαίτους ἑκατόμβας.[28]
ἀλλὰ μάλ' οὔ πως ἔστι Διὸς νόον αἰγιόχοιο
οὔτε παρεξελθεῖν ἄλλον θεὸν οὔθ' ἁλιῶσαι.[29]

[17] εἰρωτᾷς is contracted from εἰρωτάεις, 2nd person singular of the present indicative active of εἰρωτάω = I ask, enquire of, question (+ acc. of person). μ' stands for με and is qualified by θεόν as well as ἐλθόντα, masculine accusative singular of ἐλθών, the aorist participle of ἔρχομαι ("having come", "one who has come", "your visitor"). Chantraine (op. cit. vol.ii, p.325) prefers "why I am visiting you". θεὰ refers to the subject, "you". κέλεαι is 2nd person singular.
[18] ἠνώγει = "ordered", 3rd person singular, pluperfect of ἄνωγα (p.79, footnote 54).
[19] δεῦρ' stands for δεῦρο. ἐλθέμεν, the infinitive of ἦλθον, the aorist of ἔρχομαι = "to come". οὐκ ἐθελόντα (masculine singular accusative, present participle of ἐθέλω) qualifies ἐμέ.
[20] ἂν ... διαδράμοι = "would traverse". διαδράμοι is the 3rd person singular optative of διέδραμον, the aorist of διατρέχω, I run through, traverse. With ἂν (a rare use, p.121) the optative means "would...". (τρέχω, I run, has a strong aorist, ἔδραμον.)
[21] ἑκών, ἑκοῦσα, ἑκόν = willing (qualifying τίς). Where Greek uses an adjective to qualify a subject, English often prefers an adverb.
[22] τοσόσδε, τοσήδε, τοσόνδε (here spelled τοσσόσδε) = so much.
[23] ἁλμυρός, ἁλμυρά, ἁλμυρόν = salty.
[24] ἄσπετος, ἄσπετον (feminine as masculine) = unspeakably great.
[25] οὐδέ τις πόλις (ἐστι)("and there is not any city...") = "where there is no city ..."
[26] οἵ τε ("who, of course ... ") refers to βροτῶν..
[27] ἱερά (neuter plural) = holy things, i.e. sacrifices. (ἱερός, ἱερά, ἱερόν = holy.)
[28] ἔξαιτος ἑκατόμβη = a choice hecatomb (from ἑκατὸν βόες, a sacrifice of 100 oxen).
[29] παρεξελθεῖν is the aorist infinitive of παρεξέρχομαι, I slip past (literally, go past and out). ἁλιῶσαι is the (weak) aorist infinitive of ἁλιόω, I make fruitless, frustrate. The subject of οὔ πως ἔστι is the whole clause Διὸς νόον αἰγιόχοιο οὔτε παρεξελθεῖν ἄλλον θεὸν οὔθ' ἁλιῶσαι. (οὔθ' stands for οὔτε.) This clause, being the subject, performs the function of a noun in the sentence (as does to be or not to be in the English sentence, to be or not to be, that is the question). In Greek, such noun clauses have the subject of the clause in the accusative case, and the verb of the clause in the infinitive. The subject of the clause is ἄλλον θεὸν and there are two infinitives: παρεξελθεῖν and ἁλιῶσαι. These infinitives have an object: νόον Διὸς αἰγιόχοιο. οὔ πως ἔστι means "it is not in any way possible" (literally, "it does not in any way exist"). ἄλλον θεὸν (the subject accusative) = another god. οὔτε παρεξελθεῖν οὔθ' ἁλιῶσαι = neither to slip past nor to frustrate. Διὸς νόον αἰγιόχοιο = the intention of aegis-bearing Zeus. (NB Greek has a double negative where English would not.) In English, we should begin the noun clause with "that", and the translation would then be: it is in no way possible that another god should either slip past or frustrate the intention of aegis-bearing Zeus.

Section 12   85

φησί τοι ἄνδρα παρεῖναι³⁰ ὀϊζυρώτατον ἄλλων,³¹   105
τῶν ἀνδρῶν, οἳ ἄστυ πέρι Πριάμοιο μάχοντο³²
εἰνάετες, δεκάτῳ δὲ πόλιν πέρσαντες³³ ἔβησαν
οἴκαδ᾽· ἀτὰρ ἐν νόστῳ Ἀθηναίην ἀλίτοντο,³⁴
ἥ σφιν ἐπῶρσ᾽³⁵ ἄνεμόν τε κακὸν καὶ κύματα μακρά.
ἔνθ᾽ ἄλλοι μὲν πάντες ἀπέφθιθεν³⁶ ἐσθλοὶ ἑταῖροι,   110
τὸν δ᾽ ἄρα δεῦρ᾽ ἄνεμός τε φέρων καὶ κῦμα πέλασσε.³⁷
τὸν νῦν σ᾽ ἠνώγειν³⁸ ἀποπεμπέμεν³⁹ ὅττι τάχιστα·⁴⁰
οὐ γάρ οἱ τῇδ᾽ αἶσα⁴¹ φίλων ἀπονόσφιν⁴² ὀλέσθαι,
ἀλλ᾽ ἔτι οἱ μοῖρ᾽ ἐστὶ φίλους τ᾽ ἰδέειν καὶ ἱκέσθαι
οἶκον ἐς ὑψόροφον καὶ ἑὴν ἐς πατρίδα γαῖαν.   115
    ὣς φάτο, ῥίγησεν δὲ Καλυψώ, δῖα θεάων,
καί μιν φωνήσασ᾽ ἔπεα πτερόεντα⁴³ προσηύδα·

³⁰"He" (Zeus) is the subject of φησί. παρεῖναι is the infinitive of πάρειμι, I am beside, am here. ἄνδρα παρεῖναι: "a man to be here" (i.e. "that a man is here"). φημί (I affirm) is normally followed by accusative and infinitive (i.e. "I affirm this to be so" rather than "I affirm that this is so").
³¹ὀϊζυρώτατον ἄλλων = most miserable of other (men). (ὀϊζυρός -ά -όν = woeful. -τατος, -τατη, -τατον is the equivalent of the English "-est".) ἄλλων, τῶν ἀνδρῶν in English is "more miserable than those other men who ..." (For "than", see p.31.)
³²μάχοντο is 3rd person plural imperfect of μάχομαι = I fight. (ἄστυ πέρι = περὶ ἄστυ.) εἰνάετες = for nine years (ἐννέα = nine). δεκάτῳ = in the tenth.
³³πέρσαντες is nominative masculine plural of the participle ἔπερσα, the aorist of πέρθω, I ravage, sack. οἴκαδ᾽ stands for οἴκαδε. For ἔβησαν, see footnote 12.
³⁴ἀλίτοντο is 3rd person plural of ἀλιτόμην, the (strong) aorist indicative of ἀλιταίνομαι (+ accusative), I offend. The Greek chieftain who offended Athene and was drowned on the way home was the lesser Ajax who had dragged Cassandra from the altar of Athene at the sack of Troy (Vergil, Aeneid II, 403-6, though he does not name the culprit). Hermes speaks loosely (Hainsworth (op. cit., p.265). Though Athene hated Ajax she did not kill him. Poseidon drowned him for boasting (Odyssey IV, 499-511). Odysseus and Ajax did not sail home from Troy together, and the companions in line 110 below are those of Odysseus who were drowned by Zeus. Odysseus blamed Zeus, not Athene, for his bad voyage home from Troy (Odyssey IX, 38). Hermes, as Zeus' messenger, may be deliberately shielding him.
³⁵ἐπῶρσ᾽ stands for ἐπῶρσε, 3rd person singular aorist indicative of ἐπόρνυμι, I arouse. The subject is ἥ ("who", referring to Ἀθηναίην in the previous line).
³⁶ἀπέφθιθεν is 3rd plural aorist passive (Section 18) of ἀποφθίνω, I destroy utterly: "(they) were destroyed". ἄλλοι μὲν ... τὸν δ᾽ "the others, indeed ... but him ..."
³⁷τὸν refers to Odysseus. "The wind carrying" = "the wind which was carrying him ..." πέλασσε: 3rd person singular aorist indicative active of πελάζω, I bring near. Lines 110-111 = 133-134, where Calypso says them back to Hermes.
³⁸ἠνώγειν = ἤνωγει (see footnote 18). "He" (Zeus) is the subject. σ᾽ stands for σε.
³⁹ἀποπεμπέμεν is the present infinitive active of ἀποπέμπω, I send away.
⁴⁰ὅττι τάχιστα (ὡς τάχιστα in later Greek) means "as quickly as possible".
⁴¹τῇδ᾽:τῇδε. αἶσα "share" = Fate (μοῖρα). οἱ αἰσά (ἐστι): οἱ μοῖρ᾽ ἐστι (lines 41, 114).
⁴²ἀπονόσφιν + genitive = far from. Translate in the order ἀπονόσφιν φίλων. ὀλέσθαι ("to be destroyed") is the infinitive of ὠλόμην, the aorist middle of ὄλλυμι. ἱκέσθαι ("to arrive") is the infinitive of ἱκόμην. Lines 114-5 almost repeat lines 41-2.
⁴³For φάτο see p.34, footnote 7 (the subject is Hermes). φωνήσασ᾽ stands for φωνήσασα. ἔπεα πτερόεντα = winged words. προσηύδα, 3rd person singular, imperfect of προσαυδάω: "she began to speak to".

Section 13
The Imperative Mood

The imperative mood is used for giving orders. In English, "beware" is imperative in "Beware of the dog!" and so is "stop" in "Stop, thief!"

English imperatives are in the second person: i.e. "beware!" is addressed to "you", whether "you" represents one person or many. In Greek there are also 3rd person imperatives: singular, corresponding to "let him" or "let her" or "let it", and plural, corresponding to "let them". "Let the buyer beware" can, in Greek, be expressed by an imperative.

Imperatives in Greek are either based on the <u>present</u> stem of a verb, or on the <u>aorist</u> stem (without an augment). All imperatives refer to future time, and in this respect, present and aorist imperatives are alike. The difference between them is that a <u>present</u> imperative tends to give orders or prohibitions for a continued action (e.g. "fear no more", "stop being afraid"), but an <u>aorist</u> imperative tends to give orders for a single action (e.g. "give me the money!"). Prohibitions (with the present imperative) are expressed with the negative μή.

Present imperative endings:

active

2nd person singular -ε
3rd person singular -ετω

2nd person dual -ετον
3rd person dual -ετων

2nd person plural -ετε
3rd person plural -οντων

λύε = loose! (henceforth)
λυέτω = let him/her/it loose

λύετον = may you two loose

λυέτων = let them both loose

λύετε = loose!
λυόντων = let them loose

middle

2nd person singular -εο or ευ[1]
3rd person singular -εσθω

2nd person dual -εσθον
3rd person dual -εσθων

2nd person plural -εσθε
3rd person plural -εσθων

λύεο or λύευ = loose for yourself
λυέσθω = let him/her/it loose
    for him/her/itself

λύεσθον = may you two loose
    for yourselves
λυέσθων = let them both loose
    for themselves

λύεσθε = loose for yourselves!
λυέσθων = let them loose for
    themselves

---

[1] e.g. from ἕπομαι, ἕπεο (Odyssey V, 91) and ἕπευ (Odyssey XV, 281) both = "follow!"

Section 13

Aorist imperative endings:

active	middle
2nd person singular -(σ)ον	2nd person singular –(σ)αι
3rd person singular –(σ)ατω	3rd person singular –(σ)ασθω
2nd person dual –(σ)ατον	2nd person dual -(σ)ασθον
3rd person dual -(σ)ατων	3rd person dual –(σ)ασθων
2nd person plural –(σ)ατε	2nd person plural –(σ)ασθε
3rd person plural –(σ)αντων	3rd person plural –(σ)ασθων

λῦσον = loose! (once)
λυσάτω = let him/her/it loose

λῦσαι = loose for yourself
λυσάσθω = let him/her/it loose for him/her/itself

λύσατον = may you two loose
λυσάτων = let them both loose

λύσασθον = may you two loose for yourselves
λυσάσθων = let them both loose for themselves

λύσατε = loose
λυσάντων = let them loose

λύσασθε = loose for yourselves
λυσάσθων = let them loose for themselves

Aorist imperatives are not used for prohibitions, which can be expressed by μή with the aorist subjunctive (see Section 14).

Strong aorist imperative endings are like present imperative endings, e.g. (active) λάβε = take (once), (middle) λάβεο = take hold of! grasp! The imperative of ἔειπον (I said) is εἰπέ! = say! (plural, εἴπατε).
(The accentuation of the 2nd person singular strong aorist imperatives is not consistent. Chantraine (*Grammaire Homérique* vol.i, p.467) considers that originally the accent was on the final syllable, e.g. εἰπέ (say!) and ἐλθέ (come!), but "see!" is always ἴδε. Both λάβε and λαβέ are found.)

The imperative of εἰμι (I am)

singular
[ἴσθι] = be!
ἔστω = let him/her/it be!

plural
ἔστε = be!
ἔστων = let them be!

(The second person singular and the dual are not found.)

Present imperative of -μι verbs The pattern of the **active** present imperatives of ὄρνυμι is:
    ὄρνυθι (arouse!) (singular) [ὀρνύτω] (let him, her, it arouse!),
    ὄρνυτε (arouse!) (plural) [ὀρνύντων] (let them arouse)
    (dual: [ὄρνυτον, -ων])
The pattern of the **middle** imperatives is:
    [ὄρνυσο] (arise!) (singular) [ὀρνύσθω] (let him/her/it/arise),
    ὄρνυσθε (arise!) (plural) [ὀρνύσθων] (let them arise!)
    (dual: [ὄρνυσθον, -ων]).
Some other 2nd singular imperatives active ending in -θι: δίδωθι (give!) (from δίδωμι) (δίδου is also found), ἐμπίμπληθι (fill!) (from ἐμπίμπλημι), ὄμνυθι (swear!) from ὄμνυμι, ἴθι (go!, come!) (from εἶμι (p.113), βῆθι (go!) (aorist, from ἔβην), ἴσθι (know!) from οἶδα (p.145), στῆθι (stand!) (from ἔστην, intransitive aorist of ἵστημι) and κλῦθι (listen!) from κλύω.[2]

Verbs with stems ending -α The present active imperatives end:
-α, -ατω, -ατον, -ατων, -ατε, -ωντων,
and the present middle imperatives end:
-ω (contracted from -αεο), -ασθω, -ασθον, -ασθων, -ασθε, -ασθων
e.g., from αὐδάω, I speak, utter:
αὔδα = speak!   [αὐδῶ = proclaim! (utter for yourself)]
αὐδάτω = let him/her/it speak   [αὐδάσθω = let him/her/it proclaim]

αὐδάτον = may you both speak   [αὐδάσθον = may you both proclaim]
αὐδάτων = let them both speak   [αὐδάσθων = let them both proclaim]
αὐδᾶτε = speak!   [αὐδᾶσθε = proclaim!]
αὐδώντων = let them speak   [αὐδάσθων = let them proclaim]

Verbs with stems ending -ε The present active imperatives end:
-ει, -ειτω, -ειτον, -ειτων, -ειτε, -ευντων
and the present middle imperatives end:
-ευ, -εισθω, -εισθον, -εισθων, -εισθε, -εισθων
e.g. from ποιέω, I do, make:
ποίει = make!   ποιεῦ = make for yourself
ποιείτω = let him/her/it make   ποιείσθω = let him/her/it
                                                               make for him/her
                                                               /itself

ποιεῖτον = may you two make   ποιεῖσθον = may you two
                                                               make for yourselves
ποιείτων = let them both make   ποιείσθων = let them both
                                                               make for themselves
ποιεῖτε = make   ποιεῖσθε = make for yourselves
ποιεύντων = let them make   ποιείσθων = let them make for
                                                               themselves

---

[2]Chantraine, *op. cit.* vol.i, p.466.

Section 13

The present tense of verbs with stems ending -ο is less well represented in Epic. From σαόω, I save, there is an imperative, σάω (save!):
σάω δ' ἐριήρας ἑταίρους ("and save the trusty companions!") (Iliad xvi, 363)[3] but this is irregular.

The pattern of regular present active imperative endings is:
-ου, -ουτω, -ουτον, -ουτων, -ουτε, -ουντων
and of present middle imperative endings:
-ου, -ουσθω, -ουσθον, -ουσθων, -ουσθε, -ουσθων

e.g. from κακόω, I distress:

κάκου	= distress!	[κακοῦ]	= be distressed!
[κακούτω]	= let him/her/it distress	[κακούσθω]	= let him/her/it be distressed
[κακοῦτον]	= may you two distress	[κακοῦσθον]	= may you two be distressed
[κακούτων]	= let them both distress	[κακούσθων]	= let them both be distressed
[κακοῦτε]	= distress!	[κακοῦσθε]	= be distressed!
[κακούντων]	= let them distress	[κακούσθων]	= let them be distressed

μηδὲ γέροντα κάκου: and stop distressing the old man (Odyssey IV, 754)
(γέρων, γέροντος (genitive) 3 masc. = old man)

NB Personal pronouns are often used with imperatives in Greek e.g.
ὑμεῖς ἐκεῖνο ποιεῖτε (do that!)   σὺ ἔρχεο (go! *or* go yourself!)

New words:
ἄγαμαι = I am jealous, angry[4]   δήν = for long
ἐλαύνω and ἐλαάω (aorist ἤλασα) = I drive
ἐποίχομαι = I approach, attack
ἔξοχον + genitive = far above[5]   εὐνή (1f) = bed
μέσ(σ)ος, μέσ(σ)η, μέσ(σ)ον = middle, mid
οἶνοψ, οἴνοπος = wine-faced[6]   οἶος, οἴη, οἶον = only, alone
ποιέω = I do, make   πη = in any way at all[7]
ῥεῖα = easily
ῥοδοδάκτυλος = rosy-fingered (epithet of the dawn)
σαόω[8] (aorist ἐσάωσα) = I save   τόφρα = for so long
τρέφω (aorist ἔθρεψα) = I nurture

---
[3]ἐρίηρες, 3rd declension plural adjective - trusty.
[4]Especially when the subject is any of the gods, "I envy, grudge" (with dative). Otherwise, "I wonder at", "I admire".
[5]Comparative adverb used to qualify an adjective, e.g. in ζηλήμονες ἔξοχον ἄλλων, ἔξοχον qualifies ζηλήμονες ("jealous far above others").
[6]Not found in nominative singular. Of the sea, often translated "wine-dark"; the dual, οἴνοπε βόε means "two deep red oxen" (Odyssey XII, 32, Iliad xiii, 703).
[7]In a negative sentence. In a positive sentence, "somehow".
[8]Also, at Odyssey V, 490, σώζω (which is the normal form in Attic).

What is the English for: 1.λέγε. 2.λέγετε. 3.μὴ λέγετε. 4.λεγέτω. 5.σὺ εἰπέ.
6.εἰπόντων. 7.πέμψον. 8.σὺ ἔλασον. 9.τοῦτο ποιήσατε. 10.ἐκεῖνο μὴ ποιεῖτε.
11.τοῦτο οὐ ποιεῖτε. 12.τούτου λάβεο. 13.'Οδυσσεὺς ἑταίροις μὴ ἑπέσθω.
(ἕπομαι with dative: I follow) 14.ἴδε φίλους σου. 15.θεοί, μὴ θεαῖς ἀγάασθε.
16.σχετλιοὶ⁹ μή ἐστε, θεοί· μάκαρες γάρ ἐστε ῥεῖα ζωόντες.¹⁰
17."Αρτεμίς σε ἐποιχέσθω οἷσι βέλεσσιν.¹¹
18.'Οδυσσεὺς μεγαλήτωρ ἦν πατρίδα γαῖαν ἱκέσθω εἰ τετελεσμένον ἐστίν.¹²
19.τὸν νύμφη σαούτω θρέψασα καὶ φιλήσασα.¹³
20.Ζεῦ, κέασσον νῆα θοὴν Ὀδυσσῆος ἐλάσας μέσῳ ἐνὶ οἴνοπι πόντῳ·¹⁴
βόας γὰρ Ἡελίου κατέπεφνον ἐοὶ ἑταῖροι.¹⁵

Odyssey V 118-144
"σχέτλιοί ἐστε, θεοί, ζηλήμονες¹⁶ ἔξοχον ἄλλων,
οἵ τε θεαῖς¹⁷ ἀγάασθε παρ' ἀνδράσιν εὐνάζεσθαι¹⁸
ἀμφαδίην,¹⁹ ἤν²⁰ τίς τε φίλον ποιήσετ' ἀκοίτην.   120

⁹σχέτλιος σχετλίη σχέτλιον = hard hearted, flinching from no wickedness.
¹⁰ζώω = I live (see ζῶ (ζάω) in Liddell & Scott).
¹¹βέλος, βέλους (3rd declension neuter, like λέχος) = dart, shaft, arrow.
¹²See p.79, footnote 55.
¹³φιλέω = I love, befriend. As φίλος means "own" as well as "dear", φιλέω can mean "take into one's home" (Hainsworth, *A Commentary on Homer's Odyssey* vol. i, pp.257 & 267).
¹⁴(ἐ)κέασσα is the (weak) aorist of κεάζω, I shiver, cleave. θοός, θοή, θοόν = swift (a formulaic Homeric epithet for ships). ἐνὶ stands for ἐν.
¹⁵βοῦς, (genitive βοός, 3) = ox, cow. 'Ηέλιος 2 masc.= the sun. κατέπεφνον, see p.66.
¹⁶This line echoes Apollo's complaint, at Iliad xxiv, 33, to the other gods that Hector's corpse has been left to be abused by Achilles, which begins: σχέτλιοί ἐστε, θεοί, δηλήμονες ... (Hainsworth, *op. cit.* p.265). (δηλήμων = baneful, noxious). ζηλήμων, ζηλήμονος (3rd declension adjective) = jealous. For ἄλλων, see p.31.
¹⁷θεαῖς is dative plural. This ending is rare in Homer, where -ῃς or -ῃσι is usual.
¹⁸οἵ τε = "all those who" (τε implying a characteristic or repeated action; Stanford, on Odyssey I, 52) or "you who, in fact," (p.51, above). Translate θεαῖς with ἀγάασθε (2nd person plural, present indicative of ἄγαμαι) and ἀνδράσιν (dative plural of ἀνήρ) with παρά. εὐνάζομαι παρά + dative = I go to bed with (εὐνάζεσθαι is present infinitive). ἄγαμαι + dative + infinitive is to grudge that a person does something. For a similar construction with a verb meaning "grudge" see Odyssey III, 55-6: κλῦθι, Ποσείδαον γαιήοχε, μηδὲ μεγήρῃς ἡμῖν εὐχομένοισι τελευτῆσαι τάδε ἔργα ("listen, Poseidon earth-holder, and do not begrudge us, (who are) making a vow, to finish these tasks"). γαιήοχος, earth-holder. μεγήρῃς, 2nd person singular, aorist subjunctive of μεγαίρω (+ dative, I begrudge). εὔχομαι, I pray. τελευτῆσαι, aorist infinitive active of τελευτάω, I finish. ἔργον (2 neuter), task.
¹⁹ἀμφαδίην = openly. In the Homeric Hymn to Aphrodite (281-8), which is later than the Odyssey, Zeus is said to kill mortals if they boast that they have been sleeping with goddesses but not with mountain nymphs, who are described there (line 260) as long-living, but not immortal. See Hainsworth's note (*op. cit.*, p.266).
²⁰ἤν stands for ἐάν, from εἰ ἄν, used with the subjunctive for "if" in future and general conditions in Attic. ποιήσετ' stands for ποιήσεται, 3rd person singular, aorist subjunctive middle with short vowel ending (Section 14) of ποιέω. ἤν τις ποιήσεται = "if one makes for herself ..." (τε is enclitic.)   ἀκοίτης, ἀκοίτου (1m) = bedfellow, husband.

Section 13

ὣς μὲν ὅτ' Ὠρίων²¹ ἕλετο²² ῥοδοδάκτυλος Ἠώς,
τόφρα οἱ ἠγάασθε θεοὶ ῥεῖα ζώοντες,
ἕως μιν ἐν Ὀρτυγίῃ²³ χρυσόθρονος²⁴ Ἄρτεμις ἁγνή²⁵
οἷσ' ἀγανοῖσι βέλεσσιν ἐποιχομένη κατέπεφνεν.
ὣς δ' ὁπότ'²⁶ Ἰασίωνι²⁷ ἐϋπλόκαμος Δημήτηρ,   125
ᾧ θυμῷ εἴξασα,²⁸ μίγη²⁹ φιλότητι³⁰ καὶ εὐνῇ
νειῷ³¹ ἔνι τριπόλῳ· οὐδὲ δὴν ἦεν ἄπυστος³²

²¹ὅτ' stands for ὅτε. 'Ὠρίων' (object of ἕλετο) stands for 'Ὠρίωνα, the accusative of 'Ὠρίων (3rd declension), Orion, the hunter. Only here is his death attributed to an affair with Eos (Hainsworth, *op. cit.* p.266), who though married to Tithonus was prone to affairs with attractive young mortals including Cleitus (Odyssey XV, 250). Elsewhere, Orion's death is explained differently, e.g. that Artemis killed him with an arrow when he tried to seduce her. (Horace, *Odes* iii, 4, 70-2).
²²Unaugmented 3rd person singular of εἰλόμην (p.66). τόφρα: for so long. οἱ is feminine ("of her", dative with ἠγάασθε) and stands for Eos. ἠγάασθε is 2nd person plural imperfect of ἄγαμαι. The subject is "you gods".
²³μιν ("him") refers to Orion. Ὀρτυγίη is literally "Quail Island" from ὄρτυξ, ὄρτυγος, quail, and is often identified with Delos (sacred to Apollo and Artemis, who were born there) or a nearby islet (Hainsworth, *op. cit.*, p.266, who refers to the Hymn to Delian Apollo, 16). An Ortygia in Syria is also mentioned at Odyssey XV, 404 (see Hoekstra's note, *A Commentary on Homer's Odyssey*, vol.ii, p.257), and Apollo and Artemis are said to bring a painless death to its inhabitants. There is a different Ortygia at Syracuse. (To scan this line, ἕως must be read as a monosyllable.)
²⁴χρυσόθρονος = with throne of gold, an epithet of Artemis, Hera and the dawn Goddess Eos (Hainsworth, *op. cit.*, p.267). Feminine as masculine (see p.8).
²⁵ἁγνός, ἁγνή, ἁγνόν = holy, chaste, pure. ἀγανός, ἀγανή, ἀγανόν = mild, gentle. βέλος, see footnote 11 above. κατέπεφνον - see p.66. Hainsworth notes that 124 is a formulaic line, occurring once in the Iliad (xxiv, 759) and five times elsewhere in the Odyssey. Apollo and Artemis were said to bring death to men or women respectively by shooting them with arrows (see Hoekstra on Odyssey XV 411). All the other instances refer either to Apollo killing men or Artemis killing women. However, in this passage Artemis' victim is male.
²⁶ὁπότε = "at the time when" (cf. ὅτε).
²⁷Iasion was a mortal, a Cretan. Their son was Plutus, the god of wealth (Hesiod, *Theogony*, 969-971).
²⁸εἴκω (aorist εἶξα) (with dative) = I yield (to). εἴξασα is feminine nominative singular of the aorist participle active, "having yielded to...". ᾧ is dative singular masculine of the possessive adjective "her" (p.52), qualifying θυμῷ.
²⁹μίγη is 3rd person singular of the aorist passive, (ἐ)μίγην, of μίσγω, I mix, (the Attic form of the present is μίγνυμι). With dative, it means "had intercourse with".
³⁰φιλότης, φιλότητος (3f) = love. φιλότητι καὶ εὐνῇ (literally, "in love and bed") is an example of *hendiadys*, one idea "in a bed of love" being expressed through two, "bed" and "love".
³¹νειός (2 feminine) = fallow land. τρίπολος, τρίπολον (fem. as masc.) = thrice ploughed. It probably refers to a ritual ploughing of three furrows before cultivation begins (Stanford and Hainsworth). Translate as if ἐν νειῷ τριπόλῳ.
³²ἦεν is 3rd person singular imperfect ofεἰμι. ἄπυστος, ἄπυστον (fem. as masc.) (from α-privative + the root of πυνθάνομαι = I find out by enquiry) = unaware.

Ζεύς, ὅς μιν κατέπεφνε βαλὼν ἀργῆτι κεραυνῷ.³³
ὣς δ' αὖ νῦν μοι ἄγασθε, θεοί, βροτὸν ἄνδρα παρεῖναι.³⁴
τὸν μὲν ἐγὼν ἐσάωσα περὶ τρόπιος³⁵ βεβαῶτα   130
οἶον,³⁶ ἐπεί οἱ νῆα θοὴν³⁷ ἀργῆτι κεραυνῷ
Ζεὺς ἔλσας ἐκέασσε μέσῳ ἐνὶ οἴνοπι πόντῳ.
ἔνθ' ἄλλοι μὲν πάντες ἀπέφθιθεν³⁸ ἐσθλοὶ ἑταῖροι,
τὸν δ' ἄρα δεῦρ' ἄνεμός τε φέρων καὶ κῦμα πέλασσε.
τὸν μὲν ἐγὼ φίλεόν τε καὶ ἔτρεφον ἠδὲ ἔφασκον³⁹   135
θήσειν ἀθάνατον καὶ ἀγήραον⁴⁰ ἤματα πάντα.
ἀλλ' ἐπεὶ οὔ πως ἔστι Διὸς νόον αἰγιόχοιο
οὔτε παρεξελθεῖν ἄλλον θεὸν οὔθ' ἁλιῶσαι,⁴¹

---

³³μιν ("him") refers to Iasion. βαλών is nominative masculine singular, aorist participle active of βάλλω, with the meaning "strike" here. ἀργής, ἀργῆτος = bright. κεραυνός 2m = thunderbolt. "with his shining thunderbolt" is a formulaic phrase, used also in line 131.
³⁴For παρεῖναι, see p.85, footnote 30. For the construction (ἄγασθε + dative followed by an accusative and infinitive), see footnote 18 above. Translate in the order: ἄγασθέ μοι βροτὸν ἄνδρα παρεῖναι: "you are grudging to me a mortal man to be here (that a mortal man is here)", i.e. "you are jealous of me because a mortal man is here". θεοί is vocative.
³⁵ἐγών stands for ἐγώ. ἐσάωσα is 1st person singular, aorist indicative active of σαόω. τρόπις, τρόπηος (3f) = keel, and περὶ τρόπιος means round (i.e. astride) a keel. βεβαῶτα is masculine accusative singular of βεβαώς, the perfect participle of βαίνω, I go, step, and means "having stepped". It qualifies τόν, "him" (Odysseus), the object of ἐσάωσα. περὶ τρόπιος βεβαῶτα means "having stepped round a keel" (i.e. "with his legs astride a keel"). When Zeus sank Odysseus' last ship, only the mast and keel were left (Odyssey XII, 420-5).
³⁶Note the smooth breathing, distinguishing οἶος, οἴη, οἶον = alone from οἷος, οἵη, οἷον = of which kind (Section 15, p.109). οἶον qualifies τόν (line 130). οἱ ("for him") is best translated "his" (a possessive dative), where "he" is Odysseus.
³⁷See footnote 14, above. ἐκέασσε is 3rd person singular, aorist indicative active of κεάζω. ἔλσας may be an abbreviation of ἐλάσας as there is a scholium which says: Ζεὺς ἐλάσας γράφεται ἔλσας ("Ζεὺς ἐλάσας is written ἔλσας") (Buttmann, Scholia in Homeri Odysseam, p.188) and in that case the meaning will be "Zeus, having driven the swift ship ..." ἐλαύνω is used with this meaning at Odyssey V, 313, where a great wave is driving Odysseus' raft in a storm. However, ἔλσας is the nominative masculine singular of the participle of ἔλσα, the aorist active of εἴλω, "I shut in". If it is taken in this way, the meaning is, "Zeus, having shut the swift ship in ..." νῆα θοήν is the object of ἔλσας and ἐκέασσε.
³⁸cf.110-111. Calypso repeats Hermes' words.
³⁹τόν is the object of φιλέον and ἔτρεφον. ἔφασκον (1st person singular) is used as the imperfect of φημί. θήσειν is future infinitive of τίθημι (Section 15). "I was saying to be about to make him ..." = "I was saying that I would make him ..."
⁴⁰ἀγήρων is contracted from ἀγήραον, masculine accusative singular of ἀγήραος. ἀγήραος, ἀγήραον (fem. as masc.) = immune from old age. For ἤματα πάντα (accusative indicating duration) see p.20.
⁴¹Calypso repeats Hermes' words from lines 103-4 (p.84, footnote 29).

Section 13

ἐρρέτω,⁴² εἴ μιν κεῖνος ἐποτρύνει⁴³ καὶ ἀνώγει,⁴⁴
πόντον ἐπ' ἀτρύγετον.⁴⁵ πέμψω δέ μιν οὔ πῃ ἐγώ γε·   140
οὐ γάρ μοι πάρα⁴⁶ νῆες ἐπήρετμοι καὶ ἑταῖροι,
οἵ κέν μιν πέμποιεν⁴⁷ ἐπ' εὐρέα νῶτα θαλάσσης.
αὐτάρ οἱ πρόφρων⁴⁸ ὑποθήσομαι οὐδ' ἐπικεύσω,
ὥς κε μάλ' ἀσκηθής⁴⁹ ἦν πατρίδα γαῖαν ἵκηται."⁵⁰

⁴²3rd person singular imperative of ἔρρω, (here) "I come to harm", sometimes "I wander" or "I hobble". "Let him go to his ruin." "Him" refers to Odysseus.
⁴³ἐποτρύνω = I urge. κεῖνος refers to Zeus. μιν refers to Odysseus.
⁴⁴ἀνώγει is the unaugmented form of ἠνώγει(ν) (p.84, footnote 18):"he ordered".
⁴⁵Translate in the order:ἐρρέτω ἐπ' ἀτρύγετον πόντον. Also ἐγώ γε οὔ πῃ πέμψω μιν.
⁴⁶See p. 47, footnote 34. Line 141 = line 16 except that it has μοι instead of οἱ.
⁴⁷οἵ κεν ... πέμποιεν (= "who ... might send") expresses a purpose. "Send" here implies "escort".
⁴⁸πρόφρων = kind, gracious (p.46, footnote 20). ὑποθήσομαι, the future middle of ὑποτίθημι, = I shall give advice to (him). Note the Greek preference for an adjective where English would naturally have an adverb: "kind, I shall give advice to (him) ... " = "I shall advise him kindly ..." οὐδ' stands for οὐδέ. ἐπικεύσω is future, from ἐπικεύθω, I conceal. οὐδ' ἐπικεύσω "and I shall not conceal..."
⁴⁹Line 144 = line 26.
⁵⁰ὥς = "how" (κε is enclitic). ἵκηται is 3rd person singular, aorist subjunctive (see Section 14) of ἰκνέομαι. ὥς κε ... ἵκηται: "how he would reach", i.e. "so that he would reach". μάλ' ἀσκηθής = quite unharmed (p.58, footnote 37).

ἀθάνατος καὶ ἀγήρως

The expression "immortal and unageing" is found in the Iliad: at ii, 447 of the shield of Athene, at xii, 323 where Sarpedon says that he and his friend Glaucus cannot become immortal and unageing by fleeing from battle, and at xvii, 444 of the horses of Achilles, which were a gift from the gods and are compared with their owner who is destined to die.

Odyssey V 136 is a formula associated with Calypso; Odysseus uses it at Odyssey VII, 257 when he tells Alcinous about her and to Penelope at XXIII, 336. Perhaps Calypso mentions exemption from ageing at this point to show that she is a caring and kind goddess compared with Eos, who foolishly did not ask this favour from Zeus as well as immortality for her husband Tithonus so that he, from being a handsome young prince, inexorably grew older until his deathless and perpetually youthful wife could stand his increasingly senile babbling no longer and shut him away for ever (*The Homeric Hymn to Aphrodite*, 218-238). According to Ovid (*Metamorphoses*IX,421-5), as well as Eos, Demeter and Aphrodite complained that their human consorts had got old and grey (Iasion having apparently survived his ordeal). Hesiod (*Theogony*, 947-9) says that Dionysus persuaded Zeus (the son of Cronus) to exempt Ariadne from ageing and death (τὴν δὲ οἱ ἀθάνατον καὶ ἀγήρω θῆκε Κρονίων "and for him the son of Kronos made her deathless and unageing"). But there might be a connection between killing, and making ageless and deathless which may cast a sinister light on Calypso's proposed generosity. In Homer's account, Artemis killed Ariadne in sea girt Dia "on information from Dionysus" (Odyssey XI, 324-5).

Section 14
The Subjunctive Mood

The **subjunctive** mood is used in main clauses for firm wishes and commands e.g. *may you be happy!* or *let it be done!*
and for deliberations, e.g. *what am I to do?*
The subjunctive mood is used for suppositions often where in English we say "may", e.g. *Whenever it may happen, I shall be ready,* and in purpose clauses e.g., *I have come so that I may see you.* The subjunctive mood expresses *wishes* and *possibilities*.

The normal subjunctive endings are characterised by long vowels :

		active	middle
singular	1st person	-ω *or* -ωμι	-ωμαι
	2nd person	-ῃς *or* -ῃσθα	-ηαι *or* -ῃ
	3rd person	-ῃ(σι)	-ηται
	2nd person	-ητον	-ησθον
	3rd person	-ητον	-ησθον
	1st person	-ωμεν	-ωμε(σ)θα
	2nd person	-ητε	-ησθε
	3rd person	-ωσι(ν)	-ωνται

The present subjunctive active

λύω (*or* λύωμι) = let me loose
λύῃς (*or* λύησθα) = may you loose
λύῃ (*or* λύῃσι(ν)) = let him/her/it loose
λύητον = may you both loose
λύητον = let them both loose
λύωμεν = let us loose
λύητε = may you loose
λύωσι(ν) = let them loose

The present subjunctive middle

λύωμαι = let me loose for myself
λύηαι *or* λύῃ = may you loose for yourself
λύηται = let him/her/it loose for him/her/itself
λύησθον = may you both loose for yourselves
λύησθον = let them both loose for themselves
λυώμε(σ)θα = let us loose for ourselves
λύησθε = may you loose for yourselves
λύωνται = let them loose for themselves

Section 14

The subjunctive expressing a wish is used as equivalent to an **imperative**, especially in the first person, as there are no first person imperatives.
e.g.   αἶψα δὲ πάντα φέρωμεν ἀολλέα (Odyssey VIII, 394)
      but let us bring everything together at once[1]

   τὸν ξεῖνον ἐρώμεθα εἴ τιν' ἄεθλον οἶδε (Odyssey VIII, 133-4)
   let us ask that stranger if he knows any athletics[2]

A firm negative wish (virtually a command) can be expressed by μή and the subjunctive:

   μὴ δηθὰ διατρίβωμεν ὁδοῖο (Odyssey II, 404)
   let us not lose much time from our journey
   (δηθά: for a long time διατρίβω: I waste time ὁδός, ὁδοῦ (fem.): journey, road)

What is the English for the following wishes expressed in the present subjunctive:
1.ἀμείβωμαι. 2.φιλέῃσιν (φιλέω : I love). 3.ἐλαύνωσιν. 4.βάλλωμεν. 5.μὴ γίγνηται. 6.ἔρχηται. 7.μὴ ἐθέλωμι. 8.μή σε ἴσχω. 9.μή σε τοῦτο ποιέειν κελεύῃ. 10.τοῦτον ἀνέρα πέμπωμεν.

<u>The aorist subjunctive</u> is formed by joining the subjunctive endings to the aorist stems, e.g. –λυσ–from ἔλυσα. As in the aorist optative, the augment is never used. Thus, the **weak aorist subjunctive** is

active		middle	
λύσω	= let me loose	λύσωμαι	= let me loose for myself
or λύσωμι			
λύσῃς	= may you loose	λύσηαι	= may you loose for yourself
or λύσησθα		*or* λύσῃ	
λύσῃ	= let him/her/it	λύσηται	= let him/her/it loose for
or λύσῃσι(ν)	loose		him/her/itself
λύσητον	= may you two loose	λύσησθον	= may you two loose for yourselves
λύσητον	= may those two loose	λύσησθον	= may those two loose for themselves
λύσωμεν	= let us loose	λυσώμε(σ)θα	= let us loose for ourselves
λύσητε	= may you loose	λύσησθε	= may you loose for yourselves
λύσωσι(ν)	= let them loose	λύσωνται	= let them loose for themselves

---
[1] αἶψα = at once. ἀολλής = all together, in a heap.
[2] ξεῖνος 2m = stranger. ἔρομαι = I ask. ἄεθλος (2 masc.) = athletic contest. οἶδε = he knows (Section 21).

The **strong aorist subjunctive** is formed by adding the subjunctive endings to the aorist stem (without augment). Thus, the aorist subjunctive active of ἔλαβον, I took, is:
λάβω(μι), λάβῃς(θα), λάβῃ(σιν), λάβητον, λάβητον, λάβωμεν, λάβητε, λάβωσι(ν).
The English meanings are "let me take", "may you take", etc.
The aorist subjunctive middle is:
λάβωμαι, λάβηαι, λάβηται, λάβησθον, λάβησθον, λαβώμε(σ(θα, λάβησθε, λάβωνται. The English meanings are "let me take hold (of)", "may you take hold (of)", etc.

The **aorist subjunctive has no past significance.** It tends to indicate an isolated occurrence, in contrast to the present subjunctive, which is continuous and would indicate a continued or repeated occurrence. It is often difficult to make such distinctions explicit in English.
Wishes and commands can be expressed by the aorist subjunctive, e.g. νῦν δ' ἐξέλθωμεν ("and now let us go outside") (Odyssey VIII, 100).[3]

In Homer, prohibitions are expressed by μή and the present imperative e.g. μή με, Ποσείδαον γαίοχε,[4] ταῦτα κέλευε (Odyssey VIII, 350)
Poseidon, stop ordering me (to do) these things![5]

or less commonly μή with the aorist subjunctive e.g.
Πριαμίδη, μὴ δή με ἕλωρ Δαναοῖσιν ἐάσῃς κεῖσθαι (Iliad V, 684-5)
O son of Priam, do not finally allow me to lie as a prey to the Danaans[6]
μή and the present imperative is used for general as well as continuing prohibitions (e.g. μή με ἕα κύνας καταδάψαι "do not let any dogs maul me", Iliad xxii, 339).[7] The nature of the present and aorist aspects determine whether the present imperative or the aorist subjunctive is used. The aorist imperative is not used with μή. (Chantraine (*Grammaire Homérique* vol.ii, p.230,)
What is the English for the following wishes and prohibitions expressed with the aorist subjunctive:
1.βάλω. 2.ἀφίκηαι. 3.ποιήσωμεν. 4.πέσῃσι. 5.μὴ πίῃσθα. 6.τοῦτον ἀνέρα πέμψωμεν. 7.ἴδω. 8.ἴδωμι. 9.μὴ πάθωσι. 10.μὴ ὀμόσῃς.

[3]ἐξέλθωμεν is 1st person plural subjunctive from ἐξῆλθον, the aorist of ἐξέρχομαι, I go out.
[4]Vocative singular of γαιήοχος, "earth-possessor", one who ἔχει γαῖαν.
[5]At line 347, Poseidon has just ordered Hephaestus to set Aphrodite and Ares free. He used an aorist imperative, λῦσον!
[6] ἕλωρ (3n) = prey. ἐάω = I allow. The example is from Chantraine (*op. cit.* vol.ii, pp.207-8).
[7]κύων, κυνός (3) dog. καταδάψαι: aorist infinitive active of καταδάπτω, I maul.

In Homer subjunctives are sometimes found with **short** vowels, e.g.
ἀλλ' ἄγ' ἐγὼν αὐτὸς πειρήσο̱μαι ἠδὲ ἴδωμαι. (Odyssey VI, 126)
but come, let me myself try and see for myself[8]
where πειρήσομαι by itself would be ambiguous and could be future "I shall try", except that ἴδωμαι is unambiguously aorist subjunctive, and the formula ἄγε! ("come!") is frequently followed by a subjunctive. This use, in Homer, of a short vowel where we should expect a long one in the subjunctive is especially common with weak aorist subjunctives where the aorist indicative ends -(σ)α and the aorist subjunctive ends -(σ)ω (called "sigmatised aorists" on p. 61). When the short-vowel aorist subjunctive has the same form as the future indicative, they have to be distinguished by the context e.g.
"ἀμφίπολοι, στῆθ' οὕτω ἀπόπροθεν, ὄφρ' ἐγὼ αὐτὸς
ἅλμην ὤμοιϊν ἀπολούσομαι, ἀμφὶ δ' ἐλαίῳ
χρίσομαι· ἦ γὰρ δηρὸν ἀπὸ χροός ἐστιν ἀλοιφή.
ἄντην δ' οὐκ ἂν ἐγώ γε λοέσσομαι." (Odyssey VI, 218-221)
"Maidservants, stand far away like this, so that I myself may wash the salt from my two shoulders and anoint myself around with olive oil; for indeed, for a long time from my skin embrocation is (= has been & still is) absent; but I would not wash myself in front (of you)."[9]
(Clearly, ἀπολούσομαι is the subjunctive of ἀπελουσάμην, and χρίσομαι the subjunctive of ἐχρισάμην because they come after ὄφρα, and λοέσσομαι is probably aorist subjunctive because it occurs here with ἄν ("would").)[10]

Some uses of the subjunctive (when negative, with μή).
1. <u>To express purpose</u>, with ὄφρα or ὄφρ' ἄν, ἵνα, ὥς, ὥς κε, or less commonly ὅπως, e.g. (positive):
Τηλέμαχον δὲ σὺ πέμψον ἐπισταμένως, δύνασαι γάρ,
<u>ὥς κε</u> μάλ' ἀσκηθὴς ἣν πατρίδα γαῖαν <u>ἵκηται</u>,
μνηστῆρες δ' ἐν νηΐ παλιμπετὲς <u>ἀπονέωνται</u>." (Odyssey V, 25-27)
"But send Telemachus with understanding, for you can,
<u>so that he may reach</u> his own country quite unharmed
and so that the suitors <u>may depart</u> again in (their) ship."

[8] πειραομαι = I try.
[9] ἀμφίπολος : maidservant. στῆθ' (for στῆτε, 2nd person plural imperative): stand! οὕτω: in this way ἀπόπροθεν: far away. ὄφρ': ὄφρα. ἅλμη: salt. ὦμος: shoulder. ἀπολούομαι: I wash off for myself. ἔλαιον: olive oil. χρίομαι: I anoint myself. ἦ: indeed. δηρόν: for a long time. χρώς, χροός (masc.): skin. ἀλοιφή: embrocation, ointment. ἄντην: face-to-face. λοέσσομαι is 1st person singular, subjunctive of (ἐ)λου(σ)σάμην, the aorist of λούομαι, I wash myself (but with the short vowel ending -ομαι it has the same form as the 1st person singular of the future).
[10] Chantraine, op. cit. vol.ii, p.225, notes that sometimes the future indicative occurs with ἄν or κεν, e.g. Odyssey V, 36 (p.59, above): τιμήσουσι is unambiguously future. Chantraine lists short-vowel subjunctives from sigmatised aorists (vol.i, pp.454-5).

An example including positive and negative purposes:
περὶ πομπῆς
μνησόμεθ' ὥς χ' ὁ ξεῖνος ἀπάνευθε πόνου καὶ ἀνίης
πομπῇ ὑφ' ἡμετέρῃ ἣν πατρίδα γαῖαν ἵκηται ...
μηδέ τι μεσσηγύς γε κακὸν καὶ πῆμα πάθῃσι (Odyssey VII, 191-5)
concerning the escort
let us remember so that in that case the stranger without toil and trouble
under our escort may reach his home country...
and may not on the way suffer any evil and woe[11]

The subjunctive may be used for purpose clauses in present or past time. The optative may only be used for purpose clauses in past time.

2. <u>To express a clause which is the object of a verb of fearing</u>:
δείδω μὴ θήρεσσιν ἕλωρ καὶ κύρμα γένωμαι. (Odyssey V, 473)
I am afraid that I may become a prey and spoil for wild beasts.[12]
This is a fear for the *future*, since the point of being afraid is to try to prevent the thing feared; therefore μή with the subjunctive here expresses a negative purpose, like the English "lest", or at least a future situation one wishes to avert. However, we sometimes express fears about the *present* or the *past*. These do not express any purpose, because it is too late. In Greek, such fears are expressed by μή with the indicative, e.g.
δείδω μὴ δὴ πάντα θεὰ νημερτέα εἶπεν (Odyssey V, 300)
I fear that then the goddess spoke everything sure and true.

3. <u>Deliberative questions</u>, where the speaker's mind is being made up, e.g.
Ὦ μοι ἐγὼ δειλός, τί νύ μοι μήκιστα γενήται; (Odyssey V, 299)
O woe is me, poor wretch! What now at last is to happen to me?[13]

4. <u>The subjunctive expressing an eventuality.</u>
This is found particularly often in Homer. The subjunctive is used (usually with the *modal particles* ἄν or κεν, both of which originally had the meaning "in that case") to express a possibility, e.g.

---

[11]Garvie (*Odyssey VI-VIII*, p.203) takes μνησόμεθ' (standing for μνησόμεθα) as aorist subjunctive rather than future. This is appropriate as king Alcinous is consulting his nobles about Odysseus, but μνήσομαι is ambiguous and is cited as future in Liddell & Scott from this passage (it is not in Chantraine's list of short-vowel subjunctives). χ' stands for κε. ξεῖνος (2m) = stranger. ἄνευθε + genitive = far away from. πόνος (2m) = toil. ἀνίη (1f) = trouble. μηδέ is the counterpart (where μή is the negative) of οὐδέ "and not". μεσσηγύς = in between, in the middle.
[12]δείδω = I fear. θήρ = wild beast. ἕλωρ (3n) = prey. κύρμα (3n) = spoil. γένωμαι is 1st person singular subjunctive of ἐγενόμην, the aorist of γίγνομαι (p.66).
[13]δειλός -ή -όν = wretched, cowardly, used here as part of the exclamation ὦ μοι ἐγὼ δειλός (O for me, I wretched!). μήκιστα = at last. γένηται is 3rd person singular: see γένωμαι.

αὐτὰρ ἐπὴν δή μοι σχεδίην διὰ κῦμα τινάξῃ,
νήξομαι ... (Odyssey V, 363-4)
But at such time as a wave smashes through the raft for me,
I'll swim.[14]

A negative possibility is sometimes expressed by οὐκ ἄν with the subjunctive, e.g.

οὐκ ἄν τοι χραίσμῃ κίθαρις τά τε δῶρ' 'Αφροδίτης
ἥ τε κόμη τό τε εἶδος, ὅτ' ἐν κονίῃσι μιγείης. (Iliad III, 54-5)
I tell you, the lyre and the gifts of Aphrodite would not save (you),
both that hair and that beauty, when you might be mingled in the dust.[15]

The subjunctive of εἰμί

ἔω or εἴω	let me be
[ἔῃς	may you be]
ἔῃσι(ν) or ᾖσι(ν) or ἔῃ	let him/her/it be
[ἔητον	may you two be]
[ἔητον	may those two be]
[ἔωμεν	let us be]
[ἔητε	may you be]
ἔωσι(ν) or ὦσι(ν)	let them be

New words:

ἄγε = come!, come on, then!
αἰών, αἰῶνος 3m = lifetime
ἀμφιέννυμι[17] = I put round
δείδω = I fear
εἵματα (3nplu) = clothes

ἀγχοῦ = near[16]
ἀκτή (3f) = headland
ἀπέβην = I went away[18]
δούρατα (3nplu) = timbers
ἐνθάδε = here

[14]ἐπὴν stands for ἐπεὶ ἄν (whenever). διὰ ... τινάξῃ is 3rd person singular of διατινάξω, the subjunctive of διετίναξα, the aorist of διατινάσσω, I smash through. (διὰ has been separated from τινάξῃ by tmesis; see p.78.) νήξομαι is future from νήχω, I swim (p.81).
[15](Hector to Paris.) χραισμέω = I save. κίθαρις (3f) = lyre. δῶρον (2n) = gift. κόμη (1f) = hair. εἶδος (3n, genitive εἴδεος) = beauty, form. κονίη (1f, often in plural) = dust. μιγείης is 2nd person singular, aorist passive optative of μίσγω, I mingle.
[16]Adverb, and preposition with genitive or dative.
[17]i.e. "clothe". Aorist ἀμφίεσα: future (p.81), ἀμφιέσω.
[18]Irregular (strong) aorist of ἀποβαίνω, I go away (also, "I step off"). [ἀπέβην], [ἀπέβησθα], ἀπέβη, [ἀπέβητον], ἀπεβήτην, [ἀπέβημεν], [ἀπέβητε], ἀπέβησαν.

ἠεροειδής -ες = murky[19]
κάμμορος = ill-fated[21]
νέομαι = I return[23]
ὄπισθεν = behind
οὐρανός (2m) = sky
πέτρη (1f) = rock
σῖτος (2m) = corn, food.
χαλκός (2m) = bronze

ἴκρια (2nplu) = boards[20]
μενοεικής -ές = satisfying[22]
οἶνος (2m) = wine
ὄσσε (3 n. dual) = two eyes
οὖρος (2m) = following wind
πολύτλας = much-suffering[24]
χαλεπαίνω = I am angry
(aorist, ἐχαλέπηνα)

What is the English for: 1.οἰκάδε νεώμεθα. 2.μὴ χαλεπαίνωμεν. 3.δείδω μὴ τοῦτο νημερτὲς ᾖσι· δείδω μὴ θάλασσα ἠεροειδὴς γένηται. 4.δείδω μὴ τοῦτο νημερτές ἐστι· δείδω μὴ θάλασσα ἠεροειδής ἐστι. 5.σχεδίην ποιέει 'Οδυσσεὺς ἵνα ἐκ νήσου φεύγῃ. 6.ἐκ νήσου φεύγει μὴ γλυκὺς[25] αἰὼν ἐνθάδε κατείβηται.[26]
7.'Οδυσσῆα νῦν ἀπόπεμπε[27] μὴ Ζεύς πώς τοι μετόπισθε χαλεπήνῃ.
8.'Οδυσσεῦ, εὐρεῖαν σχεδίην ἁρμόζεο[28] χαλκῷ ὄφρα σε φέρῃσιν ἐπ' οἴνοπα πόντον.
9.οὖρον ὄπισθεν πέμψει ὥς κε μάλ' ἀσκηθὴς[29] σὴν πατρίδα γαῖαν ἵκηαι.
10.ἄγε,'Οδυσσῆα ἀποπέμπωμεν, καὶ σῖτον καὶ ὕδωρ καὶ οἶνον ἐρυθρὸν μενοεικέα αὐτῷ φέρωμεν.

Odyssey V, 145-170

τὴν δ' αὖτε προσέειπε[30] διάκτορος 'Αργεϊφόντης·   145
"οὕτω νῦν ἀπόπεμπε, Διὸς δ' ἐποπίζεο[31] μῆνιν,
μή πώς τοι μετόπισθε κοτεσσάμενος[32] χαλεπήνῃ."

[19]literally, "of cloudy look", a Homeric epithet for the sea.
[20]Liddell & Scott explain ἴκρια as the half deck at the stern of a Homeric ship. Hainsworth (*A Commentary on Homer's Odyssey*, vol.i, pp.269-270) notes its use later for "platform", which is consistent with this.
[21]Compound adjective - feminine as masculine.
[22]"suitable to one's taste", from μένος "strength", and so "spirit" and ἔοικα "I suit" (perfect with present meaning, Section 21, p.145).
[23]See also p.58, footnote 48.
[24]Epithet of Odysseus.
[25]γλυκύς, γλυκεία, γλυκύ = sweet (endings like ὀξύς, Section 23, p.164).
[26]κατείβομαι ("I am shed"), used metaphorically as "I pass away", "go past".
[27]ἀποπέμπω = I send away: ἀπόπεμπε is 2nd person singular, present imperative active. μετόπισθε = hereafter. πώς: πως (enclitic): in some way. (τοι is also enclitic).
[28]ἁρμόζομαι = I equip for myself, fit together for myself.
[29]μάλ' ἀσκηθής: quite unharmed (see p.58, footnote 37).
[30]προσέειπε is 3rd person singular, aorist indicative of προσλέγω, I speak to.
[31]οὕτω: thus, so, in this way. For ἀπόπεμπω see footnote 27 above. Understand 'Οδυσσῆα as the object. ἐποπίζεο is 2nd person singular imperative of ἐποπίζομαι, I respect, regard with awe. μῆνις, μήνιος (3f) = wrath.
[32]See footnote 27. κοτεσσάμενος = resentful (it is the (weak) aorist middle participle of κοτέω, I bear a grudge).

Section 14

ὣς ἄρα φωνήσας ἀπέβη κρατὺς³³ Ἀργεϊφόντης·
ἡ³⁴ δ' ἐπ' Ὀδυσσῆα μεγαλήτορα πότνια νύμφη
ἤϊ',³⁵ ἐπεὶ δὴ Ζηνὸς ἐπέκλυεν³⁶ ἀγγελιάων. 150
τὸν δ' ἄρ' ἐπ' ἀκτῆς εὗρε καθήμενον· οὐδέ ποτ' ὄσσε³⁷
δακρυόφιν³⁸ τέρσοντο,³⁹ κατείβετο⁴⁰ δὲ γλυκὺς αἰὼν
νόστον ὀδυρομένῳ,⁴¹ ἐπεὶ οὐκέτι⁴² ἥνδανε νύμφη.
ἀλλ' ἦ τοι νύκτας⁴³ μὲν ἰαύεσκεν⁴⁴ καὶ ἀνάγκῃ
ἐν σπέεσι⁴⁵ γλαφυροῖσι παρ' οὐκ ἐθέλων ἐθελούσῃ.⁴⁶ 155
ἤματα δ' ἂμ⁴⁷ πέτρῃσι καὶ ἠιόνεσσι καθίζων
δάκρυσι καὶ στοναχῇσι καὶ ἄλγεσι θυμὸν ἐρέχθων⁴⁸
πόντον ἐπ' ἀτρύγετον δερκέσκετο δάκρυα λείβων.

³³See p. 64, footnote 27.
³⁴ἡ δὲ πότνια νύμφη: and she, the lady nymph ... πότνια (feminine adjective) mistress, lady. ἐπ' stands for ἐπὶ (here, with acc., = for (the purpose of seeing).
³⁵ἤϊ' stands for ἤϊε, "she went" (p.65, footnote 51 and Section 16). The subject is ἡ.
³⁶ἐπέκλυεν is 3rd person singular, imperfect of ἐπικλύω + genitive = I listen to. ἐπεί + aorist = "when ... had ...". The imperfect of κλύω (ἔκλυον) has the force of an aorist. "When she had listened to ..." ἀγγελία = message (cf. ἄγγελος = messenger).
³⁷εὗρε is 3rd person singular, aorist indicative of εὑρίσκω. ποτ' stands for ποτε ("ever").
³⁸δακρυόφιν: "from tears" (for -φι ending, p.69, footnote 16).
³⁹τέρσοντο is 3rd person plural imperfect of τέρσομαι = I become dry.
⁴⁰κατείβετο is 3rd person singular imperfect of κατείβομαι, I flow down, run away. γλυκύς, γλυκεῖα, γλυκύ = sweet. γλυκύς qualifies αἰών.
⁴¹ὀδυρόμενος -η -ον (participle of ὀδύρομαι) = lamenting. ὀδύρομαι + accusative = I grieve for. The object of ὀδυρομένῳ is νόστον. ὀδυρομένῳ is a possessive dative: "for him grieving for his journey home, the sweet life was flowing away ..." means "his sweet life was flowing away as he grieved for his journey home."
⁴²οὐκέτι = no longer. ἥνδανε is 3rd person singular imperfect of ἀνδάνω (with dative, οἱ being understood) = I am pleasing. Its subject is νύμφη. Hainsworth (*op. cit.*,p.269) notes that tears are not necessarily unheroic in Homer. In the Iliad, Antilochus weeps when announcing Patroclus' death (xviii, 17) and Achilles weeps (on the shore, alone) when Agamemnon humiliates him (i, 349). Odysseus is weeping with frustration. He has determined to return from the supernatural to the everyday world of heroes, and Calypso prevents him. Hence his change of mind about her.
⁴³νύκτας is accusative plural, from νύξ, night. Duration of time is expressed by the accusative; νύκτας means "for the nights"; ἤματα (line 156) means "for the days". μὲν ... δὲ ... "on the one hand ... on the other hand ..." μὲν in line 154 and δ' (δὲ) in 156 contrast the nights and the days.
⁴⁴ἰαύεσκεν is 3rd person singular of the imperfect of ἰαύω, I sleep, pass the night.
⁴⁵σπέσσι is dative plural of σπέος. Perhaps the plural is used simply for poetic style, or it may indicate several chambers inside the cave.
⁴⁶Translate in the order: (Ὀδυσσεὺς) ἰαύεσκεν οὐκ ἐθέλων παρα ἐθελούσῃ (νύμφῃ).
⁴⁷ἂμ (= ἄν') stands for ἀνά, "up", i.e., "on top of" (with dative). ν tends to become μ before β, μ, π or φ. ἂμ is taken with both πέτρῃσι and ἠιόνεσσι. ἠιών, ἠιόνος (3 fem.) = shore, beach.
⁴⁸Lines 157-8 are the same as 83-84 (see p.78, footnotes 40-43). Some manuscripts omit 157.

Beginning Greek with Homer

ἀγχοῦ δ' ἱσταμένη[49] προσεφώνεε δῖα θεάων·
'κάμμορε, μή μοι ἔτ' ἐνθάδ' ὀδύρεο,[50] μηδέ τοι αἰὼν   160
φθινέτω·[51] ἤδη γάρ σε μάλα πρόφρασσ[52] ἀποπέμψω.
ἀλλ' ἄγε δούρατα μακρὰ ταμὼν[53] ἁρμόζεο χαλκῷ
εὐρεῖαν σχεδίην· ἀτὰρ ἴκρια πῆξαι[54] ἐπ' αὐτῆς
ὑψοῦ, ὥς σε φέρῃσιν ἐπ' ἠεροειδέα πόντον.
αὐτὰρ ἐγὼ σῖτον καὶ ὕδωρ καὶ οἶνον ἐρυθρὸν   165
ἐνθήσω[55] μενοεικέ', ἅ κέν τοι λιμὸν[56] ἐρύκοι,
εἵματά τ' ἀμφιέσω· πέμψω δέ τοι οὖρον ὄπισθεν,
ὥς κε μάλ' ἀσκηθὴς σὴν πατρίδα γαῖαν ἵκηαι,[57]
αἴ κε[58] θεοί γ' ἐθέλωσι, τοὶ οὐρανὸν εὐρὺν ἔχουσιν,
οἵ μευ φέρτεροί[59] εἰσι νοῆσαί[60] τε κρῆναί τε.'   170

---

[49]ἱσταμένη: "standing", the feminine nominative singular of the participle of ἵσταμαι, the present middle of ἵστημι, I make (something or someone) to stand. It qualifies δῖα θεάων, the subject of προσεφώνεε, which is 3rd person singular of the imperfect active of προσφωνέω = I speak to.

[50]ἔτ' : ἔτι. When Calypso says μὴ ὀδύρεο, stop grieving, she may be punning on his name, 'Οδυσσεύς. At 339-340 Io, another goddess, may also be punning when she says Κάμμορε, τίπτε τοι ὧδε Ποσειδάων ὠδύσατο; "Unlucky man, why does Poseidon hate you so?" (ὀδύσσομαι: I hate) (C. Calame, *The Craft of Poetic Speech in Ancient Greece*, Cornell U.P., 1995, pp.177-8). However, 'Οδυσσεύς may be derived from neither ὀδύρομαι nor ὀδύσσομαι, but have a non-Greek origin (H. von Kamptz, *Homerische Personennamen*, Vandenhoeck & Ruprecht, Göttingen, 1982, p.156, cited by Calame).

[51]φθινέτω: 3rd sing. present imperative, φθίνω = I waste away. The subject is αἰών.

[52]ἤδη (here) = now. πρόφρασσ' stands for πρόφρασσα (feminine adjective) = kindly, gracious (an adjective where English prefers an adverb). For ἀποπέμψω, see p.81. Calypso does not mention orders from Zeus and may be trying to take the credit for herself, though Hainsworth, *op. cit.*, p.269, gives several instances where those who receive commands from gods directly, and not in dreams or omens, do not say so when they carry them out. But as Hainsworth says, Calypso does defy Zeus later when she begs Odysseus to stay. (If the poet is consistent Odysseus was not deceived: see Odyssey VII, 262-3).

[53]Nominative masculine singular participle, strong aorist of ἔταμον from τέμνω, I cut, qualifying "you" implied by the imperatives ἄγε and ἁρμόζεο (footnote 28).

[54]πῆξαι is 2nd singular imperative from ἐπηξάμην, aorist indicative middle of πήγνυμι, I fix. ὑψοῦ = aloft. φέρῃσι: 3rd person singular, present subjunctive active after ὡς. The subject is "it", meaning the raft.

[55]ἐνθήσω: "I shall put in" (1st singular future active of ἐντίθημι, I put in). (For τίθημι see section 15.) The object is σῖτον καὶ ὕδωρ καὶ οἶνον.

[56]λιμός (2m) = hunger.. ἅ κεν with ἐρύκοι (3rd person singular present optative of ἐρύκω = I keep at bay) expresses purpose. ἅ "(things) which" (neuter plural of the relative pronoun; p.50) refers collectively to the object of ἐνθήσω.

[57]ἵκηαι is 2nd person singular subjunctive of ἱκόμην, I arrived. ὥς κε ἵκηαι = so that you may arrive.

[58]αἴ is an alternative for εἰ, "if". εἴ κε or αἴ κε with the subjunctive means "if only", "provided that".

[59]φέρτερος -α -ον = stronger. For τοὶ see p.48.

[60]νοῆσαι is the infinitive of ἐνόησα, the aorist of νοέω, I perceive, think (especially of foreseeing the future). κρῆναι is the infinitive of ἔκρηνα, the aorist of κραίνω, I accomplish. "Stronger to perceive and to accomplish" means "stronger **at perceiving** (the future) and bringing it about". μευ (p.29): "than me" (see p. 31).

Section 15
Part A - Future and aorist infinitives

The future infinitive is formed like the present infinitive (see p.22) but on the future stem. Thus, as λύσω (I shall loosen) is the future of λύω, the future infinitives of λύω are λύσειν (or λυσέμεν or λυσέμεναι) "to be about to loosen", and the future infinitive of λύσομαι is λύσεσθαι, "to be about to get loosened" or "to loosen for oneself".

What is the first person singular, present indicative of the verbs (listed on p.81) from which the following future infinitives come?
1.ἀποπέμψειν 2.ἀναπλήσειν 3.νήξεσθαι 4.βουλευσέμεν 5.ὀνόσσεσθαι

The future infinitive of εἰμι (I am) is ἔσ(σ)εσθαι (to be about to be).

The aorist infinitive is not augmented.
The weak aorist infinitive active ends -αι. The infinitive of ἔλυσα, "I loosened", is λῦσαι ("to loose").
The weak aorist infinitive middle ends -ασθαι. The infinitive of ἐλυσάμην is λύσασθαι ("to loose for oneself, to be loosed").
The strong aorist infinitive active ends -έειν, -εῖν, -έμεν or -έμεναι. The infinitive of ἔλαβον is [λαβεῖν] or [λαβέμεν] ("to take"). The infinitive of ἦλθον is ἐλθεῖν *or* ἐλθέμεν *or* ἐλθέμεναι ("to come *or* to go").
The strong aorist infinitive middle ends -εσθαι. The infinitive of ἐλαβόμην is λάβεσθαι ("to take hold of").

What is the first person singular, aorist indicative and present indicative of the verbs from which the following aorist infinitives (already met in Odyssey V) come? 1.ἀποκτεῖναι (line 18). 2.ἰδέειν (line 41). 3.ἱκέσθαι (line 41). 4.τέλεσαι (line 89). 5.παρεξελθεῖν (line 104). 6.ἁλιῶσαι (line 104). 7.νοῆσαι (line 170). 8.κρῆναι (line 170).

The use of the future infinitive. The future infinitive is mainly used with verbs which express a belief, thought or saying relating to a future event, e.g. at Odyssey V, 135-6:
ἔφασκον θήσειν (αὐτὸν) ἀθάνατον καὶ ἀγήραον
I used to say (me) to be about to make (him) immortal and unageing
= I used to say that I would make him immortal and unageing.

Note that ἔλπομαι and ἔολπα (p.145) "I hope", and ἐλπωρή ἐστι ("there is hope") are sometimes followed by a future infinitive, e.g. οὐκέτι νῶϊ ἔλπομαι αὐτώ περ νοστήσεμεν ἐκ πολέμοιο (Iliad XVII, 238-9)
I am not at all any longer hopeful us two indeed to be about to return from the fighting ourselves
= I am not at all hopeful any longer that we ourselves will both indeed return from the fighting
(οὐκέτι: no longer νοστέω: I return πόλεμος, πολέμοιο (2 masculine): fighting, war)

and ἐλπωρή (ἐστί) τοι ἔπειτα κακῶν ὑπάλυξιν[1] ἔσεσθαι (Odyssey XXIII, 287)
there (is) hope, look, afterwards of evils an escape to be about to be
= look, afterwards there is hope that there will be an escape from (your) suffering
(ἔσεσθαι is future infinitive),

and sometimes with an aorist infinitive:
ἐλπωρή (ἐστι) τοι ἔπειτα φίλους τ' ἰδέειν καὶ ἱκέσθαι
οἶκον ἐϋκτίμενον καὶ σὴν ἐς πατρίδα γαῖαν (Odyssey VI, 314-5)
(there is) hope, look, (for you) then both to see (your) friends and reach
(your) house, good to dwell in, and your native land.
ἐϋκτίμενος = good to dwell in
Both ἰδέειν and ἱκέσθαι are aorist infinitives.

Sometimes a present infinitive is used after ἔλπομαι with future meaning:
οὐ νύ τι κέρδιον ἡμῖν
ἔλπομαι ἐκτελέεσθαι (Iliad vii, 352-3)
I do not hope now it to be completed at all more profitably for us (= I do not hope
now that it will be finished (i.e. will end) at all more profitably for us).
κέρδιον: more profitably ἐκτελέω: I complete (ἐκ + τελέω).[2]

The present and aorist infinitives. The present infinitive expresses,
depending on the context, the idea of an action viewed as relating to a
present or imperfect tense verb, but the aorist infinitive normally has
no connotation of time at all, and expresses the idea of the verb pure
and simple.[3]

Example of a present infinitive:
φησί τοι ἄνδρα παρεῖναι (Odyssey V, 105)
look, he affirms a man to be here (= look, he says that there is a man here (now)).

Example of an aorist infinitive:
παῖδ' ἀγαπητὸν ἀποκτεῖναι μεμάασιν (Odyssey V, 18)
they are planning to kill the beloved son.

---

[1]ὑπάλυξις (3f) = escape.
[2]When ἔλπομαι means "I expect", a present or aorist (or perfect) infinitive does not always imply something in the future: αὐτὰρ ἐπὴν ἡμέας ἔλπῃ ποτὶ δώματ' ἀφῖχθαι (Odyssey VI, 297) "but at such time as you expect us to have reached the palace" = "at such time as you expect that we have reached the palace". ἐπήν (with subjunctive): at such time as. ποτί = πρός. δώματ' stands for δώματα. ἀφῖχθαι is the perfect infinitive of ἀφικνέομαι.
[3]See Chantraine, *Grammaire Homérique* vol.ii, ch.XXII, esp. pp.305-6.

However, an aorist infinitive after a verb meaning "say" or "think" can refer to a past event, e.g.
τὸν δ' ἐς Δωδώνην φάτο βήμεναι (Odyssey XIX, 296)
He affirmed him to have gone to Dodona
= He said that he had gone to Dodona. (βήμεναι is the infinitive of ἔβην, p.83.)

Both present and aorist infinitives are found with verbs meaning "order":
τὸν νῦν σ' ἠνώγειν ἀποπεμπέμεν ὅττι τάχιστα (Odyssey V, 112)
whom now he ordered you to send away as quickly as possible (present infinitive)
αὔδα ὅ τι φρονέεις· τελέσαι δέ με θυμὸς ἄνωγεν(Odyssey V, 89)
Say whatever you are thinking; and my spirit bids me fulfil (it) (aorist infinitive).

The aorist infinitive is sometimes used instead of an imperative:
νύμφῃ ἐϋπλοκάμῳ εἰπεῖν νημερτέα βουλήν (Odyssey V, 30)
to the fair-tressed nymph tell (my) plan sure and true.

Part B - The verb τίθημι, I put

There are four common –μι verbs[4] which have reduplication (repetition) of the first syllable) in the present and imperfect:

present	imperfect	future	aorist
δίδωμι I give	ἐδίδουν I was giving	δώσω I shall give	ἔδωκα I gave
ἵημι I send	ἵειν I was sending	ἥσω I shall send	ἧκα I sent
ἵστημι I stand[5]	ἵστην I was standing	στήσω I shall stand	ἔστησα I stood
τίθημι I put	ἐτίθην I was putting	θήσω I shall put	ἔθηκα I put.

The present, imperfect, future and aorist active & middle of τίθημι are:

Present indicative active
[τίθημι = I put]
τίθησθα = you put
(singular)
τίθησι = he/she/it puts
or τιθεῖ
[τίθετον = you two put]
[τίθετον = those two put]

[τίθεμεν = we put]

[τίθετε = you put
(plural)]
τιθεῖσι = they put[6]

Present indicative middle/passive
[τίθεμαι = I put for myself, am put]
[τίθεσαι = you put for yourself,
are put]
[τίθεται = he/she/it puts for him/her/itself, is put]
[τίθεσθον = you two put for yourselves, are put]
[τίθεσθον = those two put for themselves, are put]
[τιθέμε(σ)θα = we put for ourselves, are put]
τίθεσθε = you put for yourselves, are put
τίθενται = they put for themselves, are put

---
[4]Also called "athematic verbs" (p.12). For the Homeric forms of δίδωμι, ἵημι and ἵστημι, see pp. 218-230.
[5]Transitive, i.e. with an object, e.g. "I stand the chair on the table".
[6]In Attic, τιθέασι(ν).

The imperfect active
[(ἐ)τίθην = I was putting]

[(ἐ)τίθεις = you (s) were putting]

(ἐ)τίθει = he/she/it was putting

[(ἐ)τίθετον = you two were putting]

[(ἐ)τιθέτην = those two were putting]

[(ἐ)τίθεμεν = we were putting]

[(ἐ)τίθετε = you (pl) were putting]

(ἐ)τιθέσαν = they were putting

The imperfect middle/passive
[(ἐ)τιθέμην = I was putting for myself, was being put]

[(ἐ)τίθεσο = you were putting for yourself, were being put]

[(ἐ)τίθετο = he/she/it was putting for him/her/itself, was being put]

[(ἐ)τίθεσθον = you two were putting for yourselves, were being put]

[(ἐ)τιθέσθην = those two were putting for themselves, were being put]

(ἐ)τιθέμε(σ)θα = we were putting for ourselves, were being put

[(ἐ)τίθεσθε = you were putting for yourselves, were being put]

(ἐ)τίθεντο = they were putting for themselves, were being put

The future indicative active
θήσω = I shall put

θήσεις = you (s) will put

θήσει = he/she/it will put

[θήσετον = you two will put]

[θήσετον = those two will put]

θήσομεν = we shall put

θήσετε = you (pl) will put

θήσουσι(ν) = they will put

The future indicative middle
θήσομαι = I shall put for myself

θήσεαι = you will put for yourself

θήσεται = he/she/it will put for him/her/itself

[θήσεσθον = you two will put for yourselves]

[θήσεσθον = those two will put for themselves]

θησόμεθα = we shall put for ourselves

[θήσεσθε = you will put for yourselves]

θήσονται = they will put for themselves

Section 15

The aorist indicative active
(ἔ)θηκα = I put
(ἔ)θηκας = you (singular) put
(ἔ)θηκε = he/she/it put
[(ἔ)θετον = you two put]
[(ἐ)θέτην = those two put]
(ἔ)θεμεν = we put
[(ἔ)θετε = you (plural) put]
(ἔ)θεσαν = they put
or (ἐ)θῆκαν

The aorist indicative middle
[(ἐ)θέμην = I put for myself]
(ἔ)θεο = you (singular) put for yourself
(ἔ)θετο = he/she/it put for him/her/itself
[(ἔ)θεσθον = you two put for yourselves]
(ἐ)θέσθην = those two put for themselves
(ἐ)θέμεθα = we put for ourselves
(ἔ)θεσθε = you (plural) put for yourselves
(ἔ)θεντο = they put for themselves.

Notice the change from the singular active to the dual and plural active and to the middle. Similar changes are found in the aorist of δίδωμι, ἵημι and ἵστημι.

The infinitives are as follows:
Present active
τιθήμεναι[7] = to put

Present middle
[τίθεσθαι = to put for oneself]

Future active
θήσειν = to be about to put
or θησέμεναι

Future middle
θήσεσθαι = to be about to put for oneself

Aorist active
θεῖναι or θέμεναι or θέμεν
= to put

Aorist middle
θέσθαι = to put for oneself

The present subjunctive and optative of τίθημι are not found in Homer.

The aorist subjunctive active is: θείω (let me put), θήῃς, θήῃ or θήῃσι(ν), θέωμεν or θείομεν (the 2nd & 3rd persons plural and the dual are not found).

The aorist subjunctive middle is: θείομαι (let me put for myself)
(the other persons are not found)

[7]The Attic form is τίθεναι.

The aorist optative active is: θείην (O that I might put), θείης, θείη, θεῖμεν, θεῖτε, θεῖεν (dual not found).

The aorist optative middle is only found in the 1st person singular, θείμην (O that I might put for myself) and the 3rd person singular, θεῖτο.

The participles of τίθημι

masculine	feminine	neuter
Present active		
τιθείς[8]	[τιθεῖσα]	[τιθέν]
(a) putting (man)	(a) putting (woman)	(a) putting (thing)
Present middle		
τιθήμενος[9]	[τιθεμένη]	[τιθέμενον]
putting for himself	putting for herself	putting for itself
Aorist active		
θείς	θεῖσα	[θέν]
having put	having put	having put
Aorist middle		
θέμενος	θεμένη	[θέμενον]
having put for himself	having put for herself	having put for itself

The imperatives of τίθημι

Present active   middle
τίθει = put! (singular)   [τίθεσο = put for yourself!]
[τιθέτω = let him/her/it put!]   [τιθέσθω = let him/her/it put for him/her/itself!]
[τίθετον = may you both put!]   [τίθεσθον = may you both put for yourselves!]
[τιθέτων = may they both put!]   [τιθέσθων = may they both put for themselves!]
[τίθετε = put! (plural)]   τίθεσθε = put for yourselves!
[τιθέντων = let them put!]   [τιθέσθων = let them put for themselves!]

---

[8]The full pattern of endings (p.220) is like λύσας, λύσασα, λύσαν (p.73). However, only the masculine nominative singular (τίθεις) and the masculine nominative plural (τιθέντες) are found in Homer. For the full pattern of the aorist active participle θείς, see p.223.
[9]Only found as masculine accusative singular at Iliad X, 34, where the metre requires η for ε.

Section 15

Aorist active
θές = put! (singular)
[θέτω = let him/her/it put!]
[θέτον = may you both put!]
[θέτων = may they both put!]
θέτε = put! (plural)
θέντων = let them put!

middle
θέο or θεῦ = put for yourself(singular)!
θέσθω = let him/her/it put for him/her/itself
[θέσθον = may you both put for yourselves!]
[θέσθων = may they both put for themselves!]
θέσθε = put for yourselves! (plural)
[θέσθων = let them put for themselves!]

New words:
ἀεκήτι = against the will
βαίνω = I go, I step
βουλεύω = I plan, devise, advise
ἐΐση = well-balanced, equal[11]
ἡγέομαι = I lead (the way)
καθέζομαι = I sit down
λαῖτμα, -ατος (3n) = gulf
μήδομαι = I contrive
οἷος, οἵα οἷον = of which kind, such as
ὀνομάζω = I call by name
πέλω (also πέλομαι) = I am, I become
στῆθος (3n) = breast, chest (in plural, heart, seat of feelings)
χρειώ (3f) = want, need, necessity[13]

ἀργαλέος -α -ον = troublesome, difficult to deal with.[10]
ἐδωδή (1f) = food, victuals
ἔνθεν = from there, from where
ἵζω = I sit (down)[12]
καρπαλίμως = swiftly
μέγας μεγάλη μέγα = big, great
νοέω = I think, intend, perceive
ὅρκος (2m) = oath
ῥα, ῥ' = ἄρα

What is the Greek for: 1.τίθησιν. 2.τιθεῖσιν. 3.ἔθεσαν. 4.ἔθηκαν.
5.τίθεσαν. 6.ἔθεο. 7.θέμεναι. 8.θέντες. 9.θεῦ.
10.Καλυψὼ παρὰ 'Οδυσσῆι ἐτίθει πᾶσαν ἐδωδήν ἔσθειν καὶ πίνειν.
11.παρὰ δὲ νύμφη ἀμβροσίην δμωαὶ καὶ νέκταρ ἔθηκαν.[14]
12.σύ με κέλεαι σχεδίηι περάαν[15] μέγα λαῖτμα θαλάσσης;

[10]Often with δεινός. Of things, e.g. winds, "troublesome"; of tasks, "difficult".
[11]Feminine adjective only in Homer where it is an epithet for ships and also feasts (where every participant brought an equal share) and horses (Liddell & Scott). The masculine is ἶσος and the neuter ἶσον.
[12]Also means "I seat" i.e. "I cause to sit".
[13]Sometimes neuter. Genitive, χρειοῦς (not found in Homer), and dative χρειοῖ.
[14]For ἀμβροσίη and νέκταρ, see p.79. δμωαί are properly female slaves taken in war (Liddell & Scott) but here merely "maidservants". No doubt captive princesses made good parlour maids. "all" here means "all kinds of".
[15]Present infinitive active of περάω, I cross (contracted from περάειν). μέγα is neuter singular accusative; see Section 23.

13.κελεύω σε, θεά, μέγαν ὅρκον ὁμόσσαι.[16]
14.ὁμόσσαι ἐθέλεις μή τί μοι αὐτῷ[17] πῆμα κακὸν βουλεύσεμεν ἄλλο;
15.οἷον μῦθον ἐπεφράσθης[18] ἀγορεῦσαι,[19] 'Οδυσσεῦ!

Odyssey V, 171-200

ὣς φάτο,[20] ρίγησεν δὲ πολύτλας δῖος 'Οδυσσεύς,
καί μιν φωνήσας ἔπεα πτερόεντα προσηύδα·
"ἄλλο τι δὴ σύ, θεά, τόδε μήδεαι οὐδέ τι[21] πομπήν,
ἤ με κέλεαι σχεδίῃ περάαν[22] μέγα λαῖτμα θαλάσσης,
δεινόν τ' ἀργαλέον τε· τὸ δ' οὐδ' ἐπὶ[23] νῆες ἐῖσαι   175
ὠκύποροι[24] περόωσιν, ἀγαλλόμεναι Διὸς οὔρῳ.
οὐδ' ἂν ἐγώ γ' ἀέκητι σέθεν[25] σχεδίης ἐπιβαίην,[26]
εἰ μή μοι τλαίης[27] γε, θεά, μέγαν ὅρκον ὁμόσσαι
μή τί μοι αὐτῷ πῆμα κακὸν βουλευσέμεν ἄλλο."
  ὣς φάτο, μείδησεν[28] δὲ Καλυψώ, δῖα θεάων,

[16]NB ὁμόσσα is the aorist active of ὄμνυμι. For the aorist infinitive ending (ὁμόσσαι), see p.103.
[17]μοι is enclitic. μοι αὐτῷ "against (literally, 'to') me myself". After ὁμόσσαι, μή + infinitive, "swear not to ..." For a future infinitive after a verb implying saying, see p.103. μή is the negative with the infinitive: "not to be about to plan", i.e., "that you will not plan..."(NB τι and μοι are enclitic.) πῆμα κακὸν is the object of βουλεύσεμεν.
[18]ἐπεφράσθης is 2nd person singular aorist indicative passive (Section 18) of ἐπιφράζω (meaning"I tell") "you took it into your head". Literally it would mean "you suggested to yourself"; the aorist passive is sometimes used instead of the middle (Chantraine, op. cit.,vol.i, p.406).
[19]ἀγορεύω = I say. ἀγορεῦσαι is aorist infinitive.
[20]For φάτο (also at line 180), see p.34, footnote 7. Calypso is the subject of φάτο. Lines 171-2 are the same as 116-7 except that πολύτλας δῖος 'Οδυσσεύς is the subject of ρίγησεν and προσηύδα instead of Καλυψώ, δῖα θεάων and φωνήσασ ' (feminine) has become φωνήσας (masculine).
[21]μήδεαι is 2nd. person singular, present indicative of μήδομαι, as κέλεαι is of κέλομαι. οὐδέ τι "and not in respect of anything" (accusative of respect), i.e. "and not at all". ἤ refers back to σύ, "you, who..."
[22]For περάαν, see footnote 15. περόωσιν (line 176) is 3rd person plural present indicative active: (they) cross (see p.201). μέγα (neuter singular) qualifies λαῖτμα.
[23]Translate ἐπὶ before τὸ. τὸ is demonstrative ("that") (p.49). τὸ δ' οὐδ' ἐπὶ: and over that, not even ...
[24]ὠκύπορος, ὠκύπορον (fem. as masc.) = swift-going. ἀγάλλομαι + dative = I glory in. ἀγαλλόμεναι qualifies νῆες ἐῖσαι ὠκύποροι, the subject of περόωσιν.
[25]See p.29.
[26]1st person singular aorist optative active of ἐπιβαίνω.
[27]εἰ μή = if .. not ... τλαίης is 2nd person singular of τλαίην, the optative of the aorist ἔτλην meaning "I had the heart" (the present, if found, would be τλάω). εἰ μὴ τλαίης means "if you would not have the heart".
[28]μείδησεν is 3rd person singular of (ἐ)μείδησα, aorist indicative of μειδάω = I smile.

Section 15

χειρί τέ μιν κατέρεξεν[29] ἔπος τ' ἔφατ' ἔκ τ' ὀνόμαζεν·
"ἦ δὴ ἀλιτρός[30] γ' ἐσσὶ καὶ οὐκ ἀποφώλια[31] εἰδώς,[32]
οἷον δὴ τὸν[33] μῦθον ἐπεφράσθης ἀγορεῦσαι.
ἴστω[34] νῦν τόδε γαῖα καὶ οὐρανὸς εὐρὺς ὕπερθε[35]
καὶ τὸ κατειβόμενον[36] Στυγὸς[37] ὕδωρ, ὅς τε μέγιστος[38]   185
ὅρκος δεινότατός τε πέλει μακάρεσσι θεοῖσι,
μή τί τοι αὐτῷ πῆμα κακὸν βουλευσέμεν ἄλλο.

[29] κατέρεξεν is 3rd person singular, aorist indicative of καταρρέζω = I caress. ἔπος τ' ἔφατ' ἔκ τ' ὀνόμαζεν ("both spoke a word and called out by name") is a very common formula, occurring 26 times in the Odyssey and 12 times in the Iliad (see Garvie on Odyssey VI, 254). Line 181, of which it is part, χειρί τέ μιν κατέρεξεν ἔπος τ' ἔφατ' ἐκ τ' ὀνόμαζεν is itself a powerful formula for describing a persuasive gesture; it occurs twice in the Odyssey and 4 times in the Iliad. At Odyssey IV 610, Menelaus is soothing Telemachus; at Iliad v, 372, Dione consoles her wounded daughter Aphrodite in this way; at Iliad vi, 485, it describes Hector's reassuring gesture when he leaves his wife to return to battle; most significantly, Thetis caresses Achilles in this way at Iliad i, 361, when she rises from the waves to comfort him after his humiliation by Agamemnon and again at Iliad xxiv, 127, when the gods send her to make him release the body of Hector. Here, the line reminds the audience of the nobility of Odysseus; its use recalls Achilles and Hector at crucial moments in the Iliad.
[30] ἦ δὴ = ἦ τοι. ἀλιτρός = rogue. Hainsworth (*A Commentary on Homer's Odyssey* vol.i, p.271) compares ἀλιταίνω, I sin.
[31] ἀποφώλια (neuter plural) = things that are idle, in vain. ἀποφώλιος is not in the Iliad. At Odyssey VIII, 177, Odysseus uses it in an insult: νόον δ' ἀποφώλιός ἐσσι ("you are stupid and ignorant", "ἀποφώλιος with respect to your mind"). At XI, 249, it means "fruitless" (οὐκ ἀποφώλιοι εὐναὶ ἀθανάτων = beds of the immortals are not fruitless, i.e. intercourse with a god always results in pregnancy). At XIV, 212 it means "cowardly" - οὐκ ἀποφώλιος ἦα οὐδὲ φυγοπτόλεμος = "I was not cowardly nor a runner-away from war". The derivation is uncertain; the scholia explain the word as = ἀπαίδευτος (uneducated), and ancient lexicographers as = ἀνεμώλιος, "empty as the wind", or as μάταιος "in vain", or from ἀποφεῖν an obscure word which perhaps means "to cheat" (see Hainsworth's note, *op. cit.* p.271).
[32] εἰδώς, εἰδυῖα, εἰδός = "knowing" (the participle of οἶδα = I know) (Section 22).
[33] τὸν "that" (demonstrative adjective qualifying μῦθον, the object of ἀγορεῦσαι).
[34] 3rd person singular imperative from οἶδα, I know. "let (it) know" is a formula used in oaths. "it" refers to the nominatives following, γαῖα καὶ οὐρανὸς εὐρὺς καὶ τὸ καρειβόμενον Στυγὸς ὕδωρ. τόδε is the object of ἴστω.
[35] ὕπερθε = above.
[36] κατειβόμενος -η -ον = flowing down (see κατείβομαι, p. 100, footnote 26).
[37] ἡ Στύξ, τῆς Στυγός, the River Styx, separates the underworld from this one. The name is connected with στυγέω, I hate, and means "Hateful". There is a cold spring, in Classical times called "Styx", trickling down a cliff near Nonacris in the Peloponnese (Herodotus, *Histories* vi, 74 and Pausanias, *Description of Greece* VIII, xvii, 6). A god who broke an oath by the river Styx suffered a year's trance and nine years' banishment from the Olympian Council (Hesiod, *Theogony* 793 ff) (Stanford).
[38] For ὅς τε, see p.51. μέγιστος -η -ον = greatest. δεινότατος = most terrible (see Section 25). τοι αὐτῷ: against you yourself (cf. μοι αὐτῷ, footnote 17). "not to be about to plan ..." means "that I shall not plan ..." τι, κακὸν and ἄλλο all qualify πῆμα, the object of βουλευσέμεν.

ἀλλὰ τὰ μὲν νοέω καὶ φράσσομαι,³⁹ ἄσσ' ἂν ἐμοί περ
αὐτῇ μηδοίμην, ὅτε με χρειὼ τόσον ἵκοι·
καὶ γὰρ ἐμοὶ νόος ἐστὶν ἐναίσιμος,⁴⁰ οὐδέ μοι αὐτῇ   190
θυμὸς ἐνὶ στήθεσσι σιδήρεος,⁴¹ ἀλλ' ἐλεήμων."⁴²
   ὣς ἄρα φωνήσασ'⁴³ ἡγήσατο δῖα θεάων
καρπαλίμως· ὁ δ' ἔπειτα μετ' ἴχνια⁴⁴ βαῖνε θεοῖο.
ἷξον⁴⁵ δὲ σπεῖος γλαφυρὸν θεὸς ἠδὲ καὶ ἀνήρ·
καί ῥ' ὁ μὲν ἔνθα καθέζετ' ἐπὶ θρόνου, ἔνθεν ἀνέστη⁴⁶   195
Ἑρμείας, νύμφη δ' ἐτίθει πάρα⁴⁷ πᾶσαν ἐδωδήν,
ἔσθειν καὶ πίνειν, οἷα βροτοὶ ἄνδρες ἔδουσιν·⁴⁸
αὐτὴ δ' ἀντίον⁴⁹ ἷζεν Ὀδυσσῆος θείοιο,
τῇ δὲ παρ' ἀμβροσίην δμῳαὶ καὶ νέκταρ ἔθηκαν.
οἱ δ' ἐπ' ὀνείαθ'⁵⁰ ἑτοῖμα προκείμενα χεῖρας ἴαλλον.   200

---

³⁹τὰ is demonstrative: "those things", (p.49), the object of νοέω and φράσσομαι. φράσσομαι is the future middle of φράζω, I show, point out. It means "I shall show, point out to myself" i.e. "I shall think of". τὰ νοέω καὶ φράσσομαι ("I am planning and shall think of those things") ἄσσ' ἂν ἐμοί περ αὐτῇ μηδοίμην ("whatever in such a case for myself very much I would contrive") ὅτε με χρειὼ τόσον ἵκοι ("at such time as me so great a need might reach"). ἄσσ' ἂν (= ἄσσα ἂν) = "whatever things, in that case" (for ἄσσα, see p.51, footnote 7). ὅτε: "at such time as". τόσον ("so great") is neuter, qualifying χρειώ (p.109, footnote 13). ἵκω = I come to, reach. ἵκοι (3rd person singular, present optative) expresses remote possibility.
⁴⁰καὶ immediately before γὰρ usually means "indeed". ἐναίσιμος –ον (fem. as masc.) = righteous. It is derived from αἶσα, ("fate") and also means "of good omen". ἐμοὶ νόος ἐστι = ἔχω νόον.
⁴¹σιδήρεος –η –ον = made of iron. Understand ἐστι (οὐδέ μοι αὐτῇ ἐστι θυμός...= οὐδ' ἔχω θυμόν).
⁴²ἐλεήμων –ον = merciful.
⁴³φωνήσασ' stands for φωνήσασα and qualifies δῖα θεάων, the subject of ἡγήσατο (3rd person singular, aorist indicative of ἡγέομαι). ὣς ἄρα φωνήσασα is formulaic (see lines 351 and 380).
⁴⁴ἴχνιον (2n) = footprint (plural, "track"). μετ' stands for μετά (here, with accusative). "To step after the tracks of" is to follow. θεοῖο (genitive) is feminine. βαῖνε is 3rd person singular imperfect of βαίνω (its subject is ὁ, "he").
⁴⁵ἷξον (subject θεὸς ἠδὲ καὶ ἀνήρ) is 3rd person plural aorist indicative of ἵκω and means "(they) reached". σπεῖος is a variant of σπέος. ἠδὲ καί: both ... and ...
⁴⁶ῥ' stands for ῥα. καθέζετ' stands for καθέζετο, 3rd person singular imperfect of καθέζομαι (the subject is ὁ). ἀνέστη = "had stood up" (ἀνά, "up" + ἔστη, 3rd person singular (strong, irregular) aorist indicative of ἀνίστημι, meaning"I stood"). Ἑρμείας is the subject of ἀνέστη.
⁴⁷πάρα is used as an adverb here, "beside" (him).
⁴⁸ἔδω = I eat (an old form of ἐσθίω). cf. ἐδωδή.
⁴⁹ἀντίον = opposite (adverb), here used like a preposition with genitive. Ὀδυσσῆος θείοιο: facing godlike Odysseus. Translate τῇ παρ' in the order παρὰ τῇ.
⁵⁰οἱ ("they") covers both masculine and feminine, standing for Calypso and Odysseus, the subject of ἴαλλον (3rd person plural imperfect of ἰάλλω = I send forth). χεῖρας is the object. ὀνείατα (3 n. plu.) = food, victuals (the singular, ὄνειαρ, is "something advantageous") qualified by ἑτοῖμα, neuter plural of ἑτοῖμος –η –ον = ready and προκείμενα, neuter plural of προκείμενος –η –ον = laid in front (of them). This line is formulaic, used 11 times in the Odyssey and three times in the Iliad to describe the beginning of a meal, including the solemn occasion (xxiv, 627) when Achilles and Priam dine together.

Section 16
Part A - The verb εἶμι (I go)

In the first person singular of the present indicative, εἶμι (I go)[1] is only distinguishable from εἰμί (I am) by the circumflex accent, but the endings of the other persons are different:-

present
εἶμι = I go
εἶσθα = you go
(singular)
εἶσι = he/she/it goes

[ἴτον = you two go]
[ἴτον = the two of them go]
ἴμεν = we go
[ἴτε = you go (plural)]
ἴασι = they go

imperfect
ἤϊα or ἤϊον = I was going
[ἤεισθα = you were going
(singular)]
ἤϊε or ἤει = he/she/it was going
 or ἤε(ν) or ἴε(ν)
[ἴτον = you two were going]
ἴτην = the two of them were going
ἤομεν = we were going
[ἤτε = you were going]
ἴσαν or ἤσαν = they were going
 or ἤϊον

The infinitive: ἰέναι or ἴμεν or ἴμεναι = to go

The participle: ἰών (masculine), ἰοῦσα (feminine), ἰόν (neuter)[2]
                    (going)
The imperative: ἴθι = go! (singular)   ἴτω = let him/her/it go!
                    ἴτε = go! (plural)   [ἰόντων = let them go!]
The subjunctive:
     ἴω = let me go   ἴομεν = let us go
     ἴῃς or ἴῃσθα = may you go   [ἴητε = may you go]
     ἴῃ or ἴῃσι(ν) = let him/her/it go   ἴωσι = let them go
                (the dual is not found in Homer).

---

[1] See p.81, footnote 4. In Attic Greek, εἶμι often has a future meaning "I shall go", but it is usually present in Homer (Liddell & Scott) and is classified as present in Chantraine (*Grammaire Homérique* vol.i, p.284). Liddell & Scott cite two passages where it is future: Iliad i, 426 καὶ τότ' ἔπειτά τοι εἶμι ποτὶ Διὸς χαλκοβατὲς δῶ (and then, look, I shall go to Zeus' bronze-floored hall) and xviii 280, ἄψ πάλιν εἶσ' ἐπὶ νῆας (he will go back again to the ships).
[2] The case endings are like those of λύων, λύουσα, λύον (pp.71-2).

Of the optative, only the 3rd person singular is found,
ἰείη or ἴοι = (O that) he, (she), it might go!

N.B. βῆ ῥ' ἴμεν (from (ἔβη, 3rd person singular aorist of βαίνω, I go, step) ἄρα (then and there) and ἴμεν or ἴμεναι (to go) is a formula meaning "he/she set out then and there". Similarly, βῆ δ' ἴμεναι means "and/but he/she set out (to go)".

  e.g. βῆ ῥ' ἴμεν εἰς ὕλην (Odyssey V, 475)
      he set off then and there into the wood
      βῆ δ' ἴμεναι πρὸς δῶμα (Odyssey II, 298)
      and he set off for his house.

Part B - Personal possessive adjectives

masculine	feminine	neuter	
ἐμός	ἐμή	ἐμόν	= my, mine
σός	σή	σόν	= your (when "you" is singular)
ἡμέτερος	ἡμετέρη	ἡμέτερον	= our
ὑμέτερος	ὑμετέρη	ὑμέτερον	= your (when "you" is plural)

The feminine is first declension, and the masculine and neuter second.

New words:
αἶσα (1f) = lot, destiny³   ἀναπίμπλημι = I accomplish⁴
ἄρχω, also ἄρχομαι = I begin (+ genitive), lead the way
διογενής = sprung from Zeus⁵   ἔδυν = I sank⁶
εἶδος (3n) = appearance⁷

---
³Also found at lines 40 (p.59, footnote 70) and 114 (p.85, footnote 41).
⁴ἀνέπλησα, 1st person singular, aorist indicative active, I accomplished; ἀναπλῆσαι, aorist infinitive active, to accomplish, from ἀναπίμπλημι = I fill up, accomplish. κήδεα ἀναπίμπλημι: I fill up the full measure of my woes.
⁵διογένης (3rd declension adjective), also (of kings) = "upheld and ordained by Zeus", διογενές is vocative singular.
⁶Strong aorist active of δύω, I sink, go down. Found in the following persons: ἔδυ (he, she, it sank), ἐδύτην (dual) (they both sank), ἔδυτε (plural, you sank), ἔδυν or ἔδυσαν (they sank). The 3rd person singular aorist indicative middle, (he, she, it sank) is always (ἐ)δύσετο, not (ἐ)δύσατο as we should expect.
⁷cf. εἶδον, the strong aorist of ὁράω, I see.

Section 16   115

εὔχομαι = I claim to be, promise to do, vow to do[8]
ἔμπης = all the same   ἤδη = already
ἠέλιος (2m) = the sun   μέγεθος (3n) = size, tallness
μένω = I remain, wait (for) (with accusative), withstand
νόστιμον (ἦμαρ) = day of homecoming
οἶδα = I know[9]
ὅσ(σ)οι ὅσ(σ)αι ὅσ(σ)α : as many as, how many
οὕτω = so, thus, in this way   πότν(ι)α (fem. adj.) = lady,
                                                             mistress[10]
πρίν = before,[11] formerly   σύν + dative = with
τλήσομαι = I shall endure[12]   φυή (1f) = stature[13]
φυλάσσω = I stay in, keep in, watch over, guard
χώομαι = I am angry

What is the English for:
1.ἴμεν; 2.οὐκ εἶσθα. 3.Ζεὺς πατὴρ θεῶν Οὔλυμπόνδε[14] εἶσι. (cf.
Odyssey VI, 42, p.20) 4.θεοὶ ἀθάνατοί εἰσι. 5.σοὶ ἑταῖροι οὐ δύνανται
οἰκάδε ἰέναι. 6.ναῦν ἡμετέρην οἴκαδε ἰοῦσαν ὁράομεν.
7.τέκνα ὑμέτερα οἴκαδε ἰόντα εἶδον ἐγώ.
8. ἴθι, ταῦτα νύμφῃ εὐπλοκάμῳ εἰπεῖν. (See p.105).
9. ἐς πατρίδα γαῖαν αὐτίκα νῦν ἐθέλει ἰέναι πολύμητις[15] Ὀδυσσεύς.
10.πότνια νύμφη ἐπὶ μεγαλήτορα 'Οδυσσῆα ἤιε. (See lines 149-150.)
11.βῆ δ' ἴμεναι Καλυψώ, δῖα θεάων, πρὸς μυχὸν[16] σπείους γλαφυροῖο.
12.πότνα θεά, μή μοι τόδε[17] χώεο· εἶμι γὰρ οἴκαδε ἔμπης.

---
[8]See also A.W.H. Adkins, Εὔχομαι, εὐχωλή and εὖχος in Homer, *Classical Quarterly* vol.xix (1969) pp.20-33, cited with J.-L. Perpillou, La Signification du verbe εὔχομαι dans l' épopée, *Mélanges Chantraine*, Paris (1972) pp.170-82 by Hainsworth, *A Commentary on Homer's Odyssey* vol.i, p.272) and Jean M. Aitchison's comments on εὔχομαι in *Journal of Hellenic Studies* vol.lxxxix (1969), p.124. εὔχομαι also means "I pray" (p.90, footnote 18).
[9]οἶδα, found in the perfect tense, is connected with εἶδον, I saw, and originally meant "I have come to see", i.e., "I have got into the state of having seen", "it has dawned on me": hence, "I know". (See Section 21.)
[10]Also at line 149 above (see p.101, footnote 34). πότνα is always vocative.
[11]With infinitive (see Section 17, pp.121-2). πρὶν ἱκέσθαι: before reaching.
[12]See p.81.
[13]Connected with φύω, I grow. In Homer, always φυήν (accusative); very often, as at Odyssey V, 212 and VI, 16 and 152, "in respect of stature".
[14]Towards Olympus.
[15]πολύμητις = of many counsels, i.e. very wise.
[16]μυχός (2m) = corner.
[17]τόδε is accusative: "in respect of this". The accusative case can be used to show the part or aspect which is affected e.g., in this sentence, by "angry".

116   Beginning Greek with Homer

13.πολυμήχαν᾽ ᾽Οδυσσεῦ,[18] αὐτίκα ἴομεν· ὡς γὰρ ἐθέλω καὶ
ἐέλδομαι[19] ἤματα πάντα οἰκάδε τ᾽ ἐλθέμεναι καὶ νόστιμον ἦμαρ
ἰδέσθαι.
14.ἐμῇσι φρέσι οἶδα ὅσσα πήματά με μένει.

Odyssey V, 201-227
αὐτὰρ ἐπεὶ τάρπησαν[20] ἐδητύος ἠδὲ ποτῆτος,
τοῖσ'[21] ἄρα μύθων ἦρχε Καλυψώ, δῖα θεάων·
᾽διογενὲς Λαερτιάδη[22], πολυμήχαν᾽ ᾽Οδυσσεῦ,
οὕτω δὴ οἶκόνδε[23] φίλην ἐς πατρίδα γαῖαν
αὐτίκα νῦν ἐθέλεις ἰέναι; σὺ δὲ χαῖρε[24] καὶ ἔμπης.[25]   205
εἴ γε μὲν εἰδείης[26] σῇσι φρεσίν, ὅσσα[27] τοι αἶσα
κήδε᾽ ἀναπλῆσαι, πρὶν πατρίδα γαῖαν ἱκέσθαι,
ἐνθάδε κ᾽ αὖθι[28] μένων σὺν ἐμοὶ τόδε δῶμα φυλάσσοις

[18]πολυμήχανος -ον = "of many contrivances", "resourceful", an epithet of Odysseus used also in the Iliad, e.g. at ii, 173, which is identical with Odyssey V, 203. πολυμήχαν᾽ stands for πολυμήχανε (vocative, as is ᾽Οδυσσεῦ).
[19]ἐέλδομαι = I long to (+ infinitive), I long for (+ genitive).
[20]3rd person plural aorist passive of τέρπω, "I delight", meaning "they were delighted, had had their fill of". ἐδητύς, ἐδητύος(f) = food (also at Odyssey VI, 250). ποτής, ποτῆτος (f) drink. 201 is adapted from a formula describing the end of a formal meal; cf. Iliad XI, 780: αὐτὰρ ἐπεὶ τάρπημεν ἐδητύος ἠδὲ ποτῆτος "but when we had been delighted with eating and drinking", i.e. eaten and drunk our fill. See also Odyssey III 67, 473 and IV 68, αὐτὰρ ἐπεὶ πόσιος καὶ ἐδήτυος ἐξ ἔρον ἔντο... ("but when they (had) sent away the desire of drink and of food..."). Odyssey IV 67-8 = V 200-1 and succinctly describe a meal.
[21]τοῖσ᾽ : τοῖσι ("to them"). The plural is inappropriate, but found here as the line starts with a formula used for the beginning of a speech from an important character; cf. Odyssey I, 28 (about Zeus): τοῖσι δὲ μύθων ἦρχε πατὴρ ἀνδρῶν τε θεῶν τε, and III 68, 417 and 474: τοῖσι δὲ μύθων ἦρχε Γερήνιος ἱππότα Νέστωρ, in all of which τοῖσι is appropriate. Odyssey V 201-2 are closely modelled on III 67-8 & 473-4. ἦρχε is 3rd person singular imperfect of ἄρχω.
[22]See p.41, footnote 21.
[23]=οἴκαδε (see p.5, footnote 10).
[24]The 2nd singular present imperative active of χαίρω, "rejoice!" It sometimes means "hello!" e.g. Aristophanes, Frogs, 184: χαῖρ᾽ ὦ Χάρων, χαῖρ᾽ ὦ Χάρων, χαῖρ᾽ ὦ Χάρων ("hello Charon, hello Charon, hello Charon"), and sometimes "good-bye". Here it means "good luck" with overtones of "farewell".
[25]καὶ ἔμπης: at any rate.
[26]2nd person singular optative of οἶδα (p.145). "If you should know..."
[27]ὅσσα qualifies κήδε᾽(standing for κήδεα), the object of ἀναπλῆσαι at the beginning of 207. Understand ἐστι with αἶσα, "(your) portion is to fill up the full measure of... ", "you are fated to fill up ..." πρὶν ἵκεσθαι: before reaching (see p.121).
[28]κ᾽ stands for κε ("in that case"). αὖθι means "here", "on this spot". μένων (nominative masculine singular of the present participle of μένω) qualifies "you", the subject of φυλάσσοις and εἴης (both 2nd person singular present optative). Both express an eventuality (see p.44).

Section 16

ἀθάνατός τ' εἴης, ἱμειρόμενός²⁹ περ ἰδέσθαι
σὴν ἄλοχον,³⁰ τῆς τ' αἰὲν ἐέλδεαι ἤματα πάντα.   210
οὐ μέν θην³¹ κείνης γε χερείων³² εὔχομαι εἶναι,
οὐ δέμας³³ οὐδὲ φυήν,³⁴ ἐπεὶ οὔ πως οὐδὲ ἔοικε³⁵
θνητὰς ἀθανάτῃσι δέμας καὶ εἶδος ἐρίζειν.
  τὴν δ' ἀπαμειβόμενος προσέφη³⁶ πολύμητις Ὀδυσσεύς·
"πότνα θεά, μή μοι τόδε χώεο· οἶδα καὶ αὐτὸς³⁷   215
πάντα³⁸ μάλ', οὕνεκα σεῖο περίφρων³⁹ Πηνελόπεια
εἶδος ἀκιδνοτέρη μέγεθός τ' εἰσάντα ἰδέσθαι·

---

²⁹ἱμειρόμενος is nominative masculine singular present participle (also qualifying "you") of ἱμείρομαι = I long for, desire; followed by an infinitive (ἰδέσθαι, infinitive middle from εἶδον, the aorist of ὁράω, meaning "to look at, behold"). The middle of ὁράω is often used by poets instead of the active. Translate in the order περ ἱμειρόμενος ἰδέσθαι. For περ with a participle, see p.76.

³⁰ἄλοχος (2, always feminine) bedfellow, wife (derived from λέχος). ἐέλδεαι is 2nd person singular, present indicative of ἐέλδομαι (with genitive, = I long for). τῆς: for whom (p.49), referring to σὴν ἄλοχον. ἤματα πάντα: all your days (see p.20).

³¹θην = in truth (ironical). θην is enclitic.

³²χερείων = worse (i.e. inferior to). κείνης: than that woman (for "than" expressed by the genitive, see p.31). εἶναι: is the infinitive of εἰμί (p.22).

³³δέμας (neuter - only found in nominative and accusative) = body. δέμας and φυήν are accusatives of respect showing the point at which χερείων applies. οὐ δέμας οὐδὲ φυήν: "not in body nor in stature".

³⁴Immortals were generally thought to be taller than mortals. Hainsworth notes (op. cit.) that at Odyssey VI 107-8 Artemis is said to be taller than the nymphs, showing greater beauty and status. How tall the Greeks thought a goddess was is illustrated by a story in Herodotus, (Histories I, 60): the tyrant Peisistratus, exiled from Athens, returned in a chariot escorted by a woman called Φύη disguised as the goddess Athene in full armour. Herodotus says that she was three finger-breadths less than four cubits tall, 5 feet 10 inches.

³⁵οὔ πως οὐδὲ - "not in any way at all". In Homer, double negatives generally reinforce each other (Chantraine, Grammaire Homérique vol.ii, p.337). ἔοικε: it is likely. "It" is the clause (accusative and infinitive) θνητὰς ἐρίζειν. θνηταί: mortal (feminine plural). ἐρίζω + dative = "I compete with" (connected with ἔρις (3f) = strife). "nor is it likely mortal females to compete with immortal" = "it is not likely that mortal women would compete with goddesses ..." δέμας and εἶδος are accusative of respect: in body or in appearance.

³⁶See p.57, footnote 25. For πολύμητις, see footnote 15.

³⁷αὐτὸς qualifies "I", the subject of οἶδα. "I myself also know..."

³⁸πάντα (accusative) = in all respects. οὕνεκα = why. Understand ἐστι after περίφρων Πηνελόπεια and translate in the order: οἶδα οὕνεκα περίφρων Πηνελόπεια ἐστι ἀκιδνοτέρη σεῖο εἶδος μέγεθός τε ἰδέσθαι εἰσάντα. ἀκιδνότερος –η –ον = weaker, feebler. σεῖο: "than you" (p.31). εἶδος τε μέγεθός τε: accusative of respect. For ἰδέσθαι, see footnote 29. εἰσάντα = right opposite, in the face.

³⁹περίφρων, in Homer a feminine adjective, often an epithet of Penelope, "very thoughtful" or "careful"; also of the wife of Diomede (Iliad v, 412), of Arete, Alcinous' wife, (Odyssey XI, 345) and of Eurycleia, the housekeeper (XIX 357).

ἡ μὲν γὰρ βροτός ἐστι, σὺ δ' ἀθάνατος καὶ ἀγήρως.⁴⁰
ἀλλὰ καὶ ὣς ἐθέλω καὶ ἐέλδομαι ἤματα πάντα
οἴκαδέ τ' ἐλθέμεναι⁴¹ καὶ νόστιμον ἦμαρ ἰδέσθαι.   220
εἰ δ' αὖ τις ῥαίῃσι⁴² θεῶν ἐνὶ οἴνοπι πόντῳ,
τλήσομαι ἐν στήθεσσιν ἔχων⁴³ ταλαπενθέα θυμόν·
ἤδη γὰρ μάλα πολλὰ πάθον καὶ πολλὰ μόγησα⁴⁴
κύμασι καὶ πολέμῳ· μετὰ καὶ τόδε τοῖσι⁴⁵ γενέσθω."
ὣς ἔφατ', ἠέλιος δ' ἄρ' ἔδυ καὶ ἐπὶ κνέφας⁴⁶ ἦλθεν·   225
ἐλθόντες δ' ἄρα τώ γε μυχῷ σπείους γλαφυροῖο
τερπέσθην⁴⁷ φιλότητι,⁴⁸ παρ' ἀλλήλοισι μένοντες.

---

⁴⁰βροτός is feminine, here and line 334 where it describes Ino.   ἀγήρως = exempt from ageing (ἀθάνατος καὶ ἀγήρως occurs also in line 136;   see p.92, footnote 40 and p.93).   Understand ἐσσί after σύ.
⁴¹ἐλθέμεναι is the infinitive of ἦλθον, the strong aorist of ἔρχομαι (p.103).
⁴²Translate in the order: εἴ τις θεῶν ῥαίῃσι. ῥαίῃσι is 3rd person singular present subjunctive of ῥαίω = "I shatter" It expresses a possibility: "were to shatter (my ship)".
⁴³ἔχων, nominative singular masculine of the present participle of ἔχω here = "I keep", qualifies "I", the subject of τλήσομαι. ταλαπενθέα is accusative singular (masculine and feminine) of ταλαπενθής, a 3rd declension adjective meaning "patient in woe".   Translate in the order: τλήσομαι, ἔχων ταλαπενθέα θυμὸν ἐν στήθεσσιν.
⁴⁴πολλὰ (neuter plural) = much (many things) is the object of πάθον (1st person singular, aorist indicative of πάσχω). μόγησα is 1st person singular of the aorist indicative of μογέω = I undergo. πόλεμος (2m) = war. κύμασι and πολέμῳ are local datives; they say where something happened.
⁴⁵Translate μετὰ with τοῖσι. μετά + dative = "among (those)", i.e. "this" (another shipwreck) would simply count as one more, among the disasters he has already suffered.   τόδε is the subject of γενέσθω (3rd person singular imperative of (ἐ)γενόμην).
⁴⁶ἔφατ' stands for ἔφατο (p.34, footnote 7). κνέφας, κνέφαος (3n) = darkness. ἐπὶ is separated from ἦλθεν by tmesis. ἐπῆλθεν = "came over (them)".
⁴⁷ἐλθόντες is nominative plural masculine of ἐλθών, the aorist participle of ἔρχομαι. Note that it qualifies τώ (dual) and, as is customary (see also μένοντες in line 227), masculine refers to both masculine and feminine.   Translate in the order: ἐλθόντες μυχῷ γλαφυροῖο σπείους τώ γε τερπέσθην φιλότητι. μυχῷ is dative expressing destination.   Chantraine (op. cit. vol.ii, p.68) notes that such a dative (where πρός and the accusative might be expected) is more common in Epic poetry than in prose. τερπέσθην is 3rd person dual of the aorist indicative passive of τέρπω and means, "those two were delighted".
⁴⁸φιλότης, φιλότητος (3f) = love. Hainsworth (op. cit., p.273) notes other instances of an apparently casual attitude to sexual relations in Homer, and in his introduction to book V (p.250) observes that Calypso, as her name, The Concealer, implies, was, like Circe, an enchantress. This account of Odysseus and Calypso making love may serve to emphasise the similarity of Calypso's story with Circe's. Hesiod, Theogony (1011-1018), credits both Circe and Calypso with sons by Odysseus: Circe with Agrius and Latinus (and Telegonus, if 1014 is genuine) and Calypso with Nausithous and Nausinous.

Section 17
Clauses of time

Homer uses the following words for "when":-
ὅτε and ὁπ(π)οτε
εὖτε
ἦμος ("at the very time when...")
ὡς[1] ("as")
ἐπεί ("after")

For "since", he uses ἐξ οὗ.

For "until" or "while", he uses ἕως, εἷος [or ἧος][2] or εἵως, also εἷος ὅ or εἰς ὅ ("until or up to such time as") or ὄφρα[3] ("all the time that").
Such words are known as *temporal conjunctions*. They introduce clauses which express the relationship of an event to another in time. In Homeric Greek, the verbs in such clauses may be indicative, subjunctive or optative.

In a temporal clause which asserts that a particular event is an actual occurrence the verb is indicative, e.g.

ἤϊεν, ὄφρα μέγα σπέος <u>ἵκετο</u>, τῷ ἔνι νύμφη
ναῖεν ἐϋπλόκαμος (Odyssey V, 57-8)
he kept on going, until <u>he reached</u> the great cave in which the nymph with fair tresses was dwelling.
(It is a fact: he did reach the cave.)

ἐπεὶ δὴ πάντα ἑῷ <u>θηήσατο</u> θυμῷ,
αὐτίκ' εἰς εὐρὺ σπέος ἤλυθεν (Odyssey V, 76-7)
after <u>he had admired</u> everything in his heart, at once into the broad cave he went.
(It is a fact: he did admire everything. Notice the Greek preference for a verb in the aorist tense where in English "had" is preferred.)

---
[1] It is important to distinguish ὡς from ὥς (= thus, so).
[2] ἧος is found in the Oxford Classical Text (ed. Allen) and in Stanford's edition at Odyssey V 123, 365, 386, 424 and 429, but not in any mss. The text printed here is the version of the Oxford Classical Text in *Thesaurus Linguae Graecae*, and has ἕως at 123 and εἷος elsewhere. (The mss. differ on the spelling of this word.) ἧος and εἷος may both represent the older pronunciation which, by metathesis (switching of long and short syllables), later became ἕως. See Hainsworth, *A Commentary on Homer's Odyssey* vol.i, p.266 and Chantraine, *Grammaire Homérique* vol.i, p.11 who supports ἧος as the ancient form.
[3] Often followed by τόφρα ("for so long a time").

ἐπεί and ὅτε are sometimes used to mean "since" i.e. "for the reason that". With them, the indicative is used for future occurrences if it is asserted that they will certainly happen, e.g.

φίλε κασίγνητε, σθένος ἀνέρος ἀμφότεροί περ
σχῶμεν, ἐπεὶ τάχα ἄστυ μέγα Πριάμοιο ἄνακτος
<u>ἐκπέρσει</u>, Τρῶες δὲ κατὰ μόθον <u>οὐ μενέουσιν</u>. (Iliad xxi, 308-10)
"Dear brother, let both of us by all means hold (back) the might of the man, since soon <u>he will certainly sack</u> the city of lord Priam, and the Trojans <u>will not stand firm</u> in the din of battle."
(κασίγνητος -ου: brother   σθένος -ους (neuter) strength, might.   ἀμφότεροι, -αι -α: both   σχῶμεν is 1st plural subjunctive of ἔσχον, the aorist of ἔχω (see p.66,) τάχα: soon, quickly   ἄστυ (3n.): city   ἄναξ, ἄνακτος: lord   ἐκπέρσω is future, from ἐκπέρθω, I destroy (a city)   κατὰ μόθον: in the din of battle.)

The subjunctive, sometimes with ἄν[4] or (more often) κεν, sometimes without either modal particle, is found in temporal clauses which refer to eventualities or generalities (see also p. 98), e.g.

οὕτω νῦν κακὰ πολλὰ παθὼν ἀλόω κατὰ πόντον
εἰς ὅ κεν ἀνθρώποισι διοτρεφέεσσι <u>μιγήῃς</u> (Odyssey V, 377-8)
so now having suffered many evil things wander over the sea until such time as <u>you mingle</u> with Zeus-nurtured men.
ἀλόω: 2nd person singular present imperative of ἀλάομαι, I wander   μιγήῃς: 2nd person singular subjunctive of (ἐ)μίγην, the aorist passive of μίσγω, I mix διοτρεφής: nurtured by Zeus. (Poseidon is the speaker. He does not assert that Odysseus will mingle with Zeus-nurtured men, but regards this as a possibility.)

ὄφρα with the subjunctive correlated with τόφρα:

ὄφρ' ἄν μέν κεν δούρατ' ἐν ἁρμονίῃσιν <u>ἀρήρῃ</u>,
τόφρ' αὐτοῦ μενέω καὶ τλήσομαι ἄλγεα πάσχων (Odyssey V, 361-2)
for as long as on the one hand the timbers in the fastenings <u>are fixed</u>,
for so long on the spot I shall remain and endure, suffering woes
where the time for which the timbers remain in the fastenings is indefinite (and in fact turned out to be very short). In this example, both ἄν and κεν accompany the subjunctive ἀρήρῃ.[5]

---

[4] ἔπει ... ἄν is only found once (Iliad vi, 411-2) οὐ γὰρ ἔτ' ἄλλη ἔσται θαλπωρή, ἐπεὶ ἄν σύ γε πότμον ἐφίσπῃς ("there will be no other comfort (for me); at such time as you meet your doom"); elsewhere, ἔπει ἄν is contracted to ἐπήν. See Chantraine (*Grammaire Homérique* vol.ii, pp.258-9) where the possibility that ἐπήν may be a later modification of the original Homeric expression is discussed. θαλπωρή: comfort, πότμον ἐφέπω (2nd person singular, aorist subjunctive: ἐπίσπῃς): I meet my doom.

[5] The text of this passage, with ἄν and κεν together, is uncertain. Chantraine (*op. cit.* vol.ii, p.345) thinks ὄφρα μέν κεν possibly preferable. However, Hainsworth *A Commentary on Homer's Odyssey* vol.i, p.283, regards ὄφρ' ἄν μέν κεν as a formulaic usage found also at Iliad xi, 187 and 202 as well as Odyssey VI, 259 which should not be corrected. ἀρήρῃ is 3rd person singular (neuter plural subject) of ἤραρον, I was fixed, the aorist (strong, intransitive) of ἀραρίσκω, I fix. ἁρμονίη (1f) = the fastening.

Section 17

When the optative (most often without ἄν or κεν) is found in temporal clauses, it makes a possibility seem more remote, e.g.

ἀλλὰ τὰ μὲν νοέω καὶ φράσσομαι, ἅσσ' ἂν ἐμοί περ
αὐτῇ μηδοίμην, ὅτε με χρειὼ τόσον ἵκοι (Odyssey V, 188-9)
But I am planning and shall think of those things, whatever I would indeed contrive for myself, at such time as so great a need might reach me (Chantraine, *op. cit.*, vol.ii, p.260, points out that this is close to a condition: "if ever so great a need should reach me.")

ὦρσε δ' ἐπὶ κραιπνὸν βορέην, πρὸ δὲ κύματ' ἔαξεν,
εἷος ὃ Φαιήκεσσι φιληρέτμοισι μιγείη (Odyssey V, 385-6)
and she raised up a swift north wind, and broke (the force of) the waves in front of him, until such time as he should mingle with the Phaeacians, friends of the oar,
κραιπνός -η -όν: swift βορέης-ου: north wind πρό (adverb): in front ἔαξεν: 3rd person singular aorist of ἄγνυμι: I break. φιλήρετμος: fond of the oar (μιγείη is 3rd person singular, aorist optative passive from μίσγω)
(Chantraine notes, *op. cit.* vol.ii, p.261, that when the main verb is past (ὦρσε, she raised up) εἷος ὁ with the optative is close to expressing a purpose: "so that he should mingle".)

πρίν used as a temporal conjunction.

πρίν (= before) is often simply an adverb e.g.
ἣ πρὶν μὲν ἔην βροτὸς αὐδήεσσα (Odyssey V, 334).
who was indeed formerly a mortal endowed with human speech (αὐδήεσσα)

πρίν can also be used as a temporal conjunction. When so used, in Homer, πρίν is almost always followed by an infinitive, e.g.
εἰ γε μὲν εἰδείης σῇσι φρεσίν ὅσσα τοι αἶσα
κήδε ' ἀναπλῆσαι, πρὶν πατρίδα γαῖαν ἱκέσθαι,
ἐνθάδε κ' αὖθι μένων σὺν ἐμοὶ τόδε δῶμα φυλάσσοις...(Odyssey V, 206-8)
(= if indeed you should know in your heart how many woes destiny (is) for you to fulfil before reaching your native land. staying here with me in this place you would guard this hall...")

Occasionally it is followed by the subjunctive, especially when the main clause of the sentence is negative, e.g.
Ὦ φίλοι, οὐ γάρ πω καταδυσόμεθ ', ἀχνύμενοι περ,
εἰς Ἀίδαο δόμους, πρὶν μόρσιμον ἦμαρ ἐπέλθῃ (Odyssey X, 174-5)
O friends, we shall not indeed sink yet, though grieved,
to the halls of Hades, before the destined day comes on.
(καταδύομαι : I sink. ἄχνυμαι : I am grieved. μόρσιμος -ον : destined)
(ἐπέλθῃ is 3rd person singular, subjunctive of ἐπῆλθον, the aorist of ἐπέρχομαι)

But if πρίν is combined with ὅτε, like the other temporal conjunctions it can be followed by an indicative verb, e.g.
  ἡμεῖς δὲ μυχῷ θαλάμων εὐπήκτων
  ἥμεθ' ἀτυζόμεναι, σανίδες δ' ἔχον εὖ ἀραρυῖαι,
  πρίν γ' ὅτε δή με σὸς υἱὸς ἀπὸ μεγάροιο κάλεσσε
  Τηλέμαχος (Odyssey XXIII, 41-4)
    but we in a corner of the well-built chambers were sitting terrified, and the doors were keeping well fastened, before (the time) when finally your son Telemachus called me from the hall
μυχός -ου: corner θάλαμος -ου: chamber εὔπηκτος: well-built ἧμαι: I sit ἀτυζόμενος -η -ον: terrified σανίδες: boards (i.e. folding doors) ἀραρυῖα (fem. adj.): fastened. μέγαρον -ου: hall (ἐ)κάλεσ(σ)α: 1st person singular, aorist of καλέω, I call.

New words:
ἁρμονίη (1f) = fastening[6]   διαμπερές = right through
ἔδειξα is the aorist of δείκνυμι which means "I show"
δίδωμι (aorist ἔδωκα[7]) = I give
ἕννυμι (aorist, ἕσσα) = I clothe[8]   ἐπίκριον (2n) = yard arm
ἐπιχέω (aorist ἐπέχευσα) = I pour over, heap up over
ἔργον (2n) = work, task   εὖ = well
θοῶς = quickly   ἰθύνω = I keep straight, steer
ἵστια (2nplu) = sails   κεφαλή (1f) = head
λεπτός -ή -όν = fine-spun   ὁδός (2f) = road, way
ὅθι = where   πέλεκυς (3m) = axe
πηδάλιον (2n) = steering-oar
πούς, ποδός (3m) (dative plural πόδεσσι(ν), πόσι(ν) or πόσσι(ν)), =
    foot, also sheet (the rope fastened to the bottom corner of a sail)
φᾶρος (3n, like λέχος) = robe, cloth
χιτών, χιτῶνος (3m) = tunic   χρύσειος -α -ον = golden

What is the English for:
1.ἐπεὶ νύμφη 'Οδυσσῆι μήδετο πομπήν,[9] δῶκέν οἱ πέλεκυν μέγαν.
2.ὅτε ἡ ἧρχεν ὁδοῖο νήσου ἐπ' ἐσχατίης,[10] 'Οδυσσεὺς ὄπισθεν ἔβαινε.

[6]Autenrieth, *Homeric Dictionary* p.54, translates ἁρμονίαι as "bands, slabs, one side flat, the other curved, serving to bind together the raft." Stanford, quoting W.H.D. Rouse's translation, takes ἁρμονίαι as "joints". Liddell & Scott cite a later use of ἁρμονίαι (Herodotus II, 96) as seams in Egyptian river boats which are caulked with tow. ἁρμονίη is derived from ἁρμόζω, I fit together.
[7](ἔ)δωκα (ἔ)δωκας (ἔ)δωκε (ἔ)δομεν [(ἔ)δοτε] (ἔ)δοσαν *or* ἔδωκαν (cf. ἔθηκα).
[8]The middle (ἕννυμαι) means "I put on".
[9]Here, πομπή means not "an escort home" but "a means of getting home".
[10]ἐπ' stands for ἐπί. ἐσχατιή (1f) = far end.

Section 17 123

3.τέτρηνεν¹¹ δ' 'Οδυσσεὺς ἄρα δούρατα πρὶν ἁρμόζειν¹² ἀλλήλοισι.
4.αὐτὰρ ὄφρα ὁ τάμνετο¹³ δοῦρα, τόφρα¹⁴ ἔνεικε¹⁵ τέρετρα¹⁶
Καλυψώ, δῖα θεάων.
5.ἐπεὶ δ' ἱστὸν ποίησε καὶ ἐπίκριον ἄρμενον¹⁷ αὐτῷ, πρός¹⁸ ἄρα
πηδάλιον ποιήσατο, ὄφρ' ἰθύνοι.

Odyssey 228-261
ἦμος δ' ἠριγένεια¹⁹ φάνη²⁰ ῥοδοδάκτυλος Ἠώς,
αὐτίχ' ὁ μὲν χλαῖνάν²¹ τε χιτῶνά τε ἔννυτ' Ὀδυσσεύς,²²
αὐτὴ δ' ἀργύφεον²³ φᾶρος μέγα ἔννυτο νύμφη,   230
λεπτὸν καὶ χαρίεν,²⁴ περὶ δὲ ζώνην²⁵ βάλετ' ἰξυῖ
καλὴν χρυσείην, κεφαλῇ δ' ἐπέθηκε²⁶ καλύπτρην.
καὶ τότ'²⁷ Ὀδυσσῆϊ μεγαλήτορι μήδετο πομπήν·
δῶκε μέν οἱ πέλεκυν μέγαν, ἄρμενον²⁸ ἐν παλάμῃσι,²⁹
χάλκεον,³⁰ ἀμφοτέρωθεν³¹ ἀκαχμένον· αὐτὰρ ἐν αὐτῷ   235

¹¹3rd person singular aorist indicative of τετραίνω, I bore through, I pierce.
¹² ἁρμόζω, I fit together (cf. ἁρμονίη). The aorist (line 247) is ἥρμοσα.
¹³τάμνομαι = I cut for myself   δοῦρα = δούρατα.
¹⁴Here, τόφρα = "then", "at that point".
¹⁵ἔνεικα (augmented form ἤνεικα) is aorist active of φέρω (also at line 258). ἔνεικε is 3rd person singular.
¹⁶ τέρετρον (2n) = gimlet
¹⁷ἄρμενος -η -ον "fitted" is the aorist middle participle of ἀραρίσκω, I fit.
¹⁸πρός is used as an adverb; "as well", "in addition".
¹⁹ἠριγένεια = child of morn (epithet of dawn). (ἔαρ, contracted to ἦρ, is when things are fresh and bright, usually spring; in this context, early morning.)
²⁰φάνη = "appeared", 3rd person singular, aorist passive of φαίνω (Section 18).
²¹χλαῖνα (1f) = cloak, upper garment thrown over body like a blanket.
²²ἔννυτ' stands for ἔννυτο, 3rd person singular imperfect of ἔννυμαι (middle).
²³ἀργύφεος -η -ον = silver-shining, silver-white.
²⁴χαρίεις, χαρίεσσα, χαρίεν = graceful, elegant.
²⁵ζώνη (1f) = girdle, belt (cf English "zone"). βάλετ' stands for βάλετο. βάλλομαι (aorist ἐβαλόμην) here means merely "I put on". ἰξύς, [ἰξύος] (3f) = waist (of women). ἰξυῖ is contracted from ἰξύϊ because υι are sounded together. Lines 230-2 are used again, of Circe, at Odyssey X, 543-5.
²⁶ἐπέθηκε = "placed on", 3rd singular aorist active of ἐπιτίθημι. Aristarchus of Samothrace, (ὁ γραμματικώτατος - "the greatest scholar"), Head of the Library at Alexandria c. 153 BC, changed ἐπέθηκε to ἐφύπερθε ("on top") and made καλύπτρην, as well as ζώνην, an object of βάλετ', perhaps because a veil is not put on like a helmet; but this scene where Calypso gets ready for work imitates the arming scene in the Iliad where Paris prepares for his duel with Menelaus: κρατὶ δ' ἐπ' ἰφθίμῳ κυνέην εὔτυκτον ἔθηκεν/ ἵππουριν "and on his mighty head he put a well-made helmet with a horse's tail crest" (Iliad iii, 336-7). (Hainsworth, A Commentary on Homer's Odyssey, vol. i, p.273.) καλύπτρη (1f) = veil.
²⁷τότ' stands for τότε.
²⁸For ἄρμενος -η -ον (also at line 254), see footnote 17 above.
²⁹παλάμη (1f) = palm of the hand
³⁰χάλκεος, χάλκεια, χάλκεον = made of bronze
³¹ἀμφοτέρωθεν = from both sides. ἀκαχμένος -η -ον = sharp-edged.

στειλειόν[32] περικαλλές[33] ἐλάϊνον, εὖ ἐναρηρός·[34]
δῶκε δ' ἔπειτα σκέπαρνον[35] ἐΰξοον· ἦρχε δ' ὁδοῖο
νήσου ἐπ' ἐσχατιήν, ὅθι δένδρεα μακρὰ πεφύκει,[36]
κλήθρη τ' αἴγειρός τ', ἐλάτη[37] τ' ἦν οὐρανομήκης,[38]
αὖα[39] πάλαι, περίκηλα,[40] τά οἱ πλώοιεν ἐλαφρῶς.[41]   240
 αὐτὰρ ἐπεὶ δὴ δεῖξ'[42] ὅθι δένδρεα μακρὰ πεφύκει,
ἥ[43] μὲν ἔβη πρὸς δῶμα Καλυψώ, δῖα θεάων,
αὐτὰρ ὁ τάμνετο[44] δοῦρα· θοῶς δέ οἱ ἤνυτο[45] ἔργον.
εἴκοσι δ' ἔκβαλε[46] πάντα, πελέκκησεν[47] δ' ἄρα χαλκῷ,

[32]στειλειόν (2 neuter) = haft, shaft. Understand ἦν ("there was").
[33]περικαλλής -ές = very fine. ἐλάϊνος -η -ον = made of olive wood (fem. not found in Homer).
[34]ἐναρηρώς -υῖα -ός = fitted in (perfect participle (Section 22) of ἐναραρίσκω).
[35]σκέπαρνος (2 masculine) = carpenter's axe or adze for smoothing tree trunks (Liddell & Scott). Stanford notes that an adze differs from an axe as the cutting edge is at right angles to the handle. The adze is still used for shaping boat keels e.g. on the Moray Firth. ἐΰξοος -ον = well polished.
[36]δένδρεον (2 neuter) = tree. πεφύκει = had grown (3rd person singular pluperfect (NB, neuter plural subject) of πέφυκα which means "I (have) grow(n)" (intransitive), and is the perfect of φύω, I bring forth). For the pluperfect, see Section 22.
[37]ἐλάτη = fir (Liddell & Scott: "silver fir", *Abies cephalonica*). (In Euripides' *Alcestis* (438 B.C.), at line 444 the chorus call Charon's boat "a two-oared fir".)
[38]οὐρανομήκης = "sky-tall", i.e. shooting up into heaven.
[39]αὖος -η -ον = dry. Hainsworth (*op.cit.*, p.274) notes, citing Theophrastus, *Historia Plantarum* v, 7, 3, that dried-out timber was not used for shipbuilding, and that this may suggest that the poet is still thinking in terms of a raft. πάλαι = long ago.
[40]περίκηλος -ον (fem as masc) = well seasoned.
[41]3rd person plural, present optative active of πλώω, I sail. (οἱ is dative; "for him".) ἐλαφρῶς = lightly. "which might sail" expresses a purpose.
[42]δεῖξ' stands for ἔδειξεν, 3rd person singular of ἔδειξα.
[43]ἥ = "*she*", Calypso. The article is used here to point the contrast with "he".
[44]For τάμνομαι, see footnote 13 above. δοῦρα (neuter plural) = spars.
[45]ἤνυτο is 3rd person singular imperfect middle of ἄνυω = I complete, "was getting completed" (the subject is ἔργον). οἱ is dative.
[46]εἴκοσι = twenty. ἔκβαλε is 3rd person singular (unaugmented) of ἐξέβαλον, the aorist of ἐκβάλλω, which really means "I throw out", but is used here to mean "I fell (trees)" in the sense of "cast them out of the plantation". πάντα, as we say "in all" (neuter plural), implies δένδρεα (trees).
[47]πελέκκησεν is 3rd person singular (unaugmented) of ἐπελέκκησα, the aorist of πελεκκάω = I shape with an axe.

Section 17

ξέσσε⁴⁸ δ' ἐπισταμένως⁴⁹ καὶ ἐπὶ στάθμην⁵⁰ ἴθυνε. 245
τόφρα⁵¹ δ' ἔνεικε τέρετρα Καλυψώ, δῖα θεάων·
τέτρηνεν⁵² δ' ἄρα πάντα καὶ ἥρμοσεν ἀλλήλοισι,
γόμφοισιν⁵³ δ' ἄρα τήν⁵⁴ γε καὶ ἁρμονίῃσιν ἄρασσεν.⁵⁵
ὅσσον⁵⁶ τίς τ' ἔδαφος⁵⁷ νηὸς τορνώσεται⁵⁸ ἀνὴρ
φορτίδος⁵⁹ εὐρείης,⁶⁰ εὖ εἰδὼς⁶¹ τεκτοσυνάων,⁶² 250
τόσσον ἐπ'⁶³ εὐρεῖαν σχεδίην ποιήσατ' Ὀδυσσεύς.

⁴⁸ξέσσε is 3rd person singular of (ἔ)ξεσσα, the aorist active of ξέω, I smooth (wood), i.e. remove twigs, bark etc. Here the process described changes from making a rough-and-ready raft into the construction of a sea-going ship. At Odyssey XXIII, 196-9 Odysseus says "having shortened a tree stump I smoothed it all round from the root (up) with bronze (κορμὸν ἐκ ῥίζης προταμὼν ἀμφέξεσα χαλκῷ) well and skilfully (εὖ καὶ ἐπισταμένως) and I made it straight to the line (καὶ ἐπὶ στάθμην ἴθυνα) working it into a bed post (ἑρμῖν' ἀσκήσας) and I bored everything through with the drill (τέτρηνα δὲ πάντα τερέτρῳ). And beginning from that I went on making (the woodwork of) the bed smooth (ἐκ δὲ τοῦ ἀρχόμενος λέχος ἔξεον) until I had finished it (ὄφρ' ἐτέλεσσα)."
⁴⁹ἐπισταμένως = skilfully (literally, with understanding). As a true Homeric hero, Odysseus is good at whatever he does; this passage establishes his credentials as a craftsman and we are not surprised when, at Odyssey XXIII, 189-201, he says that he constructed his own bed and bed chamber in his palace. (Froma I. Zeitlin, *The Distaff Side,* p.139, Oxford, 1995, ed. Beth Cohen.)
⁵⁰στάθμη = carpenter's line (Liddell & Scott explain this as a string rubbed with red ochre or chalk; it was distinct from κανών, the carpenter's rule.) Translate as: ξέσσε δ' ἐπισταμένως καὶ ἐπὶ στάθμην ἴθυνε (δοῦρα) "and he planed skilfully and upon the line made straight (the timbers)".
⁵¹See footnotes 14-16.
⁵²See footnotes 11-12. Hainsworth compares the description in Odyssey IX, 384-6 of drilling ship timbers, which needed several men.
⁵³γόμφος (2m) = peg, dowel. Hainsworth translates "treenail". He notes (*op. cit.*, pp.274-5) that the ancient Greek shipwright, having constructed the keel with the stem and sternpost, built up the hull with planks first and then inserted the ribs and decking; modern practice is to proceed with the ribs first and then cover them with planks. Hainsworth mentions the possibility that the description of boat building may be borrowed from another poem.
⁵⁴τήν, "it", stands for the raft (σχεδίην).
⁵⁵ἀράσσω, I clash together. ἄρασσεν (3rd person singular, imperfect), "he was clashing it together".
⁵⁶ὅσσον ... τόσσον ... = "how great... so great ... ", i.e., "as great as". ὅσσον introduces a *simile*. Similes (often more elaborate than this) are a feature of the Homeric style. This one extends over two lines (249-250) and applies to what Odysseus does in 251. Translate in the order: (and) ὅσσον ἀνήρ τις εὖ εἰδὼς τεκτοσυνάων τορνώσεται ἔδαφος εὐρείης φορτίδος, ἐπὶ τόσσον Ὀδυσσεὺς ἐποιήσατο εὐρεῖαν σχεδίην.
⁵⁷ἔδαφος, ἐδάφεος = floor, and so here, "bottom" (of a ship).
⁵⁸τορνώσεται, 3rd person singular, future indicative of τορνόομαι, I round off.
⁵⁹φορτίς, φορτίδος (3f) = merchant ship (broader in the beam than a warship).
⁶⁰εὐρείη is feminine of εὐρύς.
⁶¹εἰδώς (nominative masculine singular, see Section 22) + genitive, knowledgeable of.
⁶²τεκτοσυνή = the carpenter's skill (the plural is poetical ornament).
⁶³τόσσον ἐπ' = ἐπὶ τόσσον, to such an extent, i.e. so large. ποιήσατ' stands for (ἐ)ποιήσατο, 3rd person singular, (ἐ)ποιησάμην, aorist indicative middle of ποιέω.

ἴκρια δὲ στήσας,⁶⁴ ἀραρὼν θαμέσι⁶⁵ σταμίνεσσι,
ποίει· ἀτὰρ μακρῇσιν ἐπηγκενίδεσσι⁶⁶ τελεύτα.
ἐν δ' ἱστὸν ποίει καὶ ἐπίκριον ἄρμενον αὐτῷ·
πρὸς δ' ἄρα πηδάλιον ποιήσατο, ὄφρ' ἰθύνοι.   255
φράξε⁶⁷ δέ μιν ῥίπεσσι διαμπερὲς οἰσυΐνῃσι,
κύματος εἶλαρ⁶⁸ ἔμεν πολλὴν δ' ἐπεχεύατο⁶⁹ ὕλην.
τόφρα δὲ φάρε' ἔνεικε Καλυψώ, δῖα θεάων,
ἱστία ποιήσασθαι· ὁ δ' εὖ τεχνήσατο⁷⁰ καὶ τά.
ἐν δ' ὑπέρας⁷¹ τε κάλους⁷² τε πόδας τ' ἐνέδησεν ἐν αὐτῇ,⁷³   260
μοχλοῖσιν⁷⁴ δ' ἄρα τήν γε κατείρυσεν εἰς ἅλα δῖαν.

⁶⁴στήσας "having set up" (the nominative masculine singular of the aorist participle active of ἵστημι, I set up). ἀραρών is nominative masculine singular of the participle of ἤραρον, the (strong) aorist active of ἀραρίσκω (footnote 17 above): "having fitted". θαμέσι σταμίνεσσι is dative plural, and ἴκρια ("the deck") is the object of ποίει (standing for ἐποίει, 3rd person singular, imperfect active). θαμέες (always plural) = "close set". σταμίνες (3m) are taken to be the ribs, or frame timbers of a ship (so called because they stand up (ἵστημι = I make to stand) from the keel) (Liddell & Scott). Translate in the order: στήσας ἴκρια ποίει (it) ἀραρὼν θαμέσι σταμίνεσσι. There is still much discussion about what the various names used here for parts of a ship actually mean, and Hainsworth's notes (*op. cit.* pp.274-5) should be consulted. If this description is partly borrowed from a much earlier traditional poem, they may perhaps originally have been terms referring to parts of bronze age ships. (There are extant representations of bronze age ships e.g. in the fresco of the Naval Campaign from room 5 of the West House at Thera (c.1500 BC) in the National Museum at Athens; but even if this should be the kind of ship in the poet's mind here, or described in a traditional poem he is quoting, there may still be obscurities in the fresco.)

⁶⁵τελεύτα is 3rd person singular imperfect, from τελευτάω = I finish.

⁶⁶ἐπηγκενίδες = long planks bolted to the upright ribs (Liddell & Scott) or "wales" (ridges of planking along the rail of a ship) (Casson, cited by Hainsworth).

⁶⁷φράξε is 3rd person singular of (ἔ)φραξα, aorist of φράσσω = I fence. ῥίπεσσι is dative plural of ῥίψ, ῥιπός (3f) = mat. οἰσυΐνος -η -ον = made of wickerwork (οἰσύα, osier). διαμπερές = throughout.

⁶⁸εἶλαρ (only in nominative & accusative) = protection. ἔμεν = εἶναι, to be.

⁶⁹ἐπεχεύατο is 3rd person singular of [ἐπεχευάμην], the aorist middle of ἐπιχέω, I pour (or throw) over. Some scholia suggest Odysseus was using the wood with sand and stones as ballast, but a better explanation would be as dunnage (planks to prevent the cargo from getting wet in the bilges)(Hainsworth). Rouse, quoted by Stanford, translates ὕλην as "brushwood", an alternative meaning of ὕλη. φάρε' stands for φάρεα. For ἔνεικε, see footnote 15.

⁷⁰τεχνήσατο is 3rd person singular from (ἐ)τεχνησάμην, the aorist indicative of τεχνάομαι = I devise. Note the gender change (change of subject) indicated by ὁ. τά ("them") refers to ἱστία. ποιήσασθαι is aorist infinitive of ποιέομαι ("to make for himself"). καί here = also.

⁷¹ὑπέραι = the braces (attached to the ends of the yard arms, to move the sail fore and aft according to the direction of the wind).

⁷²κάλος = reefing rope, reef (usually κάλως in later Greek). ἐνέδησεν is 3rd person singular of ἐνέδησα, the aorist indicative of ἐνδέω = I tie in.

⁷³αὐτῇ is feminine because it refers to σχεδίη, as does τήν in line 261.

⁷⁴μοχλός (2m) = crowbar. κατείρυσεν is 3rd person singular of κατείρυσα, the aorist indicative of κατερύω = I launch (literally, I haul down).

Section 18
The aorist passive tense

The aorist passive tense expresses a simple act that was done or suffered, e.g.
κινήθη δ' ἀγορὴ φὴ κύματα μακρὰ θαλάσσης (Iliad ii, 144)
and the meeting was moved like the long waves of the sea.[1]
The aorist passive endings are: –(θ)ην, —(θ)ης, -(θ)η, -(θ)ητον, -(θ)ητην, -(θ)ημεν, -(θ)ητε, -(θ)ησαν. They are like active endings.

(ἐ)λύθην	I was loosed	(also	(ἐ)λύμην)
(ἐ)λύθης	you were loosed		
(ἐ)λύθη	he/she/it was loosed	(also	(ἔ)λυτο)

(ἐ)λύθητον	you two were loosed
(ἐ)λυθήτην	those two were loosed

(ἐ)λύθημεν	we were loosed		
(ἐ)λύθητε	you were loosed		
(ἐ)λύθησαν	they were loosed	(also	(ἔ)λυντο)
or (ἔ)λυθεν			

NB1. Some verbs do not have θ in the aorist passive. For example, (ἔ)φανην ("I was shown") is the aorist passive of φαίνω ("I show"). Some have the ending –σθην instead of –θην.

NB2. -μι verbs have similar aorist passive endings, e.g. the aorist passive of πίμπλημι (I fill) is (ἐ)πλήσθην:
τῶν δ' ἄπαν ἐπλήσθη πεδίον καὶ λάμπετο χαλκῷ
ἀνδρῶν ἠδ' ἵππων (and all the plain was filled with their bronze and was shining, of men and horses) (Iliad xx, 156-7)
(πεδίον: plain, λάμπομαι: I shine, ἵππος (2m or f): horse)

NB3. The form (ἐ)λύμην which is a strong aorist middle with passive meaning is peculiar to λύω. It is found especially in the formula γούνατα λύτο meaning "his knees were loosed", i.e. "(his) knees buckled", as we say "his knees were knocking".

---
[1]ἀγορή (1 f) = meeting φή = like. κινέω = I move.

Some aorist passives in Homer are best translated by active verbs in English; e.g. from φαίνω, I show: (ἐ)φάνην often means "I appeared"; from χαίρω, I rejoice: (ἐ)χάρην ("I was made glad") = "I was glad".

New words:
ἄγκιστος -η -ον = nearest   ἄμαξα (1f) = waggon[2]
ἅπας ἅπασα, ἅπαν = every (in plural, all) (like πᾶς)
ἀσκός (2m) = wineskin   δύω = I sink
λούω = I wash[3]   μέλας μέλαινα μέλαν = dark[4]
ὄρος, ὄρεος (3n) = mountain   ὀψέ = late
ὄψον (2n) = cooked dish, food
πετάννυμι (aorist πέτασα or πέτασσα) = I spread
ὕπνος (2m) = sleep   φαίνω = I show
What is the English for:
(a)1.οὐκ ἐλύθησαν. 2.Ὀδυσσεὺς οὐκ ἐχάρη. 3.πῦρ ἐκάη. 4.ἐφάνη ὄρεα. 5.δμωαὶ (the maidservants) θεὸν ἰδοῦσαι τάρφθεν. 6.εὖ τελέσθη πάντα;

(b)1.ἤδη ἦμαρ ἔεν καὶ τῷ ἐτελέσθη ἅπαντα.
2.ἐν δέ νηΐ οἱ ἀσκὸς ἐτέθη μέλανος οἴνοιο.
3.ἐν δέ νηΐ οἱ ὄψα τέθη μενοεικέα πολλά.
4.Ὀδυσσῆι ὁράοντι φάνησαν Πληϊάδες.[5]
5.Ὀδυσσεὺς δ' ἑπτὰ[6] καὶ δέκα ἤματα ἐτέρπετο ποντοπορεύων,[7] ὀκτωκαιδεκάτῳ[8] δ' ἐφάνη ὄρεα γαίης Φαιήκων.

[2](in Attic Greek, ἄμαξα); in astronomy, cf. English "Charles's Wain", meaning Charles's Wagon, an old name for the constellation of the Plough.
[3]Usually λούω = "I wash people". πλύνω = "I wash things", e.g. clothes. In Homer, men are often washed by women, normally in preparation for a meal. Telemachus is washed by Polycaste, Nestor's eldest daughter, at Odyssey III, 464-5. At IV, 252, Helen says she washed Odysseus in Troy; at X 361 and 450, Circe washes Odysseus and his companions. Sometimes the washing is by slave women rather than the mistress of the house personally. At Odyssey XIX, 317 ff., Penelope invites the beggar (really Odysseus in disguise) to have a rinse down (for his feet) by the maids before going to bed, and a bath next morning before breakfasting with Telemachus. See West, *A Commentary on Homer's Odyssey* vol.i, p.189.
[4]μέλας also = "black".
[5]The Pleiades.
[6]ἑπτά = seven. δέκα = ten. ἤματα is accusative. The accusative case is used to express duration of time, where in English "for" is used.
[7]ποντοπορεύω = I rove across the sea.
[8]ὀκτωκαιδέκατος -η -ον = eighteenth. The dative case is used to denote the time of an occurrence, like the English "on".

Section 18   129

Odyssey V, 262-281
τέτρατον⁹ ἧμαρ ἔην,¹⁰ καὶ τῷ τετέλεστο¹¹ ἅπαντα·
τῷ δ' ἄρα πέμπτῳ¹² πέμπ' ἀπὸ νήσου δῖα Καλυψώ,
εἵματά τ' ἀμφιέσασα θυώδεα¹³ καὶ λούσασα.
ἐν δέ οἱ ἀσκὸν ἔθηκε¹⁴ θεὰ μέλανος οἴνοιο   265
τὸν ἕτερον,¹⁵ ἕτερον δ' ὕδατος μέγαν, ἐν δὲ καὶ ἧα¹⁶
κωρύκῳ,¹⁷ ἐν δέ οἱ ὄψα τίθει μενοεικέα πολλά·
οὖρον δὲ προέηκεν¹⁸ ἀπήμονά¹⁹ τε λιαρόν τε.
γηθόσυνος²⁰ δ' οὔρῳ πέτασ' ἱστία δῖος Ὀδυσσεύς.
αὐτὰρ ὁ πηδαλίῳ ἰθύνετο²¹ τεχνηέντως   270
ἥμενος·²² οὐδέ οἱ ὕπνος ἐπὶ βλεφάροισιν ἔπιπτε
Πληϊάδας τ' ἐσορῶντι²³ καὶ ὀψὲ δύοντα Βοώτην²⁴

⁹τέτρατος -η -ον (also τέταρτος) = fourth.
¹⁰For ἔην, see p.9, footnote 10.
¹¹τετέλεστο is 3rd person singular (because the subject, πάντα, is neuter plural) of the pluperfect passive (see Section 22) of τελέω. "Everything had been finished for him."
¹²πέμπτος = fifth τῷ πέμπτῳ = "on the fifth (day)" (p.49). πέμπ' stands for (ἔ)πεμπε, 3rd person singular imperfect of πέμπω.
¹³θυώδης = smelling of incense (for θύον, see line 60). ἀμφιέσασα is feminine nominative singular of the aorist participle active of ἀμφιέννυμι. λούσασα is feminine nominative singular of the aorist participle active of λούω.
¹⁴For ἔθηκε see p.107. θεά is the subject.
¹⁵ἕτερος -α -ον = the other (of two) (cf. English "heterodox" = "holding the other (i.e. the wrong) opinion"). ὁ ἕτερος ... (ὁ) ἕτερος means "the one ... the other"... or "the first (of two) ... the second (of two)..." Hainsworth (op. cit., vol.i, p.275) notes this as one of the few "acephalic" Homeric lines (i.e. "headless", without a proper beginning). The first syllable (τὸν) is short, but treated as if it were long, perhaps because the is emphasised.
¹⁶Contracted form of ἤϊα (neuter plural), found only in nominative and accusative, meaning "provisions for a journey".
¹⁷κώρυκος (2m) = leather food-bag. τίθει: see p.106.
¹⁸προέηκεν: 3rd person singular, aorist indicative active, προΐημι:"she sent forth".
¹⁹ἀπήμων (3rd declension; so ἀπήμονα is accusative masculine singular) = "tireless". λιαρός -ά -όν = warm, soft.
²⁰γηθόσυνος -η -ον = "glad". πέτασ': (ἐ)πέτασε, 3rd person singular of (ἐ)πέτασα.
²¹ἰθύνετο is 3rd person singular, imperfect middle of ἰθύνω: "he was steering a straight course for himself". τεχνηέντως = skilfully.
²²ἥμενος -η -ον = sitting down. βλεφάρα (n plu) = eyelids. ἔπιπτε is 3rd person singular imperfect from πίπτω.
²³ἐσοράω = I look at. ἐσορῶντι is dative masculine singular (qualifying οἱ in line 271) of the present participle of ἐσοράω. Assuming that Odysseus watched the Pleiades all night and that ὀψὲ δύοντα ("late setting") is a *significant* epithet of Bootes, it is possible to work out that Odysseus' trip is described as taking place between 1 September and 21 October. However, there is a conventional description of the Pleiades, Orion and the Great Bear at Iliad xviii 486-9, on the shield of Achilles, and lines 274-5 = Iliad xviii 488-9. (See Hainsworth, op. cit., pp.276-7, whose note discusses the astronomical considerations.)
²⁴The constellation Bootes, "the Ploughman or Ox-driver". (Liddell & Scott suggest that here Arcturus, the most brilliant of its stars, is meant.)

130 Beginning Greek with Homer

Ἄρκτον²⁵ θ', ἥν καὶ ἅμαξαν ἐπίκλησιν καλέουσιν,
ἥ τ' αὐτοῦ²⁶ στρέφεται καί τ' Ὠρίωνα δοκεύει,²⁷
οἴη δ' ἄμμορός²⁸ ἐστι λοετρῶν²⁹ Ὠκεανοῖο· 275
τὴν γὰρ δή μιν ἄνωγε³⁰ Καλυψώ, δῖα θεάων,
ποντοπορευέμεναι ἐπ' ἀριστερὰ³¹ χειρὸς ἔχοντα.
ἑπτὰ δὲ καὶ δέκα μὲν πλέεν³² ἤματα ποντοπορεύων,
ὀκτωκαιδεκάτῃ³³ δ' ἐφάνη ὄρεα σκιόεντα³⁴
γαίης Φαιήκων, ὅθι τ' ἄγχιστον πέλεν³⁵ αὐτῷ· 280
εἴσατο³⁶ δ' ὡς ὅτε ῥινὸν³⁷ ἐν ἠεροειδέϊ πόντῳ.

The night sky - northern hemisphere

---

²⁵ Ἄρκτος (2 feminine)= the she bear (the Great Bear). ἐπίκλησις (3 feminine) = title (translate: "as a title"). καλέω = I call.
²⁶ἥ "she" is Ἄρκτος. αὐτοῦ = just there. στρέφεται is 3rd person singular present indicative of στρέφομαι = I turn (myself).
²⁷δοκεύει: 3rd person singular of δοκεύω = I watch out for (Orion was a hunter).
²⁸ἄμμορος -ον (fem. as masc.) + genitive = without a share in. The Great Bear is the only constellation mentioned by Homer or Hesiod as not sinking below the horizon.
²⁹λουτρόν = bath, bathing place. Ὠκεανός = Ocean. "The bathing places of Ocean" implies that the Homeric view of the world is a flat disc around which Ocean runs like a river, and that when stars set, they disappear into its water.
³⁰ἄνωγε is the 3rd person singular of ἄνωγα, I order (Section 21).
³¹ἐπ' ἀριστερά χειρός = on the left. ἀριστερός -όν = left (δεξιός = right). Literally, the expression is "against the things left of hand", and so "on the left hand". ποντοπορευέμεναι is present infinitive active of ποντοπορεύω (for which, see footnote 7). Translate in the order: γὰρ δή Καλυψώ, δῖα θεάων, ἄνωγέ μιν ποντοπορευέμεναι ἔχοντα τήν ἐπ' ἀριστερὰ χειρός. μιν stands for "him", Ὀδυσσεύς and τήν for "it", Ἄρκτος.
³²πλέεν is 3rd person imperfect of πλέω = I sail
³³ὀκτωκαιδέκατος -η -ον = eighteenth. ὀκτωκαιδεκάτη is feminine because ἡμέρῃ (the dative of ἡμέρη, a feminine word for "day") is understood. ἐφάνη, and εἴσατο are singular because their subject (ὄρεα) is neuter plural.
³⁴σκιόεις, σκιόεντος = shadowy. ἄγχιστον used as an adverb: most near.
³⁵πέλεν is 3rd person singular imperfect of πέλω. The subject is "it", i.e. γαῖα Φαιήκων.
³⁶εἴσατο is 3rd person singular aorist indicative of εἴδομαι meaning "I seem, appear".
³⁷ῥινόν (2n) = shield. Stanford notes that Aristarchus' text of Homer had ἐρινόν, a wild fig tree, instead of ῥινόν; but if the shield is imagined lying flat, and Odysseus is looking at it from the edge, the simile is striking. Translate as: εἴσατο δ' ὡς ὅτε ῥινὸν (κεῖται) ἐν ἠεροειδέϊ πόντῳ.

Section 19
The aorist passive tense (continued).
The aorist passive participle.

The aorist passive participle is formed by adding –θείς, –θεῖσα, –θέν to the stem, e.g.

λυθείς	λυθεῖσα	λυθέν
(a man)	(a woman)	(a thing)
being loosed or	being loosed or	being loosed or
having been loosed	having been loosed	having been loosed.

The declension is as follows:

	masculine	feminine	neuter
singular			
nominative	λυθείς	λυθεῖσα	λυθέν
accusative	λυθέντα	λυθεῖσαν	λυθέν
genitive	λυθέντος	λυθείσης	λυθέντος
dative	λυθέντι	λυθείσῃ	λυθέντι
dual			
nominative & accusative	λυθέντε	λυθείσα	λυθέντε
genitive & dative	λυθέντοιιν	λυθείσῃιν	λυθέντοιιν
plural			
nominative	λυθέντες	λυθεῖσαι	λυθέντα
accusative	λυθέντας	λυθείσας	λυθέντα
genitive	λυθέντων	λυθεισάων	λυθέντων
dative	λυθεῖσι[1]	λυθείσης	λυθεῖσι

The infinitive and imperatives have no past meaning, but refer to the simple meaning of the verb. The infinitive is:
λυθῆναι or λυθήμεναι = to be loosed (once).
The imperative is:

singular	λύθητι	be loosed! (singular)
	λυθήτω	let him/her/it be loosed
dual	λυθῆτον	be loosed, both of you!
	λυθήτων	let them both be loosed
plural	λύθητε	be loosed! (plural)
	λυθέντων	let them be loosed.

---
[1] or λυθέντεσσι

There are also an aorist passive subjunctive and optative, referring to the simple meaning of the verb, as follows:

subjunctive		optative	
λυθῶ	let me be loosed	λυθείην	O that I might be loosed
λυθῇς	may you be loosed (singular)	λυθείης	O that you might be loosed (singular)
λυθῇ	let him, her, it be loosed	λυθείη	O that he/she/it might be loosed
λυθῆτον	may you both be loosed	λυθεῖτον	O that you might both be loosed
λυθῆτον	let them both be loosed	λυθείτην	O that they might both be loosed
λυθῶμεν	let us be loosed	λυθεῖμεν	O that we might be loosed
λυθῆτε	may you be loosed (plural)	λυθεῖτε	O that you might be loosed (plural)
λυθῶσι(ν)	let them be loosed[2]	λυθεῖεν	O that they might be loosed[3]

The aorist imperative passive is not found in Odyssey V and VI.

The aorist subjunctive passive is found at Odyssey V, 378:
εἰς ὅ κεν ἀνθρώποισι διοτρεφέεσσι μιγήῃς
until such time as you should mingle (be mixed) with Zeus-nurtured men
(μιγήῃς, 2nd person singular subjunctive of (ἐ)μίγην, aorist passive of μίσγω, I mix)

and the aorist optative passive at 386-7:
εἷος ὅ Φαιήκεσσι φιληρέτμοισι μιγείη διογενὴς 'Οδυσσεύς ...
until such time as Odysseus, descended from Zeus, might mingle (be mixed) with the Phaeacians, friends of the oar ...
(μιγείη, 3rd person singular optative of (ἐ)μίγην.)

The aorist infinitive passive is found at 384:
παύσασθαι δ' ἐκέλευσε καὶ εὐνηθῆναι ἅπαντας
and she ordered them all to cease and to be lulled
(εὐνηθῆναι is the infinitive of εὐνήθην, the aorist passive of εὐνάω, I lull literally, I put to bed)[4]

---

[2] A longer form, λυθέω, λυθέῃς, λυθέῃ, λυθέωμεν, λυθέητε, λυθέωσι is occasionally found, e.g. ἐπεί κε πυρὸς θερέω ("at such time as I am warmed from the fire") (Odyssey XVII, 23). θερέω is 1st person singular, subjunctive, from ἐθέρην, "I was warmed", the aorist passive of θέρομαι, I am being warmed.
[3] Or λυθείημεν (O that we might be loosed), λυθείητε (O that you might be loosed (plural), λυθείησαν (O that they might be loosed)(given in Pfarr, *Homeric Greek*, p.262).
[4] A cognate verb, εὐνάζομαι, is used at line 65 of birds roosting and at 119 meaning "go to bed (with)".

Section 19   133

Aorist participles passive are found at 325:
ἀλλὰ μεθορμηθεὶς ἐνὶ κύμασι ἐλλάβετ' αὐτῆς
but dashing (having been set in rapid motion) amid the waves, he got hold of it
(μεθορμηθείς: nominative masculine singular, participle of μεθωρμήθην, the aorist passive of μεθορμάω I cause to rush.)[5]

and at 462-3: ὁ δ' ἐκ ποταμοῖο λιασθεὶς σχοίνῳ ὑπεκλίνθη
and he, having turned aside from the river, lay down on a bed of rushes
(λιασθείς: nominative masculine singular, participle of (ἐ)λιάσθην, the aorist passive of λιάζω, I pull back (found mostly as λιάζομαι (passive), I turn aside (from), depart (from). ποταμός (2 m) river. σχοῖνος (2 m *or* f): rush-bed. ὑπεκλίνθην, aorist passive of ὑποκλίνω, I bend; ὑποκλίνομαι (passive) is used for "I lie down".)

New words:
βορέης, βορέου (1m) = north wind
γούνατα (3 neuter plural) = knees   ἐκφεύγω = I escape
ἐνοσίχθων = earth-shaker[6]   εὖρος (2m) = the east wind
ζέφυρος (2m) = the west wind[7]   ἦτορ (3n) = heart[8]
ἱκάνω = I come, (w. acc.) approach   κακότης (3f) = distress[9]
καλύπτω = I hide (aorist active (ἐ)κάλυψα) (συγκαλύπτω: I cover completely)
κάρη, κάρητος (n) = head   κρείων, κρείοντος = lord
νέφος, -εος (3n) = cloud   νότος (2m) = south wind
νύξ, νυκτός (f) = night   ὀχθέω = I am vexed
παντοῖος -α -ον = all kinds of   σχεδόν = near
ταράσσω = I stir up, disturb (aorist active, ἐτάραξα)
τηλόθεν = from afar

What is the English for:
1. νύμφης ἐνὶ σπῆι (dative of σπέος) εὐνηθῆναι οὐκέτι (no longer) ἐθέλει δῖος Ὀδυσσεύς.
2. ἀπὸ σπείους λιασθεὶς Ὀδυσσεὺς πρὸς σχεδίην θόως εἶσιν.
3. κρείων ἐνοσίχθων, Ὀδυσσῆα ἰδὼν ποντοπορεύοντα, πόντον ἐτάραξε.
4. Ὀδυσσῆος δὲ λύτο γούνατα καὶ φίλον ἦτορ· ἀπὸ σχεδίης πέσε.
5. ἐν κύμασι, μετὰ σχεδίην μεθορμηθείς, ἐσαώθη.
6. Ὀδυσσεῦ, εἴ ὅς κεν αὖτε ἀνθρώποισι μίγῃς, κάμμορος ἔσσῃ.
7. θεὰ παύσασθαι (to cease) καὶ εὐνηθῆναι κέλευε πάντας ἀνέμους εἴος ὅ (until such time as) Φαιήκεσσι μιγείη διογενὴς Ὀδυσεύς.

---
[5] μεθορμάομαι (passive) stands for an English active verb, "I dash".
[6] Traditional epithet (in the form κρείων ἐνοσίχθων) of Poseidon who presided over earthquakes, as well as being the god of horses and chief god of the sea.
[7] cf. English "zephyr".
[8] Found only in nominative and accusative singular in Homer.
[9] Genitive, κακότητος. κακότης can also mean "cowardice"; literally "badness" either of fortune or of morale.

Odyssey V, 282-296

τὸν δ' ἐξ Αἰθιόπων[10] ἀνιών[11] κρείων ἐνοσίχθων
τηλόθεν ἐκ Σολύμων[12] ὀρέων ἴδεν· εἴσατο[13] γάρ οἱ
πόντον ἐπιπλείων. ὁ δ' ἐχώσατο κηρόθι[14] μᾶλλον,
κινήσας[15] δὲ κάρη προτὶ[16] ὃν μυθήσατο θυμόν·   285

[10]Αἰθίοψ originally probably meant "with burnt face" (see West's notes on Odyssey I, 22-4 (*A Commentary on Homer's Odyssey* vol.i, p.75).) The Aethiopians were distinguished for their justice and piety, and so were intimate friends of the gods. They may have been thought of as living in the remote east before they were located south of Egypt. Poseidon had been absent from the first council of the gods because he was visiting the Aethiopians (Odyssey I, 20-26).
[11]ἀνιών is nominative masculine singular of the participle of ἄνειμι, I return (also "I go up" and "I go near").
[12]ὀρέων is genitive plural from ὄρος. Mount Solyma (presumably connected with the Solymi mentioned at Iliad vi, 184 and 204) is in Lycia, in the south of Asia Minor and while it is a good place to observe the sea routes between Greece and Egypt or Syria, it seems far from where Odysseus was sailing if he was going eastwards towards Greece. As Hainsworth notes (*op. cit.*, p.279), gods could see a very long way. ἴδεν: εἶδεν without augment (3rd person singular of ἴδον, for which see p.67). τὸν (line 282) is the object of ἴδεν (κρείων ἐνοσίχθων is the subject). τὸν denotes Odysseus, and its position shows that it is emphasised.
[13] εἴσατο: "he (Odysseus) appeared", "became visible". ἐπιπλώων is nominative masculine singular of the present participle active of ἐπιπλώω (with accusative) = I sail over. ὁ δ' refers to Poseidon. ἐχώσατο is 3rd person singular, aorist indicative (middle) of χώομαι.
[14]The ending -θι is locative (v. Chantraine, *Grammaire Homérique*, vol.i, p. 245): "in his heart". In Homer κηρόθι is always followed by μᾶλλον, "all the more" (Liddell & Scott). ("locative", indicating where something is done, is the name of an earlier case in nouns and adjectives which is obsolete in Epic and later Greek; other obsolete cases in Greek, whose functions are shared between the genitive and dative, are "ablative", indicating separation, and "instrumental", indicating the means by which a thing is done.)
[15]κινήσας is nominative masculine singular of the aorist participle active of κινέω = I move. Stanford notes that shaking the head was a sign of anger. The genitive of κάρη is κάρητος, for which see Odyssey VI, 230:['Αθηναίη] κὰδ δὲ κάρητος ['Οδυσσῆος] οὔλας ἧκε κόμας ("Athene let crisp, curly hair grow down (Odysseus') head"). A good head of hair was a sign of a warrior and κάρη κομόωντες Ἀχαιοί (= *Achaeans with long hair as to the head*) is often found in Homer (Aristotle later remarked at *Rhetoric* I, 1367a, that Spartan warriors had long hair because no one with long hair could do a slave's work easily).
[16]προτί = πρός. προτὶ ὃν θυμόν means "to his own spirit". μυθήσατο is 3rd person singular, aorist indicative of μυθέομαι = I speak, express (cf. μῦθος). Line 285 is repeated at 376, and is found at Iliad xvii 200 and 442, where Zeus begins a soliloquy.

"ὢ πόποι,[17] ἦ[18] μάλα δὴ[19] μετεβούλευσαν[20] θεοὶ ἄλλως
ἀμφ' Ὀδυσῆϊ ἐμεῖο μετ' Αἰθιόπεσσιν ἐόντος·[21]
καὶ δὴ Φαιήκων[22] γαίης σχεδόν, ἔνθα οἱ αἶσα

[17]ὢ πόποι is a conventional expression of anger, pain or surprise in Homer. "Bah!"

Both Hainsworth and Stanford note that there are six soliloquies in this episode of Odyssey V, and only four in the rest of the Odyssey. The Greeks connected epic closely with drama (cf. Aristotle's *Poetics*); speech is therefore an important element in it. The reason for so many soliloquies here is no doubt that both Poseidon and Odysseus are alone, and if they did not talk to themselves it would have been difficult for the bard to describe their feelings. In Iliad xvii, two soliloquies are spoken by Zeus, pitying first (201-208) Hector, who is putting on Achilles' armour and does not realise that his own death is near, and second (443-455) the horses of Achilles, who stand stock still on the battlefield, weeping for their dead driver, Patroclus. (Both soliloquies are preceded by the line: κίνησας ῥα κάρη προτὶ ὃν μυθήσατο θυμόν.) Had Zeus not spoken to himself, how could Homer have told us his feelings? However, Rutherford, *Odyssey XIX and XX*, p.205, on Odyssey XX, 18-21, notes that there is another kind of soliloquy, one appropriate for battlefields, where a hero urges himself to endure or take a great risk, as the Trojan Agenor does at Iliad xxi, 552 before confronting Achilles. Odysseus' soliloquy at 356-364 in book V is of this kind. He is encouraging himself to greater feats of endurance, and his soliloquy is introduced with the same line, ὀχθήσας δ' ἄρα εἶπε πρὸς ὃν μεγαλήτορα θυμόν, "vexed, he said to his great-hearted spirit", repeated also as lines 298, 355, 407 and 464.

[18]ἦ = in truth, of a certainty. μάλα here qualifies ἄλλως "very differently".
[19]δὴ = of course (ironically).
[20]μετεβούλευσαν is 3rd person plural, aorist indicative of μεταβουλεύω = I change my plans. ἄλλως = "differently", "in another way".
[21]For ἐών, ἐοῦσα, ἐόν see Section 11, p.72. The genitive case is used in Greek to express the time during which something happens, e.g., τῆς νυκτός = "during the night". The two genitives ἐμεῖο ... ἐόντος (literally, "of me ... being") mean "during me being", i.e., "during the time that I was". Such an expression, employing a genitive noun or pronoun and a participle, frequent in Greek, is called "genitive absolute".
[22]Understand ἐστι with σχεδόν and again with αἶσα. Scheria, the land of the Phaeacians, was sometimes identified with Corcyra (Corfu) in antiquity. Thucydides (I, 25) speaks of the Corcyreans claiming that the Phaeacians had preceded them as inhabitants of the island, and (III, 70) mentions a shrine of Alcinous there. Others thought that Scheria was fictitious. (See A.F. Garvie, *Odyssey VI-VIII*, pp.19-20.)

ἐκφυγέειν μέγα πεῖραρ ὀϊζύος,²³ ἥ μιν ἱκάνει.
ἀλλ' ἔτι μέν μίν φημι ἄδην²⁴ ἐλάαν κακότητος. 290
ὣς εἰπὼν σύναγεν²⁵ νεφέλας,²⁶ ἐτάραξε δὲ πόντον
χερσὶ τρίαιναν²⁷ ἑλών· πάσας δ' ὀρόθυνεν²⁸ ἀέλλας
παντοίων ἀνέμων, σὺν δὲ νεφέεσσι κάλυψε
γαῖαν ὁμοῦ καὶ πόντον· ὀρώρει²⁹ δ' οὐρανόθεν³⁰ νύξ.
σὺν δ' εὖρός τε νότος τ' ἔπεσον ζέφυρός τε δυσαὴς³¹ 295
καὶ βορέης αἰθρηγενέτης,³² μέγα κῦμα κυλίνδων.³³

---

²³ἐκφυγεῖν is the infinitive of ἐξέφυγον, the aorist of ἐκφεύγω. μέγα πεῖραρ ὀϊζύος is obscure. Hainsworth (*op. cit.*, p.280) compares Fitzgerald's translation, "bondage of exile", with Lattimore's "great trial of misery". ὀϊζύς, (gen. ὀϊζύος, fem.) = "woe", but πεῖραρ (gen. πείρατος, neuter) is more difficult to understand. Citing Ann L.T. Bergren, *The Etymology and Usage of ΠΕΙΡΑΡ in Early Greek Poetry*, American Classical Studies 2, New York, 1975, Hainsworth notes that the meaning of πεῖραρ, "boundary", might be extended to "bondage" so that πεῖραρ ὀϊζύος ἐκφυγέειν might mean "escape the bondage of woe". (But compare Iliad xviii, 501, where πεῖραρ means "final decision, verdict" (Liddell & Scott) in the context of the decoration of the shield made for Achilles by Hephaestus. in which two disputants in a lawsuit appear: ἄμφω δ' ἱέσθην ἐπὶ ἴστορι πεῖραρ ἐλέσθαι ("both were setting their hearts to get a final decision in the power of an arbitrator"). (ἄμφω: both ἵεμαι (middle of ἵημι): I set my heart on ἴστωρ: arbitrator ἑλέσθαι, aorist infinitive of αἱρέομαι, p.66 above). If πεῖραρ means "final decision" here, ἔνθα οἱ αἶσα ἐκφυγέειν μέγα πεῖραρ ὀϊζύος, ἥ μιν ἱκάνει means "where for him destiny is to escape once for all the great final decision of the woe which is approaching him", i.e. "and if he reaches there, he is destined to be clear of the great final decision (on him) which consists of the woe which is approaching him". (In later Greek, e.g. at Aristophanes, *Wasps* 157, ἐκφεύγω means "I am being acquitted" at a trial.) This translation is close to Lattimore's. What is to follow will be the severest test of Odysseus' will; if he does not succumb, he will face no more perils until he reaches Ithaca.)

²⁴ἄδην + genitive = to one's fill, until one is fed up with a thing. ἐλάαν is the future active infinitive of ἐλαύνω (σ having been lost from ἐλά(σ)ω) (Liddell & Scott and Chantraine, *op. cit.* vol.I, p.448). μίν is the object of ἐλάαν. Translate, φημι (I declare) (myself, ἐμέ being understood) ἐλάαν to be going to drive) μίν (him) ἄδην (until he has had enough) κακότητος (of misery).

²⁵εἰπὼν is nominative singular masculine of the participle of ἔειπον (p.66). σύναγεν is 3rd person singular, imperfect of συνάγω = I drive together.

²⁶νεφέλη = cloud, mass of clouds.

²⁷For χερσί see p. 40. τρίαινα = the trident. ἑλών is nominative masculine singular of the participle of εἷλον (p.66).

²⁸ὀρόθυνεν:3rd person singular imperfect, ὀροθύνω = I arouse. ἀέλλη = whirlwind. σὺν ... κάλυψε (line 293): συνεκάλυψε (tmesis). The subject is Poseidon.

²⁹ὁμοῦ = together. ὀρώρει = (it) had arisen (νύξ is the subject). ὀρώρει is 3rd person singular pluperfect (see Section 22) of ὄρνυμι: "had arisen".

³⁰The ending -θεν means "from", and οὐρανόθεν means "from heaven". The blackness of the clouds above causes darkness to cover the sea.

³¹σὺν ... ἔπεσον: συνέπεσον (tmesis), 3rd person plural of the aorist of συμπίπτω = I collide, meet violently (cf. ἔπεσον, p.67). δυσαής = ill-blowing, stormy.

³²αἰθρηγενέτης = "born of the ether" (Hainsworth).

³³κυλίνδων is nominative masculine singular of the present participle of κυλίνδω = I roll (cf. English "cylinder").

Section 20

The Perfect Tense

active	middle/passive
[λέλυκα = I have loosed	λέλυμαι = I have loosed for myself, I have been loosed
λέλυκας = you have loosed (singular)	λέλυσαι = you have loosed for yourself, you have been loosed (singular)
λέλυκε = he/she/it has loosed	λέλυται = he/she/it has loosed for him/her/itself, he/she/it has been loosed
λελύκατον = you two have loosed	λέλυσθον = you two have loosed for yourselves, you two have been loosed
λελύκατον = those two have loosed	λέλυσθον = those two have loosed for themselves, those two have been loosed.
λελύκαμεν = we have loosed	λελύμε(σ)θα = we have loosed for ourselves, we have been loosed
λελύκατε = you have loosed	λελύσθε = you have loosed for yourselves, you have been loosed
λελύκασι(ν) = they have loosed][2]	λελύνται[1] = they have loosed for themselves, they have been loosed.

Notes (i) The perfect tense describes a present state arising from a past action,[3] e.g.

ἐννέα δὴ βεβάασι Διὸς μεγάλου ἐνιαυτοί
καὶ δὴ δοῦρα σέσηπε[4] νεῶν καὶ σπάρτα λέλυνται. (Iliad ii, 134-5)
indeed, nine years of great Zeus have gone, and finally the timbers of the ships have become rotten and the cables have become loosened.

[1]Some verbs have 3rd person plural perfect middle & passive ending -αται instead of -νται, e.g. βεβλήαται ("they have been pelted", or "they have been thrown") from βέβλημαι, the perfect middle/passive of βάλλω (Iliad xi, 657 and Odyssey XI 194). See Chantraine, *Grammaire Homérique* vol.i, p.435.
[2]The perfect active of λύω is not found in Homer, but it shows the pattern of active perfects which do occur, e.g. βέβηκα or βέβαα, from βαίνω.
[3]Le rôle du parfait est d' exprimer un état acquis. Chantraine, *op.cit.* vol.ii, p.197 (the illustration is also his).
[4]Perfect of σήπω, I make rotten, putrefy (NB the perfect of σήπω has a passive meaning). ἐνιαυτός (2m) = year, anniversary σπάρτον (2n) = cable.

In English, this is the perfect tense expressed with "have", sometimes called the present perfect.

(ii)In most Greek verbs, the perfect is formed by *reduplication*, that is, by repeating the opening letter of the verb stem with ε, e.g. λέλυκα and λέλυμαι from λύω, and, in Homer,
βέβηκα *or* βέβαα (I have stepped, or I have gone) from βαίνω,
βέβληκα (I have thrown) from βάλλω,
δείδοικα *or* δείδια(I (have come to) fear) from δείδω,
μέμιγμαι (passive) (I have been mingled) from μίσγω, I mix,
πέπονθα (I have suffered) from πάσχω,
πέπταμαι[5] (I have been spread) (passive) from πετάννυμι,
πεποίημαι (I have been made) from ποιέω,
τετάνυσμαι (I have been stretched) from τανύω, I stretch,
τέτρηχα[6] (I have been troubled, am in uproar) from ταράσσω, I trouble,
τέτροφα (I have nurtured) from τρέφω (I nurture).

When the first letter of the stem is an aspirated consonant (θ, φ or χ), the corresponding unaspirated consonant is used for reduplication, e.g. τέθνηκα (I have died and so am dead) from θνήσκω, I die,
πέφασμαι (I have appeared) from φαίνω, I show,
πέφευγα (I have fled) from φεύγω, I flee,
κέχυμαι (I have been poured) from χέω, I pour.

When the first letter is a double consonant, e.g. ζ, ξ or ψ, or if the first letter is σ and it is followed by another consonant, ε is prefixed instead of reduplication. From ζεύγνυμι = I yoke or I join, there is ἔζευγμαι (passive).[7] Some verbs beginning σ- have perfects beginning ἐσσ-, e.g. from σεύω, I hasten, there is ἐσσύμενος -η -ον "having been hastened" and so "rushing" or "eager".[8]

---

[5]See p. 20.
[6]Used by Homer in passive sense; I have been thrown into disorder (and so) I am in disorder.
[7]"long planks, well planed, joined together (ἐζευγμέναι)" (Iliad xviii, 276, describing the gates of Troy).
[8]Also, from ἐπισσεύομαι, I am being set in motion (perfect ἐπέσσυμαι, I am in motion, rush, hasten), ἐπεσσύμενον meaning "onrushing" (Odyssey V, 314) and ἐπέσσυτο (pluperfect), meaning "she hastened" (VI, 20).

When the first letter is a vowel, in some verbs ε is prefixed. This may be a true reduplication, and at one time ε may have been followed by ϝ (digamma), a letter which dropped out of use.[9] In other verbs with stems beginning with vowels, the stem is either lengthened or repeated, e.g.

ἐλήλαμαι, I have been driven (passive) from ἐλαάω, I drive,
ὄλωλα,[10] I am ruined, I have perished, from ὄλλυμι, I destroy,
ὄρωρα,[11] I have arisen, from ὄρνυμι, I arouse.

If a verb has a preposition as a prefix, reduplication follows the prefix, e.g. ἀμφιβέβηκα, I have stepped around, from ἀμφιβαίνω, I step around.

What is the present tense (active) of: ἐπικέχυμαι, δέδυκα, τετέλεσμαι, πεφύλαγμαι.[12]

The perfect infinitive
The perfect infinitive active ends -(ε)μεν or -εμεναι
e.g. [λελύκεμεν] or [λελυκέμεναι], to have loosed.

The perfect infinitive middle/passive ends -(σ)θαι
e.g. λελύσθαι, to have loosed for oneself, to have been loosed.[13]

What is the English for: 1.βεβάμεν, 2.πεφευγέμεναι, 3.τετελέσθαι, 4.πεφάσθαι.

---

[9]Chantraine, *Grammaire Homérique*, vol.1, p.422. Note that the initial ε continued to be pronounced separately and so has the breathing, which does not go back to the following vowel. Examples of such perfects are ἔοικα and ἔολπα (see section 21). For digamma, see p.1, footnote 1.
[10]Note that the meaning of the perfect is *passive*, "I have been ruined, am dead" although the form is active. Other perfects with active-type endings which have intransitive or passive meanings, though the present tense of the verb is active, include ὄρωρα, from ὄρνυμι, and τέτρηχα from ταράσσω.
[11]The pluperfect of this verb (Section 22) occurs in line 294 (p.136, footnote 29).
[12]Verbs ending -σσω have perfect middle and passive ending -αγμαι.
[13]The perfect of ἀφικνέομαι is ἀφῖγμαι, formed by treating ἀφ- as a prefix and lengthening ι. The perfect infinitive, ἀφῖχθαι ("to have arrived") is found at Odyssey VI, 297.

Beginning Greek with Homer

New words:

αἶψα = quickly, suddenly
δοῦρα (n plu) = spears, spars[14]
ἐπισσεύω = I set in motion against
θάνατος (2m) = death
θύελλα (1f) = hurricane, squall[15]
ὄλεθρος (2m) = ruin, destruction
ὀχθέω = I am vexed
τῆλε, τηλοῦ = far off
χρόνος (2m) = time

ἅλμη (1f) = brine, salt water
ἔαξα (aorist of ἄγνυμι) = I broke
θνήσκω, aorist (ἐ)θάνον) = I die
μίσγω = I mix
ὁρμή (1f.) = effort, onset, rush.
στόμα, στόματος (3n) = mouth
χάρις (3f) = favour, kindness[16]
ὤ μοι (ἐγώ) expresses surprise or pain

What is the English for:
1. ὤ μοι ἐγὼ δειλός,[17] γούνατά μου νῦν λέλυται.
2. πόντος αἶψα τέτρηχε· οἵοισιν νεφέεσσι Ζεὺς περιστέφει[18] οὐρανὸν εὐρύν.
3. δεινὴ θύελλα ὄρωρε, τῆλε δ' ἀπὸ σχεδίης με βέβληκε.
4. θυέλλῃ σχεδίη ἐλήλαται· ἁρμονίαι σχεδίης κύμασι λελύνται.
5. νῦν δέ μοι σῶς[19] αἰπὺς[20] ὄλεθρος καὶ θάνατος πέφανται· ὄλωλα.

Odyssey V 297-332
καὶ τότ' Ὀδυσσῆος λύτο[21] γούνατα καὶ φίλον ἦτορ,
ὀχθήσας δ' ἄρα εἶπε[22] πρὸς ὃν μεγαλήτορα θυμόν·
"ὤ μοι ἐγὼ δειλός, τί νύ μοι μήκιστα[23] γένηται;
δείδω μὴ[24] δὴ πάντα θεὰ νημερτέα εἶπεν,   300
ἥ μ' ἔφατ' ἐν πόντῳ, πρὶν[25] πατρίδα γαῖαν ἱκέσθαι,

[14]Alternative to δούρατα.
[15]Genitive: θυέλλης.
[16]i.e. act of kindness. Accusative singular: χάριν, genitive singular: χάριτος. The plural, χάριτες, is often found (as at Odyssey VI, 18) meaning "The Graces".
[17]δειλός -ή -όν = "wretched" or "cowardly". "Woe is me, how wretched I am!"
[18]περιστέφω = I enwreathe, surround (στέφανος = wreath, as worn by Olympic victors).
[19]σῶς, σῶν (masculine as feminine) = "safe and sound", but here it is used ironically, and means "certain".
[20]αἰπύς, αἰπεῖα, αἰπύ = sheer, utter (often found with ὄλεθρος in Homer).
[21]For λύτο (also at 406, where this line is repeated) see p.127.
[22]See p. 135, footnote 17. ὀχθήσας is nominative masculine singular, participle of ὤχθησα, the aorist of ὀχθέω. εἶπε stands for ἔειπε (p.66). Although "to" is usually expressed by the dative in Greek with a verb implying speaking, πρός with the accusative is often used instead, as here and in line 338 below, and in 355, 407 and 464, where line 298 is repeated. Odyssey V 298 = Iliad xxi 552.
[23]μήκιστα = at last. γένηται (3rd person singular, subjunctive of ἐγενόμην the aorist of γίγνομαι) is deliberative: Odysseus wonders what is to become of him. Translate "What is to happen to me at last?"
[24]See p.98.
[25]See p.121.

Section 20

ἄλγε' ἀναπλήσειν·²⁶ τὰ δὲ δὴ νῦν πάντα τελεῖται.²⁷
οἵοισιν νεφέεσσι περιστέφει οὐρανὸν εὐρὺν
Ζεύς, ἐτάραξε δὲ πόντον, ἐπισπέρχουσι²⁸ δ' ἄελλαι²⁹
παντοίων ἀνέμων· νῦν μοι σῶς αἰπὺς ὄλεθρος.³⁰   305
τρὶς³¹ μάκαρες Δαναοὶ καὶ τετράκις,³² οἳ τότ' ὄλοντο³³
Τροίῃ ἐν εὐρείῃ, χάριν Ἀτρεΐδῃσι φέροντες.
ὡς δὴ ἐγώ γ' ὄφελον³⁴ θανέειν καὶ πότμον³⁵ ἐπισπεῖν
ἤματι τῷ ὅτε μοι πλεῖστοι³⁶ χαλκήρεα³⁷ δοῦρα

²⁶ἀναπλήσειν is the infinitive of ἀναπλήσω, the future of ἀναπίμπλημι, "I fill up" (p.114). The infinitive goes with the accusative μ' (standing for με) in line 301. Translate "who (ἥ) said me ... to be going to fill up woes" (i.e., that I would have my fill of woes). The reference is to line 207.

²⁷τελεῖται is contracted from τελέεται, 3rd person singular, present indicative middle (used as passive) of τελέω.

²⁸ἐτάραξε is 3rd person singular of ἐτάραξα, the aorist indicative of ταράσσω. ἐπισπέρχω = I rage furiously (Liddell & Scott), I rush to the spot (Autenrieth).

²⁹ἄελλη (1f) = gust, whirlwind.

³⁰Understand φαίνεται "appears" (the subject is σῶς αἰπὺς ὄλεθρος).

³¹τρὶς μάκαρες = three times blessed. Understand "were" as the verb of which Δαναοί is the subject. Δαναοί really means "subjects of Danaos", a mythical king of Argos in Greece, but is often used by Homer to mean the Greeks at Troy generally; Agamemnon, the chief Greek king at Troy, is spoken of as king of Argos as well as Mycenae.

³²τετράκις = four times.

³³ὄλοντο is 3rd person plural of ὀλόμην (augmented, ὠλόμην) aorist indicative middle of ὄλλυμι. The aorist middle of ὄλλυμι has a passive meaning in English: always "I was destroyed" or "I was killed". Τροίη = Troy (as at line 39). εὐρείῃ is dative of εὐρείη (p.125, footnote 60) and qualifies Τροίη. Translate as ἐν εὐρείῃ Τροίῃ. φέροντες is nominative masculine plural of φέρων, the participle of φέρω. χάριν φέρειν + dative, "to bear favour for somebody", means "to win their gratitude". Ἀτρεΐδαι are the sons of Atreus, Agamemnon and Menelaus.

³⁴ὡς here introduces a wish, "O that!", "if only" (Chantraine, *op. cit.* vol.ii, p.214). The verb that follows is aorist indicative (not optative) to show that the wish, which relates to the past, cannot be fulfilled. ὄφελον (or ὤφελον) is 1st person singular, (strong) aorist of ὀφείλω, I owe. It is used, followed by an infinitive, to mean "I ought to have ..." ὡς ὄφελον θανέειν = "if only!, I ought to have died", i.e. "if only I had died". θανέειν is the infinitive of (ἔ)θανον.

³⁵πότμος (2m) = doom, destiny. πότμον ἐπισπεῖν is "to come face to face with one's destiny", "to meet one's doom". ἐπισπεῖν is the infinitive of ἐπέσπον, the aorist of ἐφέπω, I encounter.

³⁶ἤματι τῷ = on that day (dative expressing "time when"). πλεῖστοι -αι -α = very many, qualifying Τρῶες (3 masculine plural, Trojans). μοι = at me .

³⁷χαλκήρεα is neuter plural accusative of χαλκήρης, "tipped with bronze".

Τρῶες ἐπέρριψαν³⁸ περὶ Πηλεΐωνι³⁹ θανόντι.   310
τῷ⁴⁰ κ' ἔλαχον⁴¹ κτερέων,⁴² καί μευ κλέος⁴³ ἦγον Ἀχαιοί·⁴⁴
νῦν δέ με λευγαλέῳ⁴⁵ θανάτῳ εἵμαρτο⁴⁶ ἁλῶναι.' ⁴⁷
  ὣς ἄρα μιν εἰπόντ'⁴⁸ ἔλασεν μέγα κῦμα κατ' ἄκρης,⁴⁹
δεινὸν ἐπεσσύμενον,⁵⁰ περὶ δὲ σχεδίην ἐλέλιξε.⁵¹
τῆλε δ' ἀπὸ σχεδίης αὐτὸς πέσε,⁵² πηδάλιον δὲ   315
ἐκ χειρῶν προέηκε· μέσον δέ οἱ⁵³ ἱστὸν ἔαξε

---

³⁸ἐπέρριψαν, 3rd person plural of the (weak) aorist active of ἐπιρρίπτω (with accusative of missile and dative of target (μοι)), I hurl (at).
³⁹Odysseus implies that defending Achilles' corpse was his most dangerous exploit at Troy. Πηλεΐων "son of Peleus" refers to Achilles, shot in the heel (his only vulnerable part) by Paris perhaps with the aid of Apollo; the dying Hector prophesied Achilles' death in the Scaean gate at the hands of Paris and Apollo (Iliad xxii 359-60). Achilles' death, the battle over his corpse, and his funeral (see Odyssey XXIV, 35-94) were probably included in the lost epic *Aethiopis*, attributed to Arctinus of Miletus or Homer (*Homeri Opera* V p.126, Oxford Classical Texts, and Hainsworth *A Commentary on Homer's Odyssey* vol.i, p. 281). θανόντι (dative singular masculine, from θανών, the participle of ἔθανον, the aorist of θνήσκω, meaning "having died", i.e. "when he had been killed") qualifies Πηλεΐωνι, dative with περί.
⁴⁰τῷ = "by that".
⁴¹ἔλαχον is 1st person singular, (strong) aorist of λαγχάνω (+ genitive, = I have the benefit of"). κ' ἔλαχον means "in that case, I should have had the benefit of ...". The effect of κε with the aorist is to give the result that would have happened if a past condition which is unfulfilled had been fulfilled.
⁴²κτέρεα (plural of κτέρας, 3 neuter) = funeral gifts.
⁴³κλέος (3n) = fame. κλέος ἄγω τινος: I celebrate someone's glory. ἦγον is 3rd person plural, imperfect active. The imperfect expresses what would have followed if the condition had been fulfilled: "the Greeks would have been celebrating ..." (See p.172, footnote 7.)
⁴⁴Ἀχαιοί = "the Greeks" (used in Homer especially of Agamemnon's and Achilles' men; Scullard, *Oxford Classical Dictionary*, 2nd edition, "*Achaea*").
⁴⁵λευγαλέος, λευγαλέα, λευγαλέον = wretched, pitiable.
⁴⁶εἵμαρτο: "it was decreed (by fate)". This is 3rd person singular pluperfect (see Section 22) of μείρομαι (= I receive as my portion). (The 3rd person singular perfect, εἵμαρται, was used for "it has been decreed by fate".)
⁴⁷ἁλῶναι is the infinitive of the aorist (ἥλων) of ἁλίσκομαι = I am caught, and means "to be caught". Translate closely with με: "it was decreed me to be caught", i.e. "it was decreed that I should be caught ... "
⁴⁸εἰπόντ' stands for εἰπόντα (accusative, qualifying μιν): "him saying", i.e., "as he was speaking thus". ἔλασεν (subject, μέγα κῦμα) is 3rd person singular of ἔλασα, the aorist of ἐλαάω, here = I smite, strike.
⁴⁹κατ' ἄκρης = down from above. (ἄκρη, ἄκρης fem. = top, highest part.)
⁵⁰ἐπεσσύμενον is neuter (qualifying κῦμα) of the past participle passive of ἐπισσεύω) and means "having been set in motion", i.e. "swift", "onrushing".
⁵¹ἐλέλιξε is 3rd person singular, aorist (weak) active of ἐλελίζω, I whirl round. The subject is still κῦμα. περί is adverbial: "whirled the raft round".
⁵²πέσε: 3rd person singular, (ἔ)πεσον (p.67). αὐτός, the subject of πέσε and προέηκε (3rd person singular, aorist active, προίημι, I let go) refers to Odysseus.
⁵³οἱ is dative, "for him", but in English it would be more natural to say "his". μέσον ἱστον is, in English, the middle *of* the mast. The subject of ἔαξε is δεινὴ ἐλθοῦσα θύελλα. ἐλθοῦσα is feminine from ἐλθών, the participle of ἦλθον, the aorist of ἔρχομαι. It does not express past time (see pp.73-4.)

Section 20

δεινὴ μισγομένων⁵⁴ ἀνέμων ἐλθοῦσα θύελλα·
τηλοῦ δὲ σπεῖρον⁵⁵ καὶ ἐπίκριον ἔμπεσε⁵⁶ πόντῳ.
τὸν δ' ἄρ' ὑπόβρυχα⁵⁷ θῆκε πολὺν χρόνον, οὐδὲ δυνάσθη
αἶψα μάλ' ἀνσχεθέειν⁵⁸ μεγάλου ὑπὸ κύματος ὁρμῆς·   320
εἵματα γάρ ἐ βάρυνε,⁵⁹ τά οἱ πόρε⁶⁰ δῖα Καλυψώ.
ὀψὲ δὲ δή ῥ' ἀνέδυ,⁶¹ στόματος δ' ἐξέπτυσεν⁶² ἄλμην
πικρήν,⁶³ ἥ οἱ πολλὴ⁶⁴ ἀπὸ κρατὸς κελάρυζεν.⁶⁵
ἀλλ' οὐδ' ὧς σχεδίης ἐπελήθετο,⁶⁶ τειρόμενός⁶⁷ περ,
ἀλλὰ μεθορμηθεὶς⁶⁸ ἐνὶ κύμασιν ἐλλάβετ αὐτῆς,   325
ἐν μέσσῃ δὲ καθῖζε⁶⁹ τέλος⁷⁰ θανάτου ἀλεείνων.⁷¹

⁵⁴μισγομένων is masculine genitive plural, present participle middle of μίσγω, and means "getting mixed", "mingling", qualifying ἀνέμων.
⁵⁵σπεῖρον (2 neuter) = sail.
⁵⁶πόντῳ (dative) expresses the end of the motion implied by ἔμπεσε. ἔμπεσε is 3rd singular (strong) aorist of ἐμπίπτω (+ dative) = "I fall into".
⁵⁷τὸν, "him", refers to Odysseus. ὑπόβρυχα (adverb) = under water. θῆκε is 3rd person singular of (ἐ)θηκα, the aorist of τίθημι. Its subject is θύελλα. πολὺν χρόνον (the accusative marks duration; see p.128, footnote 6): "for much time", i.e. "for a long time". (For πολύν and πολλή below, see Section 23.) The subject of ἐδυνάσθη (3rd person singular of (ἐ)δυνάσθην, the aorist of δύναμαι) is "he" (Odysseus). ἐδυνάσθη is exceptional in Homer, where (ἐ)δυνήσατο (aorist middle) is usual for "he could".
⁵⁸ἀνσχεθέειν is the infinitive of ἀνέσχον, the aorist of ἀνέχω, I emerge. μεγάλου is genitive singular neuter of μέγας. Translate as: ὑπὸ ὁρμῆς μεγάλου κύματος.
⁵⁹βάρυνε is 3rd person singular imperfect of βαρύνω = I weigh down. The subject (neuter plural) is εἵματα and the object ἐ. τά is relative (p.49 (e)).
⁶⁰πόρε is 3rd person singular of (ἐ)πορον, a verb only found as (strong) aorist, "I provided". The English pluperfect ("had provided") would be appropriate.
⁶¹ἀνέδυ is 3rd person singular of ἀνέδυν, the (irregular) aorist of ἀναδύομαι = I pop up. ὀψὲ (here) = at last. ῥ' stands for ἄρα.
⁶²ἐξέπτυσεν is 3rd person singular of ἐξέπτυσα, the (weak) aorist active of ἐκπτύσσω (+ accusative of what is spat out and genitive of what it is spat out of) = I spit out.
⁶³πικρός -ή -όν = bitter. πικρήν qualifies ἄλμην.
⁶⁴πολλή (feminine) qualifies ἥ, which refers to ἄλμην, and means "in great quantity".
⁶⁵κρατός is the genitive singular of κράς, "head", a poetical synonym of κάρη. κελάρυζεν is 3rd person singular imperfect of κελαρύζω = I gush, run gurgling.
⁶⁶ἐπελήθετο is 3rd person singular of ἐπεληθόμην, the (strong) aorist of ἐπιλανθάνομαι (+ genitive) meaning "I forget", "I cease to be mindful of".
⁶⁷τειρόμενος is nominative masculine singular of the participle of τείρομαι = I am distressed.
⁶⁸See p.133.
⁶⁹καθῖζε is 3rd person singular imperfect of καθίζω = I sit. ἐν μέσσῃ stands for ἐν μέσῃ σχεδίῃ (cf. μέσον ἵστον line 316).
⁷⁰τέλος, τέλους (3n) = end, consummation. τέλος θανάτου means little more than "death"; cf. Iliad v, 553 (cited by Autenreith), of Crethon and Orsilochus, who were killed by Aeneas: τὼ δ' αὖθι τέλος θανάτοιο κάλυψεν – "and the two of them on the spot (the consummation of) death did cover".
⁷¹ἀλεείνων is masculine nominative singular of the (present active) participle of ἀλεείνω = I avoid, I shun.

τὴν⁷² δ' ἐφόρει μέγα κῦμα κατὰ ῥόον⁷³ ἔνθα καὶ ἔνθα.
ὡς⁷⁴ δ' ὅτ' ὀπωρινὸς⁷⁵ βορέης φορέῃσιν ἀκάνθας⁷⁶
ἂμ πεδίον,⁷⁷ πυκιναὶ δὲ πρὸς ἀλλήλῃσιν ἔχονται.
ὣς τὴν ἂμ πέλαγος⁷⁸ ἄνεμοι φέρον ἔνθα καὶ ἔνθα·   330
ἄλλοτε μέν τε νότος βορέῃ προβάλεσκε⁷⁹ φέρεσθαι,⁸⁰
ἄλλοτε δ' αὖτ' εὖρος ζεφύρῳ εἴξασκε⁸¹ διώκειν.

---

⁷²τὴν stands for σχεδίην. ἐφόρει (contracted from ἐφόρεε) is 3rd person singular imperfect active of φόρεω = I bear along. The subject is μέγα κῦμα.
⁷³κατὰ ῥόον = down the current (ῥόος is a stream in a river, or a current in the sea). ἔνθα καὶ ἔνθα = hither and thither.
⁷⁴ὡς δ' ὅτ', "and as when", introduces a simile (see also p.125, footnote 56). These are a feature both of the Iliad and the Odyssey and contain much subtlety (for a general discussion, see e.g. G.S. Kirk, *Homer and the Epic* (Cambridge, 1965) p. 107f). They are often extended beyond obvious points of resemblance, frequently with surprising images, to stimulate the imagination of the bard's listeners by reference to everyday sights and sounds of their own time or perhaps making references which were traditional in epic poetry. Here, Odysseus' raft is depicted as the plaything of the elements; other similes in books 5 and 6 include: 368-9 (the end of the raft, scattered like chaff); 394-8 (Odysseus' relief, at sighting land, like that of a family whose father recovers from a serious illness); 432-3 (Odysseus sucked off the rocks like an octopus); 488-90 (Odysseus sleeping, saved from the storm, like a spark of fire saved under a heap of dust at the edge of a field); book 6, 130-5 (Odysseus having, though naked, to approach young ladies for help, like a mountain lion in winter forced to raid farm stock); 232-5 (Athene making Odysseus handsome, like a skilful craftsman gilding a statue). ὅτ' stands for ὅτε.
⁷⁵ὀπωρινός (-ή-όν) "of late summer" qualifies Βορέης, the subject of φορέῃσιν (= φορέῃ), 3rd person singular, present subjunctive of φορέω: "whenever ... bears ...". ἀκάνθας is the object.
⁷⁶ἄκανθα = thorn, prickle, or prickly plant. ἄκανθαι are "thorny thistle stalks which gather into balls" (Stanford) or "thistles" (Autenrieth), not thistledown, the Greek for which is πάππος.
⁷⁷πεδίον (2n) = "plain", "field". ἂμ stands for ἄνα (+ accusative, = "up", "along"). ἂμ πεδίον = "along the plain". πρός with dative means "upon". ἔχονται = they cling. "they" stands for ἄκανθαι and is qualified by πυκιναί.
⁷⁸ὣς... ἄνεμοι ... (ὣς with accent) = so... the winds ... (τὴν ("it") stands for σχεδίην). πέλαγος πελάγους (3n) = the open sea. For ἂμ πέλαγος, compare ἂμ πεδίον. φέρον is 3rd person plural, imperfect of φέρω, and its subject is ἄνεμοι.
⁷⁹ἄλλοτε ... ἄλλοτε ... = at one time ... at another time ... μέν ... δέ ... = on the one hand ... on the other hand ... προβάλεσκε is 3rd person singular of the imperfect of προβάλλω, I throw to. The –σκον form of the imperfect denotes repetition: "kept on throwing" (Chantraine, *op. cit.*, vol. i, p.318).
⁸⁰The present passive infinitive of φέρω: "to be carried", expressing a purpose, as does διώκειν in line 332.
⁸¹εἴξασκε is 3rd person singular aorist of εἴκω (+ dative) = "I make way for". The –ασκε ending is frequentative. διώκειν is the (present active) infinitive of διώκω = I chase.

Section 21
The perfect tense (2)

The perfect tense describes a present state which has been acquired through a previous action; however, in the case of many verbs expressing feelings, positions of the body, sounds and conditions, the reference to a previous action is not apparent and the Greek perfect is expressed by an English present (a common example is ἕστηκα, I stand). The following examples are found in Odyssey V and VI:

     ἄνωγα = I command
     γέγωνα = I make myself heard
     ἔϊκα or ἔοικα = I am like (+ dative)
     ἔολπα = I hope (have come to hope)
     μέμονα = I am eager[1]
     οἶδα = I know.

Also found in Homer is: εἴωθα, I am accustomed (to).

What is the English for:
1. τὰ δέ σε φράζεσθαι[2] ἄνωγα. (Odyssey XXIII, 122)
2. σμερδαλέον[3] δ' ἐβόησε, γέγωνέ τε πᾶσι θεοῖσι. (Odyssey VIII, 305)
3. οὔτε κακῷ οὔτε ἄφρονι[4] φωτὶ ἔοικας (Odyssey VI, 187)
4. ...μέμαμεν δέ τοι ἔξοχον[5] ἄλλων
 κήδιστοί τ' ἔμεναι καὶ φίλτατοι, ὅσσοι Ἀχαιοί. (Iliad ix, 641-2)

οἶδα (which is derived from *εἴδω, I see (with the mind's eye), a verb not found in the present tense) is irregular:
 οἶδα = I know   ἴδμεν = we know
 οἶσθα *or* οἶδας = you know (sing.) ἴστε = you know (plu.)
 οἶδε(ν) = he/she/it knows   ἴσασι(ν) = they know[6]

The 2nd person imperative is ἴσθι (know!), and the 3rd person imperative is ἴστω (let him/her/it know).

[1]This is irregular: 1st person plural ("we are eager") is μέμαμεν, the 2nd person plural ("you are eager") is μέματε and 3rd person plural ("they are eager") is μεμάασι. The participle, "eager" is μεμαώς. (Chantraine, *Grammaire Homérique* vol.i, p.425)
[2]φράζομαι = I consider, ponder, think over.
[3]σμερδαλέον = fearfully. βοάω = I shout.
[4]ἄφρων (3rd declension adjective) = senseless. φώς, φωτός (3m) = man, fellow.
[5]τοι: to you ἔξοχον = more than (+ genitive) κήδιστος = most worthy of care
φίλτατος = dearest.
[6]The dual is not found in Homer.

The subjunctive is εἰδῶ or εἰδέω or ἰδέω (let me know), εἰδῇς (may you know), εἰδῇ (may he/she/it know), εἴδομεν (let us know), εἴδετε (may you know) (plural), εἰδῶσι (let them know).

The optative is only found in the 2nd person singular, εἰδείης (O that you might know!) and 3rd person singular, εἰδείη (O that he/she/it might know!)

The infinitive is ἴδμεναι or ἴδμεν, to know.[7]

New words:
ἀλάομαι = I wander   ἀλύσκω (aorist ἤλυξα) = I escape
ἀπινύσσω = I lack understanding
αὐδήεις, αὐδήεσσα, αὐδῆεν = speaking with human voice[8]
ἄψ = back again   δέος, δέους (3n) = fear, alarm
δοκέω = I seem   εἰκώς, εἰκυῖα, εἰκός (+ dat.) = like
ἤπειρος (1f) = land, mainland
θυγάτηρ, θυγατρός (3f) = daughter
κρήδεμνον -ου = women's headdress[9]
νέω (also νήχω) = I swim
στέρνον -ου (2n) = breast[10]   τανύω[11] = I stretch
ὧδε = thus, so, in this way

---

[7]For ἤδεα, the past tense of οἶδα, see Section 22, p.154.
[8]This adjective is used to describe two goddesses, Circe and Calypso, as well as Ino in her human form. It has been suggested that the other gods had a distinctive intonation (Hainsworth, *A Commentary on Homer's Odyssey* vol.i, p.282, cites J. Clay, *Hermes* cii, pp.129-36). The special word - ὀμφή - used in Homer only for the speech of the gods, may have meant a kind of chanting. It is found at Iliad ii, 41 (the voice of Zeus heard by Agamemnon in a dream), Iliad xx, 129 (used by Hera of the gods generally) and Odyssey III, 215, (but here Nestor uses it for a proclamation by the gods, not for their intonation, and it could have that meaning in the Iliad also) and in the same formulaic couplet addressed to Telemachus, by Odysseus at XVI, 96. In later Greek, ὀμφή is used for oracles, and human voices, e.g. Euripides, *Medea* 175 μύθων τ' αὐδαθέντων δέξαιτ' ὀμφάν; "and would she welcome the sound of myths being uttered?" (referring to the singing of the chorus) cited in Liddell & Scott. Greek seems to have been the language of Olympus, although gods and people had different names for some things, e.g. Iliad xx 73-4: ποταμὸς βαθυδίνης, ὃν Ξάνθον καλέουσι θεοί, ἄνδρες δὲ Σκάμανδρον "the river, deep-eddying, which the gods call Xanthus, but men (call) Scamander".
[9]Liddell & Scott suggest "veil" or "mantilla"; it was, however, substantial enough to serve Odysseus as a kind of lifebelt.
[10]In Homer, always of males (Liddell & Scott).
[11]Aorist active, ἐτάνυσσα.

Section 21

What is the English for: 1.ταῦτα ἴστε; 2.ταῦτα εὖ ἴδμεν. 3.ταὐτά σε ἴδμεναι ἔολπα. 4.ἔολπας θεούς σε σαωσέμεν; ὧδε ἔρδειν (to act) σε ἄνωγα. 5.ὑμεῖς αὐτοὶ τόδε ἴστε; 6.ἴδμεν· ἡμεῖς γὰρ αὐτοὶ τόδε ἴδομεν. 7.πῶς ἴδεν ᾿Οδυσσῆα καλλίσφυρος᾿Ινω; τοῦτο οὐκ ἴδμεν. 8.σοὶ δ᾿ ὧδε μνηστῆρες[12] ὑποκρίνονται, ἵν᾿ εἰδῆς αὐτὸς σῷ θυμῷ, εἰδῶσι δὲ πάντες ᾿Αχαιοί. (Odyssey II, 111-2)

Odyssey V, 333-353
τὸν δὲ ἴδεν Κάδμου θυγάτηρ, καλλίσφυρος[13] ᾿Ινώ,[14]
Λευκοθέη, ἣ πρὶν μὲν ἔην βροτὸς αὐδήεσσα,
νῦν δ᾿ ἁλὸς ἐν πελάγεσσι[15] θεῶν ἐξέμμορε[16] τιμῆς.   335
ἥ ῥ᾿ ᾿Οδυσῆ᾿ ἐλέησεν[17] ἀλώμενον, ἄλγε᾿ ἔχοντα·
[αἰθυίῃ[18] δ᾿ εἰκυῖα ποτῇ ἀνεδύσετο λίμνης,]

[12]μνηστῆρες = the suitors ὑποκρίνομαι = I answer.
[13]τὸν, "him", stands for Odysseus. For ἴδεν, see note on line 283. καλλίσφυρος = with beautiful ankles, (epithet of women, Iliad ix, 557 and 560, and xiv, 319).
[14]Ino, a daughter of Cadmus the founder of Thebes, was the second wife of Athamas, the king of Orchomenos in Boeotia, who had previously married Nephele ("Cloud"), a phantom created by Zeus to deceive Ixion when he tried to seduce Hera. Athamas had a son, Phrixus and a daughter, Helle, by Nephele, and two sons, Learchus and Melicertes, by Ino. Nephele resented the second marriage and complained to Hera who swore vengeance. Meanwhile, through the intrigues of Ino, Phrixus was to be sacrificed to Zeus, but escaped with his sister (who was to fall into the Hellespont) on the miraculous flying ram with the golden fleece. Hera sent a fit of madness upon Athamas who attacked his second family and killed Learchus; Ino and Melicertes only evaded Athamas' assault by leaping into the sea from the Molurian Rock near Megara (Pausanias, *Description of Greece* I, xliv, 7). As Ino was a sister of Semele, the mother of Dionysus, she was not sent to Hades but changed into a sea goddess known as Leucothea. (Hainsworth, *op. cit.*, p.282.) See also Ovid, *Metamorphoses* IV, 416-562.) For ἔην, see p.9, footnote 10.
[15]For πέλαγος, see p.144, footnote 78. ἁλὸς ἐν πελάγεσσι "on the high seas".
[16]ἐξέμμορε is 3rd person singular of ἐξέμμορον, strong aorist of ἐκμείρομαι (+ genitive) = I obtain for my lot. τιμή, τιμῆς (1 fem.) = honour (here, "status").
[17]᾿Οδυσῆ᾿ stands for᾿Οδυσῆα. ἐλέησεν is 3rd person singular of ἐλέησα, the aorist of ἐλεέω = I pity (the subject is ἥ). ἀλώμενον is accusative masculine singular of ἀλώμενος (contracted from ἀλαόμενος), the (present) participle of ἀλάομαι, and ἔχοντα is accusative masculine singular of ἔχων, the (present) participle of ἔχω. Both qualify ᾿Οδυσῆα.
[18]This line, though not excised by Aristarchus, is bracketed as many early editors thought it an interpolation inspired by line 353. Hainsworth (*op. cit.*, p.283) prefers to retain it, as it shows Leucothea coming out of the sea. αἴθυια probably = shearwater (Liddell & Scott, and Stanford). The context requires a diving bird, and the Manx shearwater (*Puffinus puffinus*) is found in the Mediterranean. ποτή = flight (ποτῇ: in flight). ἀνεδύσετο is 3rd person singular of ἀναδύομαι = I rise up. For ἀνεδύσετο, see footnote 38 below. λίμνη (properly = "marsh") here = "sea". The use of the genitive indicates "out of".

ἷζε[19] δ' ἐπὶ σχεδίης καί μιν πρὸς μῦθον ἔειπε·
"κάμμορε,[20] τίπτε τοι ὧδε Ποσειδάων ἐνοσίχθων
ὠδύσατ'[21] ἐκπάγλως, ὅτι τοι κακὰ πολλὰ φυτεύει;[22]   340
οὐ μὲν δή σε καταφθείσει,[23] μάλα περ μενεαίνων.[24]
ἀλλὰ μάλ' ὧδ' ἔρξαι,[25] δοκέεις δέ μοι οὐκ ἀπινύσσειν·
εἵματα ταῦτ' ἀποδὺς[26] σχεδίην ἀνέμοισι φέρεσθαι
κάλλιπ',[27] ἀτὰρ χείρεσσι νέων ἐπιμαίεο[28] νόστου
γαίης Φαιήκων, ὅθι τοι μοῖρ' ἐστὶν ἀλύξαι.[29]   345
τῆ[30] δέ, τόδε[31] κρήδεμνον ὑπὸ στέρνοιο τανύσσαι
ἄμβροτον·[32] οὐδέ τί[33] τοι παθέειν δέος οὐδ' ἀπολέσθαι.

[19]ἷζε is 3rd person singular, imperfect indicative active of ἵζω. Translate in the order ἔειπε μῦθον πρός μιν.

[20]κάμμορε is vocative masculine singular of κάμμορος, "unfortunate", formed from κακός ("bad") and μόρος ("fate", "doom", "lot"). τίπτε is a shortened form of τί ποτε; (= why ever?)

[21]ὀδύσσομαι (found only in aorist, ὠδυσάμην) = I am vexed at, I feel hatred for (with dative). ὠδύσατ' stands for ὠδύσατο, 3rd person singular, indicative. Although most aorists in Homer refer to past occurrences, this is an example of a timeless aorist, referring to Poseidon's attitude in isolation, i.e. in an absolute sense. It is better translated as present in English. See p.32 and especially pp.189-90. For a possible double meaning in ὠδύσατο, see p.102, footnote 50. ἐκπάγλως = outrageously (Hainsworth). τοι: "for you".

[22]φυτεύει is 3rd person singular of φυτεύω = I cause (literally, "I plant").

[23]καταφθείσει is 3rd person singular of καταφθείσω, future (active) of καταφθίνω, I destroy utterly.

[24]μενεαίνων is nominative singular masculine of the present participle of μενεαίνω = I desire eagerly.

[25]ἔρξαι is the aorist infinitive of ἔρδω, I do, used as an imperative. (Many mss. show this verb with a rough breathing, present ἕρδω, aorist active ἕρξα.) μάλ' ὧδ' = just like this. μάλ ' stands for μάλα.

[26]ἀποδύς is nominative masculine singular (qualifying "you", implied by ἔρξαι) of the participle of ἀπέδυν, aorist of ἀποδύομαι, I take off.

[27]κάλλιπ' is short for κατάλιπε, the 2nd person singular imperative from κατέλιπον, the aorist of καταλείπω, I leave behind, abandon.

[28]νέων is nominative masculine singular of the present active participle of νέω. ἐπιμαίεο is 2nd person singular, present imperative of ἐπιμαίομαι (+ genitive) = I strive after, make for. νόστος + genitive = "arrival at" rather than "voyage home" (Hainsworth, op. cit., p.283). "arrival of" = "arrival at".

[29]See page 10. μοῖρ ' stands for μοίρα. ἀλύξαι is the infinitive of ἤλυξα.

[30]τῆ = here! (always followed by a command).

[31]See Section 8, p.52.

[32]τάνυσσαι is aorist infinitive of τανύω used as imperative (see p.105), as are βαλέειν (line 349) and τράπεσθαι (line 350). ἄμβροτος, ἄμβροτον (fem. as masc.) = immortal, divine, qualifying κρήδεμνον.

[33]τοι is enclitic; this explains the accent on τί, which is to be translated as τι, "any" (neuter, qualifying δέος). Understand ἐστι with δέος τι and translate in the order: οὐδέ ἐστί τι δέος τοι παθέειν οὐδέ ("nor") ἀπολέσθαι. ("fear for you to suffer: = "fear that you will suffer"). παθέειν is the infinitive of ἔπαθον, the aorist active of πάσχω. ἀπολέσθαι is the infinitive of ἀπωλόμην, the strong aorist middle (with passive meaning) of ἀπόλλυμι, I destroy, and means "to be destroyed".

Section 21

αὐτὰρ ἐπὴν³⁴ χείρεσσιν ἐφάψεαι ἠπείροιο,
ἂψ ἀπολυσάμενος³⁵ βαλέειν εἰς οἴνοπα πόντον
πολλὸν³⁶ ἀπ' ἠπείρου, αὐτὸς δ' ἀπονόσφι τραπέσθαι.   350
  ὣς ἄρα φωνήσασα θεὰ κρήδεμνον ἔδωκεν,³⁷
αὐτὴ δ' ἂψ ἐς πόντον ἐδύσετο κυμαίνοντα³⁸
αἰθυίῃ εἰκυῖα· μέλαν δέ ἑ κῦμ' ἐκάλυψεν.³⁹

---

³⁴ἐπήν = ἐπεί + ἄν = whenever, at such time as. ἐφάψεαι is 2nd person singular (with short vowel - ε - instead of ἐφάψηαι, see p.97) of ἐφάψωμαι, the aorist subjunctive of ἐφάπτομαι (+ genitive) = I touch, grasp: After ἐπήν, it means "at such time as you may grasp ...". χείρεσσιν is dative plural of χείρ.

³⁵The masculine singular nominative of the participle of ἀπελυσάμην, the aorist of ἀπολύομαι = I undo, release. βαλέειν (see footnote 32) is the infinitive of (ἐ)βαλον, the aorist of βάλλω.

³⁶πολλόν = far. ἀπ ' stands for ἀπό. ἀπονόσφι = away. τραπέσθαι is the infinitive of ἐτραπόμην, the aorist of τρέπομαι, I turn (myself). αὐτὸς refers to "you" implied by the imperatives: "as for you yourself, turn away".

³⁷For ὣς ἄρα φωνήσασα, see line 192. ἔδωκε is 3rd person singular of ἔδωκα, the aorist of δίδωμι.

³⁸ἐδύσετο is 3rd person singular of ἐδυσάμην, the aorist middle of δύω (the subject is θεὰ αὐτή, i.e. Ino). We should expect ἐδύσατο, but the 3rd person singular ("he/she/it sank") is always (ἐ)δύσετο in the Iliad and Odyssey (see Chantraine, *Grammaire Homérique* vol.i, pp.416-7), and this also applies to compounds such as ἀνεδύσετο ("she popped up") in line 337. κυμαίνοντα (accusative masculine singular of the present participle of κυμαίνω, I surge) qualifies πόντον. κῦμ ' stands for κῦμα.

³⁹For αἰθυίῃ εἰκυῖα, see line 337. ἐκάλυψεν is the 3rd person singular of ἐκάλυψα, the aorist (active) of καλύπτω. The subject is μέλαν κῦμα.

Hainsworth (*op. cit.*,p.282) notes that Leucothea was a generic name for sea goddesses. Ino was worshipped in several other places as well as Megara, and it was said that she came up from the sea at Corone in Messenia after her name had been changed from Ino to Leucothea (Pausanias, *Description of Greece*, IV, xxxiv, 4). A scholium on Apollonius Rhodius, *Argonautica* I, 917, cited by Hainsworth and by W. Buckert in *Greek Sanctuaries* (ed. Marinatos & Hägg, Routledge, 1993, p.187) mentions that in the mysteries of Samothrace the initiates wore a talisman against drowning, as Odysseus had worn the veil of Leucothea. *Argonautica* I, 915-8 is as follows:

ἑσπέριοι δ' 'Ορφῆος ἐφημοσύνῃσιν ἔκελσαν
νῆσον ἐς 'Ηλέκτρης 'Ατλαντίδος, ὄφρα δαέντες
ἀρρήτους ἀγανῇσι τελεσφορίῃσι θέμιστας
σωότεροι κρυόεσσαν ὑπεὶρ ἅλα ναυτίλλοιντο.

"In the evening, at the suggestion of Orpheus, they beached the ship at Samothrace, the island of Electra daughter of Atlas. He wished them, by a holy initiation, to learn something of the secret rites, and so sail on with greater confidence across the formidable sea." (tr. Rieu)

Beginning Greek with Homer
Section 22
Part A - The Perfect Participle

The perfect participle active of λύω is λελυκώς (masculine), λελυκυῖα (feminine), λελυκός (neuter), meaning "having loosed" (not found in Homer). The commonest perfect participles are those of verbs which are perfect in form but have present meanings in English; and the commonest of these is the participle of οἶδα, εἰδώς, "knowing", which has already been met three times:

1. μή τις ἔτι πρόφρων ἀγανὸς καὶ ἤπιος ἔστω
σκηπτοῦχος βασιλεύς, μηδὲ φρεσὶν αἴσιμα εἰδώς (OdysseyV, 8-9)
let not any sceptre-bearing king be gracious, gentle and kind, nor _knowing_ things that are agreeable

2. ἦ δὴ ἀλιτρός γ' ἐσσὶ καὶ οὐκ ἀποφώλια εἰδώς (Odyssey V, 182)
Indeed, you are a rogue, and _knowing_ things that are not in vain

3. ὅσσον τίς τ' ἔδαφος τορνώσεται ἀνὴρ
φορτίδος εὐρείης, εὖ εἰδὼς τεκτοσυνάων (Odyssey V, 249-250)
as big as a man will round off the bottom of a wide freighter, a man well _knowledgable_ (knowing) of skills
and is also found at Odyssey VI, 12.

μεμαώς (eager), from μέμονα, occurs at V, 375.

ἐοικώς or εἰκώς (like), from ἔοικα (I am like)[1] occurs in the masculine at V, 51 σεύατ' ἔπειτ' ἐπὶ κῦμα λάρῳ ὄρνιθι ἐοικώς ("then he dived down on to the wave _like_ a bird (that is) a gull"), in the feminine (εἰκυῖα) at V, 337 and 353 αἰθυίῃ εἰκυῖα ("_like_ a shearwater"), and in the neuter (plural) at VI, 301:
οὐ μὲν γάρ τι ἐοικότα τοῖσι τέτυκται
δώματα Φαιήκων, οἷος δόμος Ἀλκινόοιο
ἥρως[2] ("for indeed for them the houses of the Phaeacians have been built not at all _like_ such as the house of the hero Alcinous (is).").

γεγαώς, from γέγονα, the perfect of γίγνομαι, occurs in the form ἐκγεγαυῖα ("sprung from") at VI, 229, where Διὸς ἐκγεγαυῖα ("sprung from Zeus" = "daughter of Zeus") is an epithet of Athene.

---
[1] As well as "like", ἐοικώς sometimes means "suitable", "seemly" or "reasonable".
[2] ἥρως is genitive singular here, contracted from ἥρωος. Hainsworth (*A Commentary on Homer's Odyssey* vol.i, p.312) and Garvie (*Homer, Odyssey Books VI-VIII*, p.156) note this as a unique example. τέτυκται is 3rd person singular (neuter plural subject) of τέτυγμαι, the perfect middle/passive of τεύχω, I make, build. δόμος (2m) = house.

Section 22   151

Other active perfect participles found frequently[3] in Homer include:
τεθνηώς ("dead"), from τέθνηκα, the perfect of θνήσκω
ἀρηρώς ("fitting", "having been made to fit")[4]
κεκμηκώς ("weary") from κάμνω ("I toil").

The declension of εἰδώς is:

SINGULAR	masculine	feminine	neuter
nominative	εἰδώς	(ἐ)ἰδυῖα	[εἰδός]
	(a) knowing (man)	(a) knowing (woman)	(a) knowing (thing)
accusative	εἰδότα	(ἐ)ἰδυῖαν	[εἰδός]
	(a) knowing (man)	(a) knowing (woman)	(a) knowing (thing)
genitive	εἰδότος	[(ἐ)ἰδυίης]	[εἰδότος]
	of (a) knowing (man)	of (a) knowing (woman)	of (a) knowing (thing)
dative	[εἰδότι]	[(ἐ)ἰδυίῃ]	[εἰδότι]
	to/for (a) knowing (man)	to/for (a) (woman) knowing	by (a) knowing (thing)
DUAL nom & acc	εἰδότε	[(ἐ)ἰδυία]	[εἰδότε]
	two knowing (men)	two knowing (women)	two knowing (things)
gen & dat	[εἰδότοιιν]	[(ἐ)ἰδυίῃιν]	[εἰδότοιιν]
	of, *or* to/for two knowing men	of, *or* to/for two knowing men	of, *or* by two knowing men
PLURAL nominative	εἰδότες	[(ἐ)ἰδυῖαι]	[εἰδότα]
	knowing (men)	knowing (women)	knowing (things)
accusative	[εἰδότας]	(ἐ)ἰδυίας	[εἰδότα]
	knowing (men)	knowing (women)	knowing (things)
genitive	[εἰδότων]	[(ἐ)ἰδυίων]	[εἰδότων]
	of knowing (men)	of knowing (women)	of knowing (things)
dative	εἰδόσι	(ἐ)ἰδυίῃσι	[εἰδόσι]
	to/for knowing (men)	to/for knowing (women)	by knowing (things)

---
[3]δεδαηκώς *or* δεδαώς, "knowing about", "having been taught", from *δάω, "I learn, I teach" is found twice in the Odyssey (II, 61 and XVII, 519).
[4]from ἀραρίσκω, I join, fit together. The perfect, ἄρηρα, has an intransitive meaning, "I (have been made to) fit."

Some active perfect participles have endings formed from -ηω or -εω, e.g. τεθνηώς, dead, having died:

	masculine	feminine	neuter
SINGULAR nominative	τεθνηώς having died	[τεθνυῖα] having died	[τεθνηός]
accusative	τεθνηῶτα or τεθνηότα having died	τεθνηυῖαν having died	[τεθνηός]
genitive	τεθνηῶτος or τεθνηότος of(a man) having died	τεθνηυίης of a woman having died	[τεθνηότος]
dative	τεθνηῶτι to/for (a man) having died	[τεθνηυίῃ]	[τεθνηκότι]
PLURAL nominative	[τεθνηῶτες] [dead (men)]	[τεθνηυῖαι] [dead (women)]	[τεθνηῶτα] [dead (things)]
accusative	τεθνηῶτας or τεθνηότας dead (men)	[τεθνηυίας]	[τεθνηῶτα]
genitive	τεθνηώτων of dead men	[τεθνηυίων]	[τεθνηώτων]
dative	[τεθνηῶσι(ν)] to/for dead (men)	[τεθνηυίῃσι(ν)]	[τεθνηῶσι(ν)]

The dual is not found.
Like τεθνηώς is [ἑστηώς] ("standing"), from ἵστημι.[5]
Perfect participles active occasionally have the same ending pattern in Homer as present participles active, e.g.
τοὶ δ' ἅμ' ἕποντο ὀξέα κεκλήγοντες and they were following, having begun to scream shrilly (Iliad xii, 124-5) (ἕπομαι - I follow ὀξύς - sharp) κεκλήγοντες is nominative plural masculine of the perfect participle of κλάζω, I scream. The nominative singular masculine is κεκληγώς. The present form is only used when -οντ- appears in the ending. Chantraine (*Grammaire Homérique* vol.i, p.430) gives this as an example of Aeolian usage, noting that it is not consistent: κεκληγῶτες and κεκληγῶτας also occur.

There is a perfect participle middle/passive,
λελυμένος (masc.), λελυμένη (fem.), λελυμένον (neut.)
(having loosed for oneself, having been loosed)
which is declined like καλός, καλή, καλόν (as is the present participle middle/passive; see section 11, p.71).

[5]See p.224. Nom. sing. not used by Homer, but by Hesiod (*Theogony*, 747).

Section 22

What is the English for: 1.εἰδυῖα. 2.ἐοικός. 3.γεγαότες. 4.μεμαὼς τέκνον. 5.σκηπτοῦχος βασιλεὺς⁶ Διὸς ἐκγεγαώς. 6.ἄνεμος θυέλλῃ ἐοικώς. 7.κούρη (a girl) πολλὰ εἰδυῖα. 8.ἀνὴρ βοάων γεγωνώς.⁷ 9.ἵκεται ἐσθλὰ ἐολπότες.
10.θεὸς λαρῷ ὄρνιθι ἐοικώς. 11.τετελεσμένον ἐστίν. (Odyssey V, 90)
12.μεμαότες ἵκεται.
13.κρῆναι τετραμμέναι ἄλλυδις ἄλλη. (Odyssey V, 70-1)
14.Κίρκη ἑταίρους ἐξέλασεν σιάλοισιν ἐοικότας ἐννεώροισιν.⁸
15.νεκρὸν⁹ τεθνηῶτα φέρειν εἰς δώματα Κίρκης ἑταίρους ἄνωγε ’Οδυσσεύς.
16.αὐτὸς δὲ πρηνὴς ἁλὶ κάππεσε,¹⁰ νηχέμεναι μεμαώς.
17.κλυτὰ εἵματα μοι ῥερυπωμένα¹¹ κεῖται.
18.ἀμφοτέρῃσι δὲ χερσὶν ἐπεσσύμενος¹² λάβε πέτρης.
19.ἐν πελέκει στειλειόν ἐστι περικαλλὲς ἐλάϊνον, εὖ ἐναρηρός.
20.τὸν μὲν ’Αθηναίη θῆκεν, Διὸς ἐκγεγαυῖα, μείζονά εἰσιδέειν.¹³

Part B - The pluperfect tense - active.

The pluperfect stands to the perfect as the imperfect stands to the present. Therefore it is often augmented, but not always in Homer. It signifies an occurrence which is previous to a past action. In English, it is equivalent to "had" in "(Sarpedon and Tlepomenos) threw their spears at the same time; Sarpedon killed Tlepomenos) then, however, Tlepomenos had hit his left thigh with the long spear" (... Τληπόμενος δ' ἄρα μηρὸν ἀριστερὸν ἔγχεϊ μακρῷ βεβλήκειν) (Iliad v, 660-1). (μηρός (2m) = thigh ἔγχος (3n) = spear ἀριστερός: see line 277)

The pluperfect is comparatively uncommon in Greek compared with English because Greek regularly has an aorist after "when"; "when I had reached the river, I sat down and wept" is, in Greek, ἐπεὶ εἰς τὸν ποταμὸν ἱκόμην, καθήμενος (ἐ)δάκρυσα (literally, when I *reached* the river, sitting down, I wept.). (ποταμός (2m) = river δακρύω = I weep)

---
⁶Odyssey V,9, p.46 above.
⁷From γέγωνα, I make myself heard (see p. 165).
⁸ἐξέλασα is aorist (unaugmented) from ἐξελαύνω, I drive out (for ἐλαύνω or ἐλαάω, see Section 13). σίαλος, σιάλου = fat hog. ἐννέωρος = nine seasons old (from Odyssey X, 388-90, adapted).
⁹νεκρός (2m): corpse, body.
¹⁰κάππεσε = κατέπεσε, he fell down (3rd person singular, aorist active of καταπίπτω). ἁλὶ is dative of end of motion, "into the sea". πρηνής = face down.
¹¹ῥυπόω = I make dirty. κλυτός : famous, but here perhaps "glorious". μοι (possessive dative) : my. (adapted from Odyssey VI, 58-9)
¹²For ἐπεσσύμενος, see line 314. . For ἐλαβόμην, see p.66.
¹³τὸν : him. τίθημι (here) : I make (i.e., alter so as to become). μείζονα is accusative singular masculine of μείζων, "bigger". εἰσοράω : I behold. For εἰσιδέειν, see section 10, p.67 and section 15, p.103.

Example: αὐτὰρ ἐπεὶ δὴ πάντα ἐῷ θηήσατο θυμῷ
αὐτίκ' ἄρ' εἰς εὐρὺ σπέος ἤλυθεν. (Odyssey V, 76-7)
but when then he had beheld everything in his mind straightaway then into
the broad cave he went (θηήσατο is 3rd person singular, aorist).

The pluperfect active
SINGULAR [(ἐ)λελύκη *or* ἐλελύκεα   I had loosed
(ἐ)λελύκης *or* ἐλελύκεας you had loosed (sing.)
(ἐ)λελύκει(ν) *or* ἐλελύκεε he/she/it had loosed

DUAL	(ἐ)λελύκετον	you two had loosed
	(ἐ)λελυκέτην	those two had loosed
PLURAL	(ἐ)λελύκεμεν	we had loosed
	(ἐ)λελύκετε	you had loosed (plu)
	(ἐ)λελύκεσαν	they had loosed.]

If a verb found in the perfect in Greek is equivalent to an English present, its pluperfect is equivalent to an English past, e.g. οἶδα (perfect in Greek) = I know (present in English), and ᾔδεα (pluperfect in Greek) = I knew (past in English):

ᾔδεα   I knew
ᾔείδεις *or* ᾔδησθα   you knew
ᾔδη *or* ᾔδεε *or* ᾔείδει   he, she, it knew
(the dual, and 1st and 2nd persons plural are not found in Homer)
ἴσαν   they knew

Examples: (1) ὣς φάτο, καὶ Παιήον' <u>ἀνώγειν</u> ἰήσασθαι (Iliad v, 899)
So he said, and he <u>ordered</u> Paeon to heal him. (ἰάομαι: I heal, cure)

(2) ᾤμωξεν δ' ὁ γέρων, κεφαλὴν δ' ὅ γε κόψατο χερσὶν
ὑψόσ' ἀνασχόμενος, μέγα δ' οἰμώξας <u>ἐγεγώνει</u>
λισσόμενος φίλον υἱόν· ὁ δὲ προπάροιθε πυλάων
<u>ἑστήκει</u>, ἄμοτον μεμαὼς Ἀχιλῆϊ μάχεσθαι (Iliad xxii 33-36)
And the old man wailed, and (his) head he indeed did beat with his hands holding them up above, and greatly having wailed, <u>he made himself heard</u> entreating his own dear son; but he, in front of the gates <u>was standing</u>, incessantly being eager with Achilles to fight.[14]

---

[14]οἰμώζω: I wail κόπτομαι: I knock, strike ὑψόσε: aloft, up high ἀνεσχόμην is the aorist of ἀνέχομαι: I hold up ἐγεγώνει is pluperfect λίσσομαι: I entreat υἱός (2m): son προπάροιθε (with genitive): in front of πυλή (1f): gate ἑστήκει is pluperfect ἄμοτον: incessantly μεμαώς is a perfect participle μάχομαι: I fight.

Section 22

The pluperfect middle/passive

SINGULAR
(ἐ)λελύμην — I had loosed for myself/had been loosed
(ἐ)λέλυσο — you (sing.) had loosed for yourself, had been loosed
(ἐ)λέλυτο — he/she/it had loosed for himself/herself/itself, he/she/it had been loosed

DUAL
(ἐ)λέλυσθον — you two had loosed for yourselves/had been loosed
(ἐ)λελύσθην — those two had loosed for themselves, had been loosed

PLURAL
(ἐ)λελύμε(σ)θα — we had loosed for ourselves/had been loosed
(ἐ)λέλυσθε — you (plu.) had loosed for yourselves/had been loosed
(ἐ)λέλυντο or (ἐ)λελύατο — they had loosed for themselves/had been loosed

Example: ἡ δ' αὐτοῦ τετάνυστο περὶ σπείους γλαφυροῖο ἡμερὶς ἡβώωσα, τεθήλει δὲ σταφυλῇσιν (Odyssey V, 68-9) and just there was stretched around the hollow cave a vine, luxuriant, and it was blooming with bunches of grapes.
Here, τετάνυστο means literally "it had been stretched" (τείνω = I stretch) and τεθήλει means literally, "it had come into bloom" (θάλλω = I come into bloom).

What is the English for:
1. ὕλη πεφύκει. (Odyssey V, 63)(NB πέφυκα is the perfect of φύω, I grow.)
2. Ζεὺς ἠνώγει. (Odyssey V, 99) 3. τετέλεστο ἅπαντα. (Odyssey V, 262)
4. ἀλὶ γὰρ δέδμητο φίλον κῆρ. (Odyssey V, 454) (δέδμημαι is the perfect passive of δαμάζω: I subdue) 5. θύραι δ' ἐπέκειντο φαειναί. (Odyssey VI, 19) (κεῖμαι, I lie, is used as the perfect passive of τίθημι, I put; so ἐπίκειμαι is the perfect passive of ἐπιτίθημι, I put together, I close. θύρα = door φαεινός = shining) 6. ἡ δ' ἀνέμου ὡς πνοιὴ ἐπέσσυτο δέμνια κούρης. (Odyssey VI, 20). (ἐπέσσυμαι is the perfect middle/passive of ἐπισεύω, I excite, set on, and means "I rush".) πνοιή = breath. δέμνια (neuter plural) = bed) 7. ἕποντο Ἀργείων βασιλῆες, ὅσοι κεκλήατο βουλήν. (Iliad x, 194-5) (ἕπομαι: I follow βασιλεύς: king καλέω with 2 accusatives = I call somebody to something (perfect middle/passive κέκλημαι) βουλή (1f) = council.) 8. κεῖνο ἰδὼν ἐτεθήπεα θυμῷ δήν. (Odyssey VI, 166) (τέθηπα is the perfect of θάμβω, I wonder, am amazed)

Beginning Greek with Homer

New words:
ἄριστος, ἀρίστη, ἄριστον = best, very good
ἄνωγα = I command
ἑκάς = far away
ἵππος (2m) = horse
κλυτός, κλυτόν[17] = famous
κραιπνός, κραιπνή, κραιπνόν = swift, rushing
μερμηρίζω = I am in doubt about (+ accusative)[18]
μυθέομαι = I speak, say
ὁρμαίνω = I debate anxiously, ponder
οὔπω or οὔ πω = not yet
πόρον or ἔπορον (found only in aorist) = I provided
τινάσσω = I shake[19]

διασκεδάννυμι[15] = I scatter
ἱμάσσω[16] = I flog, whip up
κέλευθος (2f) = road, path
κούρη (1f) = maiden

παύομαι = I cease

Odyssey V, 354-387

αὐτὰρ ὁ μερμήριξε πολύτλας δῖος Ὀδυσσεύς,
ὀχθήσας[20] δ' ἄρα εἶπε πρὸς ὃν μεγαλήτορα θυμόν· 355
'ὤ μοι ἐγώ, μή τίς μοι ὑφαίνῃσιν[21] δόλον[22] αὖτε
ἀθανάτων, ὅ τέ με σχεδίης ἀποβῆναι[23] ἀνώγει.[24]
ἀλλὰ μάλ' οὔ πω πείσομ',[25] ἐπεὶ ἑκὰς ὀφθαλμοῖσι
γαῖαν ἐγὼν[26] ἰδόμην, ὅθι μοι φάτο φύξιμον[27] εἶναι.
ἀλλὰ μάλ' ὧδ' ἔρξω,[28] δοκέει δέ μοι εἶναι ἄριστον· 360

[15]Aorist active, διεσκέδασα.
[16]Aorist active: ἵμασα.
[17]Feminine as masculine.
[18]Aorist active (ἐ) μερμήριξα.
[19]Aorist active : ἐτίναξα.
[20]Line 355 = line 298.
[21]Understand δείδω before μή (see p.98). ὑφαίνω = I weave (-ῃσιν is the longer form of the 3rd person singular present subjunctive active, p.94).
[22]δόλος (2m) = deceit.
[23]ἀποβῆναι is the infinitive of ἀπέβην, the irregular strong aorist of ἀποβαίνω, I step off (see p.99, footnote 18).
[24]The subject of ἀνώγει (3rd person singular pluperfect, and standing for an imperfect) is "she" (Ino). μοι is enclitic, which explains the accent on τίς. ὅ is neuter. ὅ τε = "with regard to which point, to be sure", but it might be better to translate as if we read ὅτε ("when"/"since"). Translate in the order: (δείδω) μή τις ἀθανάτων αὖτε ὑφαίνῃσι δόλον μοι, ὅτε ἀνώγει με ἀποβῆναι σχεδίης.
[25]Stands for πείσομαι, the future of πείθομαι, I obey. οὔ πω = not yet.
[26]Stands for ἐγώ. ἰδόμην is 1st person singular, aorist middle; ὁρῶμαι, the middle of ὁράω, is often used for the active by poets.
[27]φύξιμον (neuter) = refuge. For φάτο, see p.34. The subject is "she". μοι φύξιμον εἶναι, "to be a refuge for me" = "that there was a refuge for me". For accusative-with-infinitive construction with φημί, see p.85, footnote 30.
[28]μάλ' ὧδε: just like this. ἔρξω is future of ἔρδω, I do (some mss. have ἕρξω, as here). (The subject of δοκέει is "it": ἄριστον is neuter.)

Section 22

ὄφρ' ἂν μέν κεν²⁹ δούρατ' ἐν ἁρμονίῃσιν ἀρήρῃ,³⁰
τόφρ' αὐτοῦ³¹ μενέω³² καὶ τλήσομαι ἄλγεα πάσχων·
αὐτὰρ ἐπὴν³³ δή μοι σχεδίην διὰ κῦμα τινάξῃ,
νήξομ',³⁴ ἐπεὶ οὐ μέν τι πάρα³⁵ προνοῆσαι³⁶ ἄμεινον."
 εἷος ὁ ταῦθ' ὥρμαινε³⁷ κατὰ φρένα καὶ κατὰ θυμόν,   365
ὦρσε³⁸ δ' ἐπὶ³⁹ μέγα κῦμα Ποσειδάων ἐνοσίχθων,
δεινόν τ' ἀργαλέον τε, κατηρεφές, ἤλασε⁴⁰ δ' αὐτόν.
ὡς δ' ἄνεμος ζαὴς⁴¹ ἠίων θημῶνα⁴² τινάξῃ

²⁹ὄφρ' ἂν μέν κεν + subjunctive is a formula for "as long as". For ἄν and κεν, see Section 14, pp. 98 and 99. Hainsworth (*A Commentary on Homer's Odyssey* vol. i, p.283) notes that the use of ἄν and κεν together elsewhere in Homer (e.g. at Odyssey VI, 259: ὄφρ' ἂν μέν κ ' ἀγροὺς ἴομεν καὶ ἔργ' ἀνθρώπων = *for as long as we go (through) fields and the work of men*) forbids us to correct the apparent repetition. For lines 361-2, see p.120.
³⁰δούρατ' stands for δούρατα. ἀρήρῃ is 3rd person singular subjunctive of ἄρηρα, the perfect of ἀραρίσκω, I join together, with intransitive meaning, "stay joined together". The subject is δούρατα.
³¹τόφρ' stands for τόφρα. αὐτοῦ = here (in the same place).
³²μενέω is 1st person singular, future of μένω (future with -ε: see p.82, NB5). πάσχων is nominative masculine singular of the participle of πάσχω (present).
³³ἐπήν = ἐπεὶ ἄν (+ subjunctive), "at such time as". τινάξῃ is 3rd person singular subjunctive of ἐτίναξα. διά + genitive: through. διά has become separated from τινάξῃ by tmesis. διατινάσσω + accusative: I smash through. κῦμα is the subject. Translate as if: αὐτὰρ ἐπὴν κῦμα τινάξῃ διὰ σχεδίην μοι (μοι is a dative denoting possession, "my".)
³⁴νήξομ' stands for νήξομαι, the future of νήχω (p.81).
³⁵πάρα stands for πάρεστι, "there is at hand", i.e. "(it) is possible" (προνοῆσαι ἄμεινον is the subject). cf. lines 16 and 141, where πάρα stands for πάρεισι.
³⁶προνοῆσαι is the infinitive of προνόησα, aorist active of προνοέω, I think ahead, take precautions. ἄμεινόν τι προνοέω = I think ahead of something better. ἄμεινον is the accusative neuter singular of ἀμείνων, better.
³⁷ὥρμαινε is 3rd person singular imperfect of ὁρμαίνω.
³⁸ὦρσε is 3rd person singular of ὦρσα, aorist indicative active of ὄρνυμι. δὲ links the whole sentence to the previous one, and is best translated after εἷος.
³⁹Understand "him". Ποσειδάων ἐνοσίχθων is the subject of ὦρσε. δεινόν, ἀργαλέον and κατηρεφές (neuter of κατηρεφής = overhanging) qualify κῦμα, the object.
⁴⁰ἤλασε is 3rd person singular of ἤλασα the aorist indicative active of ἐλαύνω (ἐλαάω). The subject is "it", standing for κῦμα. αὐτόν: "him" (Odysseus).
⁴¹ζαής, ζαές = stormy. "And as a stormy wind ..." introduces a simile.
⁴²θημών, θημῶνος (masculine) = heap (from the same root as τίθημι). ἠων is the genitive of ἤα (neuter plural) = "chaff". (Liddell & Scott lists this word under ἤια (= "(I) provisions for a journey, (II) heap of husks, chaff"). Hainsworth (*op. cit.* p.284) suggests that "chaff" is ἤια, and "provisions" is ἠα. If ἠίων is right, the two vowels ηϊ must be merged in scanning the line, as follows:

$$- \; - | - \; - | - \; - | - \; - | - \; \smile \; \smile | - - \|$$

 ὡς δ' ἄνεμος ζαῆς ἠίων θημῶνα τινάξῃ
The running together of two vowels which would normally be separate (i.e. would not form a diphthong) is called *synizesis*.
For τινάξῃ ("smashes") see footnote 33 above.

καρφαλέων,⁴³ τὰ μὲν ἄρ τε διεσκέδασ' ἄλλυδις ἄλλῃ,⁴⁴
ὡς τῆς⁴⁵ δούρατα μακρὰ διεσκέδασ'. αὐτὰρ Ὀδυσσεὺς   370
ἀμφ'⁴⁶ ἑνὶ δούρατι βαῖνε, κέληθ' ὡς⁴⁷ ἵππον ἐλαύνων,
εἵματα δ' ἐξαπέδυνε,⁴⁸ τά οἱ πόρε δῖα Καλυψώ.
αὐτίκα δὲ κρήδεμνον ὑπὸ στέρνοιο τάνυσσεν,
αὐτὸς δὲ πρηνής⁴⁹ ἁλὶ κάππεσε, χεῖρε πετάσσας,⁵⁰
νηχέμεναι μεμαώς.⁵¹ ἴδε δὲ κρείων ἐνοσίχθων,   375
κινήσας⁵² δὲ κάρη προτὶ ὃν μυθήσατο θυμόν·
'οὕτω νῦν κακὰ πολλὰ παθὼν ἀλόω⁵³ κατὰ πόντον,
εἰς ὅ κεν⁵⁴ ἀνθρώποισι διοτρεφέεσσι⁵⁵ μιγήῃς.

⁴³καρφαλέος, καρφαλέα, καρφαλέον = dry, parched. καρφαλέων qualifies ᾗ ὧν.
⁴⁴διεσκέδασ' stands for διεσκέδασε, 3rd person singular of διεσκέδασα, the aorist of διασκεδάννυμι. διεσκέδασε in line 369 is a timeless aorist, saying what a violent wind generally does to a heap of chaff. διεσκέδασε in line 370 is an aorist referring to a single action in the past: what the wave did on this occasion to the timbers of Odysseus' raft. ἄλλυδις ἄλλῃ = this way and that, hither and thither, now this way, now that. The dative ἄλλῃ shows that this is an adverbial use, whereas at lines 70-1, where there is κρήναι ... τετραμμέναι ... ἄλλυδις ἄλλη, ἄλλη is nominative singular, adjectival qualifying κρήνη (implied by κρήναι).
⁴⁵Note that ὡς has an accent. τῆς (genitive feminine singular) stands for σχεδίης, i.e. the English "its" meaning "belonging to the raft". Hainsworth notes (op. cit.p.280) that the raft wreck echoes the wreck of Odysseus' last ship (Odyssey XII 420-5), to which Calypso alludes at Odyssey V, 130.
⁴⁶ἑνὶ is the dative (neuter) of εἷς, "one". The meaning is that Odysseus got his legs round one timber (from the shattered raft). βαῖνε is 3rd person singular of the imperfect of βαίνω, with the meaning "step" here.
⁴⁷ὡς introduces another simile "like a man driving..." ἐλαύνων is nominative masculine singular of the participle (present) of ἐλαύνω. κέλης, κέλητος (ἵππος) = riding horse, courser. κέληθ' stands for κέλητα. To drive a riding horse is of course the same as to ride a horse.
⁴⁸ἐξαπέδυνε is 3rd person singular imperfect active of ἐξαποδύνω = I take off.
⁴⁹πρηνής = face downwards ἁλὶ is dative of end of motion, "into the sea" (Chantraine, op. cit. vol.ii, p.68, who cites this passage). See also p.143, footnote 56. κάππεσε is short for κατέπεσε, he fell down (3rd person singular, aorist active of καταπίπτω).
⁵⁰πετάσσας is nominative masculine singular of the participle of (ἐ)πέτασ(σ)α, the aorist active of πετάννυμι. Note that χεῖρε is dual.
⁵¹For μεμαώς, see p.150. νηχέμεναι is the infinitive (see p. 22) of νήχω. ἴδε is 3rd person singular of ἴδον, aorist of ὁράω.
⁵²Line 376 = line 285 (section 19, p.134).
⁵³παθών is nominative singular masculine of the participle of ἔπαθον, the aorist of πάσχω. ἀλόω is 2nd person singular present imperative from ἀλάομαι, I wander. The form we should expect in Attic would be ἀλάου, contracted to ἀλῶ (cf. αὐδῶ, p.88). However, in Homer ω as the ending of a contracted verb is sometimes lengthened to -οω to suit the metre (see p.201 and Chantraine, op. cit. vol.i, pp.76-7). Hainsworth (op. cit., p.284) notes that there is no example exactly parallel to ἀλόω. The meaning is "Carry on wandering!".
⁵⁴For lines 377-8, see p. 120.
⁵⁵διοτρεφής, διοτρεφές (dative plural, διοτρεφέεσσι(ν)) = fostered by Zeus.

Section 22

ἀλλ' οὐδ' ὥς σε ἔολπα ὀνόσσεσθαι[56] κακότητος.·
  ὣς ἄρα φωνήσας ἵμασεν καλλίτριχας[57] ἵππους,   380
ἵκετο δ' εἰς Αἰγάς, ὅθι οἱ κλυτὰ δώματ' ἔασιν.
αὐτὰρ Ἀθηναίη, κούρη Διός, ἀλλ' ἐνόησεν·[58]
ἣ τοι τῶν ἄλλων ἀνέμων κατέδησε[59] κελεύθους,
παύσασθαι δ' ἐκέλευσε καὶ εὐνηθῆναι[60] ἅπαντας·
ὦρσε δ' ἐπὶ[61] κραιπνὸν βορέην, πρὸ[62] δὲ κύματ' ἔαξεν   385
εἷος ὃ Φαιήκεσσι φιληρέτμοισι[63] μιγείη
διογενὴς Ὀδυσεύς, θάνατον καὶ κῆρας[64] ἀλύξας.

[56]οὐδ' (for οὐδέ) = "not even". ὀνόσσεσθαι is the infinitive of ὀνόσσομαι, the future of ὄνομαι (here + genitive, usually + accusative) = "I find fault with". (For the use of a future infinitive with a verb meaning "hope" or "expect", see pp. 103-4.) Poseidon is bitterly sarcastic.
[57]ὣς ἄρα φωνήσας is the masculine form of ὣς ἄρα φωνήσασ(α) (lines 192 and 351). καλλίθριξ, καλλίτριχος (3) = with beautiful manes (from καλός, and θρίξ, τριχός (3f) = a hair). ἵκετο is 3rd person singular of ἱκόμην, the aorist of ἱκνέομαι. At Iliad xiii. 21 Poseidon goes off in a huff to Aegae, ἔνθα οἱ κλυτὰ δώματα βένθεσι λίμνης χρύσεα μαρμαίροντα τετεύχαται "where for him a beautiful palace in the depths of the mere, golden and sparkling has been built". λίμνη ("marsh") is often used for "sea" in Homer, and Liddell & Scott take it in this sense here. Aegae is therefore somewhere on the coast and according to the passage from Iliad xiii, four god's steps from the island of Samothrace in the northern Aegean sea. There is an Aegae on the southern shore of the Gulf of Corinth with a famous temple of Poseidon conveniently near where Odysseus presumably was, but the reference in Iliad xiii raises the possibility that somewhere in the Aegean is meant. For ἔασιν, see p.9, footnote 12.
[58]ἐνόησεν is 3rd person singular of ἐνόησα, the aorist of νοέω. ἀλλ' ἐνόησεν : formed other intentions.
[59]ἣ τοι : of a certainty. κατέδησε is 3rd person singular of κατέδησα, the aorist of καταδέω = I tie down, stop.
[60]παύσασθαι is the aorist infinitive of παύομαι. εὐνηθῆναι is the aorist passive infinitive of εὐνάω = I put to bed. For line 384, see p. 132.
[61]ἐπῶρσε is 3rd person singular, aorist active of ἐπόρνυμι: I arouse. The prefix ἐπί has become detached by tmesis and placed after δέ. κύματ' stands for κύματα.
[62]πρό (adverb) = before, in front. ἔαξε is 3rd person singular of ἔαξα.
[63]For lines 385-6, see p.121. Hainsworth notes (op. cit., p.284) that though διοτρεφής (used by Poseidon in line 378) is the Homeric epithet generally applied to noblemen and kings, φιλήρετμος is a special epithet for the Phaeacians.
[64]Κῆρες are the fates, the goddesses of doom, and so simply "doom". ἀλύξας is nominative masculine singular of the participle of ἤλυξα, the aorist active of ἀλύσκω.

Section 23
Adjectives

Adjectives qualify nouns, e.g. ὑψιβρεμέτης in Ζεὺς ὑψιβρεμέτης, "high-thundering Zeus". Sometimes they are used instead of nouns, e.g. ἦ δὴ ἀλιτρός γ' ἐσσὶ καὶ οὐκ ἀποφώλια εἰδώς (Odyssey V, 182) decidedly you are a rogue and (a man) knowing not unfruitful (things), where ἀλιτρός[1] is the masculine of an adjective meaning "sinful" and means "a sinful man" (cf. "imp" from "impious").

Greek adjectives fall into the same declensions as nouns; most of the adjectives met in Odyssey V have masculine and neuter endings in the second declension and feminine endings in the first, e.g. φίλος (masculine) φίλη (feminine) φίλον (neuter). Other adjectives are third declension in all genders, e.g. μεγαλήτωρ (genitive μεγαλήτορος), "great-hearted", and others have third declension masculine and neuter, but first declension feminine, e.g., ὀξύς, ὀξεῖα, ὀξύ, "sharp".[2] An adjective has the same case and gender as the noun it qualifies, and is singular, dual or plural according to the noun. So we have φίλην ἐς πατρίδα[3] γαῖαν, where a first declension noun (γαῖαν) is qualified by one first declension adjective (φίλην) and one third declension adjective (πατρίδα), all accusative singular and all feminine.

Irregular adjectives of the first and second declensions:
In πολλός ("much") the nominative and accusative masculine and neuter sometimes have a shorter form (which is the normal form in Attic Greek).[4]

---
[1] See p. 111, footnote 30.
[2] Also γλυκύς, γλυκεῖα, γλυκύ : sweet (see p.100, footnote 25) and many others.
[3] πατρίς, genitive πατρίδος, is a third declension adjective meaning "of one's fathers", but when it is used without a noun, γαῖα is understood, and it becomes a substantive (a word that can be used in the place of a noun or pronoun) meaning "fatherland".
[4] Chantraine (*Grammaire Homérique* vol.i, p.253) describes πολύς as "athematic" and πολλός as "thematic"; compare this with thematic and athematic verbs.

Section 23

	masculine	feminine	neuter
SINGULAR			
nominative	πολλός *or* πολύς *or* πουλύς much	πολλή much	πολλόν *or* πολύ *or* [πουλύ] much
accusative	πολλόν *or* πολύν *or* πουλύν[5] much	πολλήν much	πολλόν *or* πολύ *or* πουλύ much
genitive	πολέος of much	πολλῆς of much	πολέος of much
dative	[πολλῷ] to/for much	πολλῇ to/for much	πολλῷ by much
PLURAL			
nominative	πολλοί *or* πολέες *or* πολεῖς many	πολλαί many	πολλά many
accusative	πολλούς *or* πολέας many	πολλάς many	πολλά many
genitive	πολλῶν *or* πολέων of many	πολλάων *or* πολλέων of many	πολλῶν of many
dative	πολλοῖσι *or* πολέσι *or* πολέεσι to/for many	πολλῇσι *or* πολλῇς to/for many	πολλοῖσι *or* πολέεσι by many

The genitive singular, masculine and neuter, of πολλός is 3rd declension (πολέος), and there are alternative 3rd declension endings (πολέες, πολέας, πολέων, πολέσι) for the whole of the masculine plural of πολλός. There is no dual of πολύς.

Short forms for the masculine and neuter nominative and accusative singular are also always found in μέγας ("big"), the singular of which is:

---

[5]πουλύν is feminine at Iliad v, 776 and viii, 50 in the formula ἠέρα πουλὺν ἔχευε ("was pouring a thick mist") and at Iliad x, 27 πουλὺν ἐφ' ὑγρήν ("over much water").

	masculine	feminine	neuter
nominative	μέγας	μεγάλη	μέγα
	big	big	big
accusative	μέγαν	μεγάλην	μέγα
	big	big	big
genitive	μεγάλοιο *or* μεγάλου	μεγάλης	μεγάλοιο *or* μεγάλου
	of big	of big	of big
dative	μεγάλῳ	μεγάλῃ	μεγάλῳ
	to/for big	to/for big	by big

The plural, μέγαλοι, μέγαλαι, μέγαλα and dual have endings like the dual and plural of φίλος.

What is the English for:
1. πολέεσσιν ὀχήσατο κύμασιν Ἑρμῆς. (Odyssey V, 54)
2. ἦ γὰρ τούσδε γ' ἀτιμάζει[6] κατὰ δῆμον[7]
Φαίηκας, τοί μιν μνῶνται πολέες τε καὶ ἐσθλοί. (Odyssey VI, 283-4)[8]
3. Ἀρτέμιδί σε ἐγώ γε, Διὸς κούρῃ μεγάλοιο, ἐΐσκω. (Odyssey VI, 151-2)[9]
4. τὸν δὲ μέγα κῦμ' ἐκάλυψεν.(Odyssey V, 435)
5. αὐτὰρ ὁ βῆ διὰ δῶμα πολύτλας δῖος Ὀδυσσεὺς πολλὴν ἠέρ' ἔχων, ἥν οἱ περίχευεν Ἀθήνη. (Odyssey VII, 139-40)[10]
6. "τίς δ' ὅδε Ναυσικάᾳ ἕπεται καλός τε μέγας τε ξεῖνος;" (Odyssey VI, 276-7) (ἕπομαι with dative: I follow. ξεῖνος, 2 masc.: stranger)
7. ἔστι δέ τις νῆσος μέσσῃ ἁλὶ [11]πετρήεσσα ...
Ἀστερίς, οὐ μεγάλη. (Odyssey IV, 844-6) πετρήεσσα (fem. adjective): rocky
8. ἔνθ' ἦ τοι πλυνοὶ ἦσαν ἐπηετανοί, πολὺ δ' ὕδωρ καλὸν ὑπεκπρόρεεν. (Odyssey VI, 86-7) πλυνός -οῦ (2 masculine): rock basin for washing clothes. ἐπηετανός -όν (feminine as masculine): always full. ὑπεκπρορέω: I flow up and out.

Adjectives with third declension masculine & neuter, and first declension feminine:
In active participles, e.g. λύσας, λύσασα, λύσαν (p. 73), all cases of the masculine and neuter are 3rd declension, while the feminine endings are first declension. This pattern is followed by many adjectives including πᾶς and ἅπας ("every", "all") and μέλας (black):

---
[6] ἀτιμάζω: I dishonour (the subject of ἀτιμάζει is "she", i.e. Nausicaa).
[7] δῆμος -ου (2 masculine): the people.
[8] μνάομαι: I woo. μιν is feminine.
[9] Ἄρτεμις, Ἀρτέμιδος: Artemis. ἐΐσκω: I liken.
[10] ἀήρ, ἠέρος f: mist. περιχέω, aorist περίχευα: I pour round.
[11] μέσσῃ ἁλί is dative indicating locality; understand ἐν before μέσσῃ.

Section 23   163

SINGULAR	masculine	feminine	neuter
nominative	πᾶς	πᾶσα	πᾶν
accusative	πάντα	πᾶσαν	πᾶν
genitive	παντός	πάσης	[παντός]
dative	παντί	πάσῃ	παντί
PLURAL			
nominative	πάντες	πᾶσαι	πάντα
accusative	πάντας	πάσας	πάντα
genitive	πάντων	πασάων	πάντων
dative	πάντεσσι or πᾶσι	πάσῃσι or πάσαις[12]	πάντεσσι or πᾶσι

Similarly, μέλας, μέλαινα, μέλαν ("black" or "dark")

SINGULAR	masculine	feminine	neuter
nominative	μέλας	μέλαινα	μέλαν
accusative	μέλανα	μέλαιναν	μέλαν
genitive	μέλανος	μελαίνης	μέλανος
dative	μέλανι[13]	μελαίνῃ	μέλανι
DUAL			
nom & acc	[μέλανε]	[μελαίνα]	[μέλανε]
gen & dat	[μελάνοιιν]	[μελαίνῃιν]	[μελάνοιιν]
PLURAL			
nominative	μέλανες	μέλαιναι	[μέλανα]
accusative	[μέλανας]	[μελαίνας]	[μέλανα]
genitive	[μελάνων]	μελαινάων[14]	[μελάνων]
dative	[μελάνεσσι or μέλασι]	μελαίνῃσι	[μελάνεσσι or μέλασι]

An important group of adjectives, already noted, ends -υς in the masculine singular nominative and has first declension feminine and third declension masculine and neuter. As well as γλυκύς and ὀξύς ("sharp"), these include εὐρύς ("wide") and θηλύς ("female").

[12]Odyssey XXII, 471.
[13]Only found in the form μείλανι (Iliad xxiv, 79).
[14]Found as μελαινέων at Iliad iv, 117.

ὀξύς, ὀξεῖα, ὀξύ, sharp

	masculine	feminine	neuter
SINGULAR			
nominative	ὀξύς	ὀξεῖα	ὀξύ
accusative	ὀξύν	[ὀξεῖαν]	ὀξύ
genitive	[ὀξέος]	[ὀξείης]	[ὀξέος]
dative	ὀξέϊ	ὀξείῃ	ὀξέϊ
DUAL			
nom & acc	[ὀξέε]	[ὀξεία]	[ὀξέε]
gen & dat	ὀξέοιιν	[ὀξείῃιν]	[ὀξέοιιν]
PLURAL			
nominative	ὀξέες	ὀξεῖαι	ὀξέα
accusative	[ὀξέας]	ὀξείας	ὀξέα
genitive	[ὀξέων]	[ὀξειάων]	[ὀξέων]
dative	ὀξέσι	ὀξείῃσι	[ὀξέσι]

μάκαρ, "blessed", is always masculine in the Iliad and Odyssey, as follows:

	SINGULAR	[DUAL]	PLURAL
nominative	μάκαρ	[μάκαρε]	μάκαρες
accusative	[μάκαρα]	[μάκαρε]	[μάκαρας]
genitive	μάκαρος	[μακάροιιν]	μακάρων
dative	[μάκαρι]	[μακάροιιν]	μακάρεσσι

Where the feminine is found, at line 14 in the Homeric Hymn to Delian Apollo, it is first declension, μάκαιρα (describing Leto, the mother of Apollo and Artemis).

Adjectives which are third declension for all genders:

	masculine & feminine	[neuter]
SINGULAR		
nominative	[μεγαλήτωρ]	[μεγάλητορ]
accusative	μεγαλήτορα	[μεγάλητορ]
genitive	μεγαλήτορος	[μεγαλήτορος]
dative	μεγαλήτορι	[μεγαλήτορι]
DUAL		
nominative & accusative	[μεγαλήτορε	μεγαλήτορε
genitive & dative	μεγαλητόροιιν	μεγαλητόροιιν]

Section 23   165

PLURAL
nominative   μεγαλήτορες   [μεγαλήτορα]
accusative   μεγαλήτορας   [μεγαλήτορα]
genitive   [μεγαλητόρων]   [μεγαλητόρων]
dative   [μεγαλητόρεσσι]   [μεγαλητόρεσσι]

An important group of third declension adjectives has stems ending -ε. This includes ἀελπής ("unhoped for"), ἀληθής ("true"), ἀσκηθής ("safe and sound"), διογενής ("sprung from Zeus"), ἠεροειδής ("murky", "like mist"), μενοεικής ("plentiful", "satisfying the desires") and νημερτής ("sure and true"). Their declension pattern is as follows:

SINGULAR	masculine & feminine	neuter
nominative	νημερτής	νημερτές
accusative	νημερτέα	νημερτές
genitive	[νημερτέος]	[νημερτέος]
dative	[νημερτέϊ]	[νημερτέϊ]
DUAL		
nom., acc.	[νημερτεῖ]	[νημερτεῖ]
gen., dat.	[νημερτοῖν]	[νημερτοῖν]
PLURAL		
nominative	[νημερτέες]	νημερτέα
accusative	[νημερτέας]	νημερτέα
genitive	[νημερτέων]	[νημερτέων]
dative	[νημερτέσσι(ν)]	[νημερτέσσι(ν)]

New words:
ἀκούω = I hear   ἀμφότεροι, ἀμφότεραι, ἀμφότερα = both.
βοάω = I shout   γαλήνη (1f) = calm
γέγωνα = I make myself heard
δαίμων, δαιμόνος (m. or f.) = god, goddess, deity
δηρόν = (all too) long (adv.)   δύω, δύο = two
ἐφευρίσκω[15] = I discover   θύραζε = out (of doors)
λιμήν, λιμένος (m.) = harbour   ὀξύς, ὀξεῖα, ὀξύ = sharp
ὅσ(σ)ος, ὅσ(σ)η, ὅσ(σ)ον = how much, how great (plural, how many)
πάγος (2m.) = rock[16]   ποτί = πρός (with dative, near, against)
που = somewhere
προτέρω = farther   στενάχω = I groan, sigh, wail
τόσ(σ)ος, τόσ(σ)η, τόσ(σ)ον = so much, so great (in plural, so many)

[15]Aorist, ἐφεῦρον.
[16]πάγοι are crags, i.e. *fixed* rocks (πήγνυμι: I fix).

What is the English for:
1. Ναυσικάα, θυγάτηρ μεγαλήτορος 'Αλκινόοιο. 2.διογενέα 'Οδυσσῆα Λαερτιάδην ὁρόω. 3.ἐϋπλόκαμος 'Ηὼς φάος θεοῖσι μακάρεσσι φέρει. 4.'Οδυσσῆϊ γαῖαν ἀελπέα δῶκεν ἰδέσθαι Ζεύς. 5.ἔκβασις[17] οὔ πῃ φαίνεθ' ἁλὸς πολιοῖο.[18] 6. ἔκτοσθεν[19] γὰρ ἦσαν πάγοι ὀξέες. 7.δείδω μή[20] μ' ἐξαῦτις ἀναρπάξασα[21] θύελλα πόντον ἐπ' ἰχθυόεντα[22] φέρῃ. 8.κεῖται κρατέρ' ἄλγεα πάσχων. 9.ἀκταὶ προβλῆτες ἔσαν σπιλάδες[23] τε πάγοι τε. 10.τόφρα δέ μιν μέγα κῦμα φέρε τρηχεῖαν[24] ἐπ' ἀκτήν.

Odyssey V, 388-423
ἔνθα δύω νύκτας δύο τ' ἤματα κύματι πηγῷ[25]
πλάζετο,[26] πολλὰ δέ οἱ κραδίη[27] προτιόσσετ'[28] ὄλεθρον.
ἀλλ' ὅτε δὴ τρίτον[29] ἦμαρ ἐϋπλόκαμος τέλεσ' 'Ηώς,   390
καὶ τότ' ἔπειτ' ἄνεμος μὲν ἐπαύσατο[30] ἠδὲ γαλήνη
ἔπλετο νηνεμίη·[31] ὁ δ' ἄρα σχεδὸν εἴσιδε[32] γαῖαν

[17]ἔκβασις, genitive ἐκβάσεως, 3f = way out.
[18]πολιός, πολιή, πολιόν = grey.
[19]ἔκτοσθεν: outside. πάγοι: rocks (see *new words*, below).
[20]μή: lest. ἐξαῦτις: again.
[21]ἀναρπάξασα is feminine singular nominative of ἀναρπάξας, the participle of ἀνήρπαξα, the aorist active of ἀναρπάζω, I snatch up.
[22]ἰχθυόεις, ἰχθυόεσσα, ἰχθυόεν (masculine and neuter genitive singular, ἰχθυόεντος) = full of fish.
[23]προβλής, προβλῆτος (3rd declension adjective, found in masculine and feminine) = jutting out. σπιλάς, σπιλάδος 3f = rock (over which the sea dashes).
[24]τρηχύς, τρηχεῖα, τρηχύ = rugged.
[25]πηγός, πηγή, πηγόν = mighty ("solid", "strong", from πήγνυμι, I fix, stick in).
[26]πλάζετο is 3rd person singular, imperfect indicative of πλάζομαι = I wander, rove (passive of πλάζω, I turn aside).
[27]κραδίη (1 f.) = heart. οἱ is a dative denoting possession: "for him" = "his".
[28]προτιόσσετ' stands for προτιόσσετο, 3rd person singular imperfect of προτιόσσομαι (literally, I look upon in my mind's eye) = I forbode. The subject of προτιόσσετο is κραδίη and the object is ὄλεθρον. πολλά, "with regard to many things", refers here to time and means "often".
[29]τρίτος, τρίτη, τρίτον = third. τέλεσ' stands for (ἐ)τέλεσε, 3rd person singular of ἐτέλεσα, the aorist of τέλεω. τελέω here means "I finish making", and so "I bring in", "I begin".
[30]ἐπαύσατο is 3rd person singular, aorist indicative of παύομαι.
[31]νηνεμίη (1 f.) = a ceasing of winds. γαλήνη νηνεμίη: "a calm, a ceasing of winds." ἔπλετο, "there was", is 3rd person singular, aorist of πέλομαι (aorist not found in 1st person singular).
[32]εἴσιδε is 3rd person singular of εἴσιδον, aorist active of εἰσοράω, I behold.

Section 23

ὀξὺ³³ μάλα προϊδών,³⁴ μεγάλου ὑπὸ κύματος ἀρθείς.³⁵
ὡς δ' ὅτ' ἂν ἀσπάσιος³⁶ βίοτος³⁷ παίδεσσι φανήῃ
πατρός, ὃς ἐν νούσῳ³⁸ κεῖται κρατέρ'³⁹ ἄλγεα πάσχων,   395
δηρὸν τηκόμενος,⁴⁰ στυγερὸς⁴¹ δέ οἱ ἔχραε⁴² δαίμων,
ἀσπάσιον⁴³ δ' ἄρα τόν γε θεοὶ κακότητος⁴⁴ ἔλυσαν,
ὣς 'Οδυσῆ' ἀσπαστὸν⁴⁵ ἐείσατο⁴⁶ γαῖα καὶ ὕλη,

---

³³ὀξὺ μάλα is used adverbially, qualifying προϊδών, "very keenly".
³⁴προϊδών is nominative masculine singular of the participle of προεῖδον, the aorist active of προοράω, I keep a look out forward.
³⁵ἀρθείς is the nominative singular masculine of the participle of ἀέρθην, the aorist passive of ἀείρω, I raise, meaning "having been raised". ὑπὸ with the genitive means "by", expressing the agent by which he was raised. In Attic, ὑπό is normally used to express the effect of a personal agent (Mastronarde, *Introduction to Attic Greek*, p.77; Jones & Sidwell, *Reading Greek: Grammar, Vocabulary and Exercises* para.138) but in Homer ὑπό is found both with personal and impersonal agents (Chantraine, *op. cit.* vol. ii, pp.142-3). Compare the use of the dative to express an instrument; an agent acts independently, while an instrument is used. "By" in English expresses both.
³⁶ὡς δ' ὅτ' ("and as when ...") introduces a simile (cf.line 328). Hainsworth (*A Commentary on Homer's Odyssey* vol.i, p.284) notes that the connection between rescue at sea and family reunion may be traditional, since the words of this simile are echoed (with the images reversed) at Odyssey XXIII (233-240) when Penelope has finally recognised Odysseus. ἀσπάσιος, ἀσπάσια, ἀσπάσιον = gladly welcomed (ἀσπάζομαι = I greet) (also in line 397 below).
³⁷βίοτος (2 m.) = life. φανήῃ is 3rd person singular, subjunctive of ἐφάνην ("I appeared"), the aorist passive of φαίνω (Section 18, p.127). Both φάνη (e.g. at Iliad ix, 707) and φανήῃ (here, and at Iliad xix, 375) are found; the longer form is normal and the shorter contracted (Chantraine, *op. cit.* vol.i, p.459).
³⁸νοῦσος (2 f.) = disease, illness. ὅς refers to πατρός. Translate in the order: ὡς δ' ὅτ' ἂν βίοτος πατρός, ὃς κεῖται ἐν νούσῳ πάσχων κράτερα ἄλγεα τηκόμενος δηρόν, δὲ στυγερὸς δαίμων ἔχραέ οἱ, δ' ἄρα ἀσπάσιον θεοὶ ἔλυσαν τὸν κακότητος, φανήῃ ἀσπάσιος παίδεσσι, ὡς γαῖα καὶ ὕλη ἐείσατο' Ὀδυσῆι ...
³⁹κρατέρ' stands for κρατέρα, neuter plural of κρατερός, κρατερά, κρατερόν = strong, mighty (qualifying ἄλγεα). (Some scholars take κεῖται as a short-vowel subjunctive contracted from *κείεται, 3rd person singular from κεῖμαι "the kind of man who lies down...", but this is not certain and it can be translated as κεῖται (indicative): "who lies down".) (Chantraine, *op. cit.* vol.i, p.457)
⁴⁰τηκόμενος is masculine singular nominative of the participle of τήκομαι (passive of τήκω, I melt down) = I pine away.
⁴¹στυγερός = hateful, abominable.
⁴²οἱ is dative. ἔχραε is 3rd person singular of ἔχραον, the aorist of χράω, (with *dative*): I fall upon (so Liddell & Scott). (Autenreith, *Homeric Dictionary*, p.331, does not derive ἔχραε from χράω but χραύω which, with the *accusative* means "I attack". For ἔχραε with the *dative*, Autenreith suggests "has handled him hardly". However, the phrase τίς τοι (dative) κακὸς ἔχραε δαίμων; is found at Odyssey X, 64 where Heubeck (*A Commentary on Homer's Odyssey* vol.ii, p.46) accepts the translation "What evil demon has fallen upon you?")
⁴³ἀσπάσιον here: "as something gladly welcome". The object of ἔλυσαν is τόν.
⁴⁴Genitive of separation; see Section 5, p.30.
⁴⁵ἀσπαστός, ἀσπαστή, ἀσπαστόν = welcome, to be welcomed (in the neuter, "(as) something to be welcomed").
⁴⁶'Οδυσῆ' stands for 'Οδυσῆι. ἐείσατο = εἴσατο: see p.130, footnote 36.

Beginning Greek with Homer

νῆχε δ' ἐπειγόμενος⁴⁷ ποσὶν ἠπείρου ἐπιβῆναι.
ἀλλ' ὅτε τόσσον ἀπῆν,⁴⁸ ὅσσον τε γέγωνε βοήσας,   400
καὶ δὴ δοῦπον⁴⁹ ἄκουσε ποτὶ σπιλάδεσσι⁵⁰ θαλάσσης·
ῥόχθει⁵¹ γὰρ μέγα κῦμα ποτὶ ξερὸν⁵² ἠπείροιο
δεινὸν ἐρευγόμενον,⁵³ εἴλυτο⁵⁴ δὲ πάνθ' ἁλὸς ἄχνῃ·
οὐ γὰρ ἔσαν λιμένες νηῶν ὀχοί,⁵⁵ οὐδ' ἐπιωγαί,⁵⁶
ἀλλ' ἀκταὶ προβλῆτες⁵⁷ ἔσαν σπιλάδες τε πάγοι τε   405
καὶ τότ' Ὀδυσσῆος λύτο γούνατα καὶ φίλον ἦτορ,⁵⁸
ὀχθήσας δ' ἄρα εἶπε πρὸς ὃν μεγαλήτορα θυμόν·

⁴⁷νῆχε is 3rd person singular, imperfect indicative active of νήχω. ἐπειγόμενος is the nominative masculine singular of the participle of ἐπείγομαι = I am eager to (+ infinitive, in this instance ἐπιβῆναι, the aorist infinitive of ἐπιβαίνω).

⁴⁸ἀπῆν is 3rd person singular imperfect of ἄπειμι, I am distant. τόσσον ... ὅσσον (so much ... how much ...) = as far as. τε is used in Epic sometimes in general statements; τόσσον ... ὅσσον τε means "the kind of distance", "as far as, generally speaking ..." Hainsworth (*op. cit.*, p.284) notes that the whole line is an Odyssean formula, found also at IX, 473 and XII, 181, and nearly the same as VI, 294. βοήσας ("a man shouting") is nominative masculine singular of the participle of ἐβόησα, the aorist of βοάω. γέγωνε has past meaning: "(he) could make himself heard".

⁴⁹ἄκουσε is 3rd person singular of ἄκουσα, the (unaugmented) aorist indicative active of ἀκούω. δοῦπος (2m) = thudding. At Iliad xxiii, 234-5 Homer uses it for the measured tread of marching men:
τῶν μιν ἐπερχομένων ὅμαδος καὶ δοῦπος ἔγειρεν,
ἕζετο δ' ὀρθωθεὶς καί σφεας πρὸς μῦθον ἔειπεν
the noise of them coming and their measured tread aroused him (Achilles) and he sat up straight and spoke a word to them.

⁵⁰For σπιλάς, see footnote 23 above. Translate in the order: ἄκουσε δοῦπον θαλάσσης ποτὶ σπιλάδεσσι ...

⁵¹ῥόχθει is contracted from ῥόχθεε, 3rd person singular imperfect of ῥοχθέω = I dash with a roaring sound. The subject is μέγα κῦμα.

⁵²ξερόν ἠπείροιο ("the dry of the (main)land") = dry land (*terra firma*, Liddell & Scott).

⁵³ἐρευγόμενον is neuter nominative singular (qualifying κῦμα) of the participle of ἐρεύγομαι = I roar. (δεινόν is used as an adverb.) ἐρεύγομαι can mean "I spew", or "I roar" which is better here; compare Iliad xvii, 263-5: "as when at the mouth of a river fed by Zeus a great wave is roaring against the current and around it ἄκραι ἠϊόνες βοόωσιν ἐρευγομένης ἁλὸς ἔξω (the headland shores bellow beyond the roaring sea)". (See Liddell & Scott.) ἐρεύγεται also means "roar" at Odyssey V, 438.

⁵⁴εἴλυτο is 3rd person singular imperfect indicative passive of εἰλύω = I enwrap. πάνθ' stands for πάντα (neuter plural nominative), the subject of εἴλυτο. ἄχνη (1f) = foam, froth.

⁵⁵For ἔσαν, see p.9. ὀχός, ὀχοῦ (2m) = receptacle (used to describe a harbour, "capacious of", i.e. "capable of holding").

⁵⁶ἐπιωγή (1f) = roadstead, shelter for ships.

⁵⁷προβλής, προβλῆτος (3rd declension adjective) = jutting out (literally, "thrown forward"), from πρό, "forward" and βάλλω, "I throw".

⁵⁸406-7 = 297-8. See also p.135, footnote 17.

Section 23

"ὤ μοι, ἐπεὶ δὴ γαῖαν ἀελπέα⁵⁹ δῶκεν ἰδέσθαι
Ζεύς, καὶ δὴ τόδε λαῖτμα διατμήξας⁶⁰ ἐπέρησα,⁶¹
ἔκβασις⁶² οὔ πῃ φαίνεθ' ἁλὸς πολιοῖο⁶³ θύραζε·⁶⁴   410
ἔκτοσθεν⁶⁵ μὲν γὰρ πάγοι ὀξέες, ἀμφὶ⁶⁶ δὲ κῦμα⁶⁷
βέβρυχεν ῥόθιον,⁶⁸ λισσὴ⁶⁹ δ' ἀναδέδρομε⁷⁰ πέτρη,
ἀγχιβαθὴς⁷¹ δὲ θάλασσα, καὶ οὔ πως ἔστι πόδεσσι
στήμεναι⁷² ἀμφοτέροισι καὶ ἐκφυγέειν κακότητα·
μή⁷³ πώς μ' ἐκβαίνοντα βάλῃ λίθακι⁷⁴ ποτὶ πέτρῃ   415

⁵⁹ἐπεὶ, "at a time when", begins a clause which continues to ἐπέρησα. ἀελπέα is accusative singular of ἀελπής (p.165), qualifying γαῖαν. For ἰδέσθαι, see p.117, footnote 29. Ζεύς is the subject of δῶκεν (3rd person singular of δῶκα, aorist indicative active of δίδωμι).

⁶⁰διατμήξας is masculine singular nominative of the aorist participle active of διατμήγω = I cut in two, cleave, make my way through. It qualifies the subject of ἐπέρησα, "I". τόδε λαῖτμα is the object of both διατμήξας and ἐπέρησα.

⁶¹ἐπέρησα is 1st person singular, aorist indicative active of περάω = I traverse, pass right through or across.

⁶²ἔκβασις (3f) = way out, exit (from ἐκ + βαίνω). φαίνεθ' stands for φαίνεται, 3rd person singular of φαίνομαι (present). πῃ: anywhere.

⁶³See footnote 18, above. ἁλὸς πολιοῖο is genitive of separation (p.30).

⁶⁴θύραζε (derived from θύρα, door) means literally "to the door", and so "out of doors"; but here it means merely "out".

⁶⁵ἔκτοσθεν = outside. ἔκτοσθεν μὲν ... ἀγχιβαθὴς δὲ θάλασσα ... makes a comparison: "outside, on the one hand ... on the other hand, inshore the sea (is) deep". Understand εἰσιν ("there are") with πάγοι ὀξέες after ἔκτοσθεν.

⁶⁶Understand αὐτοὺς ("them", standing for "rocks") with ἀμφί.

⁶⁷κῦμα is the subject of βέβρυχε, 3rd person singular of βέβρυχα = "I bellow" (perfect with present meaning, cf. similar verbs in Section 21). In later Greek, this verb has the form βρυχάομαι, under which it is found in Liddell & Scott.

⁶⁸ῥόθιος, ῥόθιον (fem. usually as masc.) = dashing, roaring. ῥόθιον (neuter) qualifies κῦμα.

⁶⁹λισσός, λισσή, λισσόν = smooth (and so "sheer").

⁷⁰ἀναδέδρομε is 3rd person singular of ἀναδέδρομα (perfect with present meaning) = I run up. The present is ἀνατρέχω. The perfect of τρέχω (I run) in Homer is δέδρομα (I have run).

⁷¹ἀγχιβαθής = deep inshore (from ἄγχι, near, βαθύς, deep.) Understand ἐστι.

⁷²στήμεναι = στῆναι, the infinitive of ἔστην, "I stood", the strong aorist of ἵστημι, I make to stand. στήμεναι and στῆναι mean "to stand". For ἔστι "it is possible" (note the accent), see Odyssey V, 103 and p.84 above, footnote 29. ἀμφοτέροισι qualifies πόδεσσι, the dative plural of πούς. ἐκφυγέειν is the infinitive of ἐξέφυγον, the aorist of ἐκφεύγω. κακότητα is the object of ἐκφυγέειν.

⁷³Understand δείδω before μή. For "I fear that", see Section 14, p. 98. The accent on μή is from πώς (πως is enclitic) and the accent on πώς is from μ' (standing for με, which is also enclitic). πώς therefore stands for πως: "in some way". ἐκβαίνοντα is masculine singular accusative of ἐκβαίνων, the participle of ἐκβαίνω, I step out, go out, emerge. Translate in the order: (δείδω) μή πως μέγα κῦμα ἁρπάξαν μ(ε) ἐκβαίνοντα (ἐκ θαλάσσης) βάλῃ (με) ποτὶ λίθακι πέτρῃ.

⁷⁴βάλῃ is 3rd person subjunctive of ἔβαλον, the aorist active of βάλλω. λίθαξ, λίθακος (3rd declension adjective) = stony.

κῦμα μέγ' ἁρπάξαν·⁷⁵ μελέη⁷⁶ δέ μοι ἔσσεται ὁρμή.
εἰ δέ κ' ἔτι προτέρω παρανήξομαι,⁷⁷ ἤν⁷⁸ που ἐφεύρω
ἠϊόνας⁷⁹ τε παραπλῆγας λιμένας τε θαλάσσης,
δείδω μή μ' ἐξαῦτις⁸⁰ ἀναρπάξασα⁸¹ θύελλα
πόντον ἐπ' ἰχθυόεντα⁸² φέρῃ βαρέα⁸³ στενάχοντα, 420
ἠέ τί μοι καὶ κῆτος⁸⁴ ἐπισσεύῃ⁸⁵ μέγα δαίμων
ἐξ ἁλός, οἷά τε⁸⁶ πολλὰ τρέφει κλυτὸς Ἀμφιτρίτη·⁸⁷
οἶδα γὰρ ὥς μοι ὀδώδυσται⁸⁸ κλυτὸς ἐννοσίγαιος."⁸⁹

---

⁷⁵ἁρπάξαν, the neuter singular nominative of the participle of ἥρπαξα, the aorist active of ἁρπάζω, I seize, snatch up, qualifies κῦμα, the subject of βάλῃ.
⁷⁶μέλεος, μελέη, μέλεον = useless, in vain. ἔσσεται is 3rd person singular, future of εἰμι (Section 12, p.81). ὁρμή here means "effort".
⁷⁷παρανήξομαι is 1st person singular of the future of παρανήχω, I swim past.
⁷⁸ἤν = εἰ ἄν, used with the subjunctive sometimes with κε, to express a future condition (see p.172). ἐφεύρω is 1st person singular, subjunctive of ἐφεῦρον, the aorist of ἐφευρίσκω, I discover. The meaning is "to see if I would discover anywhere..." This really expresses a purpose.
⁷⁹ἠϊών, ἠϊόνος (3f) = shore, beach. παραπλήξ, παραπλῆγος (3rd declension adjective) = struck sideways, i.e. not facing the full force of the wave. Liddell & Scott suggest "on which the waves break obliquely". This would not have been as much help as a shelving beach (Hainsworth, *op. cit.* p.285).
⁸⁰ἐξαῦτις = back again.
⁸¹For ἀναρπάξασα, see footnote 21 above. It qualifies θύελλα, the subject of φέρῃ, 3rd person singular present subjunctive of φέρω.
⁸²See footnote 22.
⁸³βαρύς, βαρεῖα, βαρύ, heavy, deep-toned. βαρέα (neuter plural accusative) is used as an adverb, "deeply", qualifying στενάχοντα, the masculine singular accusative of στενάχων, the participle of στενάχω, which qualifies μ' (line 419) or perhaps πόντον (torrents groan (στενάχουσι) at Iliad xvi, 391).
⁸⁴ἠέ (more often ἤ) : or. The accent on ἠέ is from τί (enclitic). The accent on τί is from μοι (also enclitic). Translate τί as τι ("some", "a", indefinite), qualifying κῆτος. κῆτος, κήτους (3n) = sea monster.
⁸⁵ἐπισσεύῃ is 3rd person singular present subjunctive, from ἐπισ(σ)εύω = I set (something, accusative) on (someone, dative). The subject is δαίμων. μέγα (neuter) qualifies κῆτος (the object of ἐπισσεύῃ). Translate in the order: ἠέ δαίμων καὶ ἐπισσεύῃ τι μέγα κῆτος ἐξ ἁλός μοι. (καί: also.) ἅλς is used for the sea close to the shore (Liddell & Scott); this might be frequented by basking sharks. Hainsworth (*op. cit.*, p.285) refers to reports of impressively large sharks and whales in the Mediterranean.
⁸⁶οἷά τε πολλά : "such as, you may be sure, in great numbers". οἷα ("of which kind") and πολλά are neuter plural qualifying κήτεα (understood from κῆτος in the preceding line). οἷά τε πολλά is the object of τρέφει, 3rd person singular present indicative active of τρέφω. κλυτὸς Ἀμφιτρίτη is the subject.
⁸⁷Amphitrite is the wife of Poseidon and mother of Triton (Hesiod, *Theogony* 930). She is not mentioned in the Iliad, and in the Odyssey represents the sea; see West's note on Odyssey III, 91 (*op. cit.* p.166).
⁸⁸The accent on ὥς is enclitic, from μοι. ὡς (here) = "how" (introducing a clause in indirect speech, the object of οἶδα). ὀδώδυσται is 3rd person singular, perfect of ὀδύσσομαι (p.148, footnote 21). The perfect gives the meaning "has come to hate (and still does)". The subject is κλυτὸς ἐννοσίγαιος.
⁸⁹ἐννοσίγαιος like ἐνοσίχθων. means "earth-shaker". and is a title of Poseidon.

Section 24
Clauses expressing conditions.[1]

A conditional sentence has a clause stating a supposition, the "protasis", with a conclusion which can be inferred from it, the "apodosis",

e.g. *if Zeus says this* (protasis)
it is certainly true (apodosis).

Conditional clauses can be "open", i.e., not prejudging the conclusion, or they can hint that the condition is contrary to fact.

εἰ or αἰ are used for "if". "if ... not ..." is usually εἰ (or αἰ) ... μή ... ἄν is found in the clause expressing the consequence that would have followed an unlikely (or untrue) condition. The negative in an apodosis is normally οὐ.

Conditions can be expressed with verbs in the optative, subjunctive or indicative moods.

Conditions with **optative** verbs can express a wish:
  εἰ γὰρ Ζεὺς τοῦτο λέγοι - if only Zeus were to say this![2]
and also express a remote condition, not necessarily desirable:
  εἰ Ζεὺς τοῦτο λέγοι, νημερτὲς ἄν εἴη
  if Zeus were to say this, it would be certainly true.
  εἴ κε Ζεὺς τοῦτο λέγοι, νημερτὲς εἴη
  if Zeus were by any chance to say this, it would be certainly true.[3]

An optative condition can be used for the English "to see if ..."
  ἤλυθον εἴ τινά μοι κληηδόνα πατρὸς ἐνίσποις (Odyssey IV, 317)
    I came to see if you would tell me any news of (my) father
  κληηδόνα (not found in nominative): news   ἐνέπω (aorist ἔνισπον) I tell

Conditions with **subjunctive** verbs express an eventuality or a repetition:
  εἴ (κε) Ζεὺς τοῦτο λέγῃ, νημερτὲς ἔσται
  if Zeus says this in the end, it will be certainly true
  if Zeus goes on saying this, it will be certainly true.

---
[1] See Chantraine, *Grammaire Homérique*, vol. ii, ch. xix, pp.274-284.
[2] Such wishes in Homer begin either εἰ γάρ ... or εἰ μέν ... With wishes, the apodosis ("that would be fine!") is usually not expressed but understood.
[3] εἴ κε(ν) or αἴ κε(ν) is like the English "if by (any) chance"; see Odyssey XII, 345: εἰ δέ κεν εἰς Ἰθάκην ἀφικοίμεθα, πατρίδα γαῖαν, αἶψά κεν Ἠελίῳ Ὑπερίονι πίονα νηὸν τεύξομεν "but if by any chance we were to reach Ithaca, (our) native land, we would build a rich temple at once to the Sun, Hyperion". (πίων: rich   νηός: temple   τεύχω: I build. For future (τεύξομεν) with κεν, p.186, footnote 1.)   εἰ + ἄν + optative occurs once, at Iliad ii, 597-8: εἴ περ ἄν αὐταὶ Μοῦσαι ἀείδοιεν "even if by chance the Muses themselves were singing".

They can also express a generality:
εἴ (κε) Ζεὺς τοῦτο λέγῃ, νημερτές ἐστιν
if ever Zeus says this, it is certainly true.
κε is often, but not always, used with subjunctive conditions.[4]

εἰ ἄν (sometimes ἤν) and the subjunctive is rare in Homer.[5]
εἰ ἄν (or ἤν) Ζεὺς τοῦτο λέγῃ, νημερτὲς ἔσται.
Suppose that Zeus says this; then it will be certainly true.

Conditions with **indicative** verbs express real conditions:
εἰ Ζεὺς τοῦτο λέγει, νημερτές ἐστιν
if Zeus says this, it is certainly true.[6]

The indicative is also used for untrue past conditions, i.e. conditions which were not fulfilled in the past. ἄν or κε(ν) is found in the apodosis of untrue past conditions, e.g.
εἰ Ζεὺς τοῦτο εἶπεν, νημερτὲς ἂν ἦν *or* νημερτές κεν ἦν
or νημερτές κ' ἦν
if Zeus had said this, it would have been certainly true.[7]

---

[4]For an example without κεν, see Odyssey V, 221-2: εἰ δ' αὖ τις ῥαίῃσι θεῶν ἐνὶ οἴνοπι πόντῳ, τλήσομαι "suppose, moreover, that one of the gods were to shatter (my ship) in the wine-faced sea, I shall endure (it)."
[5]See Chantraine, *op. cit.*, vol.ii, p.280. ἐάν (or ἤν) and the subjunctive is the usual construction for the protasis of a future (open) condition in Attic (the dialect of Athens) and koiné, the later Common Greek dialect; where ἤν is found with the subjunctive in Homer, Chantraine suspects that sometimes the text may have been been modernised to conform to the later usage.
[6]For a future condition expressed by future indicative both in protasis and apodosis (with a subjunctive following in the apodosis), see Odyssey XII, 382-3: εἰ δέ μοι οὐ τίσουσι βοῶν ἐπιεικέ' ἀμοιβήν, δύσομαι εἰς 'Αΐδαο καὶ ἐν νεκύεσσι φαείνω "but if to me they do not pay of my cattle (= for my cattle) suitable compensation, I shall sink down into the (house of) Hades and among the dead let me shine." (τίνω: I pay βόες (plural): cattle ἐπιεικής: suitable ἀμοιβή: exchange, and so compensation νέκυς, νέκυος: dead person, corpse φαείνω: I shine (here 1st. person singular, present subjunctive.) The use of εἰ and the future indicative is found also in Attic, especially when it stresses an intention or a threat ("Future Most Vivid", Mastronarde, *Introduction to Attic Greek*, p.261)(Jones & Sidwell, *Reading Greek*, Language Survey 6). cf. Sophocles, *Antigone* 93: εἰ ταῦτα λέξεις, ἐχθαρεῖ μὲν ἐξ ἐμοῦ. "if you *will* say these things, you will receive emnity from me on the one hand ..." ἐχθαρεῖ is 2nd person singular future of ἐχθαίρομαι (= I am treated as an enemy).
[7]NB κε with imperfect indicative in an apodosis refers to *past* time in Homer: νύ κε τὸ τρίτον πάλαιον, εἰ μὴ 'Αχιλλεὺς κατέρυκε (Iliad xxiii, 733-4) ("now they would have wrestled for the third time if Achilles had not stopped them"). (πάλαιον is 3rd person plural, imperfect of παλαίω: I wrestle κατέρυκεν is 3rd person singular, imperfect of κατερύκω: I restrain).

Section 24   173

New words:
ἄναξ, ἄνακτος (3m) = lord
γλαυκῶπις = with gleaming eyes (epithet of Athene)[8]
δύστηνος, δύστηνον = wretched   ἐλεαίρω = I pity
ἐμβάλλω = I throw into
ἐπεσσύμενος, ἐπεσσυμένη, ἐπεσσύμενον = violent, hasty[9]
ἤπειρόνδε = to the (main)land   κάματος (2m) = weariness
λάϊγξ, λάιγγος (3f) = pebble   μογέω = I toil, suffer
παύω = I stop   ποταμός (2m) = river
ῥόος (2m) = stream   σκέπας (3n) = shelter
χρώς, χροός (3m) = skin, flesh

What is the English for: 1.εἰ γὰρ πατρίδα γαῖαν ἴδοιμι!
2.εἰ πατρίδα γαῖαν ἴδοιμι, τερποίμην ἄν.
3.εἴ κε πατρίδα γαῖαν ἴδω, ἱερά τε ῥέξω καὶ ἐξαίτους ἑκατόμβας.[10]
4.εἴ κε πατρίδα γαῖαν ἴδω, τέρπομαι.
5.εἰ τοῦτο νημερτές ἐστι, τέρπομαι.
6.ἔνθα κ' ἀπὸ ῥινοὺς δρύφθη,[11] σὺν δ' ὀστέ' ἀράχθη,[12]
εἰ μὴ ἐπὶ φρεσὶ θῆκε[13] θεὰ γλαυκῶπις 'Αθήνη· (Odyssey V, 426-7)
7.ἔνθα κε δὴ δύστηνος ὑπὲρ μόρον[14] ὤλετ' 'Οδυσσεύς,
εἰ μὴ ἐπιφροσύνην δῶκε γλαυκῶπις 'Αθήνη· (Odyssey V 436-7)

[8]Probably connected with γλαυκός, "bright", not with γλαῦξ, "owl", which does not occur in Homer. See West, *A Commentary on Homer's Odyssey* vol.i, p.80 (on Odyssey I, 44).
[9]Perfect participle passive of ἐπισσεύω.
[10]ῥέξω is 1st person singular, future of ῥέζω. See also line 102, p.84 above.
[11]κ' = "would" in the apodosis of an untrue past condition. ῥινός = the skin. ἀπὸ ῥινοὺς δρύφθη is tmesis (p. 78, footnote 39); ῥινοὺς is inserted between ἀπὸ and δρύφθη, which together make up ἀποδρύφθη ("he would have been stripped"), 3rd person singular of the aorist passive indicative of ἀποδρύπτω, I tear off. ῥινοὺς is accusative and shows where the passive verb, ἀποδρύφθη, applies: "he would have been stripped with respect to his skin", or "as far as his skin was concerned". ("skins" may be poetical ornament, or mean several layers of skin (at Iliad xiii, 804 ῥινοῖσι means "with layers of ox-hide").)
[12]ὀστέ' stands for ὀστέα (neuter plural). ὀστέον = the bone. συναράχθη is 3rd person singular (neuter plural subject) of συναράχθην, the aorist passive of συναράσσω, I smash, dash in pieces. σὺν δ' ὀστέ' ἀράχθη is another example of tmesis. συναράχθη is included in the apodosis with κ' and so is also untrue.
[13]For θῆκε, see p. 107; the object, "a suggestion" is understood: ἐπὶ φρεσὶ θῆκε "put a suggestion in his mind" = "made a suggestion" (Hainsworth, *op.cit.*, p.285). (The subject is θεὰ γλαυκῶπις 'Αθήνη.)
[14]ὑπὲρ μόρον = above (i.e. contrary to) his destiny (μόρος 2m = fate, destiny). ὠλόμην, the aorist middle of ὄλλυμι, has the intransitive meaning "I was destroyed". κε shows that ὤλετ' (standing for ὤλετο) is untrue ("would have been ..."). δῶκε = "gave" (3rd person singular of (ἐ)δωκα, the aorist active of δίδωμι, I give. ἐπιφροσύνη (1f) = wisdom.

Odyssey V, 424-457

εἷος ὁ ταῦθ' ὥρμαινε κατὰ φρένα καὶ κατὰ θυμόν,[15]
τόφρα δέ μιν μέγα κῦμα φέρεν τρηχεῖαν[16] ἐπ' ἀκτήν. 425
ἔνθα κ' ἀπὸ ῥινοὺς δρύφθη, σὺν δ' ὀστέ' ἀράχθη,
εἰ μὴ ἐπὶ φρεσὶ θῆκε θεὰ γλαυκῶπις Ἀθήνη·[17]
ἀμφοτέρῃσι δὲ χερσὶν[18] ἐπεσσύμενος λάβε πέτρης,
τῆς[19] ἔχετο στενάχων, εἷος μέγα κῦμα παρῆλθε.[20]
καὶ τὸ μὲν ὣς ὑπάλυξε,[21] παλιρρόθιον[22] δέ μιν αὖτις 430
πλῆξεν[23] ἐπεσσύμενον, τηλοῦ δέ μιν ἔμβαλε πόντῳ.
ὡς δ' ὅτε πουλύποδος[24] θαλάμης[25] ἐξελκομένοιο[26]
πρὸς κοτυληδονόφιν[27] πυκιναὶ λάϊγγες ἔχονται,[28]
ὥς[29] τοῦ πρὸς πέτρῃσι θρασειάων[30] ἀπὸ χειρῶν

[15]Line 424 = line 365.
[16]τρηχύς, τρηχεῖα, τρηχύ = jagged ἐπ' stands for ἐπί. Translate as if ἐπὶ τρηχεῖαν ἀκτήν. ὥρμαινε and φέρε are 3rd person singular imperfect of ὁρμαίνω and φέρω respectively.
[17]See footnotes 11-13 above.
[18]For χερσὶν, see p.40. λάβε is 3rd person singular of λάβον (Section 10, p.66.)
[19]τῆς: of which (translate with ἔχετο). ἔχετο is 3rd person singular of ἔχομην, the imperfect of ἔχομαι + genitive = I hold on to (something). στενάχων is masculine singular nominative of the participle of στενάχω.
[20]παρῆλθε is 3rd person singular of παρῆλθον, aorist of παρέρχομαι = I go past.
[21]τὸ (it) refers to μέγα κῦμα, the object of ὑπάλυξε (the subject is "he" (Odysseus)). ὑπάλυξε is 3rd person singular of ὑπάλυξα, the aorist of ὑπαλύσκω = I escape. Note that ὣς is accented.
[22]παλιρρόθιος, παλιρροθίη, παλιρρόθιον = rushing backwards (neuter here because qualifying the subject of πλῆξεν, which is "it", i.e. κῦμα).
[23]αὖτις = again. πλῆξεν is 3rd person singular of πλῆξα, the aorist active of πλήσσω, I smite. ἐπεσσύμενον (neuter singular) qualifies κῦμα. ἔμβαλε is 3rd person singular of ἔμβαλον, the aorist of ἐμβάλλω. πόντῳ (dative) indicates the end of the motion expressed by ἔμβαλε: "in the open sea". τηλοῦ: far away.
[24]For ὡς δ' ὅτε, see lines 328 and 394. πουλύποδος masculine (3rd declension) genitive singular, found only once (here) in Homer, = octopus, "many-footed", cf. English "polyp". The nominative singular would be πο(υ)λύπους (found in later writers).
[25]θαλάμη (1f) = lair, lurking place (the genitive expresses "from").
[26]ἐξελκομένοιο (qualifying πουλύποδος) is masculine genitive singular of ἐξελκόμενος, the participle of ἐξέλκομαι, the present passive of ἐξέλκω = I drag out of (+ genitive of place dragged from).
[27]κοτυληδών, κοτυληδόνος (3f) = sucker. πρὸς κοτυληδονόφιν: (close-set pebbles cling) closely to its suckers. For the ending -οφιν, see p.69, footnote 16.
[28]ἔχομαι (middle) (here) = I cling (cf. footnote 19 above).
[29]ὥς (accented: "so") gives the point of the comparison. τοῦ ("his") refers to Odysseus. πρὸς πέτρῃσι: very close to (i.e. clinging to) the rocks (translate with ῥινοὶ ἀπέδρυφθεν).
[30]θρασύς, θρασεία, θρασύ = daring, bold.

Section 24

ῥινοὶ ἀπέδρυφθεν·³¹ τὸν δὲ μέγα κῦμ' ἐκάλυψεν. 435
ἔνθα κε δὴ δύστηνος ὑπὲρ μόρον ὤλετ' Ὀδυσσεύς,
εἰ μὴ ἐπιφροσύνην δῶκε γλαυκῶπις Ἀθήνη·³²
κύματος ἐξαναδύς,³³ τά τ' ἐρεύγεται³⁴ ἤπειρόνδε,
νῆχε παρέξ,³⁵ ἐς γαῖαν ὁρώμενος,³⁶ εἴ που³⁷ ἐφεύροι
ἠϊόνας³⁸ τε παραπλῆγας λιμένας τε θαλάσσης. 440
ἀλλ' ὅτε δὴ ποταμοῖο κατὰ στόμα καλλιρόοιο³⁹
ἷξε νέων,⁴⁰ τῇ⁴¹ δή οἱ ἐείσατο⁴² χῶρος ἄριστος,
λεῖος⁴³ πετράων, καὶ ἐπὶ⁴⁴ σκέπας ἦν ἀνέμοιο·

³¹ ἀπέδρυφθεν = ἀπεδρύφθησαν (3rd person plural, aorist passive of ἀποδρύπτω, for which see footnote 11 above). Odysseus' skin, as it got torn off his hands, was clinging to the rocks like the pebbles clinging to the suckers of the octopus. τὸν ("him", Odysseus) is the object of ἐκάλυψεν (3rd person singular of (ἐ)κάλυψα, the aorist indicative of καλύπτω). μέγα κῦμα is the subject.
³²See footnote 13 above.
³³ἐξαναδύς (+ genitive) = "having popped up out of" (masculine singular nominative of the participle of ἐξανέδυν, the aorist of ἐξαναδύομαι, I emerge).
³⁴Hainsworth notes that κύματος has a collective meaning, "out of the waves". So τά (plural) refers to κύματος. τά τ' : "all those which". For this use of τ' (= τε), see p.90, footnote 18. τά is the subject of ἐρεύγεται. ἐρεύγομαι here = I roar (see p.168, footnote 53). ἤπειρόνδε: towards the land. Chantraine emphasises (*op. cit.* vol.ii, p.191) that the historic present is not found in Epic. ἐρεύγεται (present tense, singular because having a neuter plural subject (τά standing for κύματα)) is therefore descriptive: "all those which roar towards the land."
³⁵νῆχε is 3rd person singular, imperfect of νήχω (inceptive, p.32): he began to swim. παρέξ = out beside, i.e. out alongshore.
³⁶ὁρώμενος (contracted from ὁραόμενος) is masculine singular nominative of the participle of ὁράομαι, meaning "keeping an eye open".
³⁷εἴ που (indefinite), with the optative: "to see it anywhere ... ". που is enclitic, which accounts for the accent on εἴ. ἐφεύροι is 3rd person singular, optative of ἐφεῦρον, the aorist of ἐφευρίσκω.
³⁸See p.170, footnote 79 (line 440 = 418).
³⁹κατὰ with accusative (στόμα) (here) means "towards". ἷξε (line 442) is 3rd person singular of ἷξον, the aorist of ἵκω, I come. Taking κατὰ and ἷξε together, translate as "he reached". καλλιρόος, καλλιρόον = flowing beautifully (used at Odyssey XVII, 206, to describe the fountain from which the people in Ithaca town drew their water). καλλιρόοιο qualifies ποταμοῖο.
⁴⁰νέων is masculine singular nominative of the participle of νέω.
⁴¹τῇ = there.
⁴²ἐείσατο (subject χῶρος ἄριστος), see p.130, footnote 36. χῶρος 2m = place.
⁴³λεῖος, λεῖα, λεῖον = smooth, hence free (from rocks). See p.30.
⁴⁴ἐπί is used here by itself as an adverb: "on it".

ἔγνω⁴⁵ δὲ προρέοντα καὶ εὔξατο⁴⁶ ὃν κατὰ θυμόν·
"κλῦθι,⁴⁷ ἄναξ, ὅτις⁴⁸ ἐσσί· πολύλλιστον⁴⁹ δέ σ' ἱκάνω   445
φεύγων ἐκ πόντοιο Ποσειδάωνος ἐνιπάς.⁵⁰
αἰδοῖος μέν τ' ἐστὶ καὶ ἀθανάτοισι θεοῖσιν,
ἀνδρῶν ὅς τις ἵκηται⁵¹ ἀλώμενος, ὡς καὶ ἐγὼ νῦν
σόν τε ῥόον σά τε γούναθ' ἱκάνω πολλὰ μογήσας.
ἀλλ' ἐλέαιρε, ἄναξ· ἱκέτης δέ τοι εὔχομαι⁵² εἶναι."   450
ὣς φάθ', ὁ δ'⁵³ αὐτίκα παῦσεν ἑὸν ῥόον, ἔσχε δὲ κῦμα,

⁴⁵ἔγνω is 3rd person singular of ἔγνων, the strong aorist of γιγνώσκω, "I recognise." προρέοντα is accusative singular masculine of προρέων, the present participle active of προρέω, I flow forward (i.e. out into the sea) and qualifies ποταμόν, which is understood. The meaning is "he recognised that it was a river flowing into the sea". Rivers are sometimes personified in Homer (e.g. the Scamander at Troy in Iliad xxi) and so it would be natural for Odysseus to pray to the river god even though he did not know his name.
⁴⁶εὔξατο is 3rd person singular of εὐξάμην, the aorist indicative of εὔχομαι (= I pray: see p.115, footnote 8).
⁴⁷κλῦθι is 2nd person singular imperative of ἔκλυον, the aorist of κλύω, I listen. It is often found at the beginning of a line, being a bardic formula: "Hearken!"
⁴⁸ὅτις = ὅστις, whoever. ἐσσί is 2nd person singular of εἰμί.
⁴⁹πολύλλιστος, πολύλλιστον "sought with many prayers" (Liddell & Scott) is translated by Hainsworth (*op. cit.*, p.286) as "most welcome", by analogy with Iliad viii, 488, where night is ἀσπασίη (welcome) and τρίλλιστος (thrice prayed for) to the Achaeans after a hard day's fighting. Usually a suppliant would begin his plea by enunciating the titles of a god or oracle (Hainsworth).
⁵⁰φεύγων is masculine singular nominative of the participle of φεύγω. ἐνιπή = angry threat (usually "reproof"). ἐνιπάς is the object of φεύγων, "fleeing from".
⁵¹Translate in the order ὅς τις ἀνδρῶν. ὅς τις ἀνδρῶν ("whoever of men...") is the subject of ἵκηται ("may arrive") (3rd person singular, aorist subjunctive of ἱκνέομαι). The clause ὅστις ἀνδρῶν ἵκηται ἀλώμενος is the subject of ἐστι in line 447. ἀλώμενος is contracted from ἀλαόμενος, masculine nominative singular of the participle of ἀλάομαι. καὶ means "even" in καὶ ἀθανάτοισι θεοῖσιν. καὶ means "also" in καὶ ἐγώ. πολλὰ is the object of μογήσας, masculine nominative singular of the participle of (ἐ)μόγησα, the aorist of μογέω, and qualifies "I" (from the verb ἱκάνω ("I reach"), which governs the accusatives σόν τε ῥόον σά τε γούναθ'). (γούναθ' stands for γούνατα.) (A suppliant had to touch the knees of the person he was supplicating.) ἐλέαιρε is 2nd person singular imperative of ἐλεαίρω. (The repetition of ἱκ- in ἵκηται and ἱκάνω emphasises their connection with the noun ἱκέτης.)
⁵²εὔχομαι here means "I claim (to be)."
⁵³For φάθ' (which stands for ἔφατο) see p.34, footnote 7. ὁ δὲ indicates a change of subject: "but he (the river god) ..." παῦσεν is 3rd person singular of (ἔ)παυσα, the aorist of παύω. ἔσχε (3rd person singular of (ἔ)σχον, the aorist of ἔχω): "held back". κῦμα is the object.

Section 24

πρόσθε⁵⁴ δέ οἱ ποίησε γαλήνην, τὸν δ' ἐσάωσεν
ἐς ποταμοῦ προχοάς·⁵⁵ ὁ δ⁵⁶ ἄρ' ἄμφω⁵⁷ γούνατ' ἔκαμψε
χεῖράς τε στιβαράς·⁵⁸ ἁλὶ γὰρ δέδμητο⁵⁹ φίλον κῆρ·
ᾤδεε⁶⁰ δὲ χρόα πάντα, θάλασσα δὲ κήκιε⁶¹ πολλὴ   455
ἀν στόμα τε ῥῖνάς θ'· ὁ δ' ἄρ' ἄπνευστος⁶² καὶ ἄναυδος
κεῖτ' ὀλιγηπελέων,⁶³ κάματος δέ μιν αἰνὸς⁶⁴ ἵκανεν.

---

⁵⁴πρόσθε = before, in front. οἱ is dative: for him (Odysseus). ποίησε is 3rd person singular of (ἐ)ποίησα, the aorist of ποιέω. ἐσάωσεν is 3rd person singular of ἐσάωσα, the aorist of σαόω. τὸν ("him") refers to Odysseus.
⁵⁵προχοαί, "the outpourings", means the mouth of a river. "To save a person into ... " is the same as "to give someone refuge in ... ".
⁵⁶ὁ δ' changes the subject again: "but he (Odysseus) ...".
⁵⁷ἄμφω (all genders) = both (indeclinable in Homer), qualifying γούνατα. ἔκαμψε is 3rd person singular of ἔκαμψα, the aorist of κάμπτω = I bend.
⁵⁸στιβαρός, στιβαρά, στιβαρόν = sturdy. χείρ here means "arm".
⁵⁹See section 22, p. 155.
⁶⁰ᾤδεε is 3rd person singular imperfect of οἰδέω = I swell. χρόα πάντα is accusative of respect: "he was swelling with respect to all his flesh", i.e., "his whole body was becoming swollen".
⁶¹κήκιε is 3rd person singular imperfect of κηκίω = I gush, bubble forth. ἀν stands for ἀνά, here meaning "through"; cf. Iliad xvi, 349-50: τὸ (i.e. αἷμα) δ' ἀνὰ στόμα καὶ κατὰ ῥῖνας πρῆσε χανών ("and he poured it (blood) through his mouth and down his nostrils, gaping") (πρήθω (aorist πρῆσα): I pour, χαίνω (aorist ἔχανον): I gape). πολλή qualifies θάλασσα which means "sea water". ῥίς, ῥινός 3f = nose (cf rhinoceros). ῥῖνες = nostrils.
⁶²ἄπνευστος, ἄπνευστον = without breath. ἄναυδος, ἄναυδον = without voice.
⁶³ὀλιγηπελέων –ουσα –ον = weak, having little power. κεῖτ' stands for ἔκειτο, the 3rd person pluperfect of κεῖμαι. Since κεῖμαι is translated by a present tense verb ("I lie"), (ἐ)κείμην is translated as an imperfect ("I lay, was lying").
⁶⁴αἰνός, αἰνή, αἰνόν = dreadful. ἵκανεν is 3rd person singular of ἵκανον, the imperfect of ἱκάνω.

Section 25
Comparison of adjectives.

Adjectives have three degrees of comparison. The standard form.
e.g. "terrible", is the **positive** degree.
"More terrible" is the **comparative** degree.
"Most terrible" is the **superlative** degree.

With many English adjectives, the comparative degree is expressed by the suffix **-er**, and the superlative by the suffix **-est** e.g.
green *(positive)* greener *(comparative)* greenest *(superlative)*.

The regular suffixes in Greek are, for the **comparative, -τερος**, and for the **superlative, -τατος**.
Thus "more terrible" is
δεινότερος (masc.)   δεινότερα (fem.)   δεινότατον (neut.)
and "most terrible" is
δεινότατος (masc.)   δεινοτάτη (fem.)   δεινότατον (neut.)

Examples of superlatives.
1. ὅρκος δεινότατος (Odyssey V, 186) means "oath most terrible".
2. φησί τοι ἄνδρα παρεῖναι ὀϊζυρώτατον ἄλλων (Odyssey V, 105) means "he affirms, I tell you, a man to be here most wretched of (all) others".
3. μακάρτατος ἔξοχον ἄλλων (Odyssey VI, 158) means "most blessed above others".

Examples of comparatives.
1. Sometimes a comparison is implicit, i.e. the person(s) or thing(s) with which the comparison is made are not expressed, e.g.
    καὶ νύ τις ὧδ' εἴπῃσι κακώτερος (Odyssey VI, 275) means
"and now some inferior person may say as follows" (meaning "inferior to us").
2. However, if the comparison is expressed, an equivalent for "than" is needed. This can be ἤ, or the genitive[1] can be used to show the standard of comparison:

---
[1]Chantraine, *Grammaire Homérique* vol.ii, p.151.

Section 25   179

with **genitive**:
οἵ μευ φέρτεροι[2] εἰσι νοῆσαί τε κρῆναί τε (Odyssey V, 170)
"who are stronger than me both to perceive and to accomplish"
or with ἤ[3] :
οἱ (i.e. the dead warriors) ἐπὶ γαίῃ κείατο, γύπεσσι πολὺ φίλτεροι ἤ
ἀλόχοισιν (Iliad xi, 161-2)
"they, on the ground, were lying, to the vultures much dearer than to their
wives".
(γῦπες (3 plural) = vultures. ἄλοχος (2 feminine) = wife)

Some adjectives have **comparatives** ending -ιων (third declension)
and **superlatives** ending -ιστος (masc.), -ιστη (fem.), -ιστον (neut.).
χερείων ("worse") is used as a comparative of κακός.[4] Its declension
is as follows:

SINGULAR	masculine & feminine	neuter
nominative	χερείων	χερεῖον
accusative	χερείονα	χερεῖον
genitive	χερείονος	χερείονος
dative	χερείονι	χερείονι
DUAL		
nom. & acc.	[χερείονε]	[χερείονε]
gen. & dat.	[χερειόνοιιν]	[χερειόνοιιν]
PLURAL		
nominative	[χερείονες]	χερείονα
accusative	[χερείονας]	χερείονα
genitive	[χερειόνων]	[χερειόνων]
dative	[χερείοσι or χερειόνεσσι]	[χερείοσι or χερειόνεσσι]

The following comparatives and superlatives of this type are common:
ἀγαθός: good   ἀμείνων or : better   ἄριστος: best
                         ἀρείων
μέγας: big   μείζων: bigger   μέγιστος: biggest
πολύς or πολλός: much   πλέων: more   πλεῖστος: most

[2]φέρτερος ("stronger") and φέρτατος or φέριστος ("strongest") are poetical
comparative and superlative which have no corresponding positive. The
ordinary Greek for "strong" is ἰσχυρός.
[3]Note, however, that ἤ (sometimes spelled ἠέ) also means "or".
[4]χερειότερος is found meaning "inferior" at Iliad xii, 270 and "worse" at Iliad
ii, 248: οὐ γὰρ ἐγὼ σέο φημὶ χερειότερον βροτὸν ἄλλον ἔμμεναι ("for I affirm
there not to be another mortal worse than you") (Odysseus chiding Thersites).
χειρότερος is found meaning "inferior" at Iliad xv, 513 and xx 436.

The comparative of κακός, "bad", has two forms, κακίων and κακώτερος, "worse". The superlative is κάκιστος, "worst".

Examples of comparatives.

1. οὐ μέν θην κείνης γε χερείων εὔχομαι εἶναι (Odyssey V, 211)
"Indeed, I do not claim to be worse *than that woman*".

2. κέρδιον, "a more profitable thing", is a comparative of this kind,[5]
ὣς ἄρα οἱ φρονέοντι δοάσσατο κέρδιον εἶναι (Odyssey V, 474)
"to him, then, thinking thus, it seemed to be a more profitable thing".
(δοάσσατο: it seemed)

3. ἀμείνων, the comparative of ἀγαθός ("good"), e.g.
ἐπεὶ οὐ μέν τι παρὰ προνοῆσαι ἄμεινον (Odyssey V, 364)
"since (there is) not anything better at hand to plan ahead."

Examples of superlatives.

1. μέγιστος, the superlative of μέγας:
ὅς τε μέγιστος
ὅρκος δεινότατός τε πέλει μακάρεσσι θεοῖσι (Odyssey V, 185-6)
"which is, for the blessed gods both the greatest and the most terrible oath".

2. ἄριστος, the superlative of ἀγαθός:
δοκεῖ δέ μοι εἶναι ἄριστον (Odyssey V, 360)
"and it seems to me the best thing".

Degrees of comparison of adverbs.

Comparative adverbs tend to have **neuter singular** endings, and **superlative adverbs** tend to have **neuter plural** endings. Thus, from μάλα (very) the comparative is μᾶλλον (more) and the superlative is μάλιστα (most, especially).

Common superlative adverbs: τάχιστα ("very quickly", "in the quickest way") from ταχέως ("quickly"),[6] ἄγχιστα ("very near", or "very nearly") and μήκιστα ("very far"; also "last", "farthest", "at last").

What is the English for:
1. τοῦτο ποιέειν μοι φρονέοντι δοάσσατο κέρδιον εἶναι.

[5]Only in the neuter singular, as here. The superlative, κέρδιστος, means "most cunning" (good at making a profit) and qualifies Σίσυφος (Iliad vi, 153).
[6]Often found in ὅττι τάχιστα or ὡς τάχιστα, "as quickly as possible".

Section 25

2. ὕπνος πάντας ἀνθρώπους δυσπονεστάτου[7] καμάτοιο παύσει.
3. τί πάθωμεν; τί ἡμῖν μήκιστα γένηται;
4. οὐδὲν τούτου ἄμεινόν ἐστι, πατρίδα φίλην ἱκέσθαι.

New words:

ἀγρός (2m) = field   ἄλλοθεν = from another place
ἀναβαίνω (aorist participle ἀναβάς) = I go up
ἄφαρ = straightaway   δαμάζω[8] = I overcome
δοάσσατο = it seemed[9]
ἤ ... = or : ἤ ... ἤ ... (or ἠὲ ... ἠὲ ...) = either ... or ...
ἠῶθι πρό = at daybreak, early   θάμνος (2m or f) = bush
θῆλυς, (θήλεια), θῆλυ = female, soft, gentle[10]
κέρδιον = more profitable   μεθίημι (aorist μεθῆκα) = I let go
μήκιστα = as far as possible, (in this passage) at last
ὄμβρος (2m) = rainstorm, shower   ποτε = ever[11]
τάχιστα = very quickly   τρεῖς[12] = three
ὑγρός, ὑγρά, ὑγρόν = wet   φύω (perfect πέφυ(κ)α) = I grow

Odyssey V, 458-493

ἀλλ' ὅτε δή ῥ' ἄμπνυτο[13] καὶ ἐς φρένα θυμὸς ἀγέρθη,[14]
καὶ τότε δὴ κρήδεμνον ἀπὸ ἕο λῦσε θεοῖο.[15]

[7]δυσπονής, δυσπονές = toilsome. παύω with accusative of person rescued and genitive of thing rescued from, "I rescue", "I cause to cease from".
[8]Aorist active (ἐ)δάμασα, aorist passive participle, δαμείς (Odyssey VI, 11).
[9]This is an isolated Homeric form (3rd person singular aorist middle) (see Liddell & Scott and Chantraine, *op. cit.*, vol. i, p.410).
[10]θῆλυς often qualifies feminine nouns. Because of its meaning, θῆλυς seems sometimes to have been thought not to require separate feminine endings. Hainsworth (*A Commentary on Homer's Odyssey* vol.i, p.287) notes that there are seven other examples of θῆλυς as a feminine adjective. However, θήλεια is also found e.g. at Iliad viii, 7.
[11]ποτε is enclitic (see section 1, p.5). πότε (not enclitic, but with acute accent) is interrogative, and means "when?"
[12]Masculine and feminine. The neuter is τρία.
[13]ῥ' stands for ἄρα. ἄμπνυτο = he came to himself" (Chantraine, *op. cit.*, vol.i, p.382 and Liddell & Scott). It is 3rd person singular aorist middle, probably from ἀνά and πέπνυμαι (perfect with present meaning in English): I am conscious. ἄμπνυτο is found in Stanford, Thesaurus Linguae Graecae and Hainsworth (*Omero, Odissea* vol. 2 (Mondadori, 1982)) and the majority of mss. Gehring (*Index Homericus*, p.690) and Allen have ἔμπνυτο (from ἐν and πέπνυμαι), "Aristarchus' general correction" (Chantraine). The meaning is the same. ἄμπνυτο καὶ ἐς φρένα θυμὸς ἀγέρθη is used of Andromache recovering from her swoon after the death of Hector (Iliad xxii, 475).
[14]ἀγέρθη is 3rd person singular, aorist passive, ἀγείρω, I collect.
[15]θεοῖο is genitive singular, from θεός, here feminine, referring to Leucothea, and qualifies κρήδεμνον. For ἕο, see p.55. ἀπὸ ἕο = from himself.

καὶ τὸ μὲν ἐς ποταμὸν ἁλιμυρήεντα[16] μεθῆκεν,[17] 460
ἂψ δ' ἔφερεν[18] μέγα κῦμα κατὰ ῥόον, αἶψα δ' ἄρ' Ἰνὼ
δέξατο[19] χερσὶ φίλησιν· ὁ δ' ἐκ ποταμοῖο λιασθεὶς[20]
σχοίνῳ ὑπεκλίνθη, κύσε[21] δὲ ζείδωρον ἄρουραν.[22]
ὀχθήσας δ' ἄρα εἶπε πρὸς ὃν μεγαλήτορα θυμόν·[23]
"ὤ μοι ἐγώ, τί πάθω;[24] τί νύ μοι μήκιστα γένηται; 465
εἰ μέν[25] κ' ἐν ποταμῷ δυσκηδέα[26] νύκτα φυλάσσω,
μή[27] μ' ἄμυδις[28] στίβη τε κακὴ καὶ θῆλυς ἐέρση[29]
ἐξ ὀλιγηπελίης[30] δαμάσῃ κεκαφηότα[31] θυμόν·
αὔρη[32] δ' ἐκ ποταμοῦ ψυχρὴ πνέει ἠῶθι πρό.

[16]ἁλιμυρήεις, genitive singular ἁλιμυρήεντος (masculine adjective, always applies to rivers) = flowing into the sea.
[17]μεθῆκεν is 3rd person singular, aorist active of μεθίημι. The subject is "he". The object is τὸ ("it"), standing for κρήδεμνον.
[18]ἔφερεν is 3rd person singular, imperfect active of φέρω. The imperfect is used here as the meaning is inceptive: "began to..." The subject is μέγα κῦμα and the object is "it" i.e. κρήδεμνον (understood).
[19]δέξατο is 3rd person singular, aorist middle, from δέχομαι, I receive, accept.
[20]ὁ δ' ("but he") changes the subject back to Odysseus. See p. 133 for λιασθεὶς σχοίνῳ ὑπεκλίνθη.
[21]κύσε is 3rd person singular, aorist active of κυνέω = I kiss.
[22]ἄρουρα = ploughland; here, ground. ζείδωρος (fem. as masc.) = zeia-giving. (ζειά is one-seeded wheat, used as fodder for horses.) ζείδωρος ἄρουρα is a formula found 9 times in the Odyssey, and 3 in the Iliad.
[23]Line 464 = lines 298, 355 and 407.
[24]1st person singular, subjunctive of (ἔ)παθον, the aorist of πάσχω. This is a deliberative subjunctive: "What am I to ...?" γένηται (also deliberative) is 3rd person singular, subjunctive of (ἐ)γενόμην, the aorist of γίγνομαι (subject, τί).
[25]Note the antithesis between the conditions in lines 466 and 470, which he compares. εἰ μὲν ... εἰ δὲ ... = if on the one hand, ... if on the other hand ....
[26]δυσκηδής, δυσκηδές (3rd declension adjective) = full of misery. δυσκηδέα qualifies νύκτα. The accusative expresses duration of time (see p.128, footnote 6). φυλάσσω (here) "I keep watch".
[27]μή here = "lest". δείδω ("I fear") is understood before μή, and the subjunctive δαμάσῃ expresses what he fears, "lest the frost and dew may ..."
[28]ἄμυδις = at the same time, together. ἡ στίβη = frost.
[29]ἡ ἐέρση = dew. For the gender of θῆλυς, see footnote 6 above. Liddell & Scott suggest "soft" or "gentle" for θῆλυς here, which seems inappropriate. Hainsworth (*op. cit.*, p.287) notes that other commentators have preferred "moist". (*The Shield of Heracles* 395, attributed to Hesiod, says of the grasshopper πόσις καὶ βρῶσις θῆλυς ἐέρση: "his drink and food is θῆλυς ἐέρση (but he sings through the most terrible heat of the day)", where "moist dew" makes good sense.) στίβη and ἐέρση are the subjects of δαμάσῃ, and μ' is the object.
[30]ὀλιγηπελία, ὀλιγηπελίης (1 feminine) = weakness ("little-strength").
[31]δαμάσῃ is 3rd person singular subjunctive of (ἐ)δάμασα, the aorist active of δαμάζω. κεκαφηὼς θυμόν = breathing forth one's spirit, i.e. fainting. κεκαφηότα is accusative masculine singular of a perfect participle, κεκαφηώς, only found with this meaning in this phrase in Homer, at Iliad v, 698, of Sarpedon, falling unconscious when wounded by Tlepomenos at Troy,.and not connected with any other known verb. κεκαφηότα qualifies μ' (=με) in line 467.
[32]αὔρη (1 fem.) = breeze. ψυχρός, ψυχρή, ψυχρόν = cold, chilly. πνέω = I blow.

Section 25

εἰ δέ κεν ἐς κλειτὺν³³ ἀναβὰς καὶ δάσκιον³⁴ ὕλην 470
θάμνοισ' ἐν πυκινοῖσι καταδράθω,³⁵ εἴ με μεθείη
ῥῖγος καὶ κάματος, γλυκερὸς δέ μοι ὕπνος ἐπέλθοι,
δείδω μὴ³⁶ θήρεσσιν ἕλωρ καὶ κύρμα γένωμαι.
   ὣς ἄρα οἱ φρονέοντι δοάσσατο κέρδιον εἶναι·³⁷
βῆ ῥ' ἴμεν³⁸ εἰς ὕλην· τὴν δὲ σχεδὸν³⁹ ὕδατος εὗρεν 475
ἐν περιφαινομένῳ.⁴⁰ δοιοὺς⁴¹ δ' ἄρ' ὑπήλυθε⁴² θάμνους

³³κλείτυς, κλείτυος (3 fem.) = hillside. In this line, ἐς means "to". ἀναβάς, masculine nominative singular, aorist participle, ἀναβαίνω qualifies "I".
³⁴δάσκιος, δάσκιον (fem. as masc.) = thick-shaded.
³⁵καταδράθω is 1st person subjunctive of κατέδραθον, the aorist of καταδαρθάνω = I spend the night (or it could mean "I lie down and go to sleep"). ῥῖγος, ῥίγεος (3 neut.) = frost, cold   γλυκερός, γλυκερά, γλυκερόν is a lengthened form of γλυκύς, γλυκεῖα, γλυκύ, sweet. ἐπέλθοι is 3rd person singular optative of ἐπῆλθον, the aorist of ἐπέρχομαι (with dative) = I come over.

The condition beginning at εἰ δέ κεν (line 470) has a subjunctive verb (καταδράθω) and refers to a future eventuality ("If, on the other hand, in the end, I lie down and go to sleep...") (see Section 24, pp.171-2). It contains a second condition, beginning at εἰ in line 471, which has two optative verbs. The first is μεθείη ("to see if cold and weariness would release me"). μεθείη is 3rd person singular aorist optative active of μεθίημι. Its subjects (both singular) are ῥῖγος and κάματος. The second is ἐπέλθοι (3rd person singular, optative from ἐπῆλθον, the aorist of ἐπέρχομαι). Its subject is γλυκερὸς ὕπνος. The conditions in lines 470-2 run, in English, as follows: "If, on the other hand, in the end, having gone up the hill and the shady wood, I pass the night in the thick bushes, to see if the cold and weariness will release me, and to see if sweet sleep should come over me, I fear lest ..."

The poet is playing an elegant game by comparing the if-clauses with optative verbs (μεθείη, ἐπέλθοι), which express a more remote kind of contingency, with the if-clause containing the subjunctive καταδράθω (Chantraine, *op. cit.* vol.II, p.278). This has caused some trouble. Allen (Oxford Classical Text) shows μεθείη (optative) as the manuscript reading, but emends μεθείη to μεθήῃ to make all the verbs in the conditional clauses subjunctive, while Chantraine emends ἐπέλθῃ to ἐπέλθοι to make the last two both optative. (Hainsworth (*Omero, Odissea* vol. 2 (Mondadori, 1982)) has the same reading as Allen. Stanford has μεθείη and ἐπέλθῃ.)

³⁶"lest", after δείδω. θήρ, θῆρος (3 masc. or fem.) = wild animal. ἕλωρ (neuter, only in nominative & accusative) = prey. κύρμα, κύρματος (3 neut.) = spoils γένωμαι is 1st person singular subjunctive of (ἐ)γενόμην, the aorist of γίγνομαι.
³⁷See p.180.
³⁸For βῆ ῥ' ἴμεν see p.114. εἰς ὕλην: (to look) for the wood.
³⁹σχεδόν + genitive = near. τήν ("it") refers to ὕλην and is the object of εὗρεν, which is 3rd person singular of εὗρον, the aorist active of εὑρίσκω.
⁴⁰περιφαινόμενος (χῶρος): a place visible all round. περιφαίνομαι = I am visible all round. Hainsworth suggests that it was beside a clearing where Nausicaa and her maids would play ball next day.
⁴¹δοιοί, δοιαί, δοιά = two (a Homeric word).
⁴²ὑπήλυθε is 3rd person singular of ὑπήλυθον, the aorist of ὑπέρχομαι, I go under. The subject is "he" (Odysseus).

Beginning Greek with Homer

ἐξ ὁμόθεν⁴³ πεφυῶτας· ὁ μὲν φυλίης,⁴⁴ ὁ δ' ἐλαίης.
τοὺς μὲν ἄρ' οὔτ'⁴⁵ ἀνέμων διάη⁴⁶ μένος⁴⁷ ὑγρὸν ἀέντων,⁴⁸
οὔτε ποτ' ἠέλιος φαέθων⁴⁹ ἀκτῖσιν ἔβαλλεν,
οὔτ' ὄμβρος περάασκε⁵⁰ διαμπερές· ὣς ἄρα πυκνοὶ   480
ἀλλήλοισιν ἔφυν⁵¹ ἐπαμοιβαδίς· οὓς ὑπ'⁵² Ὀδυσσεὺς
δύσετ'. ἄφαρ⁵³ δ' εὐνὴν ἐπαμήσατο χερσὶ φίλῃσιν
εὐρεῖαν· φύλλων γὰρ ἔην χύσις⁵⁴ ἤλιθα πολλή,
ὅσσον τ' ἠὲ δύω ἠὲ τρεῖς ἄνδρας ἔρυσθαι⁵⁵
ὥρῃ χειμερίῃ,⁵⁶ εἰ καὶ μάλα περ χαλεπαίνοι.⁵⁷   485

⁴³ἐξ ὁμόθεν = out of the same place. ὁμός = one and the same. For the ending –θεν, see p.136, footnote 30. πεφυῶτας (qualifying θάμνους) is masculine accusative plural of πεφυώς, the perfect participle active of φύω, I grow: "having come to grow", i.e., "growing".
⁴⁴φυλίη (1 fem.) = wild olive, or perhaps a kind of fig or a thorn (Hainsworth). ἐλαίη = (cultivated) olive. ὁ (both instances) stands for θάμνος, and τοὺς in line 478 stands for θάμνους. ὁ μὲν ... ὁ δὲ ... = the one (bush)..., the other ... φυλίης and ἐλαίης are descriptive genitives ("consisting of ...").
⁴⁵οὔτ' stands for οὔτε
⁴⁶διάη is 3rd person singular, imperfect active of διάημι, I blow through.
⁴⁷μένος, μένους (3 neut.) = strength, might, force (qualified by ὑγρὸν).
⁴⁸ἀέντων is genitive plural (qualifying ἀνέμων) of the present participle active, ἀείς, of ἄημι, I blow. (cf. τιθείς, p.220.)
⁴⁹ποτ' stands for ποτε. φαέθων, φαέθουσα, φάεθον = shining (cf. Phaethon). ἀκτίς, ἀκτῖνος (3 fem.) = ray. ἔβαλλεν is 3rd person singular of the imperfect active of βάλλω (here: "I reach the middle of"). Liddell & Scott cite Apollonius Rhodius, *Argonautica* IV, 885: ἦμος δ' ἄκρον ἔβαλλε φαεσφόρος οὐρανὸν ἠώς ("and when the light-bringing dawn reached the top of heaven") (literally, "the topmost heaven"). Lines 478-80 are the same as Odyssey XIX 440-2 which describe the lair of a wild boar; if traditionally so used, they emphasise the depths to which Odysseus has been reduced (Hainsworth, *op. cit.*, p.287).
⁵⁰περάασκε is 3rd person singular, imperfect active of περάω = I penetrate. περάασκε: "used to penetrate" (p.144, footnote 79).
⁵¹πυκνοί = πυκινοί. ὣς πυκνοί means "so close-set". ἔφυν here stands for ἔφυσαν, 3rd person plural of ἔφυν, the aorist of φύω. "The aorist of a verb denoting a state or condition generally expresses the entrance to that condition" (Goodwin, *Greek Moods and Tenses*) e.g. ἐβασίλευσα, I became king. ἔφυν should therefore be translated here "they had grown". ἐπαμοιβαδίς = interchangeably, i.e. with interwoven boughs.
⁵²ὑπ' stands for ὑπό. οὓς ὑπ' stands for ὑφ' οὕς, i.e. ὑπὸ οὕς. ὑπό + accusative indicates motion towards, going to and getting underneath. δύσετ' stands for δύσετο, 3rd person singular, aorist middle of δύω: he plunged (see p.149, footnote 38.)
⁵³ἐπαμήσατο is 3rd person singular of ἐπαμησάμην, the aorist middle of ἐπαμάομαι, I scrape together for myself. φύλλον (2 neut.) = leaf. For ἔην, see p.9.
⁵⁴χύσις, χύσεως (3 fem,) = shedding, fall; in line 487, "heap". ἤλιθα = exceedingly.
⁵⁵ἔρυσθαι is the infinitive of ἐρύομαι = I protect. ὅσσον τε + infinitive: "about as much as to ...", "about enough to ..."
⁵⁶ὥρη χειμέρια = season of winter. (χειμών (3 masc.) = "winter", also "storm".)
⁵⁷χαλεπαίνοι is 3rd person singular, present optative of χαλεπαίνω = I am severe. The subject ("it") stands for ὥρη χειμέρια.

Section 25

τὴν μὲν ἰδὼν γήθησε[58] πολύτλας δῖος 'Οδυσσεύς,
ἐν δ' ἄρα μέσσῃ λέκτο,[59] χύσιν δ' ἐπεχεύατο[60] φύλλων.
ὡς δ' ὅτε[61] τις δαλὸν[62] σποδιῇ ἐνέκρυψε[63] μελαίνῃ
ἀγροῦ ἐπ' ἐσχατιῆς,[64] ᾧ μὴ πάρα γείτονες[65] ἄλλοι,
σπέρμα[66] πυρὸς σῴζων, ἵνα μή ποθεν ἄλλοθεν[67] αὔοι[68]   490
ὣς 'Οδυσεὺς φύλλοισι καλύψατο.[69] τῷ δ' ἄρ' 'Αθήνη
ὕπνον ἐπ' ὄμμασι[70] χεῦ', ἵνα μιν παύσειε τάχιστα
δυσπονέος[71] καμάτοιο, φίλα βλέφαρ' ἀμφικαλύψας.

---

[58]τὴν ("it") stands for χύσιν. ἰδὼν is masculine singular nominative of the participle of εἶδον. γήθησε is 3rd person singular of (ἐ)γήθησα, the aorist of γηθέω = I become glad.
[59]ἐν qualifies μέσσῃ. λέκτο is the 3rd person singular of (ἐ)λέγμην, the aorist of λέχομαι = I lie down (Liddell & Scott; see also Chantraine, op. cit. vol.i, p.296). λέχομαι (from the same root as λέχος) has another aorist, ἐλεξάμην. παρ' δ' Ἑλένῃ τανύπεπλος ἐλέξατο, δῖα γυναικῶν: and beside (her husband), Helen of the long robe lay down, noble of women (Odyssey IV, 305).
[60]ἐπεχεύατο (p.126, footnote 69) here means "he poured over himself". χεῦ' (line 492) is 3rd person singular of (ἔ)χευα, the aorist active of χέω, I pour.
[61]See lines 328, 394 and 432.
[62]δαλός (2 masc.) = fire brand. σποδιή (1 fem.) = heap of ashes.
[63]ἐνέκρυψε is the 3rd person singular of ἐνέκρυψα, the aorist active of ἐγκρύπτω, I hide inside, with accusative of thing hidden and dative of place inside which. The aorist is timeless, and expresses the generality of the action.
[64]ἐσχατιή (1 fem.) = edge.
[65]The antecedent of ᾧ is τις, the subject of ἐνέκρυψε. παρ' ᾧ = beside whom. γείτων, γείτονος (3 masc. or fem.) = neighbour. εἰσί needs to be understood. "Beside whom there are not other neighbours" means "who does not have other neighbours", i.e. others as neighbours. The negative μή emphasises that this is a general statement.
[66]σπέρμα, σπέρματος (3 neut.) = seed. σῴζων is masculine nominative singular of the participle of σῴζω = I save, and qualifies τις (line 488).
[67]ποθεν ἄλλοθεν = from somewhere else (for –θεν see footnote 43).
[68]αὔοι (Hainsworth, (Omero, Odissea vol. 2 (Mondadori, 1982) and also A Commentary on Homer's Odyssey vol.i, p.287, and Stanford following the mss.) is 3rd person singular present optative of αὔω, I get a light, light a fire, and is cited in Liddell & Scott from this line. αὔῃ (Allen, Oxford Classical Text) is 3rd person singular, present subjunctive of αὔω = I dry (cited once in Liddell & Scott, from Herodianus Grammaticus, 2nd century AD). αὔοι seems the better reading. A scholium on this line explains αὔω as ἐξάπτω ("I kindle"). Although αὔοι is ἅπαξ λεγόμενον (only found once), ἐναύω (I give someone a light) is well attested (Hainsworth, op. cit., p.287).
[69]καλύψατο is 3rd person singular of (ἐ)καλυψάμην, the aorist middle of καλύπτω. It means "(he) hid himself".
[70]τῷ is possessive dative. ὄμμα, ὄμματος (3 neut.) = eye. For χεῦ' v. footnote 60.
[71]παύσειε is 3rd person singular optative of (ἔ)παυσα, the aorist active of παύω meaning "I cause someone to cease from", with the genitive (δυσπονέος καμάτοιο). δυσπονής = toilsome. The subject of παύσειε is "it", meaning ὕπνος, and the object is μιν. ἀμφικαλύψας is nominative masculine singular of the participle of ἀμφικάλυψα, the aorist active of ἀμφικαλύπτω = I enfold, and qualifies ὕπνος. βλέφαρον = eyelid. φίλα βλέφαρα: "his (own) eyelids".

Appendix A
A summary of Mood, Tense, Aspect and Voice in the Greek Verb in Homer
Verbs are classified according to <u>mood</u>.

If a verb indicates a simple fact, the <u>indicative</u> mood is used.
'Ηὼς δ' ἐκ λεχέων παρ' ἀγαυοῦ Τιθωνοῖο
<u>ὄρνυτο</u>
And the dawn out of bed from beside noble Tithonus
<u>was arising</u>. (Odyssey V, 1-2)

The indicative is also used when a fact is questioned:
οὕτω δὴ οἶκονδε φίλην ἐς πατρίδα γαῖαν
αὐτίκα νῦν <u>ἐθέλεις</u> ἰέναι;
After all, <u>do you want</u> so to go home to your own country at once, now? (Odyssey V, 204-5)

The indicative is also used in a condition that can be realised in principle:
τελέσαι δέ με θυμὸς ἄνωγεν,
εἰ <u>δύναμαι</u> τελέσαι γε καὶ εἰ τετελεσμένον <u>ἐστιν</u>
but (my) heart commands me to fulfil (it)
if <u>I can</u> fulfil (it) indeed and if <u>it is</u> something to be fulfilled
(Odyssey V, 89-90)

An indicative verb can have a modal meaning (e.g. "would" or "should") if it is qualified by ἄν or κεν.
ὅσ' <u>ἄν</u> οὐδέ ποτε Τροίης <u>ἐξήρατ'</u> 'Οδυσσεύς,
εἴ περ ἀπήμων <u>ἦλθε</u>, λαχὼν ἀπὸ ληίδος αἶσαν.
as many things as not even Odysseus ever <u>would have taken away</u> from Troy
if indeed <u>he had gone</u> without trouble, having received a share from the booty.
(Odyssey V, 39-40)[1]

Chantraine, *Grammaire Homérique*, vol.ii, pp.205-6, points out that it is

---

[1]In Attic, this use of the aorist indicative is regular in past unfulfilled conditions; but in Homer κεν is also found with the future indicative, e.g. οἵ <u>κέν</u> μιν περὶ κῆρι θεὸν ὣς <u>τιμήσουσι</u> ("who <u>would honour</u> him exceedingly in their hearts like a god") (Odyssey V, 36). Note that there is no ambiguity with τιμήσουσι as the aorist subjunctive (3rd person plural) would be τιμήσωσι, but in many instances the aorist subjunctive with σ, when it has a short vowel in Homer, cannot be distinguished from the future indicative, e.g. at Odyssey VI, 221, ἄντην δ' οὐκ <u>ἂν</u> ἐγώ γε <u>λοέσσομαι</u> ("indeed, <u>I would not have a wash</u> in front (of you)"). λοέσσομαι is ambiguous and might either be future indicative or the short-vowel version of λοέσσωμαι, the aorist subjunctive. Chantraine (*op. cit.*, vol.ii p.225) prefers to take λοέσσομαι as aorist subjunctive; he explains the use of κεν, e.g. at Odyssey V, 36, to make the future modal (i.e., to mean "would") by the similarity of the future indicative to the aorist subjunctive.

Mood, Aspect, Tense & Voice 187

not easy to define hard-and-fast rules about the functions of the subjunctive, optative and imperative moods in Homer except to say that they are more subjective, while the indicative is more objective.

The <u>optative</u> mood, as its name implies, is used primarily to express <u>wishes</u> and remote suppositions.

αἰεὶ χαλεπός τ' <u>εἴη</u> καὶ αἴσυλα <u>ῥέζοι</u>
O that always <u>he might be</u> harsh and that <u>he might do</u> godless things.
(Odyssey V, 10)

τὰ μὲν νοέω καὶ φράσσομαι, ἅσσ' ἂν ἐμοί περ
αὐτῇ <u>μηδοίμην</u>, ὅτε με χρείω τόσον <u>ἵκοι</u>.
Indeed, I am planning and shall think of as many things as for myself <u>I would devise</u>, at such time as such great need <u>might reach</u> me (Odyssey V, 188-9)

The optative can be used to express a purpose in past time:
'Ἠὼς δ' ἐκ λεχέων παρ' ἀγαυοῦ Τιθωνοῖο
ὄρνυθ' ἵν' ἀθανάτοισι φόως <u>φέροι</u> ἠδὲ βροτοῖσι
And the dawn out of bed from beside noble Tithonus was arising, so that <u>she might bring</u> light to immortals and to mortals.
(Odyssey V, 1-2)

The <u>subjunctive</u> mood expresses less remote possibilities than the optative, e.g. εἰ δ' αὖ τις <u>ῥαίῃσι</u> θεῶν ἐνὶ οἴνοπι πόντῳ,
τλήσομαι
but if one of the gods <u>were to shatter</u> (my ship) in the wine-faced sea,
I shall endure (it). (Odyssey V, 221-2)
It is used to express purposes, e.g.

ἀλλ' ἕπεο προτέρω, ἵνα τοι πὰρ ξείνια <u>θείω</u> (Odyssey V, 91)
but follow first, so that <u>I may put</u> guest-presents beside you.
To express negative purposes, μή "lest" is prefaced:
οὕτω νῦν ἀπόπεμπε, Διὸς δ' ἐποπίζεο μῆνιν,
<u>μή</u> πώς τοι μετόπισθε κοτεσσάμενος <u>χαλεπήνῃ</u>
So now send (Odysseus) away, and respect the wrath of Zeus <u>so that he may not</u> in any way afterwards come to bear a grudge <u>be angry</u> with you. (Odyssey V, 146-7)
Consequently, a subjunctive verb can express negative wishes:
<u>μὴ λυώμεθα</u> ἵππους - <u>let us not loose</u> our horses. (Iliad XXIII, 7).[2]
After a verb meaning "fear", μή and the subjunctive are used:
δείδω <u>μὴ</u> θήρεσσιν ἕλωρ καὶ κύρμα <u>γένωμαι</u>. (Odyssey V, 473)
I fear <u>that I may become</u> to wild animals a prey and spoils.[3]

---

[2]"let us not loose the horses for ourselves".
[3]Compare the English expression "I fear lest ..." But note that if one fears that something is already a fact, μή with the *indicative* is used: δείδω μὴ δὴ πάντα θεὰ νημερτέα <u>εἶπεν</u> = I fear that the goddess <u>spoke</u> everything truthfully after all (Odyssey V, 300)

The verb "fear" or its equivalent may be omitted, e.g.
μή τίς μοι ὑφαίνῃσιν δόλον αὖτε
ἀθανάτων (Odyssey V, 356-7)
("I only hope that) one of the gods may not also be weaving a trap for me"
= "May one of the gods not also be weaving a trap for me ".

The imperative mood is used to express commands:
ἐρρέτω, εἴ μιν κεῖνος ἐποτρύνει καὶ ἀνώγει
let him go to his ruin, if *h e* urges him and commands. (Odyssey V, 139)[4]

The infinitive is a verbal noun which expresses the idea of the meaning of the verb. Its usual form in English is "to ..."

Verbs also have participles which are used as adjectives to qualify nouns and have gender and case endings, singular and plural. The English form of the present participle active ends in -ing, e.g. "a loving son".[5] Greek verbs have different participles for each tense and voice.

The Greek Tenses and their Aspect

The tenses are classified according to their aspect, which refers to the degree and mode of development of an action indicated by a verb. Greek has the following tenses:

Present	(λύω, λύομαι)	I am loosing, getting loosed
Imperfect	(ἔλυον, ἐλυόμην)	I was loosing, getting loosed
Future	(λύσω, λύσομαι)	I shall loose, get loosed
Aorist	(ἔλυσα, ἐλυσάμην)	*usually* I loosed, got loosed
Perfect	(λέλυκα, λέλυμαι)	I have loosed, have got loosed
Pluperfect.	(ἐλελύκη, ἐλελύμην)	I had loosed, had got loosed

All the tenses are found in the indicative.

The present, aorist and perfect tenses have subjunctive, optative and imperative moods, and have infinitives and participles.

---

[4]For prohibitions, see "aspect", below.
[5]Not to be confused with the English verbal noun ending -ing (e.g. "seeing is believing") which is often used as an alternative to the infinitive "to ...".

Mood, Aspect, Tense & Voice

The perfect subjunctive and optative are found especially in verbs like οἶδα ("I know", see p. 146) which are perfect in Greek but have meanings expressed by the present tense in English.[6]

The future is found in the indicative, and has active and middle/passive infinitives and participles.[7]

The imperfect and pluperfect are only found in the indicative.

Greek has no separate forms to correspond in the present tense to the English *I loose, I am loosing,* and *I do loose*, nor in the imperfect tense, to the English *I was loosing* or *I used to loose*.[8]

Aspect

The present aspect covers the present and imperfect tenses, and verbs with this aspect describe a continuous action or an action that is still in progress.[9]

The aorist aspect covers the aorist tense, which indicates an action pure and simple. In the indicative mood its most common use is for past actions which are complete in themselves. In Homer, the augment (ἐ)[10] may be prefixed to show that the tense of the verb is past, e.g.
"Ἕκτορα δῖον ἔλυσα πατρὶ φίλῳ
I loosed (i.e. released the body of) noble Hector to his dear father (Iliad xxiv, 593)
(the augment is sometimes omitted even when the verb expresses a past action). However, sometimes an aorist indicative is used in a

---

[6] For a perfect subjunctive from another verb, see Iliad iv, 164: ἔσσεται ἦμαρ ὅτ' ἄν ποτ' ὀλώλῃ Ἴλιος "there will be a day when (at some time) Ilios is destroyed". ὄλωλα, the perfect of ὄλλυμι, means "I am (i.e., have been) destroyed".
[7] The future optative, largely used in indirect speech, is found in Attic but not in Epic.
[8] The Greek imperfect can sometimes also mean "I began to loose".
[9] The historic present is an exception (D.J. Mastronarde, *Introduction to Attic Greek*, Univ. of California Press 1993, p.148) but it does not occur in Homer (Chantraine, *Grammaire Homérique*, vol.ii, p.191).
[10] If the initial letter of the verb is a vowel, this can be lengthened as an augment (see p. 40).

purely general sense and does not refer to a particular action completed in the past, e.g.

ὡς νῦν σε φίλησα (as I love you now) (Iliad iii, 415).[11]

The aorist imperative, subjunctive and optative do not in themselves signify time.

The aorist infinitive expresses the idea of the verb pure and simple, usually without signifying time. However, if an aorist infinitive is used with a verb which expresses an intellectual operation (e.g., believe, think, say) it can have a past sense, like the aorist indicative:

καὶ γὰρ κείνῳ φημὶ τελευτηθῆναι ἅπαντα
ὡς οἱ ἐμυθεόμην[12] (Odyssey II, 171)
and indeed I affirm everything to have been accomplished for that man as I used to speak to him
= and indeed I affirm that everything was accomplished for that man as I used to tell him

The aorist infinitive can sometimes refer to future time, e.g.

εὐχόμενος θάνατόν τε φυγεῖν καὶ μῶλον Ἄρηος (Iliad ii, 401)
praying even to escape both death and the moil of Ares.[13]

Since the present aspect expresses continuity, the present participle can express simultaneity:

τὴν δ' ἀπαμειβόμενος προσέφη νεφεληγερέτα Ζεύς
and answering her, Zeus the cloud gatherer spoke to (her) (Odyssey V, 21).

The aorist participle can express an action pure and simple, and is not always best translated by "having ...", e.g.

θηήσαιτο ἰδὼν καὶ τερφθείη φρεσὶν ᾗσιν (Odyssey V, 74)
he would be amazed seeing (these things) and would be delighted in his heart

where ἰδών refers to the simple action of seeing. However, sometimes an aorist participle does indicate an action previous to another, e.g.

Πιερίην δ' ἐπιβὰς ἐξ αἰθέρος ἔμπεσε πόντῳ (Odyssey V, 50)
and having stepped on Pieria he swooped from the sky onto the sea

where two successive actions, stepping and swooping, are referred to (in English, "stepping on Pieria, he swooped ... " refers to successive actions).

[11]μὴ μ' ἔρεθε, σχετλίη, μὴ χωσαμένη σε μεθείω/ τὼς δὲ σ' ἀπεχθήρω ὡς νῦν ἔκπαγλα φίλησα "stop provoking me, wretched woman, lest being angry I may let you go, and may treat you as an enemy in the same way as now I love you beyond all measure" (Iliad iii, 414-5) (Aphrodite threatening Helen). (ἐρέθω: I provoke σχέτλιος: wretched, persistent χώομαι: I am angry τὼς ... ὡς ...: so ... as ... ἐχθαίρω I treat like an enemy ἔκπαγλα φιλεῖν: to love beyond all measure) (Chantraine, *op. cit.* vol.ii, p.184)

[12]τελευτηθῆναι is aorist passive infinitive of τελευτάω, I accomplish. μυθέομαι: I tell.

[13] Chantraine, *op. cit.*, vol.ii, p.189. Liddell & Scott translate μῶλος as "the toil and moil of war".

Mood, Aspect, Tense & Voice   191

The constructions for prohibitions can be explained by the effect of the present and aorist aspects. Prohibitions are expressed either by μή and the present imperative e.g.

πότνα θεά, μή μοι τόδε χώεο (Odyssey V, 215)
Lady goddess, stop being angry with me (about) this
or Lady goddess, don't go on being angry with me (about) this

referring to an action (being angry) which has already begun, and so the present aspect is appropriate,

or μή and the aorist subjunctive, e.g.

'Ατρείδη, σοὶ πρῶτα μαχήσομαι ἀφραδέοντι,
ἥ θέμις ἐστίν, ἄναξ, ἀγορῇ, σὺ δὲ μή τι χολωθῇς (Iliad ix, 32-3)
Son of Atreus, with you, (because you are) being foolish, I shall first take issue, as is right, my lord, in debate, and do not be made angry at all[14]

referring to anger pure & simple which has not yet begun, and so the aorist aspect is appropriate.[15]

The imperfect tense, which has the present aspect, expresses an action which was in progress in the past, or which was just beginning, or which customarily happened.

The perfect tense, although it does not have the present aspect, expresses a present state which arises because of an action completed in the past; e.g. "I have gone to Athens" implies that that is where I am. For this reason, many Greek verbs which are found in the perfect tense correspond to English verbs in the present tense. See Section 21.

The pluperfect is used to describe the result of an earlier action still holding at a time in the past.

The aspect system does not apply to the future tense. Chantraine (*op. cit.* vol.ii, p.201) says that the future tense comes from an old desiderative, i.e. a verbal form expressing desire, and the future participle is sometimes used to express a wish or an intention:

---

[14] μάχομαι (with dative): I fight, take issue with. ἀφραδέω: I am foolish. θέμις: right. ἀγορή: meeting place, public meeting, debate. χολόω: I anger.
[15] μή is not used with either the present subjunctive or the aorist imperative to express a prohibition.

ἵνα κλυτὰ εἵματ' ἄγωμαι
ἐς ποταμὸν <u>πλυνέουσα</u> (Odyssey VI, 58-9)
so that I may take my fine clothes
to the river <u>with the intention of washing</u> (them)[16]
(because I want to wash them).

The future infinitive has a future meaning and is often found after φημί:
οὐδέ σὲ φημι
αὐτὸν <u>νοστήσειν</u>, μενέεις δὲ σύ γ' ἔνθα περ ἄλλοι (Odyssey X, 284-5)
and I affirm you yourself not
<u>to be going to return home</u>, but indeed you will stay in that place where the
others are
= and I affirm that you yourself will not
return home, but indeed you will stay in that place where the others (are).[17]

Sequence of Tenses and Moods

In subordinate clauses expressing purpose (e.g., "I have come so that I may see you") or fear ("I am afraid that you may hurt yourself") the verbs "may see", "may hurt" are naturally expressed in Greek by the subjunctive. However, if the main clause in English is past, "may" becomes "might" or "would": "I came so that I might see you", "I was afraid that you might (would) hurt yourself". In Greek, the subjunctive can still be used, but often the optative is used instead.
English main verb not past : Greek subordinate verb - subjunctive.
English main verb past : Greek subordinate verb - subjunctive or
optative.

The Voices of the Greek Verb
Verbs can be in the active, middle or passive voice.

Verbs in the <u>active</u> voice express the action of a subject. This can be transitive, i.e. the verb can have a direct object; e.g.
Achilles is eating his dinner
or intransitive, i.e. with no object expressed; e.g.
Achilles is sleeping.

Verbs in the <u>middle</u> voice can, for convenience, be said to express an action which a subject is having done or is doing for himself; e.g.
Achilles is loosing his horse

---
[16]κλυτός: famous, fine. πλυνέω is the future of πλύνω, I wash (clothes).
[17]νοστέω: I return home. ἔνθα περ : in that place where.

Mood, Aspect, Tense & Voice - Contraction 193

because it is his own horse and so he is loosing it for himself or is getting his groom to loose it. However, this distinction between the active and middle does not hold in many instances and the fact seems to be that Greek, from very ancient times, had two ending systems one of which we call active and the other middle, and verbs with either set of endings can correspond to English active verbs, e.g.
βαίνω - I am stepping, I am going (active endings)
ἔρχομαι - I am coming (middle endings).

Verbs in the <u>passive</u> voice express what is done to a subject, i.e. what a subject suffers, e.g.
τέτρατον ἦμαρ ἔην, καὶ τῷ <u>τετέλεστο</u> ἅπαντα (Odyssey V, 262)
it was the fourth day and for him everything <u>had been completed</u>.

Except in the aorist tense, passive verbs have middle endings. Some verbs have both active and middle forms, e.g.
ἔχω - I have, I hold
ἔχομαι - I hold for myself.
ἔχομαι also can mean "I am held".

This is because the passive (except for the aorist)[18] is not itself a separate voice in Homer but is expressed by the middle.[19] It is often hard to distinguish between middle and passive unless the agent (the person by whom a thing was done) is mentioned; the agent is seldom expressly stated in Homer and one might perhaps translate the passage just cited as "everything had got completed" (middle) instead of "had been completed" (passive), rather as we might say "the minstrel boy went to war and got killed" (middle) or "the minstrel boy went to war and was killed by the enemy" (passive, and the agent is stated).

Appendix B
Contraction of vowels

In Greek there is a tendency to avoid a gap or hiatus between two vowels which follow each other immediately. This can be managed in

---

[18]Chantraine notes (*op cit.* vol.i, ch. xxxv) that (a) not all aorists ending -ην have passive meanings (e.g. ἐχάρην, from χαίρω, means "I rejoiced") and (b) the aorist passive in -θην is an innovation in Greek and its counterpart is not found in other Indo-European languages. He suggests that the aorist passive forms grew out of those strong aorist middle forms which were most often used with a passive meaning; e.g. μίσγω still has two aorists passive: ἐμίγην, perhaps more like "I mingled" and ἐμίχθην, perhaps more like "I was mixed".
[19]Chantraine, *op. cit.*,vol.ii, p.180.

several ways, e.g. between words
by elision, as παρ' ἀγαυοῦ Τιθωνοῖο instead of παρὰ ἀγαυοῦ Τιθωνοῖο
or by inserting ν, as ...βροτοῖσιν· οἱ δὲ θεοὶ... instead of ...βροτοῖσι· οἱ δὲ
θεοὶ... (Odyssey V, 2-3).
Within words, hiatus tends to be avoided by contraction, when two vowels merge.

This tendency may not have been so apparent in early Greek,[20] and contraction is not found in the Mycenaean Greek so far discovered. Because Epic is a dialect which formed over centuries, and contains very old elements, in Homer successive vowels are often not contracted.[21] For instance, at Odyssey V, 5 κήδεα is used to mean "griefs" which in Attic Greek would be κήδη. At line 90, from the verb φρονέω, φρονέεις (uncontracted) is found, which would be φρονεῖς in Attic, where ει is the contracted form of εει. But instances of contraction do occur in Homer, e.g. in line 97: εἰρωτᾷς, you are asking, from εἰρωτάω, I ask. The uncontracted form for "you are asking" would be εἰρωτάεις. Some of the contractions in our text of Homer may have arisen from modernisation by later generations of Greek scholars, but not all. In this line, which scans:

- -|- -| - ˘ -|- ˘ ˘ | - ˘ ˘ |- -|
εἰρωτᾷς μ' ἐλθόντα θεὰ θεόν· αὐτὰρ ἐγώ τοι

εἰρωτάεις, having an additional syllable, could not be fitted in, and it can be concluded that εἰρωτᾷς is original.

The endings of nouns and adjectives, pronouns and verbs shown in the tables in this book are uncontracted if that form is found in our text of Homer.[22] Where contractions occur, they have been explained in the footnotes. Some of the alternative forms shown in the tables arise because both contracted and uncontracted forms are found.

The following are the contractions where the spelling of our text can be affected. (~ denotes a long vowel):

[20]Some examples of hiatus may occur because of the dropping of ϝ (digamma, pronounced w, p.1, footnote 1).
[21]See G.S. Kirk, Homer and the Epic, (Cambridge, 1965) esp. p.140 sqq.
[22]We cannot be sure of the spelling that the original bard would have used if he had known the standard Greek alphabet because it is more recent than the Iliad and the Odyssey in their original versions.

Contraction

where the first vowel is α:

αα > ᾶ	αε > ᾶ	ᾶι > ᾳ̃	αο > ω
ααι > αι	αει > ᾳ (or ᾶ)		αοι > ῳ
αᾳ > ᾳ			αου > ω
			αω > ω

where the first vowel is ε or η:

εα > η	εε > ει	ηι > η	εο > ευ[23]
εαι > η (or ᾳι)	εει > ει		εοι > οι
ηα > η	εη > η		εου > ευ
ηαι > η	εῃ > ῃ		εω > ω
	ηε > η		εῳ > ῳ
	ηει > η[24]		

where the first vowel is ι:
ιε > ῑ

where the first vowel is ο or ω:

οα > ω (or ᾶ)	οε > ου	ωι > ῳ	οο > ου	ωο > ω
οαι > αι	οει > οι (or ου)		οοι > οι	
ωα > ω	οη > ω		οου > ου	
	οῃ > οι (or ῳ)		οω > ω	
	ωε > ω		οῳ > ῳ	

Contraction does not occur where the first vowel is υ; however, the ending -υι is sometimes pronounced and scanned as a single, long syllable, e.g.

‒ ‒| ‒ ˘ ˘|‒ ˘ ˘|‒ ‒|‒ ˘ ˘|‒ ‒||
λεπτὸν καὶ χαρίεν, περὶ δὲ ζώνην βάλετ' ἰξυῖ (Odyssey V, 231).

The pronunciation together of two vowels which are normally pronounced separately and are written separately is called synizesis.[25]

Examples of contracted verbs:
Verbs with stems ending -α or -ε frequently have contraction in the present and imperfect tenses between the concluding vowel of the stem and the opening vowel of the ending, as follows:

---

[23] NB in Attic, εο contracts to ου. ευ is the Ionic contraction of εο, and the presence of ευ for εο in Homer suggests that this contraction was adopted into Epic late, after Ionic and Attic had become distinct.
[24] But if ηει stands for ηεε, it sometimes contracts to η.
[25] Chantraine, *op. cit.*, vol.i, p.50. See also p.157 above, footnote 42.

verbs with stems ending -α: e.g. τιμα- (τιμάω: I honour).

present active   middle & passive

uncontracted	contracted	uncontracted	contracted
[τιμάω]	[τιμῶ]	[τιμάομαι]	[τιμῶμαι]
[τιμάεις]	[τιμᾷς]	[τιμάηαι]	[τιμᾷ]
[τιμάει]	[τιμᾷ]	[τιμάεται]	[τιμᾶται]
[τιμάετον]	[τιμᾶτον]	[τιμάεσθον]	[τιμᾶσθον]
[τιμάετον]	[τιμᾶτον]	[τιμάεσθον]	[τιμᾶσθον]
[τιμάομεν]	[τιμῶμεν]	[τιμαόμε(σ)θα]	[τιμώμε(σ)θα]
[τιμάετε]	[τιμᾶτε]	[τιμάεσθε]	[τιμᾶσθε]
[τιμάουσι]	τιμῶσι	[τιμάονται]	[τιμῶνται]

imperfect active   middle & passive

uncontracted	contracted	uncontracted	contracted
[(ἐ)τίμαον]	[(ἐ)τίμων]	[(ἐ)τιμαόμην]	[(ἐ)τιμώμην]
[(ἐ)τίμαες]	[(ἐ)τίμας]	[(ἐ)τίμαο]	[(ἐ)τίμω]
[(ἐ)τίμαε]	(ἐ)τίμα	[(ἐ)τίμαετο]	[(ἐ)τίματο]
[(ἐ)τιμάετον]	[(ἐ)τιμᾶτον]	[(ἐ)τιμάεσθον]	[(ἐ)τιμᾶσθον]
[(ἐ)τιμαέτην]	[(ἐ)τιμάτην]	[(ἐ)τιμαέσθην]	[(ἐ)τιμάσθην]
[(ἐ)τιμάομεν]	[(ἐ)τιμῶμεν]	[(ἐ)τιμαόμε(σ)θα]	[(ἐ)τιμώμε(σ)θα]
[(ἐ)τιμάετε]	[(ἐ)τιμᾶτε]	[(ἐ)τιμάεσθε]	[(ἐ)τιμᾶσθε]
[(ἐ)τίμαον]	[(ἐ)τίμων]	[(ἐ)τιμάοντο]	[(ἐ)τιμῶντο]

The present infinitives are::
 [τιμάειν, [τιμᾶν] [τιμάεσθαι] [τιμᾶσθαι]
 τιμάεεν, τιμαέμεναι
 or τιμάεμεν]

The present imperatives are like those of αὐδάω on p.88:
(2nd person singular)
 [τίμαε] [τίμα] [τιμάεο] [τιμῶ]
(3rd person singular)
 [τιμαέτω] [τιμάτω] [τιμάεσθω] [τιμάσθω]
(2nd person plural)
 [τιμάετε] [τιμᾶτε] [τιμάεσθε] [τιμᾶσθε]
(3rd person plural)
 [τιμαόντων] [τιμώντων] [τιμαέσθων] [τιμάσθων]

The present participle active of τιμάω ("honouring") is:
   (uncontracted) τιμάων τιμάουσα τιμάον,
but is found in Homer in its contracted form,
    τιμῶν τιμῶσα τίμων.

Contraction

The present subjunctive (long vowel ending) is:

active		middle & passive	
uncontracted	contracted	uncontracted	contracted
[τιμάω(μι)]	[τιμῶ(μι)]	[τιμάωμαι]	[τιμῶμαι]
[τιμάῃς(θα)]	[τιμᾷς(θα)]	[τιμάηαι]	[τιμᾷ]
[τιμάῃ(σι)]	τιμᾷ(σι)[26]	[τιμάηται]	[τιμᾶται]
[τιμάητον]	[τιμᾶτον]	[τιμάησθον]	[τιμᾶσθον]
[τιμάητον]	[τιμᾶτον]	[τιμάησθον]	[τιμᾶσθον]
[τιμάωμεν]	[τιμῶμεν]	[τιμαώμε(σ)θα]	[τιμώμε(σ)θα]
[τιμάητε]	[τιμᾶτε]	[τιμάησθε]	[τιμᾶσθε]
[τιμάωσι(ν)]	[τιμῶσι(ν)]	[τιμάωνται]	[τιμῶνται]

The present optative is:

active		middle & passive	
uncontracted	contracted	uncontracted	contracted
[τιμάοιμι]	[τιμῷμι][27]	[τιμαοίμην]	[τιμώμην]
[τιμάοις(θα)]	[τιμῷς(θα)]	[τιμάοιο]	[τιμῷο]
[τιμάοι]	[τιμῷ]	[τιμάοιτο]	[τιμῷτο]
[τιμάοιτον]	[τιμῷτον]	[τιμάοισθον]	[τιμῷσθον]
[τιμαοίτην]	[τιμῴτην]	[τιμαοίσθην]	[τιμῴσθην]
[τιμάοιμεν]	[τιμῷμεν]	[τιμαοίμε(σ)θα]	[τιμώμε(σ)θα]
[τιμάοιτε]	[τιμῷτε]	[τιμάοισθε]	[τιμῷσθε]
[τιμάοιεν]	[τιμῷεν]	[τιμάοιντο]	[τιμῷντο]

<u>verbs with stems ending -ε</u> e.g. φιλε- (φιλέω, I love).

present			
active		middle & passive	
uncontracted	contracted	uncontracted	contracted
[φιλέω]	[φιλῶ]	[φιλέομαι]	[φιλεῦμαι]
φιλέεις	[φιλεῖς]	[φιλέηαι]	[φιλῇ]
φιλέει	φιλεῖ	[φιλέεται]	[φιλεῖται]
[φιλέετον]	[φιλεῖτον]	[φιλέεσθον]	[φιλεῖσθον]
[φιλέετον]	[φιλεῖτον]	[φιλέεσθον]	[φιλεῖσθον]
[φιλέομεν]	[φιλεῦμεν]	[φιλεόμε(σ)θα]	[φιλεύμε(σ)θα]
[φιλέετε]	[φιλεῖτε]	[φιλέεσθε]	[φιλεῖσθε]
φιλέουσι(ν)	[φιλεῦσι]	[φιλέονται]	[φιλεῦνται]

---

[26]τιμᾷ, 3rd person singular present subjunctive, at Iliad xvii, 99.
[27]Or τιμώοιμι. δρώοιμι, from δράω, I do, is found at Odyssey XV, 317, and ἡβώοιμι, from ἡβάω, I am in my prime, at Iliad vii, 157 (Chantraine, *op. cit.* vol.i, p.464).

Beginning Greek with Homer

imperfect

active		middle & passive	
uncontracted	contracted	uncontracted	contracted
[(ἐ)φίλεον]	[(ἐ)φίλευν]	[(ἐ)φιλεόμην]	(ἐ)φιλεύμην
[(ἐ)φίλεες]	[(ἐ)φίλεις]	[(ἐ)φίλεο]	[(ἐ)φίλευ]
[(ἐ)φίλεε]	(ἐ)φίλει	[(ἐ)φιλέετο]	[(ἐ)φιλεῖτο]
[(ἐ)φιλέετον]	[(ἐ)φιλεῖτον]	[(ἐ)φιλέεσθον]	[(ἐ)φιλεῖσθον]
[(ἐ)φιλεέτην]	[(ἐ)φιλείτην]	[(ἐ)φιλεέσθην]	[(ἐ)φιλείσθην]
[(ἐ)φιλέομεν]	[(ἐ)φιλεῦμεν]	[(ἐ)φιλεόμε(σ)θα]	[(ἐ)φιλεύμε(σ)θα]
[(ἐ)φιλέετε]	[(ἐ)φιλεῖτε]	(ἐ)φιλέεσθε	[(ἐ)φιλεῖσθε]
(ἐ)φίλεον	[(ἐ)φίλευν]	[(ἐ)φιλέοντο]	[(ἐ)φιλεῦντο]

The present infinitives are::
   φιλέειν   φιλεῖν *or*   [φιλέεσθαι]   [φιλεῖσθαι]
             φιλήμεναι

The present imperatives are like those of ποιέω on p.88:
(2nd person singular)
  [φίλεε]   [φίλει]   [φιλέεο]   [φιλεῦ]
(3rd person singular)
  [φιλεέτω]   [φιλείτω]   [φιλέεσθω]   [φιλείσθω]
(2nd person plural)
  [φιλέετε]   [φιλεῖτε]   [φιλέεσθε]   [φιλεῖσθε]
(3rd person plural)
  φιλεόντων   [φιλεύντων]   [φιλεέσθων]   [φιλείσθων]

The present participle active of φιλέω ("loving") is:
    (uncontracted) φιλέων φιλέουσα φιλέον,
    (contracted) φιλῶν φιλεῦσα φιλεῦν
both uncontracted and contracted forms are found in Homer.

The present subjunctive (long vowel ending) is:

active		middle & passive	
uncontracted	contracted	uncontracted	contracted
[φιλέω(μι)]	[φιλῶ(μι)]	[φιλέωμαι]	[φιλῶμαι]
[φιλέῃς(θα)]	[φιλῇς(θα)]	[φιλέῃ]	[φιλῇ]
φιλέῃσιν	[φιλῇσι(ν)]	[φιλέηται]	[φιλῆται]
[φιλέητον]	[φιλῆτον]	[φιλέησθον]	[φιλῆσθον]
[φιλέητον]	[φιλῆτον]	[φιλέησθον]	[φιλῆσθον]
φιλέωμεν	[φιλῶμεν]	[φιλεώμε(σ)θα]	[φιλώμε(σ)θα]
[φιλέητε]	[φιλῆτε]	[φιλέησθε]	[φιλῆσθε]
[φιλέωσι(ν)]	[φιλῶσι(ν)]	[φιλέωνται]	[φιλῶνται]

Contraction

The present optative is:

active		middle & passive	
uncontracted	contracted	uncontracted	contracted
[φιλέοιμι]	?[φιλοίην]	[φιλεοίμην]	[φιλοίμην]
[φιλέοις]	?[φιλοίης]	[φιλέοιο]	[φιλοῖο]
φιλέοι	φιλοίη	[φιλέοιτο]	[φιλοῖτο]
[φιλέοιτον]	[φιλοῖτον]	[φιλέοισθον]	[φιλοῖσθον]
[φιλεοίτην]	[φιλοίτην]	[φιλεοίσθην]	[φιλοίσθην]
[φιλέοιμεν]	[φιλοῖμεν]	[φιλεοίμε(σ)θα]	[φιλοίμε(σ)θα]
[φιλέοιτε]	[φιλοῖτε]	[φιλέοισθε]	[φιλοῖσθε]
[φιλέοιεν]	[φιλοῖεν]	[φιλέοιντο]	[φιλοῖντο]

Some of the entries in these tables are hypothetical; for instance, there is no example in Homer of the 1st or 2nd person singular present optative active of an -ε verb in the contracted form, and only two examples of the 3rd person singular, φιλοίη (Odyssey IV, 692) and φοροίη (Odyssey IX, 320).[28] It is more important to understand the system than to learn these tables by heart.

<u>verbs with stems ending -ο</u> In Homer, Chantraine notes that the contraction ο + vowel is only found in a small number of words.[29] The present and imperfect of -οω verbs are poorly represented.[30] Among the verbs with stems ending -ο which he lists as occurring in the present and imperfect tenses are χολόω (I anger), ἀρόω (I plough), γυμνόω (I strip naked),[31] κακόω (I distress) and δηϊόω or δηόω (I slay, cleave asunder). σαόω (I save) is irregular (see pp.89 and 200).

present indicative

active		middle & passive	
uncontracted	contracted	uncontracted	contracted
[χολόω]	[χολῶ]	[χολόομαι]	χολοῦμαι
[χολόεις]	[χολοῖς]	[χολόηαι]	[χολοῖ]
[χολόει]	[χολοῖ]	[χολόεται]	χολοῦται
[χολόετον]	[χολοῦτον]	[χολόεσθον]	[χολοῦσθον]
[χολόετον]	[χολοῦτον]	[χολόεσθον]	[χολοῦσθον]
[χολόομεν]	[χολοῦμεν]	[χολοόμε(σ)θα]	[χολούμε(σ)θα]
[χολόετε]	[χολοῦτε]	[χολόεσθε]	[χολοῦσθε]
[χολόουσι]	[χολοῦσι]	[χολόονται]	[χολοῦνται]

[28]Both may be later interpolations. See Chantraine, *op. cit.* vol.i, p.464, and Heubeck's note on IX, 320 (*A Commentary on Homer's Odyssey* vol.ii, p.31). The endings -οιην, -οιης, -οιη are found in Attic, where they are considered to be comparatively late innovations.
[29]*op. cit.* vol. i, p.54.
[30]Chantraine, *op. cit.* vol.i, p.364.
[31]γυμνοῦσθαι at Odyssey VI, 222.

Beginning Greek with Homer

present infinitive:	active	middle	& passive
uncontracted	contracted	uncontracted	contracted
[χολόειν]	[χολοῦν]	[χολόεσθαι]	[χολοῦσθαι]

imperfect	active	middle	& passive
uncontracted	contracted	uncontracted	contracted
[(ἐ)χόλοον]	[(ἐ)χόλουν]	[(ἐ)χολοόμην]	[(ἐ)χολούμην]
[(ἐ)χόλοες]	[(ἐ)χόλους]	[(ἐ)χόλοο]	[(ἐ)χόλου]
[(ἐ)χόλοε]	[(ἐ)χόλου]	[(ἐ)χολόετο]	[(ἐ)χολοῦτο]
[(ἐ)χολόετον]	[(ἐ)χολοῦτον]	[(ἐ)χολόεσθον]	[(ἐ)χολοῦσθον]
[(ἐ)χολοέτην]	[(ἐ)χολούτην]	[(ἐ)χολοέσθην]	[(ἐ)χολούσθην]
[(ἐ)χολόομεν]	[(ἐ)χολοῦμεν]	[(ἐ)χολοόμεθα]	[(ἐ)χολούμεθα]
[(ἐ)χολόετε]	[(ἐ)χολοῦτε]	[(ἐ)χολόεσθε]	[(ἐ)χολοῦσθε]
[(ἐ)χόλοον]	[(ἐ)χόλουν]	[(ἐ)χολόοντο]	[(ἐ)χολοῦντο]

The only present subjunctive is from σαόω (I save):
2nd person singular   σάῳς (Iliad ix, 681)
3rd person singular   σάῳ (Iliad ix, 424)
3rd person plural   σάωσι (Iliad ix, 393).[32]

present optative

[χολόοιμι]	[χολοῖμι]	[χολοίμην]	[χολοίμην]
[χολόοις]	[χολοῖς]	[χολόοιο]	[χολοῖο]
[χολόοι]	[χολοῖ]	[χολόοιτο]	[χολοῖτο]
[χολόοιτον]	[χολοῖτον]	[χολόοισθον]	[χολοῖσθον]
[χολοοίτην]	[χολοίτην]	[χολοοίσθην]	[χολοίσθην]
[χολόοιμεν]	[χολοῖμεν]	[χολοοίμεθα]	[χολοῖμεθα]
[χολόοιτε]	[χολοῖτε]	[χολόοισθε]	[χολοῖσθε]
[χολόοιεν]	[χολοῖεν]	[χολόοιντο]	[χολοῖντο]

present participle active: [χολῶν, χολοῦσα, χολοῦν].

From δηόω (a variant spelling of δηιόω), there are δῃῶν (nominative singular masculine, present participle active), "slaying" (Iliad xvii 65) and δῄουν (3rd person plural, imperfect active), "they were cleaving" (Iliad v 452, xi 71, xii 425(= v 452), xv 708 and xvi 771).

Some examples of -o contracted verbs have *diectasis* (a lengthening of the thematic vowel), e.g. from ἀρόω, ἀρόωσιν, "they plough" (Odyssey IX, 108) instead of ἀροῦσιν, and from δηιόω, δηιόῳεν (3rd person plural, present optative active) "(if) they should slay" (Odyssey IV, 226), δηιόων (nominative singular masculine, present participle active) (Iliad xvii 566, xviii 195 and xxiii 176), δηιώοντες (nominative plural, present participle active) ("slaying") instead of δηιοῦντες (Iliad XVII, 566) and δηιόωντο

---

[32]Apart from the 2nd person singular present imperative active, σάω, there is the irregular 3rd person singular imperfect active σάω (Iliad xvi 363 and xxi 238).

Contraction   201

("they were being slain") instead of δηιοῦντο (Iliad XIII, 675).[33]

ὁράω - I see The Greek for "I see" is ὁράω. It is found as an -α stem verb in Homer,
e.g. ὁράας "you see" at Odyssey XVII 545, but the 1st person singular is always ὁρόω
or ὁρῶ (not ὁράω). These parts of the present and imperfect tenses occur:
active: present indicative, singular -   1st person, ὁρόω or ὁρῶ:
                                            2nd person, ὁράας or ὁρᾷς:
                                            3rd person, ὁρᾷ
                    plural -   3rd person, ὁρόωσι(ν)
        present optative, 2nd person plural, ὁρόῳτε
        present infinitive, ὁρᾶν
        present participle singular   masculine   feminine
                        (nominative) ὁρόων or ὁρῶν   ὁρόωσα
                        (accusative) ὁρόωντα   ὁρόωσαν
                        (dative)   ὁρόωντι or ὁρῶντι   ὁροώσῃ
                    plural
                        (nominative) ὁρόωντες or ὁρῶντες   ὁρόωσαι
                        (accusative) ὁρόωντας
                        (dative)   ὁρόωσι
        imperfect, 3rd person singular ὅρα - 1st person plural ὁρῶμεν
middle present indicative, singular: 1st person, ὁρῶμαι - 2nd person, ὅρηαι - 3rd
                                    person, ὁρᾶται, plural: 2nd person, ὁράασθε
        present optative, singular: 3rd person, ὁρῷτο
        present infinitive, ὁράασθαι or ὁρᾶσθαι
        present participle, singular   masculine
                        (nominative) ὁρώμενος
                    plural
                        (nominative) ὁρώμενοι
        imperfect singular, 3rd person ὁρᾶται
                  plural, 3rd person ὁρόωντο or ὁρῶντο
Chantraine (op. cit. vol.i, p.76, following Wackernagel) suggests that where -οω is
found in the endings of ὁράω it is because the bard, wishing to use the contracted
form of the verb, found it a syllable too short for the verse and lengthened the
contracted ω into οω. Chantraine classifies such lengthening of verbs ending in
-αω as diectasis. ῥυπόωντα (Odyssey VI, 87) may be formed similarly from ῥυπάω
(see Garvie's note, Homer's Odyssey VI-VIII p.103 and Chantraine, op.cit. vol.i p.364).

Contraction is a factor in the general evolution of Greek; e.g. a comparison of the
Epic (uncontracted) endings of λύομαι with the Attic forms shows how contraction
modifies ending-patterns, and accounts for the apparent analogies of the 2nd
person singular indicative middle in Attic.

present		imperfect		aorist	
Epic	Attic	Epic	Attic	Epic	Attic
λύομαι	λύομαι	(ἐ)λυόμην	ἐλυόμην	(ἐ)λυσάμην	ἐλυσάμην
λύηαι	λύῃ	(ἐ)λύεο	ἐλύου	(ἐ)λύσαο	ἐλύσω
λύεται	λύεται	(ἐ)λύετο	ἐλύετο	(ἐ)λύσατο	ἐλύσατο
λυόμεθα	λυόμεθα	(ἐ)λυόμεθα	ἐλυόμεθα	(ἐ)λυσάμεθα	ἐλυσάμεθα
λύεσθε	λύεσθε	(ἐ)λύεσθε	ἐλύεσθε	(ἐ)λύσασθε	ἐλύσασθε
λύονται	λύονται	(ἐ)λύοντο	ἐλύοντο	(ἐ)λύσαντο	ἐλύσαντο.

[33]Chantraine, op. cit., vol.i, p.80.

Beginning Greek with Homer
Conspectus of Grammar
Verbs
(from section 3)   Homeric Greek ending pattern for active verbs

Person	Present indicative, future & subjunctive		Past endings weak aorist	strong aorist imperfect
1st singular (*I*)	–ω	–μι	–α (–σα)	–ν
2nd singular (*you*)	–σι, –ς,	–σθα	–ας (–σας)	–ς
3rd singular (*he/she/it*)	–ι,[1]	–σι	–ε (–σε)	–ε
2nd dual (*you both*)	–τον	–τον	–τον	–τον
3rd dual (*they both*)	–τον	–τον	–την	–την
1st plural (*we*)	–μεν	–μεν	–αμεν (–σαμεν)	–μεν
2nd plural (*you*)	–τε	–τε	–ατε (–σατε)	–τε
3rd plural (*they*)	–ουσι[2]	–ασι[3]	–αν (–σαν)	–ν

(from Section 3) <u>Present tense active verbs</u> (indicative)

λύω	I am loosing	φέρω	I am bearing
λύεις	you are loosing	φέρεις	you are bearing
λύει	he/she/it looses	φέρει	he/she/it bears
λύετον	you both are loosing	φέρετον	you both are bearing
λύετον	they both are loosing	φέρετον	they both are bearing
λύομεν	we are loosing	φέρομεν	we are bearing
λύετε	you are loosing	φέρετε	you are bearing
λύουσι	they are loosing	φέρουσι	they are bearing
ὄρνυμι	I am arousing	φημί	I am saying (yes), affirming
ὄρνυς	you are arousing	φής	you are saying (yes)
ὄρνυσι	he/she/it is arousing	φησί	he/she/it is saying (yes)
ὄρνυτον	you both are arousing	φατόν	you both are saying (yes),
ὄρνυτον	they both are arousing	φατόν	they both are saying (yes)
ὄρνυμεν	we are arousing	φαμέν	we are saying (yes)
ὄρνυτε	you are arousing	φατέ	you are saying (yes)
ὀρνύασι	they are arousing	φασί	they are saying (yes)

[1] In the subjunctive, 1st person singular can end -ωμι, 2nd singular can end -ησθα and 3rd singular can end -ησι(ν).
[2] -ωσι(ν) in the subjunctive.
[3] In the present indicative. The 3rd person plural future ends –ουσι(ν) and 3rd person plural subjunctive ends -ωσι(ν).

Conspectus of Grammar   203

(Section 4)
Active and middle/passive present indicative endings compared:
–ω verbs

	Active		Middle & Passive
singular	–ω = I		–ομαι = I
	–εις = you		–εαι = you[4]
	–ει = he she it		–εται = he, she, it
dual	–ετον = you two		–εσθον = you two
	–ετον = those two		–εσθον = those two
plural			
	–ομεν = we		–ομε(σ)θα = we
	–ετε = you		–εσθε = you
	–ουσι(ν) = they		–ονται = they

λύω	I am loosing	λύομαι	I am loosing for myself or I am being loosed
λύεις	you are loosing	λύεαι	you loosing for yourself or are being loosed
λύει	he/she/it is loosing	λύεται	he/she/it is loosing for himself, herself, itself or being loosed
λύετον	you two are loosing	λύεσθον	you two are loosing for yourselves or being loosed
λύετον	those two are loosing	λύεσθον	those two are loosing for themselves or being loosed
λύομεν	we are loosing	λυόμεθα	we are loosing for ourselves or being loosed
λύετε	you are loosing	λύεσθε	you are loosing for yourselves or being loosed
λύουσι(ν)	they are loosing	λύονται	they are loosing for themselves or being loosed

---

[4]*or* (rarely) -ῃ, e.g. at Iliad i, 160: τῶν οὔ τι μετατρέπῃ οὐδ' ἀλεγίζεις ("for those things you neither give a thought at all nor care about"). μετατρέπομαι + genitive: I give a thought for (literally, "I turn back for") ἀλεγίζω + genitive: I care about.

Active and middle/passive present endings compared –μι verbs

	active	middle & passive
singular	–μι = I	–μαι = I
	–ς = you	–σαι = you
	–σι = he, she, it	–ται = he/she/it
dual	–τον = you two	–σθον = you two
	–τον = those two	–σθον = those two
plural	–μεν = we	–με(σ)θα = we
	–τε = you	–σθε = you
	–ασι(ν) = they	–νται = they

		active		middle & passive	
singular	ὄρνυμι	I arouse	ὄρνυμαι	I arise, arouse myself, am aroused
	ὄρνυς	you arouse	ὄρνυσαι	you arise
	ὄρνυσι(ν)	he, she, it arouses	ὄρνυται	he, she, it arises
dual	ὄρνυτον	you two arouse	ὄρνυσθον	you two arise
	ὄρνυτον	those two arouse	ὄρνυσθον	those two arise
plural	ὄρνυμεν	we arouse	ὀρνύμεθα	we arise
	ὄρνυτε	you arouse	ὄρνυσθε	you arise
	ὀρνύασι(ν)	they arouse	ὄρνυνται	they arise

(from section 2)   The verb "I am".
          Present tense   Imperfect tense

singular
1 εἰμί   I am   ἦα, ἔα *or* ἔον   I was
2 ἐσσί *or* εἶς   you are   ἦσθα *or* ἔησθα   you were
3 ἐστί(ν)[5]   he/she/it is   ἦν, ἦεν, ἤην   he/she/it
                                             or ἔην   was

dual
2 ἐστόν   you two are   [ἦστον]   you two were
3 ἐστόν   the two of them are ἤστην   the two of them were

plural
1 εἰμέν   we are   ἦμεν   we were
2 ἐστέ   you are   ἦτε   you were
3 εἰσί(ν) *or* ἔασι(ν) they are   ἦσαν *or* ἔσαν   they were

[5] ν can be added if the next word begins with a vowel to avoid hiatus.

Conspectus of Grammar 205

(Section 11)   The present participle active

	masculine	feminine	neuter
singular			
nominative	λύων (loosing)	λύουσα (loosing)	λύον (loosing)
accusative	λύοντα (loosing)	λύουσαν (loosing)	λύον (loosing)
genitive	λύοντος (of loosing)	λυούσης (of loosing)	λύοντος (of loosing)
dative	λύοντι (to/for loosing)	λυούση (to/for loosing)	λύοντι (by loosing)
dual			
nominative & accusative	λύοντε (two loosing)	λυούσα (two loosing)	λύοντε (two loosing)
genitive & dative	λυόντοιιν (of/to two loosing)	λυούσηιν (of/to two loosing)	λυόντοιιν (by two loosing)
plural			
nominative	λύοντες (loosing)	λύουσαι (loosing)	λύοντα (loosing)
accusative	λύοντας (loosing)	λυούσας (loosing)	λύοντα (loosing)
genitive	λυόντων (of loosing)	λυουσάων (of loosing)	λυόντων (of loosing)
dative	λυούσι[6] (to/for loosing)	λυούσησι(ν)[7] (to/for loosing)	λύουσι[8] (by loosing)

(Section 4)   **Present infinitives**

Active infinitives:

The infinitives of -ω verbs end -ειν, -μεν, -εμεν *or* -εμεναι; so "to loose" can be λύειν, λύεμεν o r λυέμεναι.

The present active infinitive ending of -μι verbs is -ναι *or* -μεναι

or -μεν:

the present infinitive of εἰμί, "I am" is εἶναι ("to be")

the present infinitive of ὄρνυμι, "to arouse" is ὀρνύμεν *or* ὀρνύμεναι[9]

the infinitive of εἶμι ("to go") is ἴμεν *or* ἴμεναι *or* ἰέναι[10]

Middle and passive infinitives end -σθαι:

λύεσθαι = to loose for oneself, to be loosed

---

[6] or λυόντεσσι(ν).
[7] or λυούσῃς.
[8] or λυόντεσσι
[9] Homer uses the middle infinitive, φάσθαι, for "to affirm".
[10] E.g. ἴμεν ("to go"), the infinitive of εἶμι ("I (shall) go") in the expression βῆ ῥ᾽ ἴμεν ("then he proceeded to go") found at V, 475 and βῆ δ᾽ ἴμεν ("and she (he) proceeded to go") at VI 15 and 130.

(Section 13) **Present imperative endings:**

active
2nd person singular -ε
3rd person singular -ετω

middle & passive
2nd person singular -εο
3rd person singular -εσθω

2nd person dual -ετον
3rd person dual -ετων

2nd person dual -εσθον
3rd person dual -εσθων

2nd person plural -ετε
3rd person plural -οντων

2nd person plural -εσθε
3rd person plural -εσθων

λύε = loose! (henceforth)
λυέτω = let him/her/it loose

λύετον = may you both loose

λυέτων = let them both loose

λύετε = loose!

λυόντων = let them loose

λύεο = loose for yourself, be loosed
λυέσθω = let him/her/it loose
  for him/her/itself, be loosed
λύεσθον = may you both loose
  for yourselves, be loosed
λυέσθων = let them both loose
  for themselves, be loosed
λύεσθε = loose for yourselves, be
  loosed!
λυέσθων = let them loose for
  themselves, be loosed

The imperative of εἰμι (I am)

singular
[ἴσθι] = be!
ἔστω = let him/her/it be!
dual   ἔστον = may you both be!

plural
ἔστε = be!
ἔστων = let them be!
ἔστον = let them both be!

The pattern of the active present imperatives of ὄρνυμι is:
ὄρνυθι (raise!),[11] ὀρνύτω (let him, her, it arouse!), ὄρνυτε (arouse!)
(plural), ὀρνύντων (let them arouse), (dual: ὄρνυτον)
and of the middle present imperatives:
ὄρνυσο (arise!), ὀρνύσθω (let him/her/it/ arise), ὄρνυσθε (arise!)
(plural), ὀρνύσθων (let them arise!) (dual: ὄρνυσθον).

Chantraine, *Grammaire Homérique* vol.i, p.466 notes some other 2nd singular present imperatives active ending in -θι (like ἴσθι = be!), including δίδωθι (= give!), ἐμπίμπληθι (fill!), and ὄμνυθι (swear!). ἴσθι itself is not found in Homer.

---

[11]The regular 2nd singular present imperative active of -υμι verbs ends -υ. From δαίνυμι "I give a dinner" there is δαίνυ δαῖτα γέρουσι ("give a dinner for the old men") (Iliad ix, 70). δαίς, δαιτός (3f) = banquet. γέρουσι is dative plural from γέρων, γέροντος (3m) = old man.

Conspectus of Grammar 207

(Section 7) The present optative - –ω verbs:
                active   middle/passive
      endings   endings

singular

	active endings		middle/passive endings	
–οιμι	λύοιμι		–οιμην	λυοίμην
	O that I might loose!			O that I might loose for myself, be loosed
–οις	λύοις	-οιο		λύοιο
(–οισθα)	(λύοισθα)			O that you might loose for yourself, be loosed
	O that you might loose			
–οι	λύοι	–οιτο		λύοιτο
	O that he/she/it might loose			O that he/she/it might loose for him/her/itself, be loosed

dual

–οιτον	λύοιτον		–οισθον	λύοισθον
	O that you two might loose			O that you two might loose for yourselves, be loosed
–οιτην	λυοίτην		–οισθην	λυοίσθην
	O that those two might loose			O that those two might loose for themselves, be loosed

plural

–οιμεν	λύοιμεν		–οιμε(σ)θα	λυοίμε(σ)θα
	O that we might loose			O that we might loose for ourselves, be loosed
–οιτε	λύοιτε		–οισθε	λύοισθε
	O that you might loose			O that you might loose for yourselves, be loosed
–οιεν	λύοιεν		–οιντο	λύοιντο
	O that they might loose			O that they might loose x for themselves, be loosed

The present optative (active) –μι verbs (εἰμί - I am):

Singular

–ιην	εἴην	O that I might be
–ιης	εἴης[12]	O that you might be
–ιη	εἴη[13]	O that he/she/it might be

Dual

–ιτον	εἴτον	O that you two might be
–ιτην	εἴτην	O that those two might be

Plural

–ιμεν	εἶμεν	O that we might be
–ιτε	εἶτε	O that you might be
–ιεν	εἶεν	O that they might be

---

[12]ἔοις at Iliad ix, 284
[13]Occasionally ἔοι (Chantraine, *op. cit.* vol.i, p.287).

Beginning Greek with Homer

(Section 14) The present subjunctive[14]

λύω = let me loosen
(or λύωμι)
λύης = may you loosen
(or λύησθα)
λύη = let him/her/it loosen
(or λύησι(ν))

λύωμαι = let me loosen for myself, be loosened
λύηαι = may you loosen for yourself, be
(or λύη) loosened
λύηται = let him/her/it loosen for
him/her/itself, be loosened

λύητον = may you both loosen
λύητον = let them both for themselves

λύησθον = may you both loosen for yourselves, be loosened
λύησθον = let them both loosen for themselves

λύωμεν = let us loosen
λύητε = may you loosen
λύωσι(ν) = let them loosen

λυώμεθα = let us loosen for ourselves, be loosened
λύησθε = may you loosen for yourselves, be loosened
λύωνται = let them loosen for themselves, be loosened

(Section 6)   The imperfect tense (-ω verbs)
singular   active   middle/passive
  (ἔ)λυον   I was loosing   (ἐ)λυόμην   I wasloosing (for myself),
                                                          I was being loosed
  (ἔ)λυες   you were loosing   (ἐ)λύεο   you were loosing (for
                                                          yourself),
                                                          you were being loosed
  (ἔ)λυε   he/she/it was loosing   (ἐ)λύετο   he/she/itwas loosing
                                                          for himself/herself/itself,
                                                          he/she/it was being loosed

dual (ἐ)λύετον   you two were loosing   (ἐ)λύεσθον you two were loosing for
                                                          yourselves, you two were being loosed
     (ἐ)λυέτην   those two were loosing   (ἐ)λυέσθην those two were loosing
                                                          loosing for themselves,
                                                          those twowere being loosed

plural(ἐ)λύομεν   we were loosing   (ἐ)λυόμε(σ)θα we were loosing for
                                                          ourselves, we were being loosed
     (ε)λύετε   you were loosing   (ἐ)λύεσθε   you were loosing for
                                                          yourselves, you were being loosed
     (ἔ)λυον   they were loosing   (ἐ)λύοντο   they were loosing for
                                                          themselves,they were being loosed.

---

[14](1) Present subjunctives of -νυμι verbs are rare and uncertain. (2)The present subjunctive of εἶμι ("I go") (see p.113) is common, and always has a long vowel ending except for the 1st person plural, "let us go", which is always ἴομεν. Few other present subjunctives are found with short vowel endings. (Chantraine, *op. cit.,* vol.i, pp.457-8) For the present subjunctive of εἰμί ("I am"), see p.99.

Conspectus of Grammar

The imperfect tense –μι verbs:

active		middle (& passive)	
(ἔ)φην[15]	I affirmed	[ὠρνύμην	I was arising]
(ἔ)φης or (ἔ)φησθα	you affirmed	[ὤρνυσο	you were arising]
(ἔ)φη	he/she/it said	ὤρνυτο	he/she/it was arising
[ἔφατον	you two affirmed]	[ὤρνυσθον	you two were arising]
[ἐφάτην	those two affirmed]	[ὠρνύσθην	those two were arising]
(ἔ)φαμεν	we affirmed	[ὠρνύμεσθα	we were arising]
[ἔφατε	you affirmed]	[ὤρνυσθε	you were arising]
(ἔ)φασαν[16]	they affirmed	ὤρνυντο	they were arising

(Section 9)   The weak aorist tense

active
middle

singular

(ἔ)λυσα = I loosed
(ἔ)λυσας = you loosed

(ἐ)λυσάμην = I loosed for myself
(ἐ)λύσαο (or (ἐ)λύσω) = you loosed for yourself

(ἔ)λυσε(ν) = he/she/it loosed
(ἐ)λύσατο = he/she/it loosed for him/her/itself

dual

(ἐ)λύσατον = you two loosed
(ἐ)λυσάτην = those two loosed

(ἐ)λύσασθον = you two loosed for yourselves
(ἐ)λυσάσθην = those two loosed for themselves

plural

(ἐ)λύσαμεν = we loosed

(ἐ)λύσατε = you loosed

(ἔ)λυσαν = they loosed

(ἐ)λυσάμεθα = we loosed for ourselves
(ἐ)λύσασθε = you loosed for yourselves
(ἐ)λύσαντο = they loosed for themselves

<u>The weak aorist infinitive active</u> ends –αι, –αμεναι or –αμεν. λῦσαι, λύσαμεν or λυσάμεναι: to loose.

<u>The weak aorist infinitive middle</u> ends –ασθαι. λύσασθαι : to loose for oneself, to get loosed.

---
[15]See Chantraine, *op. cit.*, vol.i, p.291. ἔφην is classified as strong aorist (aor.2) in Liddell & Scott.

[16]Also ἔφαν, e.g. Odyssey IX, 413: ὣς ἄρ' ἔφαν ἀπίοντες ("so, then, they said departing") and φάν, XVIII, 342: φὰν γάρ μιν ἀληθέα μυθήσασθαι ("for they affirmed him to have spoken true things").

(Section 11) The weak aorist participle active

	masculine	feminine	neuter
singular			
nominative	λύσας (having loosed)	λύσασα (having loosed)	λῦσαν (having loosed)
accusative	λύσαντα (having loosed)	λύσασαν (having loosed)	λῦσαν (having loosed)
genitive	λύσαντος (of having loosed)	λυσάσης (of having loosed)	λύσαντος (of having loosed)
dative	λύσαντι (to/for having loosed)	λυσάσῃ (to/for having loosed)	λύσαντι (by having loosed)
dual			
nom. & acc.	λύσαντε (two having loosed)	λυσάσα (two having loosed)	λύσαντε (two having loosed)
genitive & dative	λυσάντοιιν (of, to/for two having loosed	λυσάσῃιν (of, to/for two having loosed)	λυσάντοιιν (of, by two having loosed)
plural			
nominative	λύσαντες (having loosed)	λύσασαι (having loosed)	λύσαντα (having loosed)
accusative	λύσαντας (having loosed)	λυσάσας (having loosed)	λύσαντα (having loosed)
genitive	λυσάντων (of having loosed)	λυσάσων (of having loosed)	λυσάντων (of having loosed)
dative	λύσασι(ν)[17] (to/for having loosed)	λυσάσης[18] (to/for having loosed)	λύσασι(ν) (by having loosed)

(from Section 13) Aorist imperative endings (weak)

active

2nd person singular -(σ)ον
3rd person singular –(σ)ατω

2nd person dual –(σ)ατον
3rd person dual –(σ)ατων

2nd person plural –(σ)ατε
3rd person plural –(σ)αντων

middle

2nd person singular –(σ)αι
3rd person singular –(σ)ασθω

2nd person dual -(σ)ασθον
3rd person dual –(σ)ασθων

2nd person plural –(σ)ασθε
3rd person plural -(σ)ασθων

---

[17] o r λυσάντεσσι(ν).
[18] or λυσάσης.

Conspectus of Grammar

λῦσον = loose! (once)   λῦσαι = loose for yourself
λυσάτω = let him/her/it loose   λυσάσθω = let him/her/it
                                            loose for him/her/itself

λύσατον = may you two loose   λύσασθον = may you two
                                            loose for yourselves
λυσάτων = let those two loose   λυσάσθων = let those two loose
                                            for themselves

λύσατε = loose   λύσασθε = loose for yourselves
λυσάντων = let them loose   λυσάσθων = let them loose for
                                            themselves

(Section 9)   The weak aorist optative
active   middle
λύσαιμι = might I loose   λυσαίμην = might I get loosed
λύσαις[19] *or* λύσειας = might you loose λύσαιο = might you get loosed
λύσαι *or* λύσειε = might he/she/it loose λύσαιτο = might he/she/it get loosed

λύσαιτον = might you both loose   λύσαισθον = might you both get loosed
λυσαίτην = might they both loose   λυσαίσθην = might they both get loosed

λύσαιμεν = might we loose   λυσαίμε(σ)θα = might we get loosed
λύσαιτε = might you loose   λύσαισθε = might you get loosed
λύσαιεν *or* λύσειαν = might they loose   λύσαιντο = might they get loosed

(Section 14)   The weak aorist subjunctive[20]
                    active   middle
λύσω (λύσωμι) = let me loosen   λύσωμαι = let me loosen for myself
λύσῃς (λύσησθα) = may you loosen   λύσηαι = may you loosen for yourself
λύσῃ (λύσῃσιν) = let him/her/it loosen   λύσηται = let him/her/it loosen for
                                            him/her/itself

λύσητον = may you two loosen   λύσησθον = may you two loosen for yourselves
λύσητον = may those two loosen   λύσησθον = may those two loosen for
                                            themselves

λύσωμεν = let us loosen   λύσωμε(σ)θα = let us loosen for ourselves
λύσητε = may you loosen   λύσησθε = may you loosen for yourselves
λύσωσι(ν) = let them loosen   λύσωνται = let them loosen for themselves

---
[19] *o r* λύσαισθα.
[20] The weak aorist subjunctive, especially with σ, is frequently found with a short vowel ending, and may look like the future: λύσεις, λύσει, λύσομεν, λύσετε, λύσομεν etc., e.g. εἰ μὲν γὰρ κέ σε νῦν ἀπολύσομεν ἠὲ μεθῶμεν ... ("for if indeed now we should release you or let you go ...") (Iliad x, 449). (μεθῶμεν is 1st person plural aorist subjunctive of μεθίημι.)

Beginning Greek with Homer

(from Section 10)   ˙The strong aorist indicative

	active	middle
singular	(ἐ)λαβον = I took	(ἐ)λαβόμην = I got hold of
	(ἐ)λαβες = you took	(ἐ)λαβέο = you got hold of
	(ἐ)λαβε = he/she/it took	(ἐ)λάβετο = he/she/it got hold of
dual	(ἐ)λάβετον = you two took	(ἐ)λάβεσθον = you two got hold of
	(ἐ)λαβέτην = those two took	(ἐ)λαβέσθην = those two got hold of
plural	(ἐ)λάβομεν = we took	(ἐ)λαβόμε(σ)θα = we got hold of
	(ἐ)λάβετε = you took	(ἐ)λάβεσθε = you got hold of
	(ἐ)λαβον = they took	(ἐ)λάβοντο = they got hold of

(Section 13)   The strong aorist imperative

active

λάβε = take (once)!
λαβέτω = let him/her/it take (once)!
λάβετον = may you both take (once)!
λαβέτων = let them both take (once)!
λάβετε = take (once)! (plural)
λαβόντων = let them take (once)!

middle

λάβεο = take hold of !, grasp!
λαβέσθω let him/her/it grasp!
λάβεσθον = may you both grasp (once)!
λαβέσθων = let them both grasp (once)!
λάβεσθε = grasp (once)! (plural)
λαβέσθων = let them grasp (once)!

The strong aorist optative

active

λάβοιμι = might I take
λάβοις = might you take
λάβοι = might he/she/it take

λάβοιτον = might you two take
λαβοίτην = might those two take

λάβοιμεν = might we take
λάβοιτε = might you take
λάβοιεν = might they take

middle

λαβοίμην = might I get hold of
λάβοιο = might you get hold of
λάβοιτο = might he/she/it get hold of

λάβοισθον = might you two get hold of
λαβοίσθην = might those two get hold of

λαβοίμε(σ)θα = might we get hold of
λάβοισθε = might you get hold of
λάβοιντο = might they get hold of

(from Section 14)   The strong aorist subjunctive

active

λάβω (λάβωμι) = let me take
λάβης (λάβησθα) = may you take
λάβῃ (λάβῃσιν) = let him/her/it take

λάβητον = may you both take
λάβητον = let them both take

λάβωμεν = let us take
λάβητε = may you take (plural)
λάβωσι(ν) = let them tak

middle

λάβωμαι = let me get hold of
λάβηαι = may you get hold of
λάβηται = let him/her/it get hold of

λάβησθον = may you both get hold of
λάβησθον = let them both get hold of

λαβώμε(σ)θα = let us get hold of
λάβησθε = may you get hold of (plural)
λάβωνται = let them get hold of

Conspectus of Grammar

The strong aorist infinitive active ends -έειν, -εῖν, -έμεν or -έμεναι. The infinitive ("to take") of ἔλαβον is therefore λαβέειν, λαβεῖν, λαβέμεν or λαβέμεναι.

The strong aorist infinitive middle ends -εσθαι. The infinitive of ἐλαβόμην is therefore λάβεσθαι ("to grasp").

The strong aorist participle active
(ἰδών, having seen, from ὁράω)

	masculine	feminine	neuter
singular			
nominative	ἰδών	ἰδοῦσα	ἰδόν
	(having seen)	(having seen)	(having seen)
accusative	ἰδόντα	ἰδοῦσαν	ἰδόν
	(having seen)	(having seen)	(having seen)
genitive	ἰδόντος	ἰδούσης	ἰδόντος
	(of having seen)	(of having seen)	(of having seen)
dative	ἰδόντι	ἰδούσῃ	ἰδόντι
	(to/for having seen)	(to/for having seen)	(by having seen)
dual			
nominative & accusative	ἰδόντε	ἰδούσα	ἰδόντε
	(having seen)	(having seen)	(having seen)
genitive & dative	ἰδόντοιιν	ἰδούσῃιν	ἰδόντοιιν
	(of, to/for two having seen)	(of, to/for two having seen)	(of, by two having seen)
plural			
nominative	ἰδόντες	ἰδοῦσαι	ἰδόντα
	(having seen)	(having seen)	(having seen)
accusative	ἰδόντας	ἰδούσας	ἰδόντα
	(having seen)	(having seen)	(having seen)
genitive	ἰδόντων	ἰδούσων[21]	ἰδόντων
	(of having seen)	(of having seen)	(of having seen)
dative	ἰδοῦσι(ν)[22]	ἰδούσης[23]	ἰδοῦσι(ν)
	(to/for having seen)	(to/for having seen)	(by having seen)

[21] o r ἰδουσέων o r ἰδουσῶν.
[22] or ἰδόντεσσι(ν).
[23] or ἰδούσῃσι(ν).

Beginning Greek with Homer

(Section 12)   The Future Tense
active   middle[24]

λύσω = I shall loose   λύσομαι = I shall loose for myself
λύσεις = you will loose   λύσεαι = you will loose for yourself
λύσει = he, she, it will loose   λύσεται = he, she, it will loose for him, her itself

λύσετον = you two will loose   λύσεσθον = you two will loose for yourselves
λύσετον = those two will loose   λύσεσθον = those two will loose for themselves

λύσομεν = we shall loose   λυσόμε(σ)θα = we shall loose for ourselves
λύσετε = you will loose   λύσεσθε = you will loose for yourselves
λύσουσι(ν) = they will loose   λύσονται = they will loose for themselves

<u>Future infinitives</u> end like present infinitives. The future infinitives of λύω are **λύσειν, λυσέμεν** or **λυσέμεναι** "to be about to loose", and the future infinitive of λύσομαι is **λύσεσθαι**, "to be about to get loosed" or "to loose for oneself".
The future infinitive of εἰμι (I am) is **ἔσεσθαι** (to be about to be).

(from Section 18)   The aorist passive tense
                    (ἐ)λύθην   I was loosed
                    (ἐ)λύθης   you were loosed
                    (ἐ)λύθη   he/she/it was loosed

                    (ἐ)λύθητον   you two were loosed
                    (ἐ)λυθήτην   those two were loosed

                    (ἐ)λύθημεν   we were loosed
                    (ἐ)λύθητε   you were loosed
                    (ἐ)λύθησαν[25]   they were loosed

---

[24]The future passive in Attic Greek is λυθήσομαι, but this form is not found in Homer. Some futures of the middle type however are found with passive meanings, e.g.: πέρσεται ("(this city) will be destroyed") (Iliad xxiv, 729) and φιλήσεαι ("you will be well treated" (literally, "you will be loved")) (Odyssey I, 123 and XV, 281) (Chantraine, *op. cit.*, vol,i, p.447).
[25]o r (ἐ)λυθεν.

Conspectus of Grammar 215

Some verbs do not have θ in the aorist passive. For example, ἐφάνην ("I was shown") is the aorist passive of φαίνω ("I show"). Some have the ending –σθην instead of –θην.

The aorist infinitive passive
λυθῆναι or λυθήμεναι = to be loosed (once).

The aorist imperative passsive:
λυθῆτι	be loosed! (singular)
λυθήτω	let him/her/it be loosed
λυθῆτον	be loosed, both of you!
λυθήτων	let them both be loosed
λυθῆτε	be loosed! (plural)
λυθέντων	let them be loosed.

(from Section 19) The aorist passive participle

	masculine	feminine	neuter	
singular				
nominative	λυθείς	λυθεῖσα	λυθέν	= loosed
accusative	λυθέντα	λυθεῖσαν	λυθέν	= loosed
genitive	λυθέντος	λυθείσης	λυθέντος	= (of) loosed
dative	λυθέντι	λυθείσῃ	λυθέντι	= (to/for/by) loosed
dual				
nominative & accusative	λυθέντε	λυθείσα	λυθέντε	= (two) loosed
genitive & dative	λυθέντοιιν	λυθείσηιν	λυθέντοιιν	= (of/to/for/by) (two) loosed
plural				
nominative	λυθέντες	λυθεῖσαι	λυθέντα	= loosed
accusative	λυθέντας	λυθείσας	λυθέντα	= loosed
genitive	λυθέντων	λυθεισάων	λυθέντων	= (of) loosed
dative	λυθεῖσι[26]	λυθείσῃς	λυθεῖσι[23]	= (to/for/by) loosed

[26] or λυθέντεσσι

Aorist subjunctive passive

λυθῶ	let me be loosed	λυθῶμεν	let us be loosed
λυθῇς	may you be loosed (singular)	λυθῆτε	may you be loosed (plural)
λυθῇ	let him, her, it be loosed	λύθωσι(ν)	let them be loosed

λυθῆτον may you both be loosed
λυθῆτον let them both be loosed

Section 20) The Perfect Tense

active

[λέλυκα = I have loosed

λέλυκας = you have loosed (singular)

λέλυκε = he/she/it has loosed

λελύκατον = you two have loosed

λελύκατον = those two have loosed

λελύκαμεν = we have loosed

λελύκατε = you have loosed

λελύκασι(ν) = they have loosed]

middle & passive

λέλυμαι = I have loosed for myself, I have been loosed

λέλυσαι = you have loosed for yourself, you have been loosed (singular)

λέλυται = he/she/it has loosed for him/her/itself, he/she/it has been loosed

λέλυσθον = you two have loosed for yourselves, you two have been loosed

λέλυσθον = those two have loosed for themselves, those two have been loosed.

λελύμε(σ)θα = we have loosed for ourselves, we have been loosed

λελύσθε = you have loosed for yourselves, you have been loosed

λελύνται or λελύαται = they have loosed for themselves, they have been loosed.

The irregular perfect οἶδα:

οἶδα = I know
οἶσθα[27] = you know (sing.)
οἶδε = he/she/it knows

ἴδμεν = we know
ἴστε = you know (plu.)
ἴσασι = they know

---

[27]οἶδας ("you know", singular) is found once (Odyssey I, 337) instead of οἶσθα. The dual does not occur in Homer.

Conspectus of Grammar

The perfect participle active

	masculine	feminine	neuter
singular nominative	εἰδώς (a) knowing (man)	(ε)ἰδυῖα (a) knowing (woman)	εἰδός (a) knowing (thing)
accusative	εἰδότα (a) knowing (man)	(ε)ἰδυῖαν (a) knowing (woman)	εἰδός (a) knowing (thing)
genitive	εἰδότος of (a) knowing (man)	(ε)ἰδυίης of (a) knowing (woman)	εἰδότος of (a) knowing (thing)
dative	εἰδότι to/for (a) knowing (man)	(ε)ἰδυίῃ to/for (a) (woman)knowing	εἰδότος by (a) knowing (thing)
dual nom & acc	εἰδότε two knowing (men)	(ε)ἰδυία two knowing (women)	εἰδότε two knowing (things)
gen & dat	εἰδότοιιν of, or to/for two knowing (men)	(ε)ἰδυίηιν of, or to/for two knowing (women)	εἰδότοιιν of, or by two knowing (things)
plural nominative	εἰδότες knowing (men)	(ε)ἰδυῖαι knowing (women)	εἰδότα knowing (things)
accusative	εἰδότας knowing (men)	(ε)ἰδυίας knowing (women)	εἰδότα knowing (things)
genitive	εἰδότων of knowing (men)	(ε)ἰδυίων of knowing (women)	εἰδότων of knowing (things)
dative	εἰδότεσ(σ)ι or εἰδόσι to/for knowing (men)	(ε)ἰδυιης to/for knowing (women)	εἰδότεσ(σ)ι or εἰδόσι to/for knowing (things)

The perfect participle middle/passive

λελυμένος (masc.), λελυμένη (fem.), λελυμένον (neut.)
(having loosed for oneself, having been loosed)
declined like καλός, καλή, καλόν.

The perfect infinitive active endings are -μεν *or* μεναι *or* -ναι, e.g.
λελυκέμεν *or* λελυκέμεναι *or* λελύκεναι: to have loosed

Beginning Greek with Homer

The perfect infinitive middle/passive
λελύσθαι ; to have got loosed

The pluperfect tense

active		middle & passive	
singular			
[(ἐ)λελύκη²⁹	I had loosed	(ἐ)λελύμην	I had loosed for myself/had been loosed
(ἐ)λελύκης	you had loosed (sing.)	(ἐ)λέλυσο	you (sing.) had loosed for yourself, had been loosed
(ἐ)λελύκει(ν)	he/she/it had loosed	(ἐ)λέλυτο	he/she/it had loosed for himself/herself/itself, he/she/it had been loosed
dual			
(ἐ)λελύκετον	you two had loosed	(ἐ)λέλυσθον	you two had loosed for yourselves/had been loosed
(ἐ)λελυκέτην	those two had loosed	(ἐ)λελύσθην	those two had loosed for themselves, had been loosed
plural			
(ἐ)λελύκεμεν	we had loosed	(ἐ)λελύμε(σ)θα	we had loosed for ourselves/had been loosed
(ἐ)λελύκετε	you had loosed (plu)	(ἐ)λέλυσθε	you (plu.) had loosed for yourselves/had been loosed
(ἐ)λελύκεσαν	they had loosed.]	(ἐ)λέλυντο or (ἐ)λελύατο	they had loosed for themselves/had been loosed

Verbs - active (-μι termination)

(The following verbs are frequently compounded e.g. ἐντίθημι, *I put in*. Prefixes such as ἐν are not shown in the tabulations.)

present tense active

I send	*I give*	*I set up*	*I put*
singular			
[ἵημι]	[δίδωμι]	[ἵστημι]	[τίθημι]
ἵεις	διδοῖς or διδοῖσθα	[ἵστης]	τίθησθα
ἵησι(ν)	δίδωσι(ν)	[ἵστησι(ν)]	τίθησι(ν) or τιθεῖ
dual			
[ἵετον]	[δίδοτον]	[ἵστατον]	[τίθετον]
[ἵετον]	[δίδοτον]	[ἵστατον]	[τίθετον]
plural			
ἵεμεν	δίδομεν	[ἵσταμεν]	[τίθεμεν]
ἵετε	[δίδοτε]	[ἵστατε]	[τίθετε]
ἵεισι(ν)	διδοῦσι(ν)	ἵστασι(ν)	τιθεῖσι(ν)

---

[28] ἐλελύκεα can stand for (ἐ)λελύκη, (ἐ)λελύκεας for (ἐ)λελύκης and (ἐ)λελύκεε for (ἐ)λελύκει(ν).

Conspectus of Grammar 219

Present infinitive (active)

to send	to give	to set up	to put
ἱέμεν or ἱέμεναι	διδοῦναι	[ἱστάμεν or ἱστάμεναι]	τιθήμεναι

Present imperative (active)

send!	give!	set up!	put!
ἵει	δίδου or δίδωθι	ἵστη or ἵστα	τίθει
[ἱέτω]	[διδότω]	[ἱστάτω]	[τιθέτω]
[ἵετον]	[δίδοτον]	[ἵστατον]	[τίθετον]
[ἵετον]	[δίδοτον]	[ἵστατον]	[τίθετον]
ἵετε	[δίδοτε]	[ἵστατε]	[τίθετε]
[ἱέντων]	[διδόντων]	[ἱστάντων]	[τιθέντων]

Present optative active

might I be	might I send	might I give	might I set up	might I put
εἴην	[ἱείην]	[διδοίην]	[ἱσταίην]	[τιθείην]
εἴης or ἔοις	ἱείης	[διδοίης]	[ἱσταίης]	[τιθείης]
εἴη or ἔοι	[ἱείη]	[διδοίη]	[ἱσταίη]	[τιθείη]
[εἴτον]	[ἱεῖτον]	[διδοῖτον]	[ἱσταῖτον]	[τιθεῖτον]
[εἴτην]	[ἱείτην]	[διδοίτην]	[ἱσταίτην]	[τιθείτην]
[εἴμεν]	[ἱεῖμεν]	[διδοῖμεν]	[ἱσταῖμεν]	[τιθεῖμεν]
[εἴτε]	[ἱεῖτε]	διδοῖτε	[ἱσταῖτε]	[τιθεῖτε]
εἶεν	[ἱεῖεν]	διδοῖεν	[ἱσταῖεν]	[τιθεῖεν]

Present subjunctive active

let me be	let me send	let me give	let me set up	let me put
ἔω	[ἱῶ]	[διδῶ]	[ἱστῶ]	[τιθῶ]
[ἔῃς]	[ἱῇς]	[διδῷς]	[ἱστῇς]	[τιθῇς]
ἔῃ (ἔῃσιν)	ἱῇσιν	[διδῷ]	[ἱστῇ]	[τιθῇ]
[ἔητον]	[ἱῆτον]	[διδῶτον]	[ἱστῆτον]	[τιθῆτον]
[ἔητον]	[ἱῆτον]	[διδῶτον]	[ἱστῆτον]	[τιθῆτον]
[ἔωμεν]	[ἱῶμεν]	[διδῶμεν]	[ἱστῶμεν]	[τιθῶμεν]
[ἔητε]	[ἱῆτε]	[διδῶτε]	[ἱστῆτε]	[τιθῆτε]
ἔωσι(ν)	[ἱῶσι(ν)]	[διδῶσι(ν)]	[ἱστῶσι(ν)]	[τιθῶσι(ν)]

Beginning Greek with Homer

Present participle active - εἰμι *I am*

	masculine	feminine	neuter	
singular				
nominative	ἐών	ἐοῦσα	ἐόν	being
accusative	ἐόντα	ἐοῦσαν	ἐόν	being
genitive	ἐόντος	ἐούσης	[ἐόντος]	of being
dative	ἐόντι	ἐούσῃ	[ἐόντι]	to/for being
dual				
nominative/accusative	ἐόντε	[ἐοῦσα]	[ἐόντε]	(two) being
genitive/dative	[ἐόντοιιν]	[ἐούσῃιν]	[ἐόντοιιν]	(of, to/for/by) (two) being
plural				
nominative	ἐόντες	[ἐοῦσαι]	ἐόντα	being
accusative	ἐόντας	[ἐούσας]	ἐόντα	being
genitive	ἐόντων	[ἐουσῶν]	[ἐόντων]	of being
dative	ἐοῦσι(ν)	[ἐούσης]	[ἐοῦσι(ν)]	to/for/by being

Present participle active - τίθημι:

nominative	τιθείς	[τιθεῖσα]	[τιθέν]	putting
accusative	[τιθέντα]	[τιθεῖσαν]	[τιθέν]	putting
genitive	[τιθέντος]	[τιθείσης]	[τιθέντος]	of putting
dative	[τιθέντι]	[τιθείσῃ]	[τιθέντι]	to/for/by putting
dual				
nom/acc	[τιθέντε]	[τιθείσα]	[τιθέντε]	(two) putting)
gen/dat	[τιθέντοιιν]	[τιθείσῃιν]	[τιθέντοιιν]	(to/for/by two) putting
plural				
nominative	τιθέντες	[τιθεῖσαι]	[τιθέντα]	putting
accusative	[τιθέντας]	[τιθείσας]	[τιθέντα]	putting
genitive	[τιθέντων]	[τιθεισάων]	[τιθέντων]	of putting
dative	[τιθέντεσσι(ν)]	[τιθείσῃσι(ν)]	[τιθέντεσσι(ν)]	to/for/by putting

(like τιθείς:

ἱείς	ἱεῖσα	ἱέν	sending

with vowel change to o instead of ε:

διδούς	διδοῦσα	διδόν	giving

with vowel change to α instead of ε:

ἱστάς	ἱστᾶσα	ἱστάν	setting up

Conspectus of Grammar 221

Imperfect active

I was sending	*I was giving*	*I was setting up*	*I was putting*

singular
[ἵειν]   [(ἐ)δίδουν]   [ἵστην]   [(ἐ)τίθην]
[ἵεις]   (ἐ)δίδους   [ἵστης]   [(ἐ)τίθεις]
ἵει   (ἐ)δίδου   ἵστη   (ἐ)τίθει
dual
[ἵετον]   [(ἐ)δίδοτον]   [ἵστατον]   [(ἐ)τίθετον]
[ἱέτην]   [(ἐ)διδότην]   [ἱστάτην]   [(ἐ)τιθέτην]
plural
[ἵεμεν]   (ἐ)δίδομεν   [ἵσταμεν]   [(ἐ)τίθεμεν]
ἵετε   [(ἐ)δίδοτε]   [ἵστατε]   [(ἐ)τίθετε]
[ἵεσαν]   (ἐ)δίδοσαν   ἵστασαν   (ἐ)τίθεσαν

Future indicative active

I shall be	*I shall send*	*I shall give*	*I shall set up*	*I shall put*

singular
ἔσ(σ)ομαι   ἥσω   δώσω   στήσω   θήσω
ἔσ(σ)εαι   ἥσεις   δώσεις   στήσεις   θήσεις
ἔσ(σ)εται   ἥσει or ἔσει δώσει   στήσει   θήσει
or ἔσται
dual
ἐσεσθον   [ἥσετον]   [δώσετον]   [στήσετον]   [θήσετον]
ἐσεσθον   [ἥσετον]   [δώσετον]   [στήσετον]   [θήσετον]
plural
ἐσόμεσθα   ἥσομεν   δώσομεν   [στήσομεν]   θήσομεν
ἔσεσθε   ἥσετε   [δώσετε]   [στήσετε]   θήσετε
ἔσ(σ)ονται [ἥσουσι(ν)] δώσουσι(ν) στήσουσι(ν) θήσουσι(ν)

Future participle active

about to set up
στήσων

Future infinitive active

to be about to be	*to be about to send*	*to be about to give*	*to be about to set up*	*to be about to put*
ἔσ(σ)εσθαι	ἥσειν or ἥσεμεν or ἡσέμεναι	δώσειν or δώσεμεν or δωσέμεναι	στήσειν	θήσειν or θησέμεναι

Aorist indicative active

I sent	I gave	I set up	I put
ἕηκα or ἧκα	ἔδωκα	στῆσα	ἔθηκα
ἧκας	ἔδωκας	[ἔστησας]	ἔθηκας
ἕηκε(ν) or ἧκε(ν)	ἔδωκε(ν)	ἔστησε(ν)	(ἔ)θηκε(ν)
[ἕτον]		[ἐστήσατον]	
ἕτην		[ἐστησάτην]	
ἥκαμεν or ἕμεν	(ἐ)δομεν	στήσαμεν	θέμεν
[ἥκατε or ἕτε]	[ἐδώκατε or ἔδοτε]	[ἐστήσατε]	[(ἔ)θετε]
ἧκαν or ἕσαν	ἔδωκαν or (ἔ)δοσαν	ἔστησαν	(ἔ)θεσαν or (ἔ)θηκαν

ἔστησα is the weak aorist of ἵστημι. There is also a strong aorist ἔστην, which means "I stood" and is intransitive.

Strong aorist indicative active *I stood* (intransitive)

(ἔ)στην ἔστης (ἔ)στη [ἔστητον] στήτην (ἔ)στημεν ἔστητε ἔστησαν or ἔσταν

Aorist infinitive active

to send	to give	to set up	to put
εἶναι or	δοῦναι or	στῆσαι	θεῖναι or
ἔμεναι or	δόμεναι or		θέμεναι or
ἔμεν	δόμεν		θέμεν

Strong aorist infinitive *to stand*

στῆναι or στήμεναι

Aorist imperative (duals not found)

send!	give!	set up!	put!
ἕς	δός	στῆσον	θές
ἕτω	δότω		[θέτω]
[ἕτε]	δότε		θέτε
[ἕντων]	[δόντων]		θέντων

Strong aorist imperative (duals not found)

stand!
στῆθι
στήτω
στῆτε
[στάντων]

Conspectus of Grammar   223

Aorist participle active
having put, putting

singular	masculine	feminine	neuter
nominative	θείς	θεῖσα	[θέν]
accusative	[θέντα]	[θεῖσαν]	[θέν]
genitive	[θέντος]	[θείσης]	[θέντος]
dative	[θέντι]	[θείσῃ]	[θέντι]
dual			
nom/acc	θέντε	[θείσα]	[θέντε]
gen/dat	[θέντοιιν]	[θείσην]	[θέντοιιν]
plural			
nominative	θέντες	θεῖσαι	[θέντα]
accusative	[θέντας]	[θείσας]	[θέντα]
genitive	[θέντων]	[θεισῶν]	[θέντων]
dative	[θεῖσι(ν)]	[θείσης]	[θεῖσι(ν)]

Similarly,

εἵς, εἷσα, ἕν = having sent (sending)
δούς, δοῦσα, δόν = having given (giving)
στάς, στᾶσα, στάν = having stood (standing)(strong aorist)
στήσας, στήσασα, στῆσαν = having set up (weak aorist)

Aorist optative active

might I send	might I give	might I stand	might I put
εἴην	δοίην	[σταίην]	θείην
[εἴης]	δοίης	[σταίης]	θείης
εἴη	δοίη	σταίη	θείη
[εἶτον]	[δοῖτον]	[σταῖτον]	[θεῖτον]
[εἴτην]	[δοίτην]	[σταίτην]	[θείτην]
[εἶμεν]	δοῖμεν	[σταῖμεν]	θεῖμεν
[εἶτε]	δοῖτε	[σταῖτε]	θεῖτε
[εἶεν]	δοῖεν	[σταῖεν]	θεῖεν

(strong aorist)

(The 3rd person plural of the weak aorist optative of ἵστημι is also found: στήσειεν, might they set up.)

Aorist subjunctive active

let me send	let me give	let me stand	let me put
εἵω	δω	[στῶ or στῶμι]	θείω
[ᾖς or ἧσθα]	δῷς	στήῃς	θήῃς
ᾖσι(ν)	δῶσι(ν)	στήῃ or στῇ	θῆσι(ν)
or ἔῃ or ἥῃ	or δώῃ or δώῃσιν		or θήῃ
[ἧτον]	[δῶτον]	στήετον	[θῆτον]
[ἧτον]	[δῶτον]	[στῆτον]	[θῆτον]
ὦμεν	δῶμεν or δώομεν	στέωμεν or στείομεν	θέωμεν or θείομεν
[ἧτε]	[δῶτε]	[στῆτε]	[θῆτε]
[ὦσι(ν)]	δῶσι(ν) or δώωσιν	στείωσι	[θῶσι(ν)]

Perfect indicative active

The perfect active of ἵημι, δίδωμι and τίθημι are not found in Homer. The perfect active (with present meaning in English) of ἵστημι occurs as follows:

[ἕστηκα: I am standing]   ἕσταμεν: we are standing
ἕστηκας: you are standing   ἕστατε: you are standing
ἕστηκε: he/she/it is standing   ἑστήκασι(ν) or ἑστᾶσι(ν): they are standing
{ἕστατον: you two are standing}
ἕστατον: they are both standing

The perfect subjunctive active is found in the 3rd person singular: ἑστήκῃ, "stands", i.e."has been placed" (Iliad xvii, 435 and Odyssey XXII, 469).

The perfect optative active is found once in the 3rd person singular: (ἀφ)εσταίη, "(she) would not shun (stand away from) (her husband)" (Odyssey XXIII, 101).

The perfect infinitive active is ἑστάμεν or ἑστάμεναι to stand

The perfect participle active *standing*

singular	masculine	feminine	neuter
nominative	[ἑστηώς]	[ἑστῶσα]	[ἑστός]
accusative	ἑσταότα or ἑστεῶτα		
genitive	ἑσταότος		
dative			
dual			
nominative	ἑσταότε or ἑστεῶτε		
plural			
nominative	ἑσταότες or ἑστεῶτες		
accusative	ἑστάοτας		ἑσταότα
genitive	ἑσταότων		
dative	[ἑστηῶσι}		

Conspectus of Grammar

Pluperfect indicative active
3rd person singular: ἑστήκει(ν), he, she, it stood, 1st plural: ἕσταμεν, we stood, 3rd person plural ἕστασαν, they stood.

Verbs with –μι terminations - middle and passive

Present indicative middle & passive

I am sent	*I am given*	*I am set up, I stand*	*I am put*	*I can*
[ἵεμαι]	[δίδομαι]	ἵσταμαι	[τίθεμαι]	δύναμαι
[ἵεσαι]	[δίδοσαι]	ἵστασαι	[τίθεσαι]	δύνασαι
ἵεται	[δίδοται]	ἵσταται	τίθεται	δύναται
[ἵεσθον]	[δίδοσθον]	[ἵστασθον]	[τίθεσθον]	[δύνασθον]
[ἵεσθον]	[δίδοσθον]	[ἵστασθον]	[τίθεσθον]	[δύνασθον]
[ἱέμε(σ)θα]	[διδόμε(σ)θα]	[ἱστάμε(σ)θα]	[τιθέμε(σ)θα]	δυνάμε(σ)θα
[ἵεσθε]	[δίδοσθε]	[ἵστασθε]	[τίθεσθε]	[δύνασθε]
ἵενται	[δίδονται]	ἵστανται	τίθενται	δύνανται

Present infinitive middle & passive

to get sent	*to get given*	*to get set up / to stand*	*to get put*	*to be able*
[ἵεσθαι]	[δίδοσθαι]	ἵστασθαι	[τίθεσθαι]	[δύνασθαι]

Present imperative middle & passive

be (get) sent!	*be (get) given!*	*be (get) set up! / stand!*	*be (get) put!*	
[ἵεσο]	[δίδοσο]	ἵστα(σ)ο	[τίθεσο]	
[ἱέσθω]	[διδόσθω]	[ἱστάσθω]	[τιθέσθω]	
[ἵεσθον]	[δίδοσθον]	[ἵστασθον]	[τίθεσθον]	
[ἵεσθον]	[δίδοσθον]	[ἵστασθον]	[τίθεσθον]	
ἵεσθε	[δίδοσθε]	ἵστασθε	τίθεσθε	
[ἱέσθων]	[διδόσθων]	[ἱστάσθων]	[τιθέσθων]	

(NB ἵεμαι can mean "I am set on", i.e. I desire" (+ genitive) or "I hasten (+ infinitive))

Present participle middle & passive

getting sent	*getting given*	*getting set up, standing*	*getting put*	*being able*
ἱέμενος	[διδόμενος]	ἱστάμενος	τιθήμενος	δυνάμενος

Present subjunctive middle & passive

let me get sent	let me get given	let me get set up let me stand	let me get put	let me be able
ἱῶμαι	διδῶμαι	ἱστῶμαι	τιθῶμαι	δυνῶμαι
ἱῆαι	διδῶαι	ἱστῆαι	τιθῆαι	δυνῆαι
ἱῆται	διδῶται	ἱστῆται	τιθῆται	δυνῆται
ἱῆσθον	διδῶσθον	ἱστῆσθον	τιθῆσθον	δυνῆσθον
ἱῆσθον	διδῶσθον	ἱστῆσθον	τιθῆσθον	δυνῆσθον
ἱώμε(σ)θα	διδώμε(σ)θα	ἱστώμε(σ)θα	τιθώμε(σ)θα	δυνώμε(σ)θα
ἱῆσθε	διδῶσθε	ἱστῆσθε	τιθῆσθε	δυνῆσθε
ἱῶνται	διδῶνται	ἱστῶνται	τιθῶνται	δυνῶνται

(The present subjunctive middle/passive only occurs as δύνηαι, 2nd person singular, from δύναμαι)

Present optative middle & passive

might I be (get) sent	might I be (get) given	might I be (get) set up, stand	might I be (get) put	might I be able
ἱείμην	διδοίμην	ἱσταίμην	τιθείμην	δυναίμην
ἱεῖο	διδοῖο	ἱσταῖο	τιθεῖο	δυναῖο
ἱεῖτο	διδοῖτο	ἱσταῖτο	τιθεῖτο	δυναῖτο
ἱεῖσθον	διδοῖσθον	ἱσταῖσθον	τιθεῖσθον	δυναῖσθον
ἱείσθην	διδοίσθην	ἱσταίσθην	τιθείσθην	δυναίσθην
ἱείμε(σ(θα	διδοίμε(σ)θα	ἱσταίμε(σ)θα	τιθείμε(σ)θα	δυναίμε(σ)θα
ἱεῖσθε	διδοῖσθε	ἱσταῖσθε	τιθεῖσθε	δυναῖσθε
ἱείατο	διδοίατο	ἱσταίατο	τιθείατο	δυναίατο

(The present optative middle/passive only occurs as δυναίμην, δύναιο, δύναιτο, 1st, 2nd and 3rd persons singular of δύναμαι)

Imperfect middle & passive

I was being (getting) sent	I was being (getting) given	I was being (getting) set up was standing	I was being (getting) put	I was able
[ἱέμην]	[ἐδιδόμην]	[ἱστάμην]	[(ἐ)τιθέμην]	δυνάμην
[ἵεσο]	[ἐδίδοσο]	[ἵστασο]	[(ἐ)τίθεσο]	[(ἐ)δύνασο]
ἵετο	[ἐδίδοτο]	ἵστατο	[(ἐ)τίθετο]	δύνατο
[ἵεσθον]	[ἐδίδοσθον]	[ἵστασθον]	[(ἐ)τίθεσθον]	[(ἐ)δύνασθον]
ἱέσθην	[ἐδιδόσθην]	[ἱστάσθην]	[(ἐ)τιθέσθην]	[(ἐ)δυνάσθην]
[ἱέμε(σ)θα]	[ἐδιδόμε(σ)θα]	[ἱστάμε(σ)θα]	(ἐ)τιθέμε(σ)θα	δυνάμε(σ)θα
[ἵεσθε]	[ἐδίδοσθε]	[ἵστασθε]	[(ἐ)τίθεσθε]	ἐδύνασθε
ἵεντο	[ἐδίδοντο]	ἵσταντο	(ἐ)τίθεντο	(ἐ)δύναντο

Conspectus of Grammar   227

Future indicative middle & passive

I shall be (get) sent	*I shall be (get) given*	*I shall be (get) set up, stand*	*I shall be (get) put*	*I shall be able*
ἥσομαι	[δώσομαι]	στήσομαι	θήσομαι	δυνήσομαι
[ἥσεαι]	[δώσεαι]	[στήσεαι]	θήσεαι	δυνήσεαι
[ἥσεται]	[δώσεται]	[στήσεται]	θήσεται	δυνήσεται
[ἥσεσθον]	[δώσεσθον]	[στήσεσθον]	[θήσεσθον]	[δυνήσεσθον]
[ἥσεσθον]	[δώσεσθον]	[στήσεσθον]	[θήσεσθον]	[δυνήσεσθον]
[ἡσόμε(σ)θα]	[δωσόμε(σ)θα]	στησόμεθα	θησόμεθα	[δυνησόμεθα]
[ἥσεσθε]	[δώσεσθε]	[στήσεσθε]	[θήσεσθε]	[δυνήσεσθε]
[ἥσονται]	[δώσονται]	στήσονται	θήσονται	[δυνήσονται]

Future infinitive middle & passive

to be about to be (get) sent	*to be about to be (get) given*	*to be about to be (get) set up, to be about to stand*	*to be about to be (get) put*	*to be about to be able*
[ἥσεσθαι]	[δώσεσθαι]	στήσεσθαι	θήσεσθαι	[δυνήσεσθαι]

Aorist indicative middle

I got sent	*I got given*	*I got set up, stood*	*I got put*	*I could*
[εἵμην]	[ἐδόμην]	[(ἐ)στησάμην]	[ἐθέμην]	[(ἐ)δυνησάμην]
[εἷο]	[ἔδοεο]	[(ἐ)στήσαο]	θεο	[(ἐ)δυνήσαο]
ἕτο	[ἔδοτο]	[(ἐ)στήσατο]	(ἔ)θετο	(ἐ)δυνήσατο
[εἷσθον]	[ἔδοσθον]	[(ἐ)στήσασθον]	[(ἔ)θεσθον]	[(ἐ)δυνήσασθον]
[εἵσθην]	[ἐδόσθην]	[(ἐ)στησάσθην]	θέσθην	[(ἐ)δυνησάσθην]
[εἵμε(σ)θα]	[ἐδόμε(σ)θα]	[(ἐ)στησάμε(σ)θα]	θέμεθα	[(ἐ)δυνησάμε(σ)θα]
[εἷσθε]	[ἔδοσθε]	[(ἐ)στήσασθε]	(ἔ)θεσθε	[(ἐ)δυνήσασθε]
[εἷντο or ἕντο]	[ἔδοντο]	στήσαντο	ἔθεντο	[(ἐ)δυνήσαντο]

NB1. The 3rd person singular aorist of δύναμαι is found twice (at Iliad xxiii, 465 and Odyssey V, 319) as ἐδυνάσθη ("he could"), in the form of an aorist passive.
NB2. The aorist middle of ἵστημι and δύναμαι are weak; the aorist middle of ἵημι and τίθημι are strong.

Aorist infinitive middle

to get sent	*to get given*	*to get set up to stand*	*to get put*	*to be able*
[ἕσθαι]	[δόσθαι]	στήσασθαι	θέσθαι	[δυνήσασθαι]

Aorist imperative middle

get sent!	get given!	get put!
[ἕο]	[δόο]	θέο or θεῦ
[ἕσθω]	[δόσθω]	θέσθω
[ἕσθον]	[δόσθον]	[θέσθον]
[ἕσθων]	[δόσθων]	[θέσθων]
[ἕσθε]	[δόσθε]	θέσθε
[ἕσθων]	[δόσθων]	[θέσθων]

Aorist participle middle

having got sent	having got given	standing	having got put	being able
[ἕμενος]	[δόμενος]	στησάμενος	θέμενος	[δυνησάμενος]

Aorist optative middle

might I get sent	might I get given	might I b get put
[εἵμην]	[δοίμην]	θείμην
[εἷο]	[δοῖο]	[θεῖο]
[εἷτο]	[δοῖτο]	θεῖτο
[εἷσθον]	[δοῖσθον]	[θεῖσθον]
[εἵσθην]	[δοίσθην]	[θείσθην]
[εἵμε(σ)θα]	[δοίμε(σ)θα]	[θείμε(σ)θα]
[εἷσθε]	[δοῖσθε]	[θεῖσθε]
[εἷντο]	[δοῖντο]	[θεῖντο]

Aorist subjunctive middle

let me get sent	let me get given	let me get put
[ὧμαι]	[δῶμαι]	θείομαι
[ἧαι]	[δῶαι]	[θῆαι]
[ἧται]	[δῶται]	[θῆται]
[ἧσθον]	[δῶσθον]	[θῆσθον]
[ἧσθον]	[δῶσθον]	[θῆσθον
ὥμεθα	δώμεθα or δώμεθον	[θώμε(σ)θα]
[ἧσθε]	[δῶσθε]	[θῆσθε]
[ὧνται]	[δῶνται]	[θῶνται]

(The weak aorist subjunctive of ἵστημι is found in the 3rd person plural: (ἀπο)στήσωνται, they may pay (us) back (literally, "weigh out back yesterday's debt", from ἀφίσταμαι, I weigh out ("set up on the scales").) (Iliad xiii, 745).

Conspectus of Grammar

Perfect middle & passive

I have been given	*I have been put (I lie down)*
[δέδομαι]	κεῖμαι
[δέδοσαι]	κεῖσαι
δέδοται	κεῖται
[δέδοσθον]	[κεῖσθον]
[δέδοσθον]	[κεῖσθον]
[δεδόμε(σ)θα]	[κείμε(σ)θα]
[δέδοσθε]	[κεῖσθε]
[δέδονται]	κείαται *or* κέαται *or* κέονται

NB κεῖμαι, classified by Chantraine as present middle (*op. cit.* vol.i, p.292), is used where the perfect passive of τίθημι is needed.

Perfect participle passive
put, lying
κείμενος

Perfect infinitive passive
to lie, to get put
κεῖσθαι

Perfect imperative passive

κεῖσο lie!,[be put]!   κείσθω let it lie! *or* let it be put!

Perfect subjunctive middle (and passive) (short vowel)
κεῖται *or* κῆται let him, her, it lie.

Perhaps κεῖται (subjunctive) is from κείεται (subjunctive with short vowel ending). In some passages (e.g. Odyssey V, 395) it is uncertain whether κεῖται is indicative or subjunctive (Chantraine, *op. cit.* vol.i, p.457). The other persons are not found in Homer.

Pluperfect middle (and passive)
I had been put (I lay down)
(ἐ)κείμην
κεῖσο
(ἔ)κειτο
[(ἔ)κεισθον]
[(ἐ)κείσθην]
(ἐ)κείμεθα
[(ἔ)κεισθε]
(ἔ)κειντο *or* (ἐ)κείατο

The aorist passive tense (and other aorists in -ην)
Indicative
Not found in Homer from δίδωμι, ἵστημι or τίθημι. From ἵημι and δύναμαι,

[εἵθην]
[εἵθης]
εἵθη   δυνάσθη

[εἵθητον]
[εἱθήτην]

[εἵθημεν]
[εἵθητε]
[εἵθησαν].

The aorist passive indicative of παρίημι is found at Iliad XXIII, 868-9:
ἡ δὲ παρείθη μήρινθος – but the cord was let down (i.e. fell, (suddenly) dangled).

Chantraine notes (*op. cit.*, vol.i, p.405) that δυνάσθη is not passive. It is only found twice, at Odyssey V 319 and Iliad xxiii 465, in both places meaning "he could".

Optative
The aorist optative passive of δίδωμι is found at Odyssey II, 78:
ἕως κ' ἀπὸ πάντα δοθείη - *until everything should be given back.*
The aorist optative passive of δίδωμι is:

[δοθείην]
[δοθείης]
δοθείη

[δοθεῖτον]
[δοθείτην]

[δοθεῖμεν]
[δοθεῖτε]
[δοθεῖεν].

The aorist optative passive of ἵημι, ἵστημι and τίθημι are not found in Homer.

Participle
The aorist passive participle of τίθημι is found at Iliad x 271:
δὴ τότ' Ὀδυσσῆος πύκασεν κάρη ἀμφιτεθεῖσα
then indeed having been put round Odysseus' head, it (the helmet) covered (it).

The aorist passive participle of τίθημι is:
             τεθείς   τεθεῖσα   τεθέν
like λυθείς (p.219). The aorist passive participles of δίδωμι, ἵημι and ἵστημι are not found in Homer.

Nouns

First declension

Singular

nominative			
γαῖα	θάλασσα	νύμφη	ἱκέτης
land, earth	sea	nymph	suppliant
accusative			
γαῖαν	θάλασσαν	νύμφην	ἱκέτην
land, earth	sea	nymph	suppliant
genitive			
γαίης	θαλάσσης	νύμφης	ἱκέταο *or* ἱκέτου
of land	of sea	of nymph	of suppliant
dative			
γαίῃ	θαλάσσῃ	νύμφῃ	ἱκέτῃ
(to, for) by land	(to, for) by sea	to, for nymph	to, for suppliant

Plural

nominative			
γαῖαι	θάλασσαι	νύμφαι	ἵκεται
lands	seas	nymphs	suppliants
accusative			
γαίας	θαλάσσας	νύμφας	ἱκέτας
lands	seas	nymphs	suppliants
genitive			
γαιάων	θαλασσάων	νυμφάων	ἱκετάων
of lands	of seas	of nymphs	of suppliants
dative			
γαίῃσι	θαλάσσῃσι	νύμφῃσι	ἱκέτῃσι
or γαίῃς	*or* θαλάσσῃς	*or* νύμφῃς	*or* ἱκέτῃς
(to)/for, by lands	(to)/for, by seas	to/for nymphs	to/for suppliants

The vocative case singular is like the nominative except for masculine nouns ending -ης, whose vocative singular ends -α, e.g. ἱκέτα or, for patronymics, which end -ιδης in the nominative singular, -η, e.g. 'Ατρείδη, O son of Atreus!

The vocative plural is like the nominative plural.

There are no 1st declension feminine duals in Homer. The 1st declension masculine dual is very rare. Chantraine (*op. cit.*, vol.i, p.202) notes only four examples, all in the nominative/accusative, with the ending -α, and all from the Iliad, as follows: αἰχμητά ("two spearmen") (vii, 281), 'Ατρείδα ("the two sons of Atreus") (i, 16 and 375 and xix, 310), κορυστά ("two helmeted men") (xiii, 201) and ὠκυπέτα ("two swiftly-flying", of horses) (viii, 42 and xiii, 24).

Second declension
Singular

nominative	ἑταῖρος	νῆσος	τέκνον
	companion	island	child
accusative	ἑταῖρον	νῆσον	τέκνον
	companion	island	child
genitive	ἑταίροιο or	νήσοιο or	τέκνοιο or
	ἑταίρου	νήσου	τέκνου
	of companion	of island	of child
dative	ἑταίρῳ	νήσῳ	τέκνῳ
	to/for companion	to/for/by island	to/for child

Dual

nominative	ἑταίρω	νήσω	τέκνω
	two companions	two islands	two children
accusative	ἑταίρω	νήσω	τέκνω
	two companions	two islands	two children
genitive	ἑταίροιιν	νήσοιιν	τέκνοιιν
	of two companions	of two islands	of two children
dative	ἑταίροιιν	νήσοιιν	τέκνοιιν
	to/for two companions	(to)/for/by two islands	to/for two children

Plural

nominative	ἑταῖροι	νῆσοι	τέκνα
	companions	islands	children
accusative	ἑταίρους	νήσους	τέκνα
	companions	islands	children
genitive	ἑταίρων	νήσων	τέκνων
	of companions	of islands	of children
dative	ἑταίροισι or	νήσοισι or	τέκνοισι or
	ἑταίροις	νήσοις	τέκνοις
	to/for companions	(to)/for, by islands	to/for children

The vocative singular of second declension nouns in -ος ends -ε, e.g. ἑταῖρε, o companion!

The vocative plural is like the nominative plural.

Conspectus of Grammar   233

Third declension
singular
nominative
πατήρ   πατρίς   πῆμα   λέχος   Ὀδυσ(σ)εύς
father   fatherland   woe   bed   Odysseus
accusative
πατέρα   πατρίδα   πῆμα   λέχος   Ὀδυσ(σ)έα
father   fatherland   woe   bed   Odysseus (object)
genitive
πατρός   πατρίδος   πήματος   λέχεος   Ὀδυσ(σ)ῆος
of father   of fatherland   of woe   of bed   of Odysseus
dative
πατρί   πατρίδι   πήματι   λέχει   Ὀδυσ(σ)ῆι
to/for father   to/for.by   to/for/by   to/for /by   to/for Odysseus
                 fatherland   woe   bed

Dual
nominative and accusative:
                    ὄσσε = two eyes
genitive and dative:
                    ποδοῖιν = of/with two feet

Plural
nominative   πατέρες   πατρίδες   πήματα   λέχεα
                 fathers   fatherlands   woes   beds
accusative   πατέρας   πατρίδας   πήματα   λέχεα
                 fathers   fatherlands   woes   beds
genitive   πατέρων or   πατρίδων   πημάτων   λεχέων
                 πατρῶν
                 of fathers   of fatherlands of woes   of beds
dative   (πατράσι)   πατρίσι   πήμασι   λεχέεσσι
                 to/for fathers to/for/by   to/for/by   to/for/by
                                 fatherlands   woes   beds

The irregular noun νηῦς
Singular   Plural
nominative νηῦς   ship (subject)   νῆες or νέες   ships (subject)
accusative νῆα or νέα   ship (object)   νῆας or νέας   ships (object)
genitive   νηός or νεός of ship   νηῶν or νεῶν   of ships
dative   νηΐ   (to, for) by ship   νηυσί   (to, for) by ships
                                               or νήεσσι or νεέσσι
                                               or ναῦφι (instrumental)

In most 3rd declension nouns, the vocative case (singular and plural) ends like the nominative. In a few instances there is a change in the vocative singular. In nouns ending -ηρ , the vocative singular ending is -ερ, e.g. the vocative singular of πάτηρ is πάτερ ("o father!"), and in nouns ending -ευς the vocative singular ends -ευ e.g. the vocative singular of Ὀδυσσεύς is Ὀδυσσεῦ (O Odysseus!).

Pronouns (from Section 8)

First and second person pronouns

Nominative:

| ἐγώ = I | σύ = you | ἡμεῖς or ἄμμες = we | ὑμεῖς or ὕμμες = you |

Accusative:

| (ἐ)μέ or με = me | σέ or σε = you | ἥμας or ἡμέας or ἄμμε = us | ὑμέας or ὕμμε = you |

Genitive

| ἐμεῖο or ἐμέο or ἐμεῦ or ἐμέθεν or μευ = of me, my | σεῖο or σέο or σεο or σέθεν or σευ = of you, your | ἡμείων or ἡμέων = of us, our | ὑμείων or ὑμέων = of you, your |

Dative

| (ἐ)μοί or μοι to/for me | σοί or σοι or τοι to/for you | ἡμῖν or ἄμμι to/for us | ὑμῖν or ὕμμι to/for you |

First and second person dual pronouns:

νώ or
νῶι
the two of us (nom. and acc.)

σφώ or
σφῶι
the two of you (nom. and acc.)

νῶιν
of, or to/for the two of us
(gen. and dat.)

σφῶιν or σφῷν
of, or to/for the two of you
(gen. and dat.)

Third person pronoun

accusative	ἕ or ἑ or μιν	= him, her
genitive	εἷο or ἕο or ἑο or ἕθεν or εὗ	= of him, of her
dative	ἑοῖ or οἷ or οἱ	= to/for him, to/for her

third person dual pronoun

σφωέ = the two of them (nominative & accusative)

σφωΐν = of, to, for, by the two of them (genitive & dative)

"That", 'this'; "he", "she", "it"; "the"

	masculine	feminine	neuter
singular			
nom	ὁ = that, he	ἡ = that, she	τό = that, it
acc	τόν = that, him	τήν = that, her	τό = that, it
gen	τοῦ = that's, his or τοῖο	τῆς = that's, her	τοῦ = that's its or τοῖο
dat	τῷ = to, for him	τῇ = to, for her	τῷ = by it

Conspectus of Grammar

dual
nom/acc   τώ = those two, they   -   τώ = those two, they
gen/dat   τοῖιν = of/to those two, them -   τοῖιν = of/by those two, them

plural

	masculine	feminine	neuter
nom	οἱ (τοί) = those, they	αἱ (ταί) = those, they	τά = those, they
acc	τούς = those, them	τάς = those, them	τά = those, them
gen	τῶν = of those, their	τῶν = of those, their	τῶν = of those, their
dat	τοῖσι or τοῖς = to/for them	τῇσι or τῆς = to/for them	τοῖσι or τοῖς = by them

οὗτος, αὕτη, τοῦτο   this, that

singular	masculine	feminine	neuter
nominative	οὗτος = this	αὕτη = this (woman)	τοῦτο = this (thing)
accusative	τοῦτον = this	ταύτην = this	τοῦτο = this
genitive	τούτου = of this	ταύτης	τούτου = of this
dative	τούτῳ = to/for this	[ταύτῃ = to/for this]	τούτῳ = by this

dual

nom/acc	τούτω = these two	–	τούτω = these two
gen/dat	τούτοιιν =of/to/for these two	–	τούτοιιν =of/by these two

plural

	masculine	feminine	neuter
nominative	οὗτοι = these (men)	[αὗται = these (women)]	ταῦτα = these (things)
accusative	τούτους = these	[ταύτας = these]	ταῦτα = these
genitive	τούτων = of these	[ταυτάων = of these]	τούτων = of these
dative	τούτοισι = to/for these	[ταύτῃσι = to/for these]	τούτοισι = by these

ὅδε, ἥδε, τόδε
With the suffix -δε, ὁ, ἡ, τό always means "this". So ὅδε = "this man", ἥδε = "this woman" and τόδε = "this thing".

Adjectives
First & second declension
φίλος, φίλη, φίλον = friendly, dear, own

	masculine	feminine	neuter
singular			
nominative	φίλος	φίλη	φίλον
vocative	φίλε	φίλη	φίλον
accusative	φίλον	φίλην	φίλον
genitive	φίλοιο	φίλης	φίλοιο
	or φίλου		or φίλου
dative	φίλῳ	φίλῃ	φίλῳ
dual			
nominative & accusative	φίλω	φίλα	φίλω
genitive & dative	φίλοιιν	φίληιν	φίλοιιν
plural			
nominative	φίλοι	φίλαι	φίλα
accusative	φίλους	φίλας	φίλα
genitive	φίλων	φιλάων	φίλων
dative	φίλοις	φίλης	φίλοις
	or φίλοισι	or φίλῃσι	or φίλοισι

Conspectus of Grammar 237

Irregular adjectives of the first and second declensions

singular	masculine	feminine	neuter
nominative	πολλός or πολύς or πουλύς much	πολλή much	πολλόν or πολύ or πουλύ much
accusative	πολλόν or πολύν or πουλύν much	πολλήν much	πολλόν or πολύ or πουλύ much
genitive	πολέος of much	πολλῆς of much	πολέος of much
dative	πολλῷ to/for much	πολλῇ to/for much	πολλῷ by much
plural			
nominative	πολλοί or πολέες or πολεῖς many	πολλαί many	πολλά many
accusative	πολλούς or πολέας many	πολλάς many	πολλά many
genitive	πολλῶν or πολέων of many	πολλάων or πολλέων of many	πολλῶν of many
dative	πολλοῖσι πολεέσι or πολέ(σ)σι to/for many	πολλῇσι to/for many	πολλοῖσι by many

	masculine	feminine	neuter
nominative	μέγας big	μεγάλη big	μέγα big
accusative	μέγαν big	μεγάλην big	μέγα big
genitive	μεγάλοιο or μεγάλου of big	μεγάλης of big	μεγάλοιο or μεγάλου of big
dative	μεγάλῳ to/for big	μεγάλῃ to/for big	μεγάλῳ by big

The dual and plural, μεγάλοι, μεγάλαι, μεγάλα have endings like the dual and plural of φίλος.

Adjectives with third declension masculine & neuter, and first declension feminine

πᾶς πᾶσα πᾶν every, all

singular	masculine	feminine	neuter
nominative	πᾶς	πᾶσα	πᾶν
accusative	πάντα	πᾶσαν	πᾶν
genitive	πάντος	πάσης	[πάντος]
dative	πάντι	πάσῃ	πάντι
plural			
nominative	πάντες	πᾶσαι	πάντα
accusative	πάντας	πάσας	πάντα
genitive	πάντων	πασάων	πάντων
dative	πάντεσσι *or* πᾶσι	πάσῃσιν *or* πάσαις	πάντεσσι *or* πᾶσι

Similarly, μέλας, μέλαινα, μέλαν ("black" or "dark")

SINGULAR	masculine	feminine	neuter
nominative	μέλας	μέλαινα	μέλαν
accusative	μέλανα	μέλαιναν	μέλαν
genitive	μέλανος	μελαίνης	μέλανος
dative	μέλανι[16]	μελαίνῃ	μέλανι
DUAL			
nom & acc	μέλανε	μελαίνα	μέλανε
gen & dat	μελάνοιιν	μελαίνῃιν	μελάνοιιν
PLURAL			
nominative	μέλανες	μέλαιναι	μέλανα
accusative	μέλανας	μελαίνας	μέλανα
genitive	μελάνων	μελαινάων[47]	μελάνων
dative	μελάνεσσι *or* μέλασι	μελαίνῃσι	μελάνεσσι *or* μέλασι

νημερτής sure and true

SINGULAR	masculine & feminine	neuter
nominative	νημερτής	νημερτές
accusative	νημερτέα	νημερτές
genitive	νημερτέος	νημερτέος
dative	νημερτέϊ	νημερτέϊ
DUAL		
nom., acc.	νημερτεῖ	νημερτεῖ
gen., dat.	νημερτοῖν	νημερτοῖν
PLURAL		
nominative	νημερτέες	νημερτέα
accusative	νημερτέας	νημερτέα
genitive	νημερτέων	νημερτέων
dative	νημερτέσσι(ν)	νημερτέσσι(ν)

[16]Only found in the form μείλανι (Iliad xxiv, 79).
[55]Found as μελαινέων at Iliad iv, 117.

Conspectus of Grammar

ὀξύς, ὀξεῖα, ὀξύ, sharp

SINGULAR	masculine	feminine	neuter
nominative	ὀξύς	ὀξεῖα	ὀξύ
accusative	ὀξύν	ὀξεῖαν	ὀξύ
genitive	ὀξέος	ὀξείης	ὀξέος
dative	ὀξέϊ	ὀξείῃ	ὀξέϊ
DUAL			
nom & acc	ὀξέε	ὀξεία	ὀξέε
gen & dat	ὀξέοιιν	ὀξείῃιν	ὀξέοιιν
PLURAL			
nominative	ὀξέες	ὀξεῖαι	ὀξέα
accusative	ὀξέας	ὀξείας	ὀξέα
genitive	ὀξέων	ὀξειάων	ὀξέων
dative	ὀξέσι	ὀξείῃσι	ὀξέσι

The feminine of μάκαρ, "blessed", is sometimes like the masculine, as follows:

	masculine & feminine		
	singular	[dual]	plural
nominative	μάκαρ	[μάκαρε]	μάκαρες
accusative	μάκαρα	[μάκαρε]	μάκαρας
genitive	μάκαρος	[μακάροιιν]	μακάρων
dative	μάκαρι	[μακάροιιν]	[μακάρεσσι]

but the feminine is more often 1st declension, μάκαιρα.

Adjectives which are third declension for all genders

μεγαλήτωρ, great hearted

singular	masculine & feminine	[neuter]
nominative	[μεγαλήτωρ]	[μεγάλητορ]
accusative	μεγαλήτορα	[μεγάλητορ]
genitive	μεγαλήτορος	[μεγαλήτορος]
dative	μεγαλήτορι	[μεγαλήτορι]
[dual		
nom. & acc.	[μεγαλήτορε]	[μεγαλήτορε]
gen. & dat.	[μεγαλητόροιιν]	[μεγαλητόροιιν]
plural		
nominative	μεγαλήτορες	[μεγαλήτορα]
accusative	μεγαλήτορας	[μεγαλήτορα]
genitive	[μεγαλητόρων]	[μεγαλητόρων]
dative	[μεγαλητόρεσσι]	[μεγαλητόρεσσι]

Elisions in Odyssey V

ἄλγε' : ἄλγεα
ἀλλ' : ἀλλά
ἀμφ' : ἀμφί
ἀοιδιάουσ' : ἀοιδιάουσα
ἀπ' : ἀπό
ἄρ' : ἄρα
ἀρίγνωτ' : ἀρίγνωτα (Odyssey VI, 300)
αὖτ' : αὖτε
αὐτίκ' : αὐτίκα
αὐτίχ' : αὐτίκα (before rough breathing)
βάλετ' (at 231): βάλετο
γ' : γε
γούναθ' (at 449): γούνατα
δ' : δέ
δεῖξ' : ἔδειξεν
δεῦρ' : δεῦρο
δώματ' : δώματα
δούρατ' : δούρατα
εἰπόντ' (at 313) : εἰπόντα
ἐλλάβετ' : ἐλάβετο
ἔνθ' : ἔνθα
ἔννυτ' : ἔννυτο
ἔπειθ' : ἔπειτα
ἔπειτ' : ἔπειτα
ἐπ' : ἐπί
ἐφ' : ἐπί (before a rough breathing)
ἔτ' : ἔτι
ἔφατ' : ἔφατο
ἠδ' : ἠδέ
ἤϊ' : ἤϊε(ν) (see Section 16)
κ' : κε
κερκίδ' : κερκίδι
κήδε' ; κήδεα
κῦμ' : κῦμα
κύματ' (at 385) : κύματα
μ' : με
μάλ' : μάλα
μετ' : μετά
μοῖρ' : μοῖρα
νήξομ' : νήξομαι
'Οδυσῆ' (at 336) : 'Οδυσῆα
'Οδυσῆ' (at 397) : 'Οδυσῆι
οἴκαδ' : οἴκαδε
ὀστέ' : ὀστέα
ὅτ' : ὅτε
οὐδ' : οὐδέ
οὔτ' ; οὔτε
ὄφρ' : ὄφρα
παῖδ' (at 18) : παῖδα
πάνθ' (at 403) : πάντα
παρ' : παρά
πέμπ' : (ἔ)πεμπε
πέτασ' (at 269) : (ἐ)πέτασε
ποιήσατ' : (ἐ)ποιήσατο
ποιήσετ' : ποιήσεται
πόλλ' : πολλά
ποτ' : ποτε
προτιόσσετ' : προτιόσσετο
ρ' : ρα (= ἄρα)
σ' : σε
τ' : τε
τ' ... τ' ... : τε ... τε ...
ταῦθ' : ταῦτα
τῇδ' : τῇδε
τηλόθ' : τηλόθι
τοῖσ' : τοῖσι
τότ' : τότε
τόφρ' : τόφρα
ὑπ' : ὑπό
φαθ' (at 451): (ἔ)φατο
φαίνεθ' (at 410): φαίνεται
φωνήσασ' : φωνήσασα
ὦδ' : ὦδε
ὦλετ' : ὦλετο

Answers

page 2 pseudo, character, stigma, crater, catastrophe, psyche, mania, diagnosis, phlox, Parthenon, metropolis, thermos.

Zeus, Styx, Nestor, Calypso, Zephyros, Poseid(a)on, Borees (usually Boreas), Telemachos, Cyclops, Nausicaa, Circe, Penelopeia (usually Penelope).

page 3 halma, idea, ethos, helix, Orion, hydra, epidermis, hypothesis, hippopotamos, isosceles, aer (air), horizon.

page 4 Euphrates, automaton, haimorrhagia (English, haemorrhage).

rhythm (in Greek, rhuthmos), rhododendron, rheumatism(os).
aristocracy, hypocrite, amphitheatre, apathy, rhapsody, ode, austere, sympathy, apoplexy.

Odysseus, Pallas Athene, Hermes, Artemis, Demeter, Hephaestus, Ithaca, Olympus, Heracles.

page 7 1.(the) fates. 2.(the) rooms *or* (the) houses. 3.(the) reports. 4.a messenger *or* the messenger. 5.(the) palace, *or* (the) halls. 6.(the) goddesses. 7.(the) messengers. 8.(the) gods *or* (the) goddesses. 9.a goddess *or* the goddess. 10.a god *or* the god, *or* a goddess *or* the goddess. 11.(the) two gods, (the) two goddesses. 12.a hall or the hall.

page 9 1.a *or* the beautiful land 2.a *or* the dear companion. 3.(the) sceptre-bearing gods. 4.an evil fate *or* the evil fate. 5.a *or* the noble child. 6.(the) immortal goddesses. 7.(the) evil woes. 8.a noble supplicant *or* the noble supplicant. 9.a dear fatherland *or* the dear fatherland *or* one's own fatherland 10.(the) good reports.

pages 9-10 1.The house is beautiful. 2.The report is not bad *or* it is not a bad report. 3.The friends were noble *or* they were noble friends.. 4.The gods are immortal. 5.Are you immortal? 6.Are you both immortal *or* are they both immortal? 7.Were they both immortal? 8.The children are bad *or* they are bad children. 9.The messengers are not immortal *or* the messengers are not immortals. 10.The fatherland was dear *or* it was (my, your, his, her, their) own (dear) fatherland. 11.The nymphs are noble *or* they are noble nymphs. 12.The palace was not (a) bad (one). 13 means the same as 12. 14.The woe is bad (the suffering is bad). 15.Was the bed bad? *or* was it a bad bed? 16.The bed is not bad *or* it's not a bad bed. 17.He was as (like) a kind father. (Odyssey V, 12). 18.High thundering Zeus, whose power is very great. (Odyssey V, 4) (κράτος is neuter.) 19.He came to Aegae (Aigai), where there is to him a famous palace (where he has a famous palace). (Odyssey V, 381) 20.The palace of my father great-hearted Alcinous is easily recognisable. (Odyssey VI, 299-300) 21.The land of the Phaeacians, where for you fate is for you to escape (where you are destined to escape). (Odyssey V, 345).

page 13 1.we are loosing 2.are we loosing? 3.they wish 4.he/she/it has 5.we rejoice 6.you are holding back 7.he/she/it is destroying 8.they are destroying 9. do you arouse? 10.the god swears 11.we do not wish 12.don't I rejoice? 13.the companions aren't rejoicing 14.the messengers are saying (affirming) 15.both the messengers are saying (affirming). 16.but both (your) father and (your) lady mother rejoice.(Odyssey VI, 30) 17.and (but) they always want freshly washed clothes.(Odyssey VI, 64) 18.There Calypso lives, fair-tressed, a terrible nymph. (Odyssey VII 245-6)

Beginning Greek with Homer

page 16 (i)1.I have a fine home. 2.You have an angry father. 3.Father Zeus has other children. 4.You have bad friends. 5.The people is glad; for the land is holding the sea back. 6.The sea is not destroying the land. 7.Athene is getting Nausicaa up early in the morning, but the other gods are not getting her up. 8.Nausicaa is glad; for she has a handsome father and a beautiful mother. 9.Do the children want newly-washed clothes? (Their) father and lady mother say so. 10.Zeus swears oaths, but he does not control fate. 11.The gods and goddesses are sitting down for a meeting. 12.Destiny controls men and immortals.

(ii) 1.Odysseus is sending his companions over the sea. 2.The nymph is not sending the companions into the hall. 3.The immortals are always sending messengers to men. 4.We are not sending messengers to our own country.

page 17 1.Are you sending a messenger to the gods? 2.The nymph is not sending me into the palace. 3.Alas! Odysseus and Agamemnon are sending us over the sea. 4.But they are sending you to Scylla and Charybdis. 5.I and you are glad; for the report is not true. 6.You are hardhearted, gods! 7.Son of Laertes, descended from Zeus, resourceful Odysseus, do you in this way want to go home to your own country all at once, now? 8.But harsh sorrow is reaching me. 9.The stranger is urgently requesting an escort. 10.Me does Zeus's daughter Aphrodite always dishonour, and she loves destructive Ares. 11.But (my) mother and father and all (my) other companions call me Noman. 12.He loves both your son and prudent Penelope.

page 20 1.You are loosing for yourself *or* you are being loosed (singular). 2.We loosing for ourselves *or* we are being loosed. 3.He/she/it is loosing for him/her/itself *or* he/she/it is being loosed. 4. He/she/it is being carried. 5.He/she/it is arising. 6.We are being carried. 7.You are arising. (plural) 8.You are arising. (singular) 9.You are being carried. (singular) 10.They are being carried. 11.Are you arising? (plural) 12.We are arising. 13.You are being carried. (plural) 14.They are carrying. 15.They are arousing. 16.He/she/it is arousing. 17.Are you being carried? (plural) 18.We are not being carried. 19.Aren't you arising? (plural) 20.We aren't arising.

She, in truth, then, so saying went away, (did) Athene with gleaming eyes towards Olympus, where they affirm of the gods a safe seat always to be: neither by winds is it shaken nor ever by rain is it wetted nor does snow come near, but utterly clear sky has been spread cloudless, and white radiance has spread over (it): in it the happy gods enjoy themselves all (their) days. (Odyssey VI, 41-47)

page 21 1.The nymph is lighting the fire. 2. The fire is burning. 3.The nymph is having the fire lit. 4.The god is delighted seeing Calypso's home. (τέρπεται is passive).

page 22 (a)1.You are enjoying yourself *or* You are (being) delighted.. 2.You can. 3.You remember. 4.You are answering. 5.You are coming *or* you are going. 6.You are arising. 7.You are not answering. 8.Are you coming (going)? 9.You don't remember. 10.Aren't you enjoying yourself? Aren't you delighted? (All singular)

(b) 1.We are lying down. 2.They are lying down. (*The reason why* κέαται *means "they are lying down" is that* κεῖμαι *is also a perfect passive verb meaning "I have been put", and some perfect passive verbs can have* -αται *instead of* -νται *in the third person plural ending (see p.137, footnote 1).* 3.You can.(plural) 4.He/she/it is answering. 5.They are coming (going). 6.You (singular) are burning. 7.We don't remember. 8.Are you arising? 9.Are you having the fire lit? 10.The fire is already burning.

Answers

(c) 1.We are rejoicing.   2.We are enjoying ourselves *or* We are delighted.   3.We are getting the children up.   4.The children are being got up.   5.The dawn is rising. 6.The gods are coming to a council.   7.Athene is speaking.   8.Is high-thundering Zeus answering?   9.He is not always cruel (*or* harsh, dangerous etc.)   10.Necessity and Right control the gods;   Zeus is controlled by Necessity.

page 23   1.I want to have a fine house.   2.The father wants to control the bad child. 3.The father is not able to control the bad child.   4.Odysseus wants to reach his own country.   5.High-thundering Zeus cannot control fate.   6.We can't light the fire; we are being destroyed by cold.   7.The messengers don't have horses;   they can't come.   8.The messengers are not answering;   "the reason is (γάρ), we can't remember", they say.   9.Odysseus can't arouse his companions.   10.The immortals don't want the suppliant to reach his fatherland.   11.The gods are said to be happy.   12.High-thundering Zeus is said to be the father of the gods.

page 25   κάλλιστοι πατέρες καλὰ τέκν' οὐκ αἰὲν ἔχουσιν
Ζεὺς ὑψιβρεμέτης, οὗ τε κράτος ἐστὶ μέγιστος (Odyssey V, 4) (masculine caesura after ὑψιβρεμέτης).

page 28   1.genitive singular, λέχος.   2.nominative plural, accusative   plural, πῆμα. 3.genitive plural, δῶμα.   4.accusative singular, πατήρ.   5.genitive plural, λέχος. 6.accusative plural, πατήρ.   7.nominative plural, πατήρ.   8.accusative singular, πατρίς. 9.genitive singular, δῶμα.   10.nominative plural *or* accusative   plural, δῶμα. 11.genitive plural, μάκαρ.   12.genitive singular, 'Οδυσσεύς.

page 29   1.genitive singular.   2.nominative plural.   3.accusative plural.   4.nominative singular, accusative singular.   5.accusative singular (either masculine or feminine), nominative plural (neuter), accusative plural (neuter).

1.Somebody is coming.   2.Who is coming?   3.Who is speaking?   4.What does he/she say?   5.Whose home is it?   6.It's somebody's home.   7.Some god.

page 30   1.Whose home is it?   The house of the nymph.   2.The home of the suppliant. 3.The house of the god.   4.The hall of some god.   5.Our home.   6.The child's bed. 7.The child's bed.   8.The bed of the Dawn Goddess.   9.The palace of the goddesses. 10.The palace of the gods *or* of the goddesses.   11.The island of the nymph.   12.My eye.   13.Odysseus' companions.   14.Odysseus' raft.   15.Into your country.   16.The gods and goddesses of the land are happy.   17.The nymph's palace is fine.   18.You, who are you?   We are the companions of godlike Odysseus.   But you, who are you? 19.Whose messenger are you?   20.I am the messenger of Zeus the high thunderer and of the other blessed gods.   21.Who is lord of the sea?   Poseidon the earth-shaker; he is not a friend of Odysseus.

page 31   1.The gods do not remember you.   2.Who is destroying your eye, Cyclops? Noman.   3.Our country lies far from the sea.   4.From among (*literally* out of) the Ethiopians.   5.But Dawn arises from (*literally*, out of) bed (*literally*, beds) from beside noble Tithonus.   6.Noble Calypso is sending Odysseus (away) from the island. 7.Nobody remembers godlike Odysseus.   8.And far from the raft he fell, and the steering oar did he let go out of his hands.

page 35   1.imperfect, 2nd singular active.   2.imperfect, 2nd plural active.   3.present, 3rd singular active.   4.imperfect, 2nd singular active.   5.present, 3rd singular active.   6.present.   1st singular middle/passive.   7.imperfect, 1st singular middle/passive.   8.(as no.7).   9.present, 3rd plural active.   10.(i)imperfect, 1st singular active   (ii)imperfect, 3rd plural active.   11.(as no.10).   12.present, 3rd plural active.

Beginning Greek with Homer

13.imperfect, 3rd plural middle/passive.   14.(as no.13).   15.present, 2nd singular, active.   16.imperfect, 2nd singular active.   17.(i)present, 1st plural, active (ii)imperfect, 1st plural active.   18.present, 3rd singular middle.   19.imperfect, 3rd singular middle.   20.imperfect, 3rd singular active.   21.imperfect, 3rd plural middle. 22. (as 21)   23.present, 3rd plural active.   24.imperfect, 3rd plural active.   25.imperfect, 3rd singular active.

1.You were loosing.   2.Were you loosing?   3.You are loosing.   4.You were loosing. 5.I was lighting the fire *or* they were lighting the fire.   6.The fire was burning *or* he/she was having the fire lit.   7.The fire is burning *or* he/she is having the fire lit.   8.I was lighting the fire.   9.I was having the fire lit.   10.They were having the fire lit again.   11.Zeus controls neither fate nor necessity.   12.Zeus used to control neither fate nor necessity.   13.(The) messengers used to come, but they used not to bring a report, nor used they to answer.   14.Athene was speaking, but the immortals could not hear.   15.At first the blessed immortals both rejoiced and were enjoying themselves.   16.Then they began to become angry.   17.Both the gods and goddesses were answering "we do not remember Odysseus, neither are we willing to send him home."

page 40 He is lying in an island.   In a ship.

1.The gods and goddesses are answering Zeus.   2.The companions of Odysseus are in (i.e. on board) a ship *or* The companions are on board Odysseus' ship.   3.The god is bringing a message from Zeus to the fair-tressed nymph.   4.The Cyclops is on another island.   5.There is to Odysseus a fine palace (= Odysseus has a fine palace). 6.In the sea the waves were becoming dangerous.   7.Zeus has the fate of mankind in his hand.   8.Odysseus' raft was being destroyed by the waves.   9.Furthermore, noble Odysseus is getting saved from the sea by fate.   10.Zeus was like a kind father to the suppliants.   11.Odysseus is coming to his native land after many troubles. 12.Odysseus is coming to his native land with many troubles.

page 41 1.O suppliant!   2.O goddess!   3.O messenger!   4.O messengers!   5.O companion! 6.O immortals!   7.O Priam, son of Dardanus!   8.O son of Laertes, descended from Zeus, ingenious Odysseus!

page 45 1.2nd person plural (present) optative (active).   2.1st person singular, (present) optative (middle).   3.3rd person plural (present) optative (middle).   4.3rd person plural (present) optative (active).   5.2nd person singular (present) indicative (active).   6.2nd person singular (present) optative (active).   7.2nd person singular (present) indicative (active).   8.1st person singular (present) optative (middle). 9.2nd person plural (present) indicative (middle).   10.2nd person plural (present) optative (middle/passive).

1.O that I might say (speak)!   2.O that they might answer!   3.O that you might rejoice!   4.O that I might enjoy myself/ be delighted!   5.O that he/she/it might not come!   6.O that you might be happy, O Odysseus!   7.O that Zeus the high thunderer might be kind to us!   8.The nymph wanted to send the maidservant into the palace to light the fire (so that she might light the fire).   9.The nymph wanted to send the maidservant into the palace so that the fire might be lit (*or* so that the fire might get lit).   10.The maidservant was not getting out of bed so that she might not light the fire.

pages 49 1.They, the gods remember (are mindful of) godlike Odysseus.   2.He indeed wants to arrive at his native land, but he does not have ships and companions. 3.The fair tressed nymph has (i.e. owns or possesses) that island.   4.The gods are sitting down to whom Athene is speaking.   5.The gods, whose father is Zeus the

Answers

high thunderer, are sitting down.   6.Whose is that island?   It belongs to (literally, is of) the fair-tressed nymph.

page 50 νύμφης Καλυψοῦς.

page 51 λαῶν is genitive, οἷσιν is dative.

1.The nymph who is fair-tressed owns the island.   2.Odysseus is lying in the island which the fair-tressed nymph owns.   3.Odysseus does not have companions who might take him over the wide back of the sea.   4.Zeus the high thunderer whose power is very great is lord over the other gods.   5.Athene was telling the misfortunes of Odysseus which no one remembers.   6.Hermes is coming who is in fact the messenger of the gods.

page 52 1.But, look you, he will send a following wind behind, whichever of the gods is protecting you (i.e., whichever of the gods is protecting you will send a following wind behind).   2.The messengers do not wish to say who they are.

1.The nymph is holding back her companion by necessity.   2.The nymph is keeping him in her halls.   3.But Odysseus cannot reach his native land.   4.The dawn is getting out of her bed.   5.Tithonus is not getting out of his bed.   6.The companions of Odysseus are being borne over the wide back of the sea in their ship.

page 54 1.Who is this man?   2.Who is this man?   3.This nymph is Calypso.   4.This palace is Calypso's.   5.What is this intention which Athene has?   6.I don't know this intention which Athene has.

1.He (i.e. that man) was like a kind father.   2.Zeus the high thunderer is answering her (i.e. that woman).   3.Those men do not remember Odysseus.   4.Odysseus is lord over those men.   5.Zeus is not sending those men to their native land.   6.Since then neither did I see Odysseus nor he (literally, that man) me.

page 55 1.Even I myself know.   2.Athene herself was speaking.   3.She says, "I am the child of Zeus himself."   4.The suitors themselves are in the ship.   5.Hermes, you yourself are the messenger of the immortals.

page 57 1.This (man) is Odysseus; he wants to reach his high-roofed palace.   2.Athene, are you sending him home?   Indeed, you are able (to do so).   3.I am sending him home;   for it is his destiny (destiny is for him) to go towards his native land. 4.Zeus the high thunderer was addressing Hermes, his child.   5."I want you to tell (my) sure-and-true plan to the fair-tressed nymph," he said.   6.Hermes tied on the fine sandals, divinely fair, made of gold, which used to carry him.

page 62 1.aorist.   2.imperfect.   3.aorist.   4.aorist.   5.imperfect.   6.aorist.   7.imperfect. 8.imperfect.   9.aorist.   10.aorist.   11.imperfect.   12.aorist.

1.We loosed.   2.Did they loose?   3.You loosed for yourself.   4.Did you loose for yourself?   5.O that he/she might loose for him/herself!   6.O that they might answer! 7.They sent.   8.They were lighting.   9.They lit.   10.He disobeyed.   11.He/she tied (on) for him/herself.   12.He/she/it darted.   13.He/she/it rode.   14.The man lit the fire.   15.The winds aroused the waves.   16.Did you send (your)companions into this cave?   17.Were you sending your companions into this cave?   18.Did you send your companions into this cave? (as no.16, but verb not augmented)   19.Did you tie your fine sandals under your feet, Hermes?   20.In the sea, the bird darted over the waves.   21.In the sea, the bird is darting over the waves. 22.In the sea, the bird was darting over the waves.

Beginning Greek with Homer

page 67 1.imperfect 2.aorist 3.aorist 4.imperfect 5.imperfect 6.aorist 7.aorist 8.imperfect 9.aorist 10.imperfect 11.imperfect 12.aorist

1.He/she/it threw (hit, put). 2.I was throwing (hitting, putting). 3.The companions took the gold. 4.They threw the gold into the sea. 5.We took the gold of Odysseus. 6.We took his gold. 7.The word escaped the fence of Athene's teeth. 8.Hermes saw the nymph's cave. 9.Then he spoke a word to the nymph. 10.Odysseus himself fell from the raft. 11.Did you get hold of the raft again, Odysseus? 12.Did Odysseus get hold of the raft?

page 68 1.The god came out of the violet-coloured sea towards the land. 2.But in the island he found long-winged birds. 3.Hermes reached the great cave. 4.He found the nymph at home. 5.The long-winged birds did not flee. 6.What did you see around the nymph's cave? 7.What did you say to the fair-tressed nymph? 8.Hermes told the plan of Zeus, sure and true, to the fair tressed nymph in the hollow cave in which she herself was living. 9.Hermes took his rod (for himself). 10.Poseidon grasped his trident in his hands.

page 71 1.Odysseus was weeping, sitting on the headland. 2.The god, answering with words, addressed the goddess. 3.I see trouble coming. 4.Hermes saw the nymph plying the loom.

pages 72-3 1.Suffering (nominative masculine singular). 2.The nymph singing (nominative singular). 3.The child singing (nominative *or* accusative singular). 4.The fire being lit (nominative *or* accusative singular). 5.A bird hunting fish. 6.An island being distant. 7.Odysseus suffering woes. 8.Odysseus is lying in the island suffering woes. 9.Hermes found the nymph singing in a beautiful voice. 10.The gods enjoy seeing each other. 11.Hermes reaches the islands, being distant. (Hermes reaches the islands which are distant.) 12.The Messenger, the Slayer of Argus, came into the wide cave of the nymph living far away (of the nymph who lived far away). 13.Hermes did not find Odysseus rending his spirit with woes (Odysseus who was breaking his heart with woes). 14.But Calypso was not sitting on the headland weeping. 15.The close-set feathers of birds hunting fish get wet in the salt spray. 6.The Messenger, the Slayer of Argus was gazing at the birds roosting in the wood.

page 74 1.speaking *or* having spoken (masculine singular nominative). 2.speaking *or* having spoken (feminine nominative singular). 3.sending *or* h a v i n g sent (neuter). 4.(of) having sent *or* of sending (feminine singular). 5.(of) having sent *or* of sending (masculine or neuter singular). 6.answering *or* having answered (nominative feminine singular). 7.lighting *o r* having lit (nominative masculine singular). 8.lighting *or* having lit (nominative feminine singular). 9.lighting *o r* having lit (nominative feminine plural). 10.sending *or* having sent (nominative masculine plural). 11.(to/for) sending *or* (to/for) having sent (dative feminine plural). 12.Having said this (with these words) the nymph went into the cave. 13.Then, speaking thus (*or* having spoken thus) the nymph put the table beside him. 14.The Phaeacians suffered evil things having sent Odysseus in their ship to his own fatherland. *(This could imply: because they had sent Odysseus in their ship to his own fatherland.)* 15.But Athene was telling many troubles to the gods, remembering Odysseus. 16.Zeus the cloud gatherer was answering her having spoken these things (after she had spoken these things).

page 75 1.seeing *or* having seen (masculine accusative singular *o r* neuter nominative/accusative plural). 2.(to/for *or* by) seeing *or* having seen (masculine *o r* neuter dative plural). 3.fleeing *or* having fled (masculine nominative singular). 4.fleeing (present participle) (masculine nominative singular). 6.coming/going

Answers

or having come/gone (feminine nominative singular). 7.coming/going *or* having come/gone (neuter nominative/accusative singular). 7.suffering (present participle) (masculine nominative singular). 8.suffering *or* having suffered (feminine nominative singular). 9.saying/speaking *or* having said/spoken (masculine nominative singular). 10.having/holding/keeping *or* having had/held/kept (masculine nominative singular). 11.finding *or* having found (feminine nominative singular). 12.reaching *or* having reached (feminine nominative singular)(from ἱκόμην, the aorist of ἱκνέομαι). 13.taking/accepting *or* having taken/accepted (masculine nominative plural). 14.Having come into the island, the Messenger, the Slayer of Argus was admiring the home of Calypso. 15.Seeing the god, the nymph did not fail to recognise him.

page 77 1.Zeus does not control fate although he is a god. 2.Calypso did not fail to recognise Hermes although she lives in (inhabits) a palace far away. 3.Calypso, seeing Hermes, was not glad although he is both to be respected and dear. 4.Though he had stopped while he was gazing, then at once the Messenger, the Slayer of Argus, went into the wide cave. 5.Then Hermes, though reaching (i.e. he reached) the island, did not find Odysseus. 6.Then Hermes did not find Odysseus even though he (Odysseus) was in the island. 7.Great hearted Odysseus, sitting on the headland, is breaking his heart with tears. 8.Looking at all the island, Hermes is pleased. 9.Sitting on a chair, the Messenger, the Slayer of Argus, was eating and drinking. 10.Even living in palaces far away, the immortals do not fail to recognise each other. (Not even though they live in palaces far away, do the immortals fail to recognise each other.) 11.Hermes addressed the nymph, having seated him on a chair. (After the nymph had seated him on a chair, Hermes addressed her.) 12.Then, speaking thus, the goddess mixed the red nectar. 13.But after his feast (having feasted) the Messenger, the Slayer of Argus addressed her, answering with words.

page 83 1.You will plan. (singular) 2.They will plan. 3.Will you plan? (plural) 4.We shall be. 5.Will you be friends? (plural) 6.Will it be terrible? 7.He/she/it is remaining. 8.He/she/it will remain. 9.They will send. 10.He/she/it will not send. 11.Odysseus, you will be our chief. 12.You will endure. (singular) 13.Will he/she endure? 14.We shall not endure the pain. 15.You (plural) will have the gold. 16.We do not have the gold. (NB, ἔχομεν is present.)

page 83 1.I shall shiver. 2.You will order. (singular) 3.Look you, the god will tell that story surely and truly. 4.Athene will raise up for them both an evil wind and long waves. 5.There the immortals will utterly destroy all the brave companions.

page 90 1.Say! Speak! (singular, present imperative) 2.Say! speak! *or* you are saying, you are speaking. (plural, present imperative or present indicative) 3.Stop speaking. (μή + present imperative) 4.Let him/her/it say, speak. (present imperative) 5.Say! Speak! (singular, aorist imperative) 6.Let them say, let them speak. (aorist imperative) 7.Send! (singular, aorist imperative) 8.Drive! (singular, aorist imperative) 9.Do this! (plural, aorist imperative) 10.Stop doing that! (plural, μή + present imperative) 11.You are not doing that. (plural, present indicative) (NB negative is οὐ.) 12.Take hold of this! (singular, aorist imperative) 13.Let Odysseus stop following his companions. (μή + present imperative) 14.See your friends! (singular, aorist imperative) 15.Gods, stop being jealous of the goddesses. (μή + present imperative) 16.Stop being hard-hearted, gods; for you are blessed, living easily (because you live easily, have an easy life). 17.May Artemis attack you with her arrows! 18.Let great-hearted Odysseus reach his fatherland if it is permitted by fate. 19.Let the nymph save him, having nurtured him and befriended him (taken hin into her home). 20.Zeus, smash the swift ship of Odysseus, having driven (it) in the middle of the wine-faced sea, for his companions killed the cattle of the Sun!

page 95 1.Let me answer. 2.Let hm/her love. 3.Let them drive. 4.Let us throw *or* let us hit. 5.Let it not happen. 6.May you come. 7.Let me not wish. 8.Let me not keep you. 9.Let him/her not order you to do this. 10.Let us send this man.

page 96 1.Let me throw *or* let me hit. 2.May you reach. 3.Let us do *or* let us make. 4.Let him/her fall. 5.Don't drink! (singular) 6.Let us send this man. 7.Let me see. 8.Let me see. 9.Let them not suffer. 10.Do not swear an oath! (singular)

page 100 1.Let us return home! 2.Let us not get angry. 3.I am afraid that this may be true (in the future);I am afraid that the sea may become murky. 4.I am afraid that this is (already) true; I am afraid that the sea is murky. 5.Odysseus is making a raft in order that he may escape from the island. (Odysseus is making a raft to escape from the island.) 6.He is fleeing from the island so that (his) sweet life may not slip away here. 7.Send Odysseus away now, lest Zeus, look you, may somehow afterwards get angry. (Look, send Odysseus away now so that Zeus may not somehow get angry later.) 8.Odysseus, fit a wide raft together for yourself with bronze so that it may carry you over the wine-faced sea. 9.He/she will send a following wind behind so that you may reach your fatherland quite safe and sound. 10.Come, let us send Odysseus away, and let us bring food and water and sustaining red wine for him.

page 103 1.ἀποπέμπω. 2.ἀναπίμπλημι. 3.νήχω 4.βουλεύω. 5.ὄνομαι.

1.ἀπέκτεινα ἀποκτείνω. 2.εἶδον ὁράω (p.67) 3.ἱκόμην ἱκνέομαι. (p.66) 4.(ἐ)τέλεσα τελέω. 5.παρεξῆλθον παρεξέρχομαι. 6.ἀλίωσα (ἡλίωσα) ἀλιόω. 7.(ἐ)νόησα νοέω. 8.(ἔ)κρηνα κραίνω.

pages 109-110 1.He/she/it is putting. 2.They are putting. 3.They put. 4.They put. 5.They were putting. 6.You put for yourself. 7.To put. (aorist) 8.Having put *or* putting (masculine nominative plural). 9.Put for yourself! 10.Calypso was putting all (kinds of) food beside Odysseus to eat and drink. 11.But beside the nymph the maids put ambrosia and nectar. 12.Are you ordering me to cross the great gulf of the sea by a raft? 13.I order you, goddess, to swear a great oath. 14.Are you willing to swear not to be going to devise any other trouble for me myself? 15.What kind of a word you took into your head to say, Odysseus! (=Where did you get the idea of making such a speech, Odysseus?)

page 115-6 1.Are we going? 2.You are not going. (singular) 3.Zeus, the father of the gods, is going to Olympus. 4.The gods are immortal. 5.Your companions are not able to go home. 6.We see that our ship is coming home. (We see our ship coming home.) 7.I saw your children going home. 8.Go, tell the fair-tressed nymph these things. (Go and tell the fair-tressed nymph this.) 9.The very wise Odysseus wants to go to his fatherland now, at once. 10.The lady, the nymph, was going towards great hearted Odysseus. 11.And Calypso, the noble (one) of goddesses, set off towards a corner of the hollow cave. 12.Lady goddess, stop being angry with me for this (*literally*, in respect of this (*accusative of respect*)); for I am going home all the same. 13.Ingenious Odysseus, let us go at once; for thus do I want and long both to go home and to see (for myself) the day of my homecoming. 14.In my heart I know how many troubles are awaiting me.

page 122-3 1.When the nymph was devising a means of getting home for Odysseus, she gave him a large axe. 2.When she began the road to the far end of the island, Odysseus was walking behind. 3.And then Odysseus drilled the timbers before fitting them to each other. 4.But while he was cutting the wood, at that point

Calypso, noble of goddesses, brought him gimlets. 5.But when he had made the mast, and the yardarm fitted to it, then he made the steering oar as well, so that he might keep (the raft) straight.

page 128 (a)1.They were not loosed. 2.Odysseus was not glad. 3.The (a) fire was lit. 4.(The) mountains appeared. 5.The maidservants were glad to see the god (having seen the god). 6. Was everything finished well?.

1.Already it was day and for him everything was finished. 2.And in the ship for him a wineskin was put of dark wine. 3.And in the ship for him provisions were put, many satisfying (ones). 4.To Odysseus seeing, appeared the Pleiades. (As Odysseus looked, the Pleiades appeared.) 5.And Odysseus was glad, sailing the sea for seventeen days, and on the eighteenth appeared the mountains of the land of the Phaeacians.

page 133 1.Noble Odysseus is no longer willing to have his bed in the nymph's cave. 2.Having departed from the cave, Odysseus is going swiftly towards the raft. 3.The lord, the earth-shaker, seeing Odysseus roving over the sea, stirred up the ocean. 4.Odysseus' knees and own heart were loosed; he fell from the raft. (Odysseus' knees began to knock and his heart to tremble; he fell off the raft.) 5.Amid the waves, dashing after the raft, he was saved. 6.Odysseus, until again you mingle with men, you will be unfortunate. 7.The goddess was ordering all the winds to cease and be lulled until such time as Odysseus, descended from Zeus, might mingle with the Phaeacians.

page 139 ἐπιχέω, δύω, τελέω, φυλάσσω.
1.to have gone (the perfect infinitive of βαίνω found at Iliad xvii, 359 and 510; the 1st person plural perfect, "we have gone" would be βεβάαμεν). 2.to have fled 3.to have been completed 4.to have appeared.

page 140 1.Woe is me, how wretched I am, my knees have begun to knock (*or* my knees have lost their strength; literally, my knees have now been loosed). 2.Suddenly the sea has been thrown into confusion; with what (kind of) clouds Zeus is enwreathing the broad sky! 3.A terrible hurricane has arisen, and has thrown me far away from the raft. 4.The raft has been driven by the hurricane; the fastenings of the raft have been loosened by the waves. 5.And now certain, utter destruction and death have been revealed for me; I am done for.

page 145 1.And I order you to think that (those things) over. 2.And he shouted fearfully, and made himself heard to all the gods. 3.You are neither like a bad nor a senseless man. 4.And we are striving both to be most worthy of care and dearest to you of the others, as many as (are) Achaeans (i.e. of all the Achaeans) (i.e., and we are striving to be the most worthy of care and dearest to you of all the Achaeans).

page 147 1.Do you know these things? 2.We know these things well. 3.I hope you to know these things (i.e. I hope you know these things). 4.Do you hope the gods to be going to save you? (i.e. Do you hope that the gods will save you?) (σαωσέμεν is the infinitive of σαώσω, the future of σαόω.) I order you to act thus. 5.Do you yourselves know this? 6.We know (it); for we ourselves saw this. 7.How did Ino of the fair ankles see Odysseus? We don't know this. (NB, εἶδον and ἴδον, the aorist of ὁράω, must be carefully distinguished from οἶδα.) 8.But to you do the suitors answer thus, so that you may know, yourself in your heart, and all the Achaeans may know.

page 153 1.Knowing (feminine nominative singular). 2.Being like (neuter nominative or accusative singular). 3.Having come into being, having happened (nominative masculine plural).   4.The eager child (nominative or accusative).   5.A sceptre-bearing king sprung from Zeus.   6.A wind like a hurricane.   7.A girl knowing many things.   8.A man making himself heard (by) shouting.   9.Suppliants hoping (for) good things.   10.A god like a seagull-bird.   11.It has been brought to accomplishment (by fate). (See p.79, footnote 55.)   12.Eager suppliants.   13.Fountains facing (turned) this way and that.   14.Circe drove the companions out like fat hogs nine seasons old.   15.Odysseus is ordering the companions to carry the dead body into the palace of Circe.   16.He himself fell down face down into the sea, eager to swim.   17.My glorious clothes are lying dirty.   18.And with both hands he eagerly grabbed the rock.   19.In the axe is a handle, very fine, made of olive wood, well fitted.   20.Him indeed did Athene, the offspring of Zeus, make bigger to behold.

page 155   1.A wood had grown.   (Since it was still there and had not stopped growing, we might say "a wood was growing").   2.Zeus ordered.   (ἄνωγα has present meaning in English).   3.Everything had been finished.   4.For his own heart had been subdued by the sea.   5.The shining doors were closed (had been closed).   6.And she, as a breath of wind, rushed towards the maiden's bed.   (σεύω: I set (something or someone) in motion) ἔσσυμαι (perfect middle/passive): I have been set in motion, I rush ἐσσύμην (pluperfect middle/passive): I rushed).   7.The kings of the Argives were following, as many as had been called to the council.   8.Having seen that, I was amazed in my mind for a long time (literally, I had been struck with amazement (and remained so)) (Garvie (*Odyssey VI-VIII*, p.124) notes this as a pluperfect with imperfect sense.)

page 162   1.Hermes rode over many waves.   2.Of a certainty, she is dishonouring these Phaeacians among the people who, both many and noble, are wooing her.   3,Indeed, I liken you to Artemis, the daughter of great Zeus.   4.And him did the great wave cover.   5.But he, long-suffering noble Odysseus, went through the hall in a great mist (literally, having much mist) which Athene poured over him.   6.Who (is) this stranger, both handsome and tall, (who) is following Nausicaa?   7.There is a certain rocky island in the middle of the sea ... Asteris, not large.   8.There of a certainty were rock basins for washing clothes, always full, and much fine water used to flow up and out (of them).

page 166 1.Nausicaa, the daughter of great-hearted Alcinous.   2.I see Odysseus, sprung from Zeus, the son of Laertes.   3.Fair-tressed Dawn is bringing light for the blessed gods.   4.Zeus granted Odysseus to behold an unhoped-for land.   5.A way out of the grey sea did not appear in any way.   6.For outside were sharp rocks.   7.I fear lest the hurricane having snatched me up again may carry me over the sea (which is) full of fish.   8.He is lying down, suffering mighty pains.   9.There were headlands jutting out, both rocks over which the sea dashes and crags.   10. And for so long was the great wave carrying him towards the rugged headland.

page 173   1.If only I might see my native land!   2.If I were to see my native land, I should rejoice.   3.If I see my native land, I shall perform sacrifices and choice hecatombs.   4.If ever I see my native land, I rejoice.   5.If this is really true, I am glad.   6.There he would have been stripped as far as his skin was concerned, and his bones would have been smashed, if the goddess, bright-eyed Athene, had not put a suggestion upon his mind (i.e., in his mind).   8.There would poor Odysseus have died contrary to his destiny if bright-eyed Athene had not given him wisdom.

page 180   1.To do this to me thinking seemed to be more profitable = As I thought, it seemed more advantageous to do this..   2.Sleep will cause all men to cease from the most toilsome weariness.   3.What are we to suffer?   What will happen to us in the end?   4.Nothing is better than this, to reach one's own country.

Word list
α

ἄγαμαι: I am jealous, angry[1] (13)

ἄγε : come!, come on, then! (14)

ἄγγελος 2m: messenger (2)

ἄγκιστος -η -ον: nearest (18)

ἀγρός 2m: field (25)

ἄγχι[2] : near (12)

ἀγχοῦ: near[3] (14)

ἀεκήτι: against the will (15)

ἀθάνατος -η -ον: immortal (2)

Ἀθηναίη or Ἀθήνη: Athene (7)

αἱ = εἱ

αἴγειρος 2f: black poplar (10)

αἰγίοχος: aegis-bearing[4] (12)

αἰδοῖος -α -ον: to be respected (11)

αἰεί or αἰέν: always (2, 3)

αἱρέομαι (aorist εἱλόμην): I take for myself, I choose (10))

αἱρέω: I take, grasp (aorist εἷλον) (10)

αἶσα (1f): lot, destiny (16)

αἶψα: all of a sudden (20)

αἰών, αἰῶνος 3m: lifetime (14)

ἀκουή (1f): report (2)

ἀκούω: I hear (23)

ἀκτή (3f): headland (14)

ἀλάομαι: I wander (21)

ἄλγος (3n): pain, woe (7)

ἀλλ᾽ , ἀλλά: but (6)

ἀλλήλους -ας -α: each other (10)

ἄλλοθεν: from another place (25)

ἄλλος, ἄλλη, ἄλλο: other (3)

ἄλμη (1f): brine, salt water (20)

ἅλς, ἁλός (3 m): salt, sea (9)

ἀλύσκω[5]: I escape (21)

ἅμα: at the same time, (+ dative): together with (9)

ἅμαξα (1f): waggon[6] (18)

ἀμείβομαι (aorist ἠμειψάμην): I reply, (with accusative) I answer (4)

ἀμφί + accusative: around, concerning (10)

ἀμφιέννυμι[7]: I put round (14)

ἀμφότεροι, ἀμφότεραι ἀμφότερα: both (23)

ἄν: in that case (see κεν).

ἀνά + accusative: up, along (10)

ἀναβαίνω (aorist participle ἀναβάς): I go up (25)

ἀνάγκη 1f: necessity (3)

ἄναξ, ἄνακτος (3m): lord (24)

ἀναπίμπλημι: I fulfil (16)

ἄνεμος, ἀνέμοιο (2 m): wind (9)

ἀνήρ, ἀνδρός (or ἀνέρος) (3 m): man[8] (9)

ἄνθρωπος, ἀνθρώποιο (2m): man (in plu., can mean "mankind")(3)

ἄντην (adverb): face to face (11)

ἀντίον: (with genitive) opposite, face to face(8)

ἄνωγα: I command (21 and 22)

ἅπας, ἅπασα, ἅπαν: every (plu., all) (like πᾶς) (18)

ἀπιθέω (aorist ἀπίθησα): I disobey (9)

---

[1] This is the bad sense of the word: it more often means "I wonder at", "I admire".
[2] Adverb, and preposition with genitive.
[3] Adverb, and preposition with genitive or dative.
[4] The aegis was a goatskin shield.
[5] aorist: ἤλυξα
[6] In Attic Greek, ἅμαξα.
[7] "clothe". Aorist ἀμφίεσα, future, ἀμφιέσω.
[8] For other cases, see p.63.

ἀπινύσσω: I lack understanding (21)
ἀπό (with genitive): from (5)
ἀπέβην: I went away, stepped off⁹ (14)
ἄρα, ἄρ': then, there and then, so (11)
ἀργαλέος -α -ον: troublesome, difficult to deal with (15)
Ἀργεϊφόντης (perhaps): slayer of Argus
ἄριστος, ἀρίστη, ἄριστον: best, very good (22)
ἁρμονίη (1f): fastening (17)
ἄρχω, also ἄρχομαι: I begin (+ genitive), lead the way (16)
ἀσκός (2m): wineskin (18)
ἄστυ (3n): town (12)
ἀτρύγετος, ἀτρύγετον (fem. as. masc.): barren(9)
αὖ, αὖ, αὖτε, αὖτ': again, furthermore (6)
αὐδήεις, αὐδηέσσα, αὐδηεν: speaking with human voice (21)
αὐδάω: I utter, speak (8)
ἀτάρ or αὐτάρ: but, besides, moreover (11)
αὖ: again, moreover, on the contrary (7)
αὖτε: furthermore, also (8)
αὐτίκα: immediately (9)
αὐτός, αὐτή, αὐτό: he himself, she herself, it itself (8)
ἄφαρ: straightaway (25)
ἀφικνέομαι (aorist ἀφικόμην): I reach, arrive at (10)
ἄψ: back again (21)

---

⁹Irregular (strong) aorist of ἀποβαίνω, I go away. [ἀπέβην], [ἀπέβησθα], ἀπέβη, [ἀπέβητον], ἀπέβητην, [ἀπέβημεν], [ἀπέβητε], ἀπέβησαν.

β
βαίνω: I go, I step (15)
βάλλω: I throw (aorist ἔβαλον) (also "I hit")(10)
βοάω: I shout (23)
βορέης, βορέου (1m): north wind (19)
βουλεύω (aorist, ἐβούλευσα): I plan, devise, advise (9)(15)
βουλή (1f): will, plan, design (8)
βροτός (2m or f): human, mortal (7)

γ
γαῖα 1f: land, earth (2)
γαλήνη (1f): calm (23)
γάρ : for (conjunction: "for the reason that") (2nd word in clause) (3)
γ' , γε (enclitic): indeed (8)
γέγωνα: I make myself heard (21 and 23)
γίγνομαι (aorist (ἐ)γενόμην) : I become, happen (4)
γλαυκῶπις: with gleaming eyes (24)
γλαφυρός -α -ον: hollow (10)
γούνατα (3n plu): knees¹⁰ (19)

δ
δαίμων, δαιμόνος (m. or f.): god, goddess, deity (23)
δάκρυον: the tear¹¹ (11)
δαμάζω¹²: I overcome (25)

---

¹⁰The singular is γόνυ.
¹¹In verse, the nominative and accusative singular are often δάκρυ and the dative plural δάκρυσι as if 3rd declension, to fit the metre.
¹²Aorist active (ἐ)δάμασα, aorist passive participle, δαμείς (Odyssey VI, 11). The perfect middle/passive is δέδμημαι and the aorist passive (ἐ)δμήθην.

Word list

δ', δέ: and, but, however (2nd word in clause) (3)
δείδω: I fear (14)
δεινός, δεινή, δεινόν: terrible (9)
δέομαι (aorist, ἐδησάμην): I tie on for myself (9)
δέος, δέους (3n): fear, alarm (21)
δέρκομαι: I see, look at (11)
δεῦρο: hither, to here (12)
δέομαι: I tie on myself (9)
δεύω (aorist, ἔδευσα): I dip (9)
δέω (aorist ἔδησα): I bind (9)
δή: at that point, in fact, finally(8)
δήν: for long (13)
δηρόν: (all too) long (adv.) (23)
διάκτορος: messenger, servant (11)
διαμπερές: right through (17)
διασκεδάννυμι[13]: I scatter (22)
δίδωμι (aorist, ἔδωκα): I give (17)
διογενής: sprung from Zeus (16)
δῖος, δῖα, δῖον: noble, heavenly (2)
δοάσσατο: it seemed[14] (25)
δοκέω: I seem (21)
δοῦρα (n plu): spears, spars (20)
δούρατα (3nplu): timbers (14)
δύναμαι: I can (4)
δύστηνος, δύστηνον: wretched (24)
δύω[15]: I sink (18)
δύω, δύο: two (23)
δῶμα, δώματος 3n: hall, house (plu., palace)(2)

ε

ἕ: him, her (8)
ἔαξα (aorist of ἄγνυμι): I broke (20)
ἔβην: I went[16] (12)
ἐγείρω (aorist, ἔγειρα or ἤγειρα): I wake up, arouse (9)
ἐγώ: I (3)
ἔδειξα is the aorist of δείκμυμι, "I show" (17)
ἔδυν: I sank[17] (16)
ἐδωδή (1f): food, victuals (15)
(ἔ)θανον: I died (20)[18]
ἐθέλω (aorist ἐθέλησα): I want, I wish (3)
εἰ or αἰ: if (11)
εἶδον: I saw (aorist of ὁράω) (10)
εἶδος (3n): appearance[19] (16)
ἔϊκα (see also ἔοικα): I am like (21)
εἰκώς, εἰκυῖα, εἰκός (+ dat.): like (21)
εἰλόμην: I chose (aorist of αἱρέομαι) (10)
εἷλον (aorist of αἱρέω): I took. (10)
εἰμί: I am (2)
εἶμι: I go, come (16)
εἵματα (3nplu): clothes (14)
εἷος (see ἕως)
εἶπον: I said (aorist of λέγω) (10)
εἰς (with accusative): into, to (3)
ἔϊσος, ἐΐση, ἔϊσον (always feminine in Homer): well-balanced (15)
ἐκ or ἐξ (with genitive): out of (5)

---
[13]aorist active, διεσκέδασα
[14]An isolated Homeric form.
[15]3rd person singular, aorist middle ἐδύσετο.
[16]The strong aorist of βαίνω, I go. See Section 12, p.83.
[17]Strong aorist active (intransitive) of δύω.
[18]See θάνον.
[19]cf. εἶδον.

ἑκάς: far away (22)
ἐκφεύγω (aorist ἐξέφυγον): I escape (19)
ἐλαύνω and ἐλαάω (aorist ἤλασα): I drive (13)
ἐλεαίρω: I pity (24)
ἐμβάλλω: I throw into (24)
ἐμός, ἐμή, ἐμόν: my, mine (8)
ἔμπης: in spite of all, at any rate (16)
ἐν, ἐνί (+ dative): in (6)
ἐνδόθι: within, at home (9)
ἔνδον: inside (10)
ἔνθα, ἔνθ': there, thither, where (9)
ἐνθάδε: here (14)
ἔνθεν: from there, from where (15)
ἐν(ν)έπω (+ accusative): I tell of
ἕννυμι (aorist, ἕσσα): I clothe (17)
ἐνοσίχθων: earth-shaker (19)
ἐξ: see ἐκ
ἔξοχον + genitive: far above (comparative adverb) (13)
ἔοικα: I am like (21)
ἔολπα: I expect, hope (21)
ἑός, ἑή, ἑόν: his own, her own (8)
ἔπαθον: I suffered (aorist of πάσχω) (10)
ἐπεί: when, since (11) after (17)
ἔπειτα (ἔπειτ, ἔπειθ'): then, next (6)
ἔπεσον: I fell (aorist of πίπτω) (10)
ἐπεσσύμενος, ἐπεσσυμένη, ἐπεσσύμενον: violent, hasty[20] (24)
ἐπί, ἐπ' (with accusative): against, over, to (3)

[20]Perfect participle passive of ἐπισσεύω.

ἐπι, ἐπ'(with genitive or dative): on, upon (5)
ἐπιβαίνω[21] (+ genitive): I set foot on (9)
ἐπίκριον (2n): yard arm (17)
ἐπισσεύω: I set in motion against (20)
ἐπιχέω (aorist ἐπέχευσα): I pour over, heap up over (17)
ἐποίχομαι: I approach, attack (13)
ἔπος, ἔπους (3n): word, saying, proverb, poem (8)
ἔργον (2n): work, task (17)
ἐρυθρός, ἐρυθρόν: red[22] (11)
ἔρχομαι: I come, go (aorist ἦλθον[23]) (4)
ἐς (alternative to εἰς): into, to (6)
ἐσθλός, ἐσθλή, ἐσθλόν: good, brave, noble.(12)
ἔσθω (more often ἐσθίω): I eat[24] (11)
ἔσχον: I had, I held (aorist of ἔχω) (10)
ἑταῖρος 2m: companion (2)
ἔτι: still, yet (12)
εὖ: well (17)
εὐνή (1f): bed (13)
εὐπλόκαμος –ον (fem. as masc.): with beautiful tresses (6)
εὑρίσκω: I find (aorist εὗρον) (10)
εὖρος (2m): the east wind (19)
εὐρύς, εὐρείη, εὐρύ: wide (7)
εὖτε: when (17)
εὔχομαι: I claim (to be) (16), I pray[25] (24)

[21]Aorist, ἐπέβην.
[22]The feminine is not found in Homer.
[23]Or ἤλυθον.
[24]The root is ἔδω (cf. ἐδωδή), and in later Greek, from Hesiod onwards, the form ἐσθίω is used.
[25]Its meaning in later Classical Greek.

Word list

ἐφευρίσκω[26]: I discover (23)
ἔφυγον: I fled (aorist of φεύγω) (10)
ἔχω (aorist ἔσχον): I have, hold, consider (3)
ἔωθα: I am accustomed to (21)
ἕως (sometimes εἷος or εἴως in some mss.): until, so that, while (7)[27]

ζ

Ζεύς, Ζεῦ, Δία, Διός, Διΐ: Zeus (6)
ζέφυρος(2m) : the west wind(19)

η

ἤ: or. ἤ... ἤ... *or* ἠὲ... ἠὲ...: either ... or ... (25)
ἦ τοι, ἦ γάρ: of a certainty (8)
ἡγέομαι: I lead (the way) (15)
ἠδ', ἠδέ: and (3)
ἤδη: already (16)
ἠέλιος (2m): the sun (16)
ἠεροειδής –ες: murky (14)
ἤλασα : I drove (aorist of ἐλαύνω) (13)
ἦλθον *or* ἤλυθον: I came/went (aorist of ἔρχομαι) (10)
ἦμαρ, ἤματος (3n): day (8)
ἡμεῖς: we (3)
ἦμος: at the very time when (17)
ἧος (see ἕως)
ἤπειρόνδε: to, towards the (main)land (24)
ἤπειρος (1f): land, mainland (21)
ἤπιος –α –ον : kind, gentle(6)
ἦ τοι: of a certainty (8)
ἦτορ (3n): heart[28] (19)

---

[26]Aorist, ἐφεῦρον.
[27]See p.119, footnote 2.
[28]Found only in nominative and accusative singular in Homer.

ἠῶθι πρό: at daybreak, early (25)
Ἠώς, Ἠοῦς (3fem): Dawn (5)

θ

θάλασσα 1f: sea (2)
θάμνος (2m or f): bush (25)
θάνατος (2m): death (20)
θεά 1f: goddess (2)
θεῖος –α –ον: godlike, marvellous, superhuman (5)
θέλγω (aorist, ἔθελξα): I charm, bewitch (9)
θεός: 2m: god, 2f: goddess (2)
θηέομαι[29]: I gaze at, behold (10)
θῆλυς, (θήλεια), θῆλυ: female, soft, gentle[30](25)
θνήσκω, (ἔ)θανον: I die (20)
θνητός, θνητή, θνητόν: mortal (8)
θοῶς: quickly (17)
θρόνος (2m): chair, seat (11)
θυγάτηρ, θυγατρός[31]: daughter (21)
θύελλα (1f): hurricane, squall (20)
θυμός (2m): soul, mind, spirit, heart (11)
θύραζε: out (of doors) (23)

ι

ἵζω: I sit (down)[32] (15)
ἰθύνω: I keep straight, steer straight (17)
ἱκάνω: I come, (with accusative) I approach (19)
ἱκέτης, ἱκέταο 1m: suppliant (2)

---

[29]In Liddell & Scott this verb is given as θεάομαι.
[30]The feminine is often θῆλυς.
[31]Genitive alternatively θυγατέρος.
[32]Also means "I seat" i.e. "I cause to sit".

ἱκνέομαι (aorist ἱκόμην): I come, arrive at, approach as suppliant (4)
ἴκρια (2nplu): boards[33] (14)
ἱμάσσω[34]: I flog, whip up (22)
ἵνα: where, so that (7)
ἵππος (2m): horse (22)
ἱστία (2nplu): sails (17)
ἱστός (2m): loom, mast (10)
ἴσχω: I hold (back) (3)

κ

κάθημαι: I sit (11)
καθέζομαι: I sit down (15)
καί: and, also, indeed (3)
καίομαι: I burn (intransitive), I have lit (middle) (4)
καίω (aorist, ἔκηα): I burn, light, ignite (transitive) (4)
κακός, κακή, κακόν: bad, evil (2)
κακότης (3f): distress[35] (19)
καλός, καλή, καλόν: beautiful, fine, good (2)
καλύπτω: I hide (19)
κάματος (2m): weariness (24)
κάμμορος: ill-fated (14)
κάρη, κάρητος (n): head (19)
καρπαλιμῶς: swiftly (15)
κατά (+ accusative): down, along, throughout, at, in (the heart)(9)
κε or κεν: in that case (8)[36]

---

[33]See notes in Section 17..
[34]aorist active: ἵμασα.
[35]Genitive, κακότητος. κακότης can also mean "cowardice"; literally "badness" either of fortune or of morale.
[36]Equivalent to ἄν, and used in conditional and some purpose clauses. Chantraine (*Grammaire Homérique*, vol.ii, p.345) suggests that κεν may have come from Aeolic, and ἄν from Attic/Ionic. Its effect is like the English "would".

Beginning Greek with Homer
κεῖμαι: I lie (down) (4)
κεῖνος, κείνη, κεῖνο: that (8)
κέλευθος (2f): road, path (22)
κέλομαι (also κελεύω): I order (12)
κέρδιον: more profitable (25)
κεφαλή (1f): head (17)
κῆδος (3n): anxiety, grief (7)
κῆρ, κῆρος (neuter): heart (8)[37]
κλήθρη (1f): alder (10)
κλυτός, κλυτόν[38]: famous (22)
κούρη (1f): maiden (22)
κραιπνός, κραιπνή, κραιπνόν: swift, rushing (22)
κράτος (3n): power (7)
κρείων, κρείοντος: lord (epithet of Poseidon)(19)
κρήδεμνον –ου: women's headdress (21)
κῦμα, κύματος (3 neuter): wave (6)

λ

(ἐ)λαβόμην (with genitive): I took hold of (10)
(ἔ)λαβον: I took, accepted, received (10)[39]
λάϊγξ, λάιγγος (3f): pebble (24)
λαῖτμα, –ατος (3n): gulf (15)
λαός 2m: nation, people (3)
λέγω (aorist εἶπον): I say (4)
λεπτός –ή –όν: fine-spun (17)
λέχος, λέχεος (3n): bed (2)
λιμήν, λιμένος (m.): harbour (23)
λούω: I wash, bathe (18)
λύω: I loose, loosen, undo (19)

---

[37]To be distinguished from Κήρ, Κηρός (feminine): fate, goddess of doom.
[38]Feminine as masculine in Homer.
[39]See footnote 7, p. 66.

Word list

μ

μάκαρ (3): blessed, happy (4)
μακρός, μακρά, μακρόν: long, tall (12)
μάλα: indeed, very (12)
μεγαλήτωρ: great-hearted (11)
μέγας μεγάλη μέγα: big (15)
μέγεθος (3n): size, tallness (16)
μεθίημι (aorist μεθῆκα):I let go (25)
μέλας μέλαινη μέλαν: dark[40] (18)
μέμνημαι: I remember (with genitive) (4)
μέμονα: I am eager (21)
μενοεικής –ές: plentiful, satisfying the desires (14)
μέν: indeed (7)
μένω: I remain, wait (for) (with accusative), withstand (16)
μερμερίζω: I am anxious (22)
μέσ(σ)ος, μέσ(σ)η, μέσ(σ)ον[41]: middle, mid (13)
μετά + accusative: after (7)
μετά (+ dative): accompanied by, with (6)
μή: not (with wishes, purposes and conditions and in prohibitions)
μήδομαι: I contrive (15)
μήκιστα: as far as possible, (at line 465, at last) (25)
μιν: him, her
μίσγω[42]: I mix, mingle (20)
μογέω: I toil, suffer (24)
μοῖρα 1f: fate (2)
μυθέομαι: I speak, say (22)

μῦθος (2m): word, speech, tale (12)

ν

ναίω: I dwell, inhabit (9)
νέομαι: I return (14)
νέφος, –εος (3n): cloud[43] (19)
νέω (also νήχω): I swim (21)
νημερτής (3rd declension adjective): sure and true (8)
νῆσος 2f: island (2)
νηῦς (fem., irregular): ship (6)
νήχω (see νέω)
νοέω: I think, intend (15)
νόος (2m): purpose, thought, intention (12)
νόστιμον (ἦμαρ): day of homecoming (16)
νόστος (3m): voyage home (8)
νότος (2m): south wind (19)
νύμφη 1f: nymph (2)
νῦν, νύ: now (7)
νύξ, νυκτός (f): night (19)
νῶτον (often plural, νῶτα) (2n): back (7)

ξ

ο

ὁ, ἡ, τό: that, this, he, she, it, they, the (8)
ὅδε, ἥδε τόδε: this (8)
ὁδός (2f): road, way (17)
ὅθι: where (17)
οἶδα : I know[44] (16)
οἴκαδε: homewards[45] (12)
οἶκος 2m: home or room or house (2)
οἶνος (2m): wine (14)
οἶνοψ, οἴνοπος: wine faced (13)
οἶος, οἴη, οἶον: only, alone (13)

---

[40]Also "black".
[41]Sometimes spelled μέσσος, μέσση, μέσσον.
[42]aorist passive: (ἐ)μίγην (also (ἐ)μίχθην).

[43]Often means "a mass of cloud".
[44]See Section 21, p.145..
[45]The suffix –δε means "towards".

οἷος, οἵα, οἷον: of which kind, such as (15)
ὄλεθρος (2m) : ruin, destruction (20)
ὄλλυμι (aorist ὤλεσα): I destroy (3)
ὄμβρος (2m): rainstorm, shower (25)
ὄμνυμι (aorist ὤμοσα or ὄμοσσα): I swear (a solemn oath) (3)
ὀνομάζω: I call by name (15)
ὀξύς, ὀξεῖα, ὀξύ: sharp (23)
ὄπισθεν: behind (14)
ὁπ(π)οτε: when (17)
ὅπως: how, so that (7)
ὅρκος (2m): oath (14)
ὁρμαίνω: I debate anxiously, ponder (22)
ὁρμή (1f.): effort, rush, onset, impulse (20)
ὄρνις, ὄρνιθος (3m or f): bird (9)
ὄρνυμι (aorist, ὦρσα): I arouse (3)
ὄρος, ὄρεος (3n): mountain (18)
ὁράω (aorist εἶδον) I see (10)[46]
ὅς, ἥ, ὅ: who, which (relative pronoun) (see p.50)
ὅς, ἥ, ὅν: his, her (see p.52)
ὄσσε: two eyes (6)(14)
ὅσ(σ)οι ὅσ(σ)αι ὅσ(σ)α: as many as, how many (16)
ὅσ(σ)ος, ὅσ(σ)η, ὅσ(σ)ον: how much, how great, as much as (23)
ὅστις: who, which, whoever, whichever (8)
ὅτε: when, at the time when (9)
οὐ, οὐκ, οὐχ: not (2)
οὐδέ: and not, but not, nor, not even (6)

οὔπω or οὔ πω: not yet (22)
οὐρανός (2m): sky (14)
οὖρος (2m): following wind (14)οὔτε ... οὔτε ...: neither ... nor ... (6)
οὗτος, αὗτη, τοῦτο: this, that (8)
οὕτω: so, thus, in this way (16)
ὀφθαλμός (2 masc): eye (5)
ὄφρα: while, until, so that (7)
ὀχέομαι (aorist, ὀχησάμην): I ride (9)
ὀχθέω: I am vexed (19)
ὄψον (2n): cooked dish, food (18)
ὀψέ: late (18)

π
πάγος (2m.): rock (23)
παῖς, παιδός (3 m or f): child, son, daughter (7)[47]
παντοῖος -α -ον: all kinds of (19)
παρά, παρ' (with genitive): from beside (5) + dative: beside, near (25)
πάρος (adverb): formerly (11)
πᾶς, πᾶσα, πᾶν: every (plu., all) (11)
πάσχω (aorist ἔπαθον) I suffer (7)
πατηρ, πατέρος or πατρός 3m: father (2)
πατρίς, πατρίδος 3f: fatherland (2)
παύω: I stop (24)
παύομαι: I cease (22)
πέλεκυς (3m): axe (17)
πέλω (also πέλομαι): I am, I become (15)
πέμπω (aorist, ἔπεμψα): I send (3)

[46]See p.201.

[47]Dative plural, παίδεσσι(ν).

Word list

περ: (i) very much, by all means, (ii) (with participle) though (8)
περί (preposition with accusative, genitive or dative): around (8)
περὶ κῆρι : very dear (8)
(ἔ)πεσον aorist of πίπτω
πετάννυμι (aorist, πέτασα or πέτασσα): I spread (18)
πέτρη (1f): rock, cliff (14)
πη: in any way[48](13)
πηδάλιον (2n): steering-oar (17)
πῆμα, πήματος 3n: woe (2)
πίνω (aorist ἔπιον): I drink (11)
πίπτω: I fall (aorist ἔπεσον) (10)
ποδοῖιν: by (his) two feet (6)
ποιέω: I do, make (13)
πόλις (3f)[49]: city (12)
πολλοί, πολλαί, πολλά: many (7)
πολύτλας: much-suffering (14)
πομπή (1f): a sending home, an escort (8)
πόντος (2 masc): the open sea (5)
πορον or ἔπορον (found only in aorist): I provided (22)
ποταμός (2m): river (24)
ποτε: ever[50] (25)
ποτί: πρός (23)
πότν(ι)α (fem. adj.): lady, mistress (16)
που: somewhere (23)[51]

πούς, ποδός (3m) (dative plural πόδεσσι(ν), πόσι(ν) or πόσσι(ν)): foot, and also "sheet" (rope fastened to the bottom corner of a sail) (17)
πρίν: before,[52] formerly (16)
πρός (with accusative): to, towards (3) (with dative): near, against, (close) to (23)
προτί = πρός
προσφημί: I speak to (8)
προτέρω: farther (23)
πυκινός, -ή, -όν: close set, compact, close (9)
πῦρ, πῦρος 3n: fire (4)
πω (see οὔ πω)
πῶς: how? (πως : in any way) (12)

ρ
ῥα, ῥ᾽ = ἄρα (15)
ῥέζω (aorist ἔρεξα): I perform (7)
ῥεῖα: easily (13)
ῥιγέω: I shiver (12)
ῥοδοδάκτυλος: rosy-fingered (epithet of the dawn) (13)
ῥόος (2m): stream (24)

σ
σαόω[53] (aorist ἐσάωσα): I save (13)
σεύομαι (aorist (ἐσ)σευάμην)[54]: I dart (9)
σῖτος (2m): corn, food (14)
σκέπας (3n): shelter[55] (24)
σκηπτοῦχος, σκηπτοῦχον: sceptre-bearing (2)

---

[48]In a negative sentence. In a positive sentence, "somehow".
[49]See Section 12, p.83.
[50]Enclitic. (With acute accent, πότε is interrogative and means "when?".)
[51]Enclitic. που can also mean "perhaps". (ποῦ with circumflex accent means "where?").
[52]Always found with an infinitive after a *positive* verb.
[53]Also σώζω.
[54]The active is σεύω (I put in quick motion, hunt, drive). The strong aorist middle, ἐσσύμην means "I rushed".
[55]Only the nominative and accusative singular is found in Homer.

σός, σή, σόν: your (when "you" is singular) (16)[56]
σπέος, σπείους (3 n): cavern, grotto, cave[57] (9)
στενάχω: I groan, sigh, wail (23)
στέρνον -ου (2n): breast[58] (21)
στῆθος (3n): breast, chest (in plural, heart, seat of feelings)(15)
στόμα, στόματος (3n): mouth (20)
σύ: you (singular) (3)
σύν + dative: with (16)
σφέας: them (8)
σφώ: the two of us (6)
σχεδίη (1 fem): raft (5)
σχεδόν: near (19)

τ
τανύω[59]: I stretch (21)
ταράσσω: I stir up, disturb (19)
τάχιστα: very quickly (25)
τε: and (see p.35) (6)
τε, τ' (after a relative pronoun): in fact, of course (8)
τε ... καὶ ... (or τε ... τε ...): both ... and (6)[60]
τέκνον 2n: child (2)
τελέω: I fulfil, accomplish, execute, complete, finish (11)
τέρπομαι (aorist, ἐτερψάμην): I enjoy myself (+ genitive, I enjoy to the full) (4)
τέρπω: I please, delight
(ἔ)τετμον: I found (10)
τῇδε: here (in this place) (12)

[56] p.132.
[57] At line 68, to fit the metre; normally, σπέους.
[58] Always of males.
[59] Aorist active, ἐτάνυσσα.
[60] In elision, any of these examples of τε becomes τ'.

τηλόθεν, τηλόθ ': from afar (19)
τῆλε, τηλοῦ: far off (20)
τηλόθι: afar, at a distance (9)
τίθημι: I put, make (15)
τινάσσω: I shake (22)
τις, τινος: anybody (5)
τι, τινος: anything (5)
τίς, τίνος;: who? (5)
τί, τίνος;: what? (5)
τλήσομαι: I shall endure (16)
τοι (enclitic): let me tell you! look! (12)[61]
τόσ(σ)ος, τόσ(σ)η, τόσ(σ)ον: so much, so great (in plural, so many) (23)
τότε: then (9)[62]
τόφρα: for so long (13)
τρεῖς[63]: three (25)
τρέπομαι : I turn (intransitive) (10 & 21)[64]
τρέφω (aorist ἔθρεψα): I nurture (13)

υ
ὑγρός, ὑγρά, ὑγρόν: wet (25)
ὕδωρ, ὕδατος (3n): water (10)
ὕλη (1f): wood (10)
ὑμεῖς: you (plural) (3)
ὕπνος (2m): sleep (18)
ὑπό: under (with accusative, genitive or dative); by the agency of (with genitive) (9)
ὑψιβρεμέτης, ὑψιβρεμέταο (1m): the high thunderer (2)

[61] Originally from a phrase like λέγω σοι.
[62] Often found with δή. τότε δή = and then.
[63] Masculine and feminine. The neuter is τρία.
[64] Perfect τέτραμμαι, aorist (ἐ)τραπόμην.

Word list

ὑψόροφος, ὑψόροφον (fem. as masc.): high-roofed (8)

φ

φαίνω: I show (φαίνομαι: I appear) (18)
φᾶρος (3n, like λέχος): robe, cloth (17)
φέρω: I bear, I carry (3)
φεύγω (aorist ἔφυγον): I flee(10)
φημί: I say, affirm (3)
φίλος, φίλη, φίλον: friendly, dear, own[65] (2)
φρήν, φρενός (3f): heart, mind (often plu) (7)
φρονέω: I think, I have in mind, I am wise, I am in possession of my senses.[66] (11)
φυή (1f): stature (16)
φυλάσσω: I stay in, keep in, keep watch, stay awake (16)
φύω: I put forth, grow (25)
φωνέω: I call out, speak, call by name(11)

χ

χαίρω: I rejoice (3)
χαλεπαίνω: I am angry (14)
χαλεπός, χαλεπή, χαλεπόν: difficult, dangerous, rugged, bitter, hostile, cruel (3)
χαλκός (2m): bronze (14)
χάρις (3f): (act of) kindness, favour[67] (20)

χείρ, χειρός (3 fem): hand (dative plural, χείρεσσι, χείρεσι or χερσί(ν)) (6)
χιτών, χιτῶνος (3m): tunic (17)
χρειώ (3f): want, need, necessity[68](15)
χρόνος (2m): time (20)
χρύσειος, -α -ον: golden (17)
χρυσός (2m): gold (8)
χρώς, χροός (3m)(neuter in plural) : skin, flesh (24)
χώομαι: I am angry (16)

ψ

ω

ὤ μοι (ἐγώ) conventional expression of surprise or pain (20)
ὧδε: thus, so, in this way.(21)
ὡς: as, so that, how (6, 7, 17, 23)
ὥς: thus, so (9) (note accent)

---

[65]When φίλος = "own", it does not always mean "belonging to the subject"; e.g. Iliad ii, 261: εἰ μὴ ἐγώ σε λαβὼν ἀπὸ μὲν φίλα εἵματα δύσω = if, having caught you, I do not strip off your (own) clothes" (Odysseus to Thersites).
[66]Also μέγα φρονέω (literally, "I think big") = I am presumptious.
[67]Singular only found as nominative, and accusative (χάριν), plural as dative (Odyssey VI, 237) χάρισι "with graces". Plural Χάριτες, = the Graces (Χαρίτων "of the Graces", Odyssey VI, 18).

[68]Sometimes neuter. The genitive is χρειοῦς (not found in Homer), and the dative χρειοῖ.

English Index

accents 4
accusative case 13
active voice 11, 18, 192
adjectives 8, 160
agent/instrument 167
α- privative 8
alphabet x, 1
aorist tense 11, 188, (weak, active & middle) 60, 209 (strong, active & middle) 66, 212, (passive) 127, 214
apodosis 171
Aristarchus of Samothrace 123
aspect 32, 186, 189
athematic (-μι) verbs 12
  with reduplication 105
Attic v, 172, 201
augment 34, 61, 153
books of Iliad & Odyssey, designation by letters 1
breathings 3
Common Greek (koiné) 9, 48, 172
comparative 178
comparison of adjectives 178
  of adverbs 180
compound adjectives 8
concessive clauses (although...) 76
conditions 171
correption 24
contraction of vowels 193
dactylic hexameter 23
dative case 35
declension 6
definite article ("the") 7, 48
deliberative questions 98
demonstrative pronouns 48
dialects v
diectasis 200, 201
doublets 68
dual 6, (of 3rd declension) 38, (of personal pronouns) 39, (of 1st declension) 231, (of verbs) 11.
elision 10
enclitic 5
endings (active verbs) 202 (middle & passive verbs) 203
Epic dialect v
eventualities 44, 98
fearing, construction with verbs of 98, 187
formulae vi
future tense 11, 80, 188, 214 (with ἄν or κεν) 97, 191

genitive case (possessive) 26, (other uses) 30-31
genitive absolute 135
gods, the language of 146
hendiadys 91
imperative, 46 (footnote), 86, 188, (present) 206
imperfect tense 9, 11, 33, 188, 191, 208
indefinite pronoun & adjective 29
indicative 42, 186
infinitive 188, (present) 22, 205 (future & aorist) 103, (aorist) 190, 209
instrumental 134
intransitive 13
iota subscript 3
koiné 9, 48, 172
lexicon x
locative 134
metathesis 119
-μι verbs (δίδωμι, ἵημι, ἵστημι, τίθημι) 105, 218 (see also "athematic verbs")
middle voice 18, 192
modal particles 98, 186
mood 42, 186
nominative case 14
noun clauses (accusative & infinitive) 84 (footnote 29), 85 (footnote 30)
nouns 6, (cases of) 13, 26, 35, 41, 231
numerals 1
object 14
Ogygia iii, 47, 77
optative 187, (present) 42, 207 (aorist) 62, 132,
participles 71, 188, (aorist) 190, 210, (present) 205
partitive genitive 178
passive voice 18, 193 (aorist tense of) 127, aorist participle and infinitive of 131
patronymic 41
perfect participle active 150-2, middle & passive 152
perfect tense 137, 188, 191, 216
person (of verb) 11
pluperfect tense 153-5, 188, 191, 218
possessive adjectives 52, 114
predicate 11
prepositions 16, 30, 39
present tense 9. 11, 188
prohibitions 96, 191
pronouns (1st & 2nd person) 17, 39 (3rd person) 48, 55, 234

Indices

protasis 171
punctuation 4
purpose clauses 43, 97
reduplication 138
relative pronoun 50
scholium 78, 92
sequence of tenses (primary & secondary tenses) 32, 192
sigmatised aorist 61, 97
simile 125, 144, 167
soliloquies 135
stem (noun) 28
stem (verb) 33
subject (of sentence) 11
subjunctive 43, 94, (with short vowel ending) 97, 187, (present) 208
superlative 178
synizesis 157
temporal clauses 119, (represented by participles in Greek) 76
tenses 32, 188
thema 12
time (expression of) 128 (footnotes 6 & 8)
tmesis 78, 99, 136
transitive 13, 192
transliteration 2
two termination adjectives 8
verb (persons of) 11
verbs 11, (active endings) 12 (middle/passive endings) 18-19
vocative case 41
voice 192
wishes 42-3
word order 15

Greek index

ἀθάνατος καὶ ἀγήρως 93
αἱ 171
ἄν 98, 172
ἀνήρ 63
ἄνωγα 145
Ἀργεϊφόντης 64
ἀρηρώς 151
ἄσσα 51
αὐδήεις 146
αὐτός, αὐτή, αὐτό 55
βῆ δ' ἴμεν(αι),
   βῆ ρ' ἴμεν(αι) 114
γέγωνα 145
γλαφυρός 68
δεδαώς, δεδαηκώς 151
δίδωμι 105, 122, 218

263

ἐ 55
(ἔ)βην 83
ἐγώ 17, 29
(ἔ)δωκα 122
εἰ 171
εἰδώς 150-1
ἔικα, ἔοικα 145
εἰμι 9, 204
εἰμι 113
εἷος 119
εἶπας 66
ἐξ οὗ 119
ἔοικα 139, 145
ἐοικώς 150
ἔολπα 103, 139, 145
ἐπεί 119
ἐσσύμενος, ἔσσυμαι 138
ἐστεώς 152
εὖτε 119
ἕως 44, 45, 119
Ζεύς 28
ᾔδεα 154
ἡμεῖς 17, 29
ἧμος 119
ἤν (= εἰ ἄν) 170, 172
ἧος 119
-θεν 184
θῶκόνδε 5
ἵημι 105, 218
ἵνα 44, 97
ἵστημι 105, 218
κεκμηκώς 151
κεν 98
κεῖνος 54
(ἔ)λαβον 66
μεμαώς 150
μέμονα 145
μὲν ... δὲ ... 101
μετά 40
μή 43, 44, 95, 171
μιν 55
νηῦς 39
νώ, νῶι 39
ὁ ἡ τό 48
ὅδε ἥδε τόδε 52
Ὀδυσσεύς (significance of name) 102
οἶδα 145-6, 154, 216
οἰκόνδε 5
οἷος, οἴη, οἶον 92
ὁπ(π)οτε 119

ὅπως 44, 97
ὁρόω 67, 201
ὅς ἥ ὅ (relative pronoun) 50
ὅς ἥ ὅν or ἑός, ἑή, ἑόν
  (possessive adjective) 52
ὅς τε 51
ὅσσε 38
ὅστις 51
ὅτε 119
οὗτος, αὕτη, τοῦτο 53
ὄφρα 44, 97, 119, 120
περ 76
ποδοῖιν 38
πόλις 83
πρίν 121
σαόω 89, 199
συ 17, 29
σφε or σφωε 56
σφέας 55
σφώ, σφῶι (dual) 39
τεθνηώς 152
τίθημι 105, 218
τις 29
τόφρα 120
ὑμεῖς 17, 29
(ἔ)φατο 34
φημί 12, 34, 85, 202
-φι 69
χεῖρε 38
ὡς 44, (introducing a clause expressing time) 119
ὥς κε(ν) 97